ALL THE BRIGHT COMPANY

All the Bright Company

RADIO DRAMA PRODUCED BY ANDREW ALLAN

EDITED BY HOWARD FINK AND JOHN JACKSON
(Radio Drama Project, Centre for Broadcasting Studies, Concordia University)

Quarry Press • *CBC Enterprises*

Copyright © Howard Fink and John Jackson, 1987

The acknowledgements page constitutes an extension of this copyright notice.

All rights reserved. No part of this book may be reproduced or transmitted in any form by any means, except for brief passages quoted by a reviewer, without written permission from the publisher.

Canadian Cataloguing in Publication Data

Main entry under title:

All the bright company : radio drama
produced by Andrew Allan

(Canadian radio drama series)
Co-published by CBC Enterprises.
Bibliography: p. 335

ISBN 0-919627-47-1 (bound). -
ISBN 0-919627-49-8 (pbk.)

1. Radio plays, Canadian (English). 1. Allan, Andrew, 1907-1974. 11. Fink, Howard, 1934- 111. Jackson, John 1v. CBC Enterprises v. Series

PN6120.R2A44 1987   C812'.02 C87-090020-X

Designed and typeset by ECW Production Services, Oakville, Ontario. Printed and bound by Hignell Printing Limited, Winnipeg, Manitoba. Cover design by Bette Davies.

CBC Enterprises, P.O. Box 500, Station A, Toronto, Ontario M5W 1E6

Quarry Press, Inc., P.O. Box 1061, Kingston, Ontario K7L 4Y5

ALL THE BRIGHT COMPANY

Table of Contents

Introduction by Howard Fink and John Jackson   v
Note on Texts   xvii

Andrew Allan, *All the Bright Company*   1
Fletcher Markle, *Brainstorm Between Opening and Closing Announcements*   19
W.O. Mitchell, *The Devil's Instrument*   39
Lister Sinclair, *Hilda Morgan*   67
Harry Boyle, *The Macdonalds of Oak Valley*   103
Len Peterson, *Man with a Bucket of Ashes*   135
Patricia Joudry, *Mother Is Watching*   171
Gerald Noxon, *Mr. Arcularis*   203
Reuben Ship, *The Investigator*   235
Joseph Schull, *The Jinker*   269
Tommy Tweed, *Full Speed Sideways*   301

Selected Bibliography   335

ACKNOWLEDGEMENTS

For permission to publish the production scripts of these plays, acknowledgement is made to the following copyright holders: for Fletcher Markle, "Brainstorm Between Opening and Closing Announcements," to the author; for Andrew Allan, "All the Bright Company," to Garry Allan; for Gerald Noxon, "Mr. Arcularis," to the author and to Mrs. Aiken; for W.O. Mitchell, "The Devil's Instrument," to the author; for Lister Sinclair, "Hilda Morgan," to the author; for Harry Boyle, "The Macdonalds of Oak Valley," to the author; for Len Peterson, "Man with a Bucket of Ashes," to the author; for Patricia Joudry, "Mother Is Watching," to the author; for Reuben Ship, "The Investigator," to Elaine Grand Ship; for Joseph Schull, "The Jinker," to Helene Gougeon; for Tommy Tweed, "Full Speed Sideways," to Terry Tweed and David Tweed.

The editors wish to thank, first, the authors themselves or their heirs, for their generous agreement to allow the publication of the plays, and for their further generosity with time and information; also our efficient, insightful, and energetic publisher, Bob Hilderley, who has managed to solve the multiple problems involved in bringing the volume to publication; the CBC for its generous co-operation, and CBC Enterprises for its crucial recognition and support of the project; also those in the Centre for Broadcasting Studies who helped us to prepare the manuscript; the administrators of Concordia University, who from the beginning have backed the Radio Drama Project, with understanding, encouragement, and considerable material resources; and for financial support of research useful in the preparation of the volume, both the Social Sciences and Humanities Research Council and Les fonds pour la formation de chercheurs et l'aide á la recherche du Gouvernement du Québec.

The publishers thank the Canada Council and the Ontario Arts Council for assistance in producing and distributing this book.

INTRODUCTION

Andrew Allan's Role in the History
of Canadian Radio Drama

I

Born in the summer of 1907, the son of a Presbyterian minister, in Arbroath, Scotland, Andrew Allan died in Toronto in 1974, a giant of Canadian drama, with the reputation of having established our first genuine trans-continental professional theatre. In the year of his death, Allan's friend, colleague, and boss, Harry J. Boyle, brought out a posthumous volume of Allan's biographical essays, called *A Self-Portrait* (Macmillan, 1974), still the best description of his personality, early literary influences, and extraordinary achievements. As Allan playfully observes in *A Self-Portrait*, his father, the Reverend William Allan, was "gifted with curiosity," which is the son's explanation for the father's wanderlust. In his first seventeen years, Allan lived in ten different cities on two different continents. While a child he moved to Australia, then to the United States; while a teenaged boy he moved to Canada, first to Peterborough and then to Toronto as a student at University of Toronto.

Though his first contact with the theatre was at high-school in New York, carrying a musket in Sheridan's play *St. Patrick's Day*, Allan's involvement as an actor in Hart House Theatre at university marked his real dedication to the craft. His other interest was writing. He became editor of the University newspaper, the *Varsity*, and helped pay his expenses at college through professional newspaper work. This experience, together with his dramatic aptitude, prepared him for his future radio career. His creative writing insights were valuable in the 1940s when he was responsible as a producer and director for choosing original plays for his major radio drama series. He actively advised his playwrights and exercised his prerogative as producer to give scripts their final pre-broadcast editing. Allan's early writing career, however, was short-lived. The coming of the depression in 1929 soon cut short his schooling, and he began working in the theatre in earnest, where he met Jane Mallet and others in the Toronto stock-theatre scene. In 1932, after failing to find enough work as an actor, he applied for and won the job as announcer-writer for Toronto radio station CFRB. He soon found his dramatic talents put to good use, writing and producing plays for the station. This was the beginning of Allan's career as a radio-drama director-producer. He wrote and directed everything from soap operas through dramatic documentaries to adaptations from popular movies — the last done freelance for the newly-established CBC after 1936. During this time, Allan kept his contacts with legitimate theatre, as an actor and writer.

At the beginning of 1938, Allan set off for England. He started work as a producer of commercial radio drama and variety programs for the independent stations Radio Luxembourg and Radio Normandie, broadcasting over the Channel to England. He spent almost two years in London, gaining valuable experience not only with commercial and serious radio drama, but with such variety stars as George Formbie and Gracie Fields. In September 1939, the war began. Allan was offered a job as Vancouver producer for the CBC, and he accepted. He survived the torpedoing of his homeward-bound ship and assumed his Vancouver work at the end of the year. In 1943 Allan transferred to the CBC Drama Department in Toronto, where he served as National Drama Supervisor, producing the prestigious *Stage* and *Wednesday Night* series until he retired from this position in 1955. During his tenure as National Drama Supervisor, Allan nurtured Canadian radio drama into maturity and founded our first national theatre on the air. His achievement in doing so is truly remarkable given the history of Canadian radio drama and Canadian stage theatre in the 1920s, 1930s, and 1940s.

II

The first radio drama series in Canada was created and produced by Jack Gillmore starting in 1927. This series was broadcast over our first national radio network, the Canadian National Railway Radio Department, by Gillmore's repertory troupe, the CNRV Players. Gillmore's CNRV *Players* series predated the first American radio network series, the NBC *Radio Guild*, by several years. Gillmore produced over one hundred plays from 1927 to 1932, including adaptations from the current repertory of the European and American stage, the first radio versions of Shakespeare in America, as well as a number of original plays by local authors. Gillmore's work was innovative by necessity and temperament: in important ways, he was inventing the radio drama genre, the language of dramatic communication through sound alone. Gillmore's series did not survive the nationalization of CN Radio in 1932, when its resources were taken over by the Canadian Radio Broadcasting Commission, which in turn became the CBC at the end of 1936.

The most famous drama series broadcast over CN Radio was *The Romance of Canada* during 1931. This was the first complete series on the full national network dedicated wholly to original Canadian plays. Written by the well-known Canadian radio-playwright Merrill Denison, the series celebrated the great figures of Canadian history. In its first season, *The Romance of Canada* was produced by the young Tyrone Guthrie, who was already beginning to gain his reputation as an innovative director. Denison chose Guthrie for this task because he was familiar with Guthrie's early work at the BBC, where he worked in the Drama Department during the early 1920s producing radio plays, including several of his own experimental works. Guthrie's work on *The Romance of Canada* series significantly influenced the theories of stage architecture and Shakespearean production which informed his creation of the Stratford theatre and its Shakespeare repertory company in the 1950s. When Guthrie left *The Romance of Canada* series at the end of that extremely successful 1931 season, Rupert Caplan, a young Montreal actor, became the producer of the second series in 1932. Caplan's subsequent career as a radio drama producer spans the history of Canadian radio drama: from the CN radio play experiments to the more ambitious drama series of the CRBC after 1932; and then from the so called Golden Age of CBC radio drama in the 1940s and 50s to the relative decline of radio drama in the shadow of television drama during the 1960s. Caplan provided an important link between Guthrie's original insights into the nature of radio drama in 1931 and the mature art of CBC radio drama in the Golden Age.

The CN network and its successor the CRBC were also producing a fair quantity of radio drama outside of Montreal and Vancouver in the 1930s, especially in Toronto, where the CN Radio script editor, Horace Brown, made a significant creative contribution as a drama-script writer. Paralleling the radio drama activities on the national network during these years were the drama productions on private stations. Perhaps the most impressive of these productions were on CKUA, the radio station of the University of Alberta at Edmonton, which broadcast radio dramas from 1928 to 1941. These plays, part of CKUA's unique cultural programming, were directed from 1929 on by Sheila Marryat. They included a good proportion of original plays by regional dramatists. Also during the 1930s, Esse W. Ljungh was producing original radio dramas in Winnipeg, first on private stations and then on the CBC. In Toronto, CFRB broadcast plays directed by John Holden and Andrew Allan. Holden also played roles in CFRB dramas and later founded several theatres, including the famous Muskoka summer stock theatre and a professional full-season repertory theatre in Winnipeg. Holden's 1939 season provided a number of drama broadcasts on CBC.

III

When Andrew Allan returned to Canada in 1939 to become Head of Drama at CBC Vancouver, he gradually built up a repertory team of actors and writers, with whom he began to fashion a new kind of drama: people like John Avison, Bernard Braden, Fletcher Markle, John Drainie, and Lister Sinclair. It was soon clear to the CBC what kind of talent they had in Allan — as it was clear to those who had the chance to hear his productions. The best-remembered of these seems to be the experimental series written by Markle, *Baker's Dozen*, which startled people across the country with its new and imaginative uses of the radio medium. It was no surprise, then, when Allan was named National Supervisor of the CBC Drama Department at the end of 1943. In January 1944 Allan began producing the national drama series, *Stage*, and thereby began to fulfil his dream of creating a professional national Canadian theatre.

Before Allan's initiative, there had never been a permanent professional theatre institution in Canada. That is not to say that there were no professional *theatres* before Allan's initiative: there were indeed a number of very good stock companies in the 1920s and 1930s, with which such pioneer professionals as Dora Mavor Moore, Norma Springford, Herman Voaden, and John Holden were involved. These companies were spread across the country, but they often worked on an intermittent basis. There were also significant amateur theatre companies in Canada, drawn together by the annual Dominion Drama Festivals. Yet there was nothing like the continuity of an indigenous professional theatre network in Canada at that time. Much of the professional theatre available to Canadians was in the form of touring American or British companies.

The depression in 1929–30 had negative effects on both our indigenous stock companies and the foreign touring companies. Many of the theatres in the larger cities either darkened their marquees or offered moving pictures — the first "talkies." These films, together with the new American (and occasionally Canadian) network drama series available to Canadian radio listeners, began to supplant live theatres as the major sources of dramatic entertainment. Canadian professional companies, like the Holden Players, continued to mount productions in the late 1930s, as did a number of high-quality amateur theatres. On the whole, though, whatever indigenous legitimate theatre had existed in Canada during the previous decades had almost died out by the end of the 1930s. The coming of the War in 1939 was the final blow — even the Dominion Drama Festival closed for the duration in 1940. In this frustrating atmosphere, the dream of a Canadian national theatre *on the air* grew in Andrew Allan's imagination.

One reason for Allan's choice of medium — apart from necessity — was that radio drama had been rapidly developing, in exciting ways, on the big American networks since the late 1920s. The American Golden Age of serious radio drama began in 1929 with the NBC *Radio Guild* series; matured with CBS *Playhouse* in 1933; and culminated with Orson Welles' *Mercury Theatre* in 1939. Meanwhile, valuable contributions to radio-drama techniques were being made by such popular variety dramas as *The Fred Allan Show* and *George Burns and Gracie Allan*. (Andrew Allan's own parallel 1938–39 work in England with George Formbie and Gracie Fields is significant.) There were also innovative American models in the writing of experimental radio scripts: not only Welles but also Arch Oboler and Norman Corwin, among others. One of Oboler's experimental plays was featured by Allan while he was still in Vancouver. The Golden Age of American radio drama came to an end, however, during World War II because of the dedication of broadcasting to war propaganda after 1940. More important, the big networks were winding down the commercial program structure of American radio as early as 1939 in preparation for television broadcasting; it was only the unforseen circumstance of the war which delayed the beginning of television until 1947.

For Canadian radio drama, however, the situation and the timing were different. The major professional outlet for the talents of many Canadian dramatists and actors from the middle 1930s on was radio drama. Moreover, with the almost complete shut-down of legitimate theatre activities at the beginning of the war, the CBC gained a clear monopoly over resources and audiences in the area of drama. The process of centralization of CBC dramatic productions gained real impetus after 1939. First, a new policy was established, cancelling existing contracts for the rebroadcast of plays from regional drama producers like CKUA Edmonton and the live drama broadcasts of the Holden Players. In such cases, the result was a reduction in the quantity of locally-produced Canadian plays. A countervailing force was the establishment of a set of weekly radio drama series in CBC regional production centres — in Montreal, Winnipeg, Halifax, Toronto, and Vancouver — between 1939 and 1943. Prime resources and talent were being invited from the regions to create several national radio-drama series produced in Toronto. The key move was bringing Andrew Allan from Vancouver to Toronto at the end of 1943 to become National Drama Supervisor. Allan had the responsibility not only for producing the major national series, but for administrative planning for the whole department, national and regional.

Allan's first major weekly national series was *Stage*, beginning in January 1944. It was followed in 1947 by the *Wednesday Night* series. For the success of these series, CBC brought to Toronto not only Allan but also the producers J. Frank Willis from Halifax and Esse W. Ljungh from Winnipeg. Rupert Caplan, however, preferred to continue producing in Montreal. Only *Stage* and *Wednesday Night* were an hour or more long;

the regional series were at most a half-hour in length. *Wednesday Night* featured mainly adaptations. On the *Stage* series, though, about half of the productions were hour-length Canadian plays written for radio.

Though Allan shared the *Wednesday Night* productions with his colleagues, Ljungh, Caplan, and Willis, he himself produced and directed virtually all the plays in the *Stage* series for its first twelve seasons, with the exception of part of the 1951–52 season. Allan produced 408 *Stage* plays during his tenure. He called the *Stage* series "A Report on the State of Canadian Drama." As he describes this series in *A Self-Portrait*, it was to be a writers' theatre: "My idea of being 'definitive' was to give the *writers* their head — to let them write what they wanted to write, and in the way they wanted to write it. . . . In twelve seasons we found over seventy of them — all, I think, but two of them Canadian." The other outstanding quality of the series was its function on the leading edge of contemporary social analysis and commentary.

When Allan came to Toronto as National Drama Supervisor, he managed to bring with him from Vancouver many of his repertory group of actors and writers, among them John Drainie, Lister Sinclair, and Fletcher Markle. To Allan's Vancouver band were added Alan King, who was already working in Toronto, and Tommy Tweed, who came from Winnipeg with Esse Ljungh. Among those preceding Allan to the Department in Toronto was Alice Frick. She was a young graduate in drama at University of Alberta in 1941 when she was given the position of National Script Editor under Allan's predecessor Rupert Lucas. Frick assisted Allan in script selection, editing, and production during the whole period of his tenure.

As producer, Allan was in control of the financial, technical, artistic, and personnel aspects of each play. He chose the plays, encouraging and supporting a group of dramatists whose creations satisfied his artistic standards and his urge to social commentary. He worked with his author on changes to the script before the preparation of the production script. He arranged for the composition of the musical arrangements and supervised their live playing during the broadcast — usually by Lucio Agostini. He cast the parts from his repertory group of actors. He rehearsed the actors, musicians, and sound technicians, and he directed the whole team in the actual live broadcast. Given the large measure of Allan's artistic control, the aesthetic unity of each play can be imagined; and while each play was of course in some measure different, there was a recognizable Andrew Allan style to all of them. Allan's control also led to an unusually concentrated development of the techniques and "language" of radio drama.

Radio drama is a very particular form of drama, with specific limitations and strengths, as well as a technical "language" or set of "signs" related to the medium. The major limitation, of course, is simply that everything must be communicated through the sound medium. There is no recourse to any of the visual resources of the stage: not sets, nor the physical presence of the actors; not physical action, nor facial expression, nor gesture. There can be no simultaneity of multiple impressions such as are available on television and in film. Everything passes in sequence through the funnel of the radio loud-speaker.

Yet these limitations also represent an astounding dramatic potential. First, each sequence of sounds, without the other dramatic distractions, commands an unmatched attention by the listener. Moreover, the lack of a mimetic visual reality gives the radio play a tremendous freedom from the mundane physical world. The radio play can represent any location, including the interior of the human mind. It can also move instantaneously from one place to another, and from the external to the interior world, and back. The representations of human beings and landscapes are communicated through distinctive vocal expression and accent, by narrative description and by sound effects.

As for the typical acting style, intimacy is inevitable, because of the directness of radio communication and the closeness of the listener to the sound source. The effect is of a more refined emotional communication. Mood and emotion are also carefully controlled by the musical backgrounds and bridges. By these means the radio play can stimulate the audience's imagination to fill in the effects, resulting in a relatively authentic subjective representation of reality for each listener. This is a dramatic communication ultimately more convincing than any stage representation. And Allan developed these techniques to a refinement not previously achieved.

Though reel-to-reel tape came into use in the CBC as early as 1951, Allan's plays in the *Stage* series were all played straight to live broadcast. Almost all the plays were produced in the old CBC Toronto Concert Studio on McGill Street. Though the Studio had both a stage and an auditorium, Allan (unlike Orson Welles) never invited an audience. When the production scripts had been corrected, typed, and distributed (sometimes during the very week of the broadcast), the company met for first rehearsals on Saturday morning. The process began with Allan's opening remarks on the play, its background and meaning. That afternoon there was a further rehearsal, this time with music played in a separate studio, while Allan directed from the window of the sound-booth. During this rehearsal, Allan was also timing the production, for the play as broadcast would have to fit into the CBC program slot of 29:44 or 59:44 minutes.

By Sunday afternoon Allan had made any necessary changes and cuts to the script, and there was a final dress rehearsal, followed by Allan's last-minute instructions. Though there were no spectators present, there were hundreds of thousands of listeners across the country tuned to the national network. The tension of a live performance was tangible: Allan notes in *A Self-Portrait* how, as they began, the "studio was alive with anticipation and concern, eagerness and love." The popularity of the *Stage* series, its power, and its effects on Canadian drama attest to the quality of the performances.

There was a marked team spirit among the *Stage* staff, based on Allan's long acquaintance with most of his troupe, and on their close identification with this elite enterprise. They were quite aware that they were making genuine theatre history. There was also the element of their fellow-feeling under stress. No matter how formally they worked at rehearsals — Allan insisted that they address one another as "Mr" and by their family names — their association was nevertheless a very close and personal one. There was another factor in the team spirit of the *Stage* troupe. They shared a sense of urgency about current concerns: the depression, the war, and the post-war dislocations of life. And they likewise shared a feeling of achievement in discussing these social concerns. The strongly-held conviction that they had the responsibility to communicate social truth in their broadcasts gave an added sense of identity to the team, an added edge of moral conviction to their performances.

This team created a powerfully innovative national radio drama institution. The two major national series, *Stage* and *Wednesday Night*, complemented one another admirably. While *Stage* became the showcase for Canadian playwrighting and acting talents, *Wednesday Night* was Canada's window on the whole tradition of drama, from the classics to the latest American and European dramatic experiments. Together, these series employed and trained many prominent theatre professionals. The series played live weekly over the national network to audiences often in the millions during the whole period of the Golden Age of Canadian radio. They are the clearest proofs that by the mid-1940s Canada had replaced the United States as the premiere creator of serious North American radio drama. This was acknowledged not only by the large and enthusiastic international audiences these series gained, but also by the appreciations of the theatre critics — not just the Canadians like Nathan Cohen and Robert Fulford, but the New York critics as well — and by the frequent Ohio State University Radio Drama Awards given to these productions.

IV

It was no coincidence that Allan retired as National Drama Supervisor in 1955, though he did subsequently direct several radio dramas, notably in the *Stage* season of 1961–62. A number of radical changes in our cultural institutions which had taken place since 1952 were beginning by the mid-1950s to have negative effects on the position previously enjoyed by the

CBC Drama Department. The creation of the new arts-granting agency, the Canada Council, which assumed some of the CBC's benevolent support of the arts; the beginnings of an indigenous Canadian stage network funded by the Council, which was crowned by the Stratford Festival; the founding of Canada's first national television network, complete with drama series — all these made serious, indeed irreversible, inroads into the Radio Drama Department's monopoly on resources and audiences. It was the beginning of the end of the Golden Age.

Some clear reasons can be adduced for the fact that Andrew Allan's career never leapt from radio to television. He had learned to exploit all the potentials of radio drama, had indeed invented a whole new set of techniques to exploit the medium and the genre. He had been a radio man since the early 1930s, and since 1944 the master of the network. Now, with the coming of television, the conditions under which he had worked were abruptly transformed. Allan's very mastery of the radio medium was a major stumbling block to his adapting to television. He explains in *A Self-Portrait* why he abandoned the new role the CBC offered him as a television drama director: "I had spent a dozen years learning the skills needed for radio drama, and I didn't feel that I had that kind of time for television. Also, I found not being able to control script material vastly inhibiting. The style of a show is its body; the content is its soul." Harry Boyle in his Introduction to *A Self-Portrait* further explains: "Andrew found himself expected to go through the same mill as the 21-year-old fresh out of college. He also found that television was hostile to the principle of translating the writer as fully as possible." Television simply denied the cornerstones of Andrew Allan's radio-drama goals: a writers' theatre, a theatre of social commentary, and a theatre in which the director's monopoly of the elements of production guarantees the fulfillment and unity of his artistic vision. Those goals, abundantly achieved in Allan's Golden-Age radio drama productions, had become practically impossible within the new structures of television.

Nevertheless, Allan left his strong mark on the theatre professionals who followed him. Many of the graduates of Allan's Drama Department were instrumental in the success of the very institutions which broke the Drama Department's monopoly on Canadian theatre. The new CBC television network made particularly extensive use of Radio Department personnel, not only actors like John Drainie and writers like Joseph Schull and Len Peterson, but also directors like Robert Allan, Peter Macdonald, Mavor Moore, and Esse Ljungh. The influences spread out to British and American television as well, and to their film industries. The Stratford Shakespeare Festival under Tyrone Guthrie made use (not surprisingly) of actors trained in the drama department, notably Frances Hyland, Douglas Rain, William Shatner, John Colicos, and Christopher Plummer. Many other theatres also benefitted, not only Canadian but

xiii

American and British. Our theatre schools have also been frequent beneficiaries. Allan's influence, the extent of which is only now becoming clear, has had an incalculable and invaluable effect on our theatre, especially important in the 1940s and 1950s. The Golden Age of Canadian radio drama was virtually over by the time of Allan's retirement in 1955; but the waves of Allan's talent spread far and wide in the Canadian and, indeed, the whole English-speaking theatre community. The plays collected here in *All the Bright Company* are a part of that legacy.

v

The invitation for Andrew Allan to head a national theatre on the air in 1943 was a major step in the decades-long effort to implement a conservative national policy welding Canada into a unified country. In its 19th-century form this policy was political and economic. Its implementation involved Confederation itself, the subsequent centralization of the Canadian banking system, the building of the CPR across the continent, and the development of our wheat-based economy. The entry of the CNR into broadcasting in the mid-1920s, even though tied to the economic goals of immigration, was inevitably an extension of the original policy into the cultural domain. The nationalization of Canadian radio transformed the structure of broadcasting from CNR radio and multiple private broadcasting stations to the Canadian Radio Broadcasting Commission and its affiliates. This eventually moved the production of radio-theatre from a relatively large number of local centres across the country to a monopoly (with rare exceptions) of only five or six regional centres, under the control of the CRBC and later of the CBC. The centralizing cultural trend was no less "establishment" than the economic version had been.

When Allan became CBC National Drama Supervisor in 1943, CBC regionalization became national centralization. Allan himself certainly had a national vision, as his concept of *Stage* clearly indicates. Equally important, a concentration of the best Canadian drama resources in Toronto was necessary for the flowering of a national Canadian theatre. However, the results in relation to the national policy were far from those anticipated: for Allan's nationalism was mainly on the other side of the establishment fence. His concept of the *Stage* series was, as noted above, consciously informed by an acute awareness of national social issues, issues which had become critical as a result of the crises of the 1930s. As Allan says in *A Self Portrait*: "If many of our plays in the first years had what was called 'social content,' this was because the writers — in fact, all of us — were products of a Depression and a War. Ideas bred from these twin phenomena were inevitable, unless you put artificial curbs on them. And we had determined not to apply those curbs."

And Allan was aware of the power both of the national radio network and of the dramatic mode to communicate these issues. Allan shared these views with his repertory team of writers and performers. It is clear from the contents of the plays that Allan and his team worked in opposition to the dominant establishment of the country. And the establishment reaction to the plays was not surprising. Irate listeners wrote CBC officers, Members of Parliament, and the Prime Minister. To give an example: Allan King's "Who Killed Cock Robin" is an ironic satire on prevailing economic and social assumptions. The play, aired on 11 May, 1952, despite its popularity among the general audience, drew considerable negative reaction. Letters in the Concordia Radio Drama Archives show how the writer, the producer, and the CBC were accused of being purveyors of communist propaganda. Allan had to smooth the waters with the CBC "brass"; as he says, "keeping the 'Stages' on the air, through most of those years called for the low cunning I possessed. One of the tricks was to follow an especially dangerous piece with something bland, to allow for a cooling off period."

One line of research in this area by the Concordia Radio Drama Project was to subject the Allan plays in the *Stage* series to a set of questions, the major ones being: was a play critical of particular current social practices; and were alternative practices suggested? The answers were clear: slightly more than half of the sampled plays were critical, especially with respect to social class and the economy. Of the critical plays addressing social class, almost half articulated an alternative vision. Of those plays critical to the economy, 30 percent suggested a counter-vision. Only slightly lower proportions applied to those plays in which the condition of women was questioned; and this pattern mainly held through the other categories studied. There was a tendency for more of the critical works to be found in the period 1945 to 1950, the period of post-war reconstruction, during which the directions Canada was to take concerning its social and economic organization and its relations with the United States were very much under discussion. The incidence of social and political criticism in the plays decreased in the decade of the 1950s, though, as the plays here show, there was no backing off by Allan from his general position.

It would be useful to inquire as to the effects on Canadian audiences of this didactic content in the *Stage* plays: how much of the success of Allan's productions depended on his genius in the arts of the theatre, and how much on the relevance of the issues addressed? It is certain that both elements played important roles in the popularity of the *Stage* series. Andrew Allan had a national dream, but it was not an establishment dream. With his ideals and his social consciousness he countered the establishment ideology for twelve seasons. And yet his informed nationalism not only played a major role in the creation of a genuine national Canadian theatre, but it was instrumental in the fostering of a powerful and concerned Canadian consciousness, a consciousness distinct from the British and American colonial visions of Canada. It was the development of just such a Canadian identity which, after all, was one of the major goals of the original national policy.

Howard Fink and John Jackson
Centre for Broadcasting Studies
Concordia University
Montreal, Quebec

ALL THE BRIGHT COMPANY

Note on Texts

The texts of the plays presented here are essentially those of the first as-broadcast production scripts, with all of Andrew Allan's own markings, as befits the goal of this anthology. Allan's own copy of the production script was available in every case, identified by his initials, "AA," scrawled large at the top of the first page. It is assumed, on good evidence, internal and external, that all the changes to the typed text were by Allan himself. An author was sometimes consulted on his script, however, so it is possible that a few changes were initiated by the author — though Allan's final control was never in question. We have attempted to retain the appearance of the script as well as its text and organization, in order to give as complete and accurate an impression of the broadcast as possible on paper. All the typed sub-dialogue instructions in the scripts are included, as well as all of the hand-written production notes.

In those instances in which additional pages, usually opening and closing announcements, were available, they have been included; they offer valuable information about the plays, including actors' lists, and they give a further authentic flavour of the actual broadcasts.

The plays Andrew Allan produced were, as we have suggested, fully collective creations, under the control of a superbly talented dramatic director, and one must, while reading, imagine such a production as unfolding in one's ear and mind. Only then will Allan's achievement be completely appreciated.

All the Bright Company

ANDREW ALLAN

Production

Producer: Andrew Allan
Music: Lucio Agostini
Sound: James Gilmore
Operator: Don Horne
Announcer: Arthur Hill
Program: Theatre Time
Broadcast: August 4, 1942 (DISC) 9:00–9:30 pm PDT
Studios: A and C Vancouver
Network: CBC Western

Cast

Larry McCance *as* George Manners
Alan Pearce *as* Charlie Beddoes
Bernard Braden *as* Jack Henderson
and
Peggy Hassard *as* Sylvia Hayward

•

ALL THE BRIGHT COMPANY

Preface

This is one of the many plays produced by Andrew Allan during the 1940s addressing the problem of war, and one of the thirty original dramas which he himself wrote for broadcast. "All the Bright Company" was written just three years after Allan had lost his father in the sinking of the *Athenia* in the Irish Sea. Both were aboard that first passenger liner to fall victim to German U-Boats at the opening of World War II. Perhaps out of this experience came the apocalyptic vision of the Manitou legend central to "All the Bright Company," a play in which hope and despair struggle for expression.

Listeners preoccupied with World War II and the sombre events of August 1942 were shifted to the opening days of World War I. One can imagine that feelings of despondency would have dominated the sentiments of those who tuned in for a half-hour of entertainment. The summer of 1942 was truly a summer of despair. All of Western Europe was under German control. German and Italian armies were poised for their march into Alexandria, the German assault on Stalingrad opened in August, and Japan, controlling most of Southeast Asia during the summer of 1942, had consolidated its positions in New Guinea and the Solomons, thus posing a threat to Australia.

Within the play, the opening selections from Grenfell's poem would perhaps console, but the introduction of the Manitou legend serves to express an agony of spirit. The Manitou, god of the Algonkian-speaking Amerindian peoples native to the Lake Superior region, represented both the good and the evil in their spiritual and corporeal worlds. Jack Henderson's vision, based on his knowledge of the legend of the Manitou, gives the play a mythic quality by means of which the listener is invited to consider war as a part of the human condition.

The nature-civilization opposition in the play — in some respects a culture-technology opposition — is expressed through the narrator, George Manners, whose materialism, ideological commitment to science, and

3

urbanism contrast with those of Jack Henderson and Sylvia Hayward, a young woman born of the apocalyptic vision, who carry the values of spirituality and artistic imagination. George Beddoes, the young banker, an objective observer, avoids argument and appears to keep each set of values in its place; he is the man for all seasons.

The opposing values are articulated on the realistic level in discussion and argument. The relation of the argument to the problem of war, however, can only be understood at the mythic level, where the fury of an electrical storm signals the presence of the spirit, Manitou. Likewise, Jack's vision represents the arrival of war: "The sky was filled with sheets of fire. The clouds were like the smoke from a million guns. . . . And I thought . . . I thought I saw troops of armed cavalry ride through the night." But the vision is tempered by the presence of Manitou: "something had taken charge of me . . . something strong and fierce and terrible and — *kindly*. . . . In a way I was frightened, and yet there was such an air of *compassion*."

The play expresses the dilemma of war: it appears as destiny, it offers greatness; but it maims and kills; can it be avoided? Allan answers, perhaps not — but it can be dealt with and survived if life is built around spirituality, imagination, and nature. In the dark days of 1942, this was the most positive vision possible for Allan. His courage and insight in dealing so frankly with this subject is a foretaste of the quite unique frankness and social concern characterizing many of the plays he chose to produce for the CBC in the next dozen or so years.

ANDREW ALLAN

All the Bright Company

Reader.   The fighting man shall from the sun
  Take warmth, and life from the glowing earth;
Speed with the light-foot winds to run,
  And with the trees to newer birth;
And find, when fighting shall be done,
  Great rest, and fulness after dearth.

¶ MUSIC: *sneak background.*

Reader. All the bright company of Heaven
  Hold him in their high comradeship,
The Dog-Star and the Sisters Seven,
  Orion's Belt and sworded hip.

The woodland trees that stand together,
  They stand to him each one a friend,
They gently speak in the windy weather;
  They guide to valley and ridges' end.

The thundering line of battle stands,
  And in the air Death moans and sings;
But Day shall clasp him with strong hands,
  And Night shall fold him in soft wings.

¶ MUSIC: *up to end.*

Announcer.   Vancouver *Theatre Time* tonight presents — especially transcribed for this broadcast — a play written and produced by Andrew Allan . . . "All the Bright Company."

¶ MUSIC: *narrative theme.*

George.   Good evening. My name is George Manners. I have a story I'd like to tell you. It's been on my mind all day . . . and perhaps when

I've finished, you'll realize why. On the other hand, you may think it a pretty thin story, and wonder why I bother to tell it at all. I suppose it just depends on whether or not it strikes a responsive chord in you. When it happened, it didn't seem very important to me. But, in the light of later events, it seems fraught with poignant meaning . . . . Twenty-eight years ago it happened. Twenty-eight years ago today. Jack Henderson, Charlie Beddoes, and I were camping at a place called Manitou Point in Northern Ontario. It was a hot summer, as some of you will remember — but of course the nights up there were cool. We had a lazy time of it — Charlie and Jack and I — and, though the holiday hours lumbered by slowly, the days seemed to pass all too quickly . . . . On the particular night I'm speaking of, we were sitting out on the point . . . our pipes lighted . . . the three of us gazing out across the lake. There was moonlight on the water, and a light breeze blowing from the north-west. How clearly I seem to remember it all! Much more clearly than I remember things that happened only last week. . . . For a long time none of us had spoken a word. [*BOARD FADE*] Then Jack took his pipe out of his mouth and said . . .

¶ MUSIC: *music out . . . night noises background.*

Jack.   Do you believe it?
Charlie.   Believe what?
Jack.   The legend.
Charlie.   The legend of the Manitou?
Jack.   Yes.
Charlie.   Not when I'm in Toronto, I don't.
   Pause.
Jack.   [*CASUALLY*] But up here . . .
Charlie.   I dunno.
George.   Up here you don't worry about whether you believe it or not. You just accept what you find and let it go at that.
Jack.   Mm . . . It isn't just accepting what you find. What I'm thinking about is accepting what you don't find . . . what you can hardly even imagine.
Charlie.   Jack's off again.
George.   Haven't seen any spooks, have you, Jack?
Jack.   No. Don't know as I expect to, George. But there are times when I think — with just a turn of the screw — that I might see something even more wonderful than a . . . spook.
Charlie.   More useful, too, I hope.
George.   Materialist. Just because you work in a bank, Charlie —
Charlie.   Okay! I'll conform. Believe in Jack's ghosts or anything. Only don't remind me I work in a bank.
George.   Burn incense to the presiding deity of the woods and groves?

Charlie. Anything! Don't remind me I work at all. I'm a big man up here. I don't want to remember I'm just a cog in the machine down in Toronto.

George. [CHUCKLES] I thought the open spaces made a man feel small, Charlie.

Charlie. Well —

Jack. They make him realize he's a man, though, George.

George. Uh-huh. Lord of Creation.

Jack. No. Just that he's a man . . . has a place in the scheme of things . . . a work to do . . . a life to live.

Charlie. I don't know how, but when I'm up here, I feel as if I belonged in these woods and lakes. Even when I dump the canoe or can't tell poison ivy from sumach or act like a city slicker about snakes and bugs and getting the fire started —

Jack. Even then you feel like a man, Charlie.

Charlie. I feel as if I belonged here . . . as if I'd fit in . . . if only —
Pause.

Jack. If only —

Charlie. If only I could remember something I'd forgotten . . . think my way back . . .

Jack. There! That's it!

George. Think your way back . . .

Charlie. Yes.

Jack. Even Charlie's an earth-man at heart.

Charlie. Whaddaya mean . . . *earth-man?*

Jack. I wonder just how much men have lost by cooping themselves up in cities.

George. Lost a bit, I expect. But they've gained something too.

Jack. What, for example?

George. Well . . . the social sense, I guess . . . the knack of working together side by side —

Jack. Have they?

George. Well, haven't they? They do work together side by side.

Jack. They do, because they're afraid not to. They're like rats in a wheel. They can't escape. They don't know how.

Charlie. They can always go for holidays. Like this.

Jack. Just to find out they can't light fires or tell poison ivy from —

Charlie. We're all in the same boat. The three of us. City guys. I'm no worse than you two.

Jack. No.

George. I don't imagine any of the guides down at Nemo Falls would be any great shakes at city life, if it comes to that.

Jack. Why should they be?

George. Well, is there any more reason why we should reproach ourselves for not being backwoods guides than that they should reproach themselves for not working in a ba — er — in an office?

Jack.   Maybe there is. Perhaps they've held on to the best things — the real things. Perhaps we've paid too much for our penny whistle.

¶ SOUND: *distant thunder.*

Charlie.   [AFTER A PAUSE] Pipe's out.

Jack.   Have a fill of this shag, Charlie.

Charlie.   Thanks.

George.   Almost too much breeze to light a match.

Jack.   Uh-huh.
   Pause.

Jack.   So city folks have learned to work together side by side, George.

George.   Sure. That's something anyway. An improvement over the rule of the claw . . . the law of the jungle . . . "the strong eat the weak and the weak are eaten."

Charlie.   Unless they've got good legs for running.

Jack.   George is a born optimist, Charlie. Believes in progress and everything.

George.   I believe in a lot of this "back to the simple life" stuff is just tommyrot. Sentimentality.

Jack.   Yes. But how about Charlie and his "thinking your way back . . . remembering something you'd forgotten?"

Charlie.   Don't drag me into it.

¶ SOUND: *distant thunder.*

George.   Interesting . . . if you can do it.

Charlie.   Wasn't that thunder?
   Pause.

¶ SOUND: *nearer thunder.*

Jack.   In for a storm, I guess.

Charlie.   Maybe that'll rouse the Manitou, Jack. They say thunder used to wake up the old Indian spirits.

Jack.   If he does wake up, I'd just as soon be asleep in my cot. They say no man ever saw Manitou and lived.

George.   What was he supposed to look like, Jack. Or is it an "it?"

¶ SOUND: *thunder.*

Jack.   Pretty hard to say, since no one ever lived to tell.

Charlie.   Then you can just let your imagination run riot.

Jack.   I gather old Manitou had many shapes. Most of the old legends put him in the form of a fearsome beast.

George.   The evil genius of the forest and lake . . .

Charlie.   I'll skip it when it comes my turn.
Jack.   You might not have a chance, Charlie.
Charlie.   You mean, to skip it?

¶ SOUND: *thunder.*

Jack.   Yes.
George.   All very unscientific.
Jack.   "There are more things in earth and heaven — "
George.   I know. I know.
Charlie.   The storm's going to hit us awful sudden when it comes. We'd
better get set.
Jack.   "I heard what was said of the universe,
Heard it and heard it of several thousand years;
It is middling well as far as it goes — but is that all?"
George.   Who's that?
Jack.   Walt Whitman.
Charlie.   Say, Jack, suppose old Manitou or whatever his name is,
wanted to get in touch with me, could I fix it so he'd send a messenger
instead of coming in person?
Jack.   Might. In the form of a dream, maybe. A vision.
Charlie.   Would I be awake or asleep?
Jack.   Hard to say, Charlie. A sort of half-way state, I should guess.
Afterwards you might have difficulty in deciding whether you'd had a
dream or . . . or just imagined it.

¶ SOUND: *loud thunder.*

Charlie.   What kind of a vision? Chief Big-Cow sitting on a cloud shooting arrows at things?

¶ SOUND: *very loud thunder.*

George.   Here it comes!
Charlie.   Whoops, the gear!

¶ SOUND: *downpour and wind.*

Jack.   Going to be a bad one!
George.   Better see the tents are fast in a hurry!
Charlie.   The pleasures of outdoor life, eh?
George.   It's every man for himself now!
Jack.   Right!

¶ SOUND: *montage of thunder storm, into storm music: effect of trumpet calls
and warfare through storm, segue into calm, then morning sounds, birds, &c.*

Charlie.   [CALLING OFF] Good morning, George! What're you up to?
George.   [OFF] Taking inventory of last night's damage.

Charlie. Talk about havoc! Look at that tree!

George. [COMING IN] Torn up by the roots. We were pretty lucky, Charlie. If the wind had been another point to the east, that tree would have fallen right across our tents.

Charlie. [WHISTLES] Wouldn't have done us a bit of good, would it?

George. Well, you wouldn't have to worry about going back to the bank.

Charlie. Or you about going back to the —

George. Say! Where's Jack?

Charlie. Don't know. Haven't seen him.

George. Isn't he in his tent?

Charlie. No. I thought he was out here with you.

George. Haven't seen a trace of him.

Charlie. His cot was empty when I woke up at dawn.

George. Here was I thinking I was first up.

Charlie. I just thought, "Oh, what's the use?" and rolled over and went to sleep again.

George. Holy smoke! you don't suppose —

Charlie. Wait a minute, George. The canoe's gone.

George. Oh.

Charlie. Guess Jack's gone for one of his solitary paddles.

George. [LAUGHS] For a minute I thought maybe the Manitou had got him.

Charlie. How about some breakfast?

George. Coffee's on. You're elected to fry the eggs and bacon.

Charlie. No sooner said than done. [FADE] I'm the meanest frier in the business.

George. [CALLING] And see that you do mine on both sides this time.

Charlie. [OFF] Never spoiled an egg yet.

George. [TO HIMSELF, GOOD-HUMOURED] That's a matter of opinion. . . . Hullo! . . . [CALLING] There's Jack paddling around the point now!

Charlie. [OFF] Yes! Who's that with him?

George. [SOTTO, SURPRISED] Looks like a girl with him. [CALLING] Oh! Jack!

Jack. [IN FAR DISTANCE SHOUTS SOMETHING LIKE "HULLO!"]

Charlie. [FADING IN] What do you suppose is up? Didn't know there was a girl nearer than Nemo Falls.

George. Maybe it's Mrs. Manitou.

Charlie. Well, I'd never have believed it of Jack Henderson, would you? Goes out in the canoe at dawn and comes back for breakfast with a beautiful squaw.

George. That's no squaw.

Charlie. No, but — poetic license.

George. Poetic nothing! That girl's hurt. She's got something wrong with one of her legs. [FADING] I'm going down to help.

Charlie. Hey! [*SOTTO*] Oh, well, guess I'll get back to frying eggs. It's safer. [*BOARD FADING*] Set another cover, Meadows, we're expecting Lady Mountebanks.
    Pause.
George. [*BOARD FADING IN*] Can I be of any help there, Jack?
Jack. [*BACK*] Grab the bow, George.

¶ SOUND: *water lapping: canoe bumping.*

George. Don't stand up yet, Miss.
Jack. If you'll just help me get Miss Hayward out of the canoe, George. She has a game leg.
Sylvia. [*BACK*] Sorry to be such a bother to everyone.
Jack. Sylvia, this is George Manners. Sylvia Hayward, George.
George. How do you do, Miss Hayward.
Sylvia. Sylvia. How do you do, George. I'm teetering.
Jack. If you'll give Miss — er — Sylvia a hand on that side, George, I'll support her from this side.
George. [*THROUGH BIZ*] Right. Easy does it. . . . Up! . . . There you are.
Sylvia. Thank you, kind sirs, for helping a damsel in distress. I think I can get the rest of the way with the aid of my cudgel.
Jack. It's a little rocky. Can you manage?
Sylvia. Sure of it. [*FADING*] I'll soon be able to navigate with this stick like an expert.
George. [*FADING*] If you stumble, we'll be here to catch you.
Jack. [*BOARD FADING*] I gather Charlie has breakfast under way.
    Pause.

¶ SOUND: *fade out lapping.*

George. [*FADING IN*] And this is our mutual friend, Charlie Beddoes. Miss Sylvia Hayward.
Sylvia. How do you do, Charlie Beddoes.
Charlie. Hullo there . . . Sylvia.
George. And this, madam, is our breakfast.
Sylvia. Hullo, breakfast.
Jack. To which you are most welcome.
Charlie. I've slipped in another couple of eggs and a rasher or two.
Sylvia. Mmmm! . . . What a lovely spot for a camp.
Jack. Manitou Point.
Sylvia. It *is* nice, Jack. . . . You know, George, if it hadn't been for your friend Jack, I'd have been a desolate creature by now.
George. How's that?
Sylvia. Well, you see, my father and mother and I are camping down in Deer Bay —
Jack. About six miles from here by water.

11

Sylvia. Dad went down to Toronto on Thursday. He can't keep away from business for more than a couple of weeks at a time, and we'd been here almost a month. We thought he'd be back by now — but no sign of him. So last night when the storm broke, mother and I were alone. And that storm did plenty of damage to our little place!

Jack. Made pretty much a mess of it, George. I tell you, after some of the wreckage I've seen this morning, we were mighty lucky here!

Sylvia. Anyway, my tent blew over . . . and my trophy is this sprained ankle. Silly — but as soon as it was light, nothing would stop Mother from taking off through the woods to Nemo Falls. The boat was smashed, so she couldn't row. I tried to tell her I was all right, but she lit off for a doctor. Is there a doctor in Nemo Falls?

George. Judging by the number of children I've seen hanging around door-ways . . . yes.

Sylvia. [*LAUGHING A LITTLE*] Well, anyway, I was alone and feeling sorry for myself . . . when who should paddle along in his birch-bark canoe but the brave chief of the Manitous —

Jack. Young Lochinvar.

Sylvia. And here we are!

¶ SOUND: *knocking in tin tray.*

George. And here — if I'm not mistaken — is breakfast.

Sylvia. To make life complete.

Charlie. [*BACK*] Come and get it!

Sylvia. I hope Mother finds that note I pinned to what was left of the tent flap. Otherwise, she'll think I'm kidnapped and have a posse out.

George. Maybe she'll think the pixies have got you. [*LAUGHTER INTO:*]

¶ MUSIC: *bridge.*

Charlie. Look, I'm all for a peaceful life. Must we top off our breakfast with a philosophical discussion.

Sylvia. But, Charlie! it's interesting!

Charlie. Well, if George would rather live in town, that's okay with me. As far as I'm concerned, this is the life every time.

Sylvia. That's not what you meant, though, is it, George?

George. No. All I said was . . . even if people have lost a certain amount of freedom by being cooped up in cities . . . they've gained other things. They've learned to work together . . . to abolish the old law of the jungle.

Sylvia. Do you really believe that?

George. Of course I do.

Jack. The trouble is, the law of the jungle hasn't been abolished at all. It still applies.

Sylvia. Of course it does. "The survival of the fittest" . . . that holds good today, even in cities.

Jack.   Especially in cities.

Sylvia.   People talk of it as if it were a virtue.

Jack.   Some people preach it as if it were a gospel. You take that book by von Bernhardi. The only weakness he admits is the failure to take what you can grab. Death and destruction for your neighbour is a very small cost if *you* get what you want. That's the philosophy they're preaching in the cities of the world today.

George.   Not all of them. I think you're making too *much* of an isolated case.

Charlie.   People are always coming out with theories like that. But they wouldn't dare put them into practice.

Jack.   Wouldn't they!

George.   Perhaps a certain amount of that kind of thing is necessary. A sort of antidote for the sentimentality of the times.

Sylvia.   [SADLY] Oh, George!

George.   Why not? You take that storm last night. Very terrible while it lasted . . . an upheaval of nature. Uprooted trees, blasted under-growth, wreckage —

Sylvia.   Sprained ankles —

George.   And yet, perhaps it's necessary. Perhaps it's nature's way of making a necessary adjustment. Perhaps human beings have to go through the fire and storm every so often, to burn away the dross. To bring us back to sanity — to realize what are the important things after all . . . what is noble and brave.

Jack.   [QUIETLY] Were you awake during the storm last night, George?

George.   [HESITATING] Part of the time, Jack. Why?

Jack.   Did you . . . did you notice anything?

George.   [CONSIDERING] No. . . . Only that it was uncomfortably close to us. I remember congratulating myself on the way we'd pitched our tents.

Jack.   You didn't notice . . .

   Pause.

George.   What?

Jack.   Nothing . . . I was . . . I only wondered —

Charlie.   [SUDDENLY] I noticed one thing mighty peculiar!

George.   You did?

Charlie.   There were a couple of long flashes, showed me a man standing in the middle of my tent.

Sylvia.   [SOTTO] Charlie!

Charlie.   It was Jack. What were you standing up for, Jack?

Jack.   I? Was I. . . . Oh, I don't know. Sca — er — just sort of jolted out of bed by the noise, I guess. . . . Was I — er — was I standing up, Charlie?

Charlie.   [SLOWLY] Yes. . . . And come to think of it . . . you — you did a very peculiar thing . . . at least, I *think* you — [QUICKLY] Oh, no! I must have been dreaming!

George. What in the world are you talking about, Charlie?

Charlie. Nothing. I was dreaming.

George. But what were you going to say?

Sylvia. Don't cross-examine him like a lawyer, George.

George. I wasn't. Only I wanted to know —

Charlie. I tell you, I didn't see anything. I was dreaming.

Jack. [STRONGLY] No, you weren't.

Sylvia. Jack!

George. What!

Charlie. I never sleep very well and —

Jack. Thanks, Charlie. But I might as well tell you all what happened last night.

Sylvia. Jack! *You* didn't —

Jack. I couldn't sleep. At least, I don't know. Perhaps I did doze at first — while the storm was coming nearer. I don't know. It was like the sleep you have in a fever . . . you can't tell whether it's all part of the effort to keep on breathing . . . whether any time has passed . . . what is real . . .

Sylvia. [SOFTLY] I know.

Jack. Then I was in the midst of the tent-floor. How long that was, or how I got there, I couldn't say. But there I was. I felt as if something had taken charge of me . . . something strong and fierce and terrible and — and *kindly*. I can't describe it. In a way I was frightened, and yet there was such an air of *compassion* about the — the thing there . . . I don't know! . . . And suddenly I was out in the rain — at the end of the point — without any volition of my own. Sleep-walking — delirium — it doesn't matter what you call it. Whatever you call it, you've only given it a name. It *happened* to me . . . I don't know. . . . But the sky was filled with sheets of fire. The clouds were like the smoke from a million guns. . . . And I thought . . . I thought I saw troops of armed cavalry ride through the night. . . . Oh, there's no need to look at me like that. I tell you, I saw it! You can say I dreamed it, or that I hypnotized myself into it with my talk of the Manitou. But till my dying moment, I'll know in my heart I saw it. . . . I was caught up, and saw the armies of destruction ride across the clouds at midnight on the storm!

❡ MUSIC: *strong cue: segue to quiet mood.*

Sylvia. Why did you tell them, Jack?

Jack. They might as well know.

Sylvia. They didn't understand.

Jack. Perhaps not, but they're my friends. I've known them all my life.

Sylvia. You can be someone all your life and not know him as well as the person you met yesterday.

Jack. Or this morning. [*LONG SILENCE*] Did you see the vision, Sylvia?

Sylvia. Yes.

Pause.

Jack. No wonder I was drawn so irresistibly to your camp this morning!

Sylvia. When I saw you paddle past the island and turn in, I knew I had expected you.

Jack. What does it mean?

Sylvia. Perhaps . . . it means you and I are tuned to something far off . . . something terrible and strong . . . that we feel the — what do you call it? —

Jack. Repercussion.

Sylvia. Yes. Of something far off, where people are caught in some agony of spirit.

Jack. But . . . what?

¶ SOUND: *distant thunder.*

Jack. [*PAUSE*] This . . . all this hasn't happened before, has it?

Sylvia. Perhaps it has.

Jack. The lake . . . and the trees . . . and you . . .

Sylvia. ''The Past and present wilt — I have fill'd them, emptied them, And proceed to fill my next fold of the future.''

Jack. Walt Whitman again.

Sylvia. Again?

Jack. Yes.

¶ SOUND: *distant thunder.*

Jack. ''I think I could turn and live with animals, they're so placid and self-contain'd,
I stand and look at them long and long.
They do not sweat and whine about their condition,
They do not lie awake in the dark and weep for their sins,
They do not make me sick discussing their duty to God,
Not one is dissatisfied, not one is demented with the mania of owning things,
Not one kneels to another, nor to his kind that lived thousands of years ago,
Not one is respectable or unhappy over the whole earth.''

¶ SOUND: *distant thunder: long silence.*

Jack. Sylvia . . . I love you.

Sylvia. I love you, Jack. . . . Always — from the beginning of things.

15

Jack.   Sylvia, my dear . . .

Sylvia.   I feel . . . why is it? . . . that we must know the whole love of our lifetime in a few short hours . . . [*SUDDENLY*] Jack! I'm afraid!

Jack.   Don't, my darling! Not afraid. That's one thing we must never be.

Sylvia.   Not afraid . . .

Jack.   Never.

Sylvia.   Tell me that often, my dear . . . even when you're far away.

Jack.   This is a world where so many things seem petty. We must raise what we have in us of nobility and flaunt it like a banner. None of us knows what heights he can reach until the times press in upon him and make him great.

Sylvia.   What . . . what is going to happen, Jack? What did you feel, last night?

¶ SOUND: *thunder.*

Jack.   I felt like a man caught in a pitiless current. I felt as if every action I should make had been ordained for me . . . that only my soul was my own.

Sylvia.   See the lake, Jack. It's the same lake. And the quiet pines. Are they guarding some secret?

Jack.   The same secret we guard in our hearts. [*PAUSE*] Sylvia! What is to prevent a man and woman from entering into the innermost secrets of these forests? Why should we go back to cities to labour like oxen at a mill? To bleed for other people we never even heard of?

Sylvia.   Because that is the way things are ordered, Jack.

Jack.   We've been here for three weeks . . . George and Charlie and I . . . and the gods have been so kind as to allow us another. In all this time we haven't heard so much as a rumour from the world of cities. We might go on living in the midst of all this grandeur to the end of our days, and never yearn for a moment to return to that fever and hatred.

Sylvia.   I know. I've been saying that to myself for the past month. I don't care what the people in the outside world do. What is it to me? I have the forests and lakes and the calm of real contentment.

¶ SOUND: *thunder.*

Jack.   Then . . . why go back? We will go back, you know. Why?

Sylvia.   Perhaps the vision told us, Jack. Lying comfortably in our beds, safe from the storm . . . yet we were drawn into it, without any will of our own, to watch the armies of the air ride across the sky . . .

¶ MUSIC: *narrative theme.*

George.   Twenty-eight years ago, that was. Twenty-eight years ago today. . . . No wonder it all seems so clear — more real than things that happened last week. That was the end of the old world, that summer

. . . the world we had known, the one we grew up in. . . . Poor Jack Henderson was killed at Vimy Ridge. His widow, Sylvia, has gone up to Manitou every summer — still does. Up until two years ago Derek went with her. Young Derek's her son — her's and Jack's. But Derek's in the Navy now — RCNVR — two stripes — and only twenty-seven. Jack would have been proud of him. Derek's married now — lovely girl, Sylvia says. But of course she would be. Things go on! . . . Haven't seen Charlie Beddoes since last summer. He came out to Vancouver from a place in Saskatchewan — a captain in the Home Guard! Quite a change from the fellow that finished the last war as Acting Lance Corporal Without Pay. . . . As for me, I'm not much use with this souvenir of mine — this empty sleeve — but I can be an Air Raid Warden, and I only hope I don't have to blow my whistle in earnest. . . . A lot has happened, but it doesn't seem so long ago . . . only twenty-eight years ago, the night we saw the storm at Point Manitou . . . the night of August the fourth, 1914.

¶ MUSIC: *up and under.*

Reader.   The fighting man shall from the sun
    Take warmth, and life from the glowing earth;
Speed with the light-foot winds to run,
    And with the trees to newer birth;
And find, when fighting shall be done,
    Great rest, and fulness after dearth.

All the bright company of Heaven
    Hold him in their high comradeship,
The Dog-Star and the Sisters Seven,
    Orion's belt and sworded hip.

The woodland trees that stand together,
    They stand to him each one a friend,
They gently speak in the windy weather;
    They guide to valley and ridges' end.

The thundering line of battle stands,
    And in the air Death moans and sings;
But day shall clasp him with strong hands,
    And night shall fold him in soft wings.

¶ MUSIC: *finale.*

Announcer.   The play was entitled "All the Bright Company." It was written by Andrew Allan and was produced to-night under the direction of the author in the series, *Theatre Time.* Featured in the cast were: Larry McCance as George Manners; Alan Pearce as Charlie Beddoes;

Bernard Braden as Jack Henderson; and Peggy Hassard as Sylvia Hayward. The poem, from which excerpts were read by E.V. Young, was "Into Battle," written by Julian Grenfell, a young poet who died in the last war. Special effects were by James Gilmore. "All the Bright Company" was especially transcribed for this broadcast in the Vancouver studios of the CBC.

Brainstorm Between Opening and Closing Announcements

FLETCHER MARKLE

Production

Producer: Andrew Allan
Music: Laurence Wilson
Sound: James Gilmore and Frank Vyvyan
Operator: Don Horne
Announcer: John Drainie
Program: Baker's Dozen
Broadcast: October 28, 1942, 7:15–7:45 pm PDT
Studios: A and C Vancouver
Network: CBC National

Cast

Bernard Braden *as* Surrealist
Fletcher Markle *as* Markle
Alan Pearce
Clare Murray
Larry McCance
Peggy Hassard   *as* Voices
John Bethune
Ruby Chamberlain
William Buckingham

•

BRAINSTORM BETWEEN OPENING AND CLOSING ANNOUNCEMENTS

Preface

The staging of the *Baker's Dozen* series, which includes "Brainstorm Between Opening and Closing Announcements," is a crucial event in Canadian broadcasting and theatre history. This weekly anthology series, written by Fletcher Markle and produced in Vancouver by Andrew Allan with his repertory team over thirteen weeks starting in the summer of 1942, electrified audiences across the country. There had been nothing quite like it since the *Romance of Canada*, that first national Canadian series, produced by Tyrone Guthrie for CNR Radio in 1931. *Baker's Dozen* brought to the Canadian public a new kind of radio drama, altogether a new kind of play; it marked the birth of the Golden Age of Canadian radio drama.

As Allan explains in his autobiography: "We had been working toward this. The first thing I found in Vancouver was a group of young actors who were chafing for a chance. But a kind of play completely unlike anything that was being done was obviously needed for them. The old habit of reading stage plays out loud was not good enough. We began to encourage new writers. *Baker's Dozen* was the climax of this. And we found an audience that had been waiting for it." What Markle provided for Allan was an imaginative new form of script, once and for all free of the limiting requirements of visual drama, and taking full advantage of the sound medium to recreate the tension and excitement of good theatre.

Baker's Dozen comprises ten plays in thirteen broadcasts; the plays are quite diverse, ranging from the most mundane realism to the most abstract impressionism, and make full use of the dramatic possibilities of radio communication. Doubtless the most imaginative of these plays is "Brainstorm," a satire on the hedonism and anti-intellectualism of the radio in those times, which will seem startlingly appropriate as a critique of modern broadcasting. Markle identifies his dramatic method here as surrealism, and the play lives up to this billing, showing just how imaginative radio drama can be.

Baker's Dozen launched the careers of both Allan and Markle. Allan was only thirty-five — in less than a year he would be invited to become National Supervisor of Drama. Markle, though, was only twenty-one when he wrote "Brainstorm" and the other plays in the series. Born in Winnipeg in 1921, Markle had moved at an early age to Vancouver, where he began his career in radio in 1940 as the writer, actor, and producer of the drama series *Imagine Please* for station CKWX. Allan soon recognized his talents and produced not only *Baker's Dozen* but also most of the other twenty-five original plays which Markle wrote for the CBC between 1941 and 1945. Markle's career soon widened to both Britain and America, to film and television writing, to production and direction. While in London in the RCAF from 1942 to 1945, Markle wrote and produced for the BBC and for documentary film. From 1946 on his career developed in New York and Hollywood: first in film writing and directing with Orson Welles and Alexander Korda, then in television. He produced and directed a number of the best-known television drama series, like *Ford Theatre, Studio One, Front Row Centre,* and *Life with Father.* By the 1960s, Markle was directing films again, both in Hollywood and for CBC-TV. He was Head of CBC Television Drama in the early 1970s, returning to Hollywood in 1976. Markle has supplied an almost literary symmetry to his career by spearheading the return of American radio drama in the early 1980s with the production of the series *Sears Radio Theatre.*

FLETCHER MARKLE

Brainstorm Between Opening and Closing Announcements

¶ SOUND: *static, swelling up then under between each of the following snatches of programs which cross-fade quickly one into another: effect to simulate the twisting of a radio dial.*

¶ MUSIC: *the momentary strains of a dance band.*

¶ SOUND: *static up.*

Newscaster. Recent communiques confirm the reports that the Allied Air Forces have gained the upper hand in the latest phases of the fighting. Under a strong . . .

¶ SOUND: *static up.*

M.C. And here's our next contestant stepping up to the microphone. Good evening, sir. Welcome to . . .

¶ SOUND: *static up.*

¶ SOUND: *large crowd.*

Commentator. I've never seen so many people. . . . We've managed to press our way through them and we're standing now with our microphone at the edge of the platform. This is one of the . . .

¶ SOUND: *static up.*

Announcer. So we suggest that you try it for yourself. Accept your dealer's free trial-offer *today.* You'll find that this reliable and economical way . . .

¶ SOUND: *static up.*

¶ MUSIC: *the dance band again.*

¶ SOUND: *static up.*

Dietitian. It is obvious that a diet supplying too many calories will cause overweight, encourage any tendencies your body may have to diabetes, and also force . . .

¶ SOUND: *static: chime.*

Announcer. From Vancouver, the Canadian Broadcasting Corporation brings you *Baker's Dozen*: a 13-week cycle of original radio diversions by the Canadian writer, Fletcher Markle. Tonight, as Program Number Eleven, we present "Brainstorm Between Opening and Closing Announcements" — being an epileptic farce in seven fits. By way of preface, here's a word from the author . . .

Markle. Dear Listener — Surrealism, authorities will tell you, is "a modern movement purporting to express the subconscious mental activities by presenting images without order or sequence, as in a dream." Mr. Salvador Dali, surrealism's widest-known exponent, applies a lighter touch and says: "Le surréalism, c'est moi." . . . Tonight's program, with a nod to approaching Hallowe'en, tends to Mr. Dali's attitude if not his explanation and introduces surrealism to radio with the . . .

¶ SOUND: *click of switch: background static out.*

Surrealist. [*AFTER A LONG PAUSE*] You turned off your radio. You were tired. You had been listening, half-listening, or listening not at all to announcers, newscasters, comedians, actors, orchestras playing music, good and bad, and people singing and people talking.
You were tired, bored, and unhappy.
You turned off your radio.
You relaxed in your chair.

¶ SOUND: *sneak tympani under:*

Surrealist. You were not asleep.
You were not awake.
You did not move.
But suddenly you were *there*!
The Scene: Cosmos. The Time: Eternity.
You were standing in space. Space, endless and empty.
But there was *something*.
There. Hanging out of nowhere ahead of you.
You moved closer.

¶ MUSIC: *strings, shrill minor see-saw effect, under:*

Surrealist. [*AFTER A MOMENT*] You could see it now.

¶ MUSIC: *guitar effect, ascending slur and out.*

24

¶ SOUND: *tympani out with guitar.*

Cast. WILLY NILLY...

Surrealist. You heard voices from somewhere.
   But you paid no attention.
   There was too much to be *seen.*
   Behold! A button-hook!
   You saw a great gleaming button-hook suspended from the
   dark shadows of a mighty ear's lobe.
   An ear-ring! you thought,
   A button-hook? you thought. Forty feet long?
   Oh, come now, you thought back at yourself —
   after all, this *is* the age of zippers.
   Oh, no!
   Interrogation, by Jupiter! The question mark's pendant!
   A l'espagnole! (That's French for Spanish).
   The thing's upside-down, you repeated to yourself.
   And what has it caught in its hook, there?
   You moved closer.

¶ MUSIC: *see-saw strings effect, in and out.*

Surrealist. Close enough, you thought. Go too far and they'll
   take away your poetic license.
   You could see what hung there in the hook now.
   Towering, monstrous, elephantine — a mighty chrome temple of
   Mazuma, the shrine of The Silver, The Copper, and The Green.
   A cash register.
   You shivered.
   Upon the huge white plate under the keys, you saw three figures
   dressed in the manner of contestants. (You did not understand how
   you knew that the manner of contestants was the manner they were
   dressed in. But you *knew* nevertheless).
   You saw three contestants placed upon the whiteness of the altar.
   Plump. Ready for sacrifice.

¶ SOUND: *the huge bell of the cash register.*

Surrealist. You heard the bell.
   The ear-ring!
   Gothic, wasn't it?
   But behold!
   You saw the contestants cross their legs, moving from left to right.
   You saw them wet their lips, wetting from right to left.
   You thought that there must be more to this than meets the eye.

Quiz Master. [FILTER: A SQUAWK]

Surrealist.   Why, of course, you thought — it meets the ear!
Quiz Master.   [*FILTER: A SQUAWK*]
Surrealist.   You saw him perched there on the hook.
   A parrot.
   The parrot.
   The Quiz Master himself — the jovial, jocular, jaunty master of the revels.
   Good old Polly, you thought, formerly known as Polyphemus. You remembered Polyphemus. (Used to run with the Cyclops mob. Big future until he started hitting the bottle).
   You wondered where he picked up those feathers?
Quiz Master.   [*FILTER: A LOUDER SQUAWK*]
Surrealist.   You saw him fly down to the altar, the white marble dais.
   The affair's going to start, you thought — on with the sacrifice.
   Polly! God Public is hungry for the fun that cupidity
   breeds of stupidity.

¶ SOUND: *applause: distant, muffled, under:*

Surrealist.   You heard applause from somewhere. But you couldn't see the audience.
   You watched Polly fly about over the contestants,
   explaining that they had been carefully chosen at random
   from the audience and that the game would now begin.
   You saw him settle on one of the lower keys of the mighty
   register and preen his feathers and his script.

¶ SOUND: *fade out applause.*

Surrealist.   You saw the game begin.
   You strained to listen as the first contestant stepped forward.
Quiz Master.   [*FILTER*] *Here's your question. Here's your question. Why was Christopher Columbus.*
Contestant 1.   Eh?
Quiz Master.   [*FILTER*] *Sorry. Sorry. Time's up. Time's up. You lose. You lose.* [*LAUGHS UPROARIOUSLY UNDER:*]
Surrealist.   You realized that the first contestant was deaf. He could not hear the question.
Quiz Master.   [*FILTER*] *You lose!*
Surrealist.   You saw him transformed into a set of books.

¶ SOUND: *a pile of books falls to the floor: the muffled applause is heard under:*

Surrealist.   You heard the unseen audience applaud the disappearance of the first contestant and the appearance of the second contestant before the Quiz Master.

¶ SOUND: *fade out applause.*

26

Quiz Master. [*FILTER*] *Here's the question. Here's the question. Why was Christopher Columbus?*

Contestant 2. [*GUTTERAL NOISES*]

Quiz Master. [*FILTER*] *Why was Christopher Columbus?*

Contestant 2. [*MORE GUTTERAL NOISES*]

Surrealist. You realized that the second contestant was dumb. He could not speak his answer and had an intense desire to say so.

Quiz Master. [*FILTER*] *You lose! You lose!* [*LAUGHS AGAIN UNDER:*]

Surrealist. You saw him transformed into a pile of silver dollars.

¶ SOUND: *silver dollars cascading onto a hard surface.*

Surrealist. You saw them spill around the dais, lie flipping and squirming like fresh herring, and fall off the edges leaving the imitation marble slippery and wet, as though it were covered with blood.

¶ SOUND: *the muffled applause again under:*

Surrealist. You heard the unseen audience again applauding the transformation and the arrival of the third contestant in front of the Quiz Master.

¶ SOUND: *fade out applause.*

Quiz Master. [*FILTER*] *Third contestant! Third contestant! How do you feel tonight? How do you feel?*

Contestant 3. I've got six months to live.

Quiz Master. [*FILTER*] *Fine! Fine! Here's the question. Why was Christopher Columbus?*

Contestant 3. Because he discovered America and could lay an egg on a table.

Quiz Master. [*FILTER*] *Correct! Correct! You win! You win the game!*

¶ SOUND: *again the applause: under:*

Surrealist. You saw that the third contestant had won the books, formerly the first contestant, and the pile of silver dollars, formerly the second contestant.

Contestant 3. But I'm blind! I can't read.

Surrealist. You heard that the third contestant was blind. He couldn't read.

Quiz Master. [*FILTER*] *Don't worry. Don't worry. Talking books. The books talk. Come here. Come here.*

¶ SOUND: *fade out applause under:*

Surrealist. You saw the third contestant introduced to the books by the Quiz Master and exchange the usual cordialities. You saw, too, that the mighty register had begun to swing, pendulum-like, on the button-hook. Swing, as if the owner of the ear-ring, lost in the dark shadows above, were slowly nodding in confirmation. You turned your attention to the contestant again.

Contestant 3. I've never spoken to a talking book before. How are you?

Book. All right, I guess. A little bound up at the back, though. My appendix has been giving me trouble. I think I'll have it taken out. And my footnotes have been simply killing me.

Contestant. Tell me, do you know William Shakespeare to speak to?

Book. Well, no. But I know his younger brother, Expurgated Shakespeare. A rather gray personality, I'm sorry to say. Most people can read him like a book.

Quiz Master. [*FILTER: A SQUAWK*]

Surrealist. You saw the Quiz Master, good old Polly, fly up to his perch on one of the keys again, looking happy to have found a lucky contestant. Polly wants a wise cracker? you thought. No. You saw him fly away as key dropped from under him and the drawer crashed open.

¶ SOUND: *cash register bell and noise of huge drawer opening.*

Surrealist. You noticed the tag which appeared behind the glass at the top of the register. NO SALE.

¶ SOUND: *confusion of voices.*

Surrealist. Then you saw the audience, pouring out of the open drawer. Squinting, you could see each one of them was clutching a memento of the occasion — a little clay effigy of the sponsor.

Surrealist. Then it happened.

¶ SOUND: *out of the voices come shouts and screams of terror.*

Surrealist. You had hardly realized that the pendulum-swing
of the register had increased its speed.
Now you saw it swinging in a high arc.
You saw the contestants, the talking book, the pile of
silver and the shrieking audience dropping into space,
into nowhere.

¶ SOUND: *slowly fade sound out under:*

Surrealist. Before you knew it, the register on its inverted button-hook pendulum had thrown them all off and was rising slowly into the black shadows where you had seen the giant ear-lobe.
In a moment, there was nothing.
You were alone, you thought.
Then you saw old Polly, the Quiz Master. He flew past you with a long, slow wink.

Then he, too, was gone.

¶ MUSIC: *guitar effect, descending slur and out.*

Cast. MUMBO JUMBO...

Surrealist. You heard more voices.
  You were in another part of space now.
  But you had not moved.
  Before you was the grotesque shape of an enormous pair
  of lips. Twice the size of the homicidal cash register.
  You shivered again.
  You saw the lips moving, slowly.
  You heard:

Critic. According to Coleridge, the style rhythm of the Captain's speeches in the second scene should be illustrated by reference to the interlude in Hamlet, in which the epic is substituted for the tragic, in order to make the latter be felt as the real-life diction. In Macbeth, the poet's object was to raise the mind at once to the high tragic tone, that the audience might be ready for the precipitate consummation of guilt in the early part of the play. It would seem then, as Coleridge says, that the true reason for the first appearance of the Witches is to strike the key-note of the character of the whole drama, as is proved by their reappearance in the third scene, after such an order of the king's as establishes their supernatural power of information . . .

Cooking Expert. [ON "DICTION": OVER CRITIC] Now you cream the cheese thoroughly, adding sugar gradually. Next the eggs, one at a time. Beat well after each. Add salt, flour, and lemon juice next and mix well. Now, then, in case some of you haven't got that quite clear, I'll repeat it . . . [SHE DOES]

Surrealist. [AS COOKING EXPERT BEGINS: OVER VOICES] Then you heard another voice.
  You saw the lips begin to move faster.

Exerciser. [ON "FASTER"] Place the hands on the hips. Knees full bend, keeping the head and shoulders well back. Return to standing position and raise the body with the toes. Ready — to the count of three. . . . One, two, three . . . [AD-LIB TO END OF EFFECT]

Surrealist. [AS EXERCISER SPEAKS: OVER VOICES] You saw the moving lips become a blur.

¶ SOUND: *voices up full: to the above are added as many recorded voices as mechanically possible: the latter's speed is slowly increased to gibberish: at peak of effect, a cut-off, knife-clean.*

Surrealist. There was a sudden silence, as if the voices had been savagely switched off.

You saw that the enormous lips had talked themselves to
a formless blubber.
You heard an epic sigh escape from them.

Cast. [*LONG CONCERTED SIGH*]

Surrealist. You find yourself sighing, too, as the bloated red mass
slowly melted away into the deep space below.

¶ MUSIC: *guitar effect, descending slur and out.*

Cast. HODGE PODGE...

Surrealist. Another place,
Yet not another.
The voices again.
After them, this time, a demented shrilling.

¶ MUSIC: *a single note: singing shrilly, expanding.*

Surrealist. You looked for its source.
You found it.
Far out in front of you were five black lines across
the chiaroscuro of emptiness.
They sang as wires in a wind and as you floated toward
them, you saw dark splotches caught fly-wise in their web.
The quintuple lines and their blobs seemed a
staff and notes of music, you thought.
But, as you neared them, you saw that the black splotches
were alive, that they were men, that they were all playing instru-
ments.
Their faces were spasmed in pain, you noticed.
It must be difficult to play music while enmeshed in those
wires, you thought.
Suddenly you felt yourself pulled into a sitting position,
though you sat upon nothing, and you heard:

¶ MUSIC: *Laurence Wilson and thirteen musicians at the mercy of a perverted
script writer's imagination.*

Surrealist. With a sharp tingling in your spine, you realized that the
wires had suddenly begun to glow — a hot, glaring red.

¶ SOUND: *short-circuit effect.*

Surrealist. There was a searing flash before your eyes.
Short circuit!
The wires and their animated splotches were smoke.
There was the stench of discord in your nostrils.

¶ MUSIC: *guitar effect, descending slur and out.*

Cast. HURLY BURLY...

¶ SOUND: *a crowd symphony of cheers, shouts applause, boos, and miscellaneous uproar: rising and falling background to:*

Surrealist.   Another celestial corner.
But somehow the same one.
Full of sound and shadow, this one, you thought as
you looked it over.
Below, above and around you swelled the cacophonous
music of Mob.
All you could see was a door. A phosphorescent square
with a handle, ahead of you.
There was no reason for it, you thought. There was
no sign of a wall around it.
Yet you noticed that an anxious figure stood before its
dazzling whiteness, clutching a metallic bulb on a wire
that trickled off into the murk.
You drifted towards him, seeking explanation.

¶ MUSIC: *see-saw strings effect, in and out.*

Surrealist.   In a moment, you heard his voice, clarion in the tumult.

Commentator.   [*FADING IN*] Well, we're still waiting, ladies and gentlemen. . . . We should have the results any time now. . . . We're standing just outside the door here — uh — waiting. . . . I'd — I'd just like to say while I have a moment that this is the most — er — unusual actuality broadcast I've ever had the privilege of reporting to you. . . . When you come right down to it — uh — I suppose this event we're — er — we're waiting to bring you is the real *reason* — the real *cause* — of all the others . . .the other — um — events. . . . The football, baseball, and, hockey games . . . the prizefights . . . banquets and parades and — er — ship-launchings . . . all of these wouldn't even — uh — exist if it weren't for the event of the kind we're waiting to bring you — to *report* to you tonight. . . . Yes, sir, this is the most exciting happening I've ever had the opportunity to broadcast. . . . I wish you could be here. . . . As I said, I'd never have been able to describe all the — the tennis matches and golf tournaments — even the unveiling of a monument — if it weren't for this — this miraculous happening we're waiting to bring you — er — tonight . . . [*GALVANIZED*] AH! Stand by! The door knob is turning! The door is opening wide . . .and here's the young lady we've been waiting for. . . . Er — won't you tell our listeners — er — in your own words — what has happened tonight. . . . Right into the microphone here . . .

Nurse.   I'd be glad to. . . . It's a boy — *and* a girl. Twins!

Commentator.   Thank you. . . . A truly blessed event!

¶ SOUND: *the twins' first vocal efforts.*

Surrealist. Bewildered, you were scarcely aware of the door's abrupt slam.

¶ SOUND: *door slam: cutting all sound.*

Surrealist. The hubbub of Special Events was gone.
   So was the door.
   It had slammed itself out of existence.
   You stood alone in the soundless jet.
   Soundless?
   No. There *was* one voice left.
   You heard it as it died.
Commentator. [*FADING*] This concludes our portion of the program. We return you now to . . .

¶ MUSIC: *guitar effect, descending slur and out.*

Cast. HOCUS POCUS . . .
Surrealist. To another place.
   The same place.
   Here you saw a glowing cornucopia, formed in Twentieth-Century style — a cross between a dollar-sign and a tuba. High on the pile of plenty spewing from its mouth, you saw three smiling young men, shoulder to shoulder.
   They spoke to you:
Trio. [*CHANTING*] X — X — X
   It calms a vex.
   It breaks a hex.
   The well-known unknown quantity
   Of long-respected quality.
   X — X — X
   The riddle of our sex!
Announcer 1. X — the harmless cosmic pill, obtainable in all reliable lifetimes:
Announcer 2. We guarantee that it produces
Announcer 3. And only one of its many uses
Announcer 1. Is treatment of your gastric juices!
Announcer 2. Soft as petals on a rose.
Announcer 3. Sweetens your breath and blows your nose.
Announcer 1. Our independent survey shows:
Trio. X is Rex!
Announcer 1. And now we know how eager everyone is's
   To hear how rapidly this pill fizzes.
Announcer 2. Standing a cup upon a blotter,

We drop a tablet in the water.

¶ SOUND: *fizz which becomes the violent hissing of steam: screams from the young men as the hissing steam becomes a bursting flood of water: bring up to maximum level and slowly fade off to:*

Surrealist.　You saw the horn and its flood fall away into the
void like a teardrop.
There *is* many a slip 'twixt the cup and lip, you thought.
But *you* hadn't even got wet.

¶ MUSIC: *guitar effect, descending slur and out.*

Cast.　R A Z Z L E D A Z Z L E . . .
Surrealist.　You saw them in this next corner.
The same corner.
They made you think of Hallowe'en, a time of noise and
fire and pumpkin heads and little old children.
And masks.
No, not the ones with the red noses and bug eyes
up in your attic, you thought.
Two other masks. Ancient masks, dating back to
Aristotle and before.
You saw them there in this corner of space, corpse-pale
against the inky curtain of emptiness.
One had a rather silly grin on its face, you thought.
An eternal grin, with a certain toothless inanity.
It was called Comedy, you remembered.
The other looked like a desperate case of dyspepsia.
Gloom with an evil smell under its nose.
Its name was Tragedy, you remembered.
It flew towards you before you knew it, this Tragedy,
and tried itself on you for size.
A perfect fit!
You heard:

¶ MUSIC: *sneak organ background to:*

Announcer.　[CLOSE] And now we bring you another episode of *Life Can Be Dreadful*. . . . As you know, John ran off with Elsie, the hired girl, after shooting her father, Hiram, in the cabbage patch. Meanwhile, Aunt Ella has fallen off the roof again, breaking her petunias. Cousin Rupert awaits execution for the murder of Mrs. Willington and her three daughters. As we drop in on the little house up the street, around the corner, and down two blocks to your left, we find Helen alone in her bedroom, sobbing quietly to herself . . .

¶ SOUND: *loud sobbing: terminated by vigorous nose-blowing.*

33

Announcer. Downstairs, Herman Herbschrieber, the smoked halibut magnet, paces the floor, nervously puffing a cigar. Rover, a dog, lurks behind the living room curtain, biding his time. . . . It's *Life Can Be Dreadful* . . .

¶ SOUND: *door opens and slams.*

¶ MUSIC: *out with slam.*

Actor. Genevieve! You've come back! After twenty-five years, you've come back. You have . . . you have — *returned!*

Actress. Oh, Ralph, I am not Genevieve. I'm her daughter, Sylvia, the one who was lost in the Chicago fire. I've come to plead with you, Anthony, to ask you to release Mrs. Mullins from her contract with your fish company.

Actor. I'm sorry, Elizabeth, but I gave my last word on that subject to your sister ten years ago — in Akron, Ohio.

Actress. But, Ernest! There's grandfather's will and Mr. Droke told me —

Actor. Never mind what Mr. Randolph told you. I, too, must think of the future. The past is passed. We can live only in the present.

Actress. No, no William — you don't know what you're saying!

Actor. I do know what I'm saying, Margaret, and that is final. I must ask you now to pick up your accordian and leave!

¶ SOUND: *door opens and slams on last line above: after a moment, there is a lingering howl from rover.*

Surrealist. You noticed that the mask had slipped around on your
face a little. The corners of its mouth had turned
up, had lifted your own.
You were suddenly grinning through Comedy whether
you liked it or not.
You heard:

¶ SOUND: *a roar of laughter.*

Psychologist. Laughter is a higher instinct, if it may be called an instinct, and one not shared by the lower animals.

¶ SOUND: *another roar of laughter which cross-fades into the chattering of monkeys under.*

Comedian 1. Well, tell me, why did the chicken cross the road?
Comedian 2. That was no chicken. That was my wife.

¶ SOUND: *monkeys up and down under:*

Comedian 1. Our goat had his nose cut off.
Comedian 2. Yeah? How did he smell?

Comedian 1.   Terrible.

¶ SOUND: *monkeys up and down under.*

Comedian 1.   Where was Moses when the lights went out?
Comedian 2.   In the dark.

¶ SOUND: *monkeys up full: they are joined by laughter: both fade under.*

Surrealist.   You saw Divine Comedy ride quickly by astride the back of
    that fierce rogue elephant, Hyperbole.

¶ SOUND: *elephant trumpeting.*

Comedian 1.   She was so fat . . .
Comedian 2.   She was so ugly . . .
Comedian 1.   He's so skinny . . .

¶ SOUND: *monkeys and laughter up and fade slowly to:*

Surrealist.   I must tear these masks off and be myself, you thought.
    You did.
    You watched them float gently back to their curtain,
    ear to ear, leering and glowering.
    They hung there in space a moment, swinging together.
    They turned to each other.
    They kissed.

¶ SOUND: *explosion.*

Surrealist.   Who said opposites attract? you wondered.

¶ MUSIC: *guitar effect, descending slur and out.*

Cast.   T O P S Y   T U R V Y . . .
Surrealist.   Still another place.
    But the same place.
    Somehow, though, you knew — the Last Place.
    You were higher up this time than you had ever been before.
    Moon-high.
    Far, far, far below you was the Earth.
    The old boomerang, still going, you thought. Spinning around the
    Sun — a great, fat, wingless moth bearding an even greater candle,
    with the same old mad intent. It was revolving in its old orbit, coming
    closer to you. Round and round she goes and where she stops nobody
    knows — yet —
    Place your bets, gentlemen! you wanted to shout. Black? Red? White?
    Red has been winning lately.

¶ SOUND: *fade in morse signals of varying tones: hold under:*

Surrealist.   You heard the Earth speak.

They seem to have something to say, you thought.
Everybody is talking at once.
The Earth was close now.

¶ MUSIC: *a swelling rumble becoming a bombastic music-cue to:*

Narrator.   Time and Tide wait for no man!

¶ MUSIC: *scream chord.*

Narrator.   At this week's beginning in a town identified by name only, a strange, world-perplexing thing occurred. So strange was this unexpected phenomenon that even we, the Editors of Tide, do not know what it was. This means that God only knows.

¶ MUSIC: *brief cue.*

Narrator.   One day, this same week, in every village, town, and city in this country, was Monday.

¶ MUSIC: *brief cue.*

Narrator.   One night, this week, a heavy fog crept over the shallow waters off the coast of Newfoundland. And then . . . it slowly crept out again.

¶ MUSIC: *brief cue.*

Narrator.   But, meantime, world-famed Greenwich mean time, a curious interlude had occurred. For, in those treacherous, ice-filled, Newfoundland waters, two ships passed in the night. We re-enact this moving scene, as the two ships pass in the night:
Ship 1.   I pass.
Ship 2.   I pass.

¶ MUSIC: *brief cue.*

Narrator.   To a spirited apathy the world of science was roused this week by the startling, almost-legendary news that a man named J. Lucius Lapse had succeeded in remaining motionless for 26 consecutive days. Unable to discover Lapse's grim, undivulged secret, New York medical circles buzzed:

¶ SOUND: *buzzing.*

Narrator.   Until suddenly, surprisingly, without fanfare, a humble country doctor provided a breathless, confused world with his amazing solution to the case. Said the doctor:
Doctor.   Lapse is dead.

¶ MUSIC: *finale up and cross-fade into morse signals again: hold under:*

Surrealist.   You waited anxiously for another voice that was bound to come.
 To the first voice, you knew it was only necessary to
 add a dash of quibble, a hint of choplogic, a soupçon
 of circumlocution and you would have your Commentator,
 sublimating the news with the views.
 You knew he would come, that clever aerial artist,
 walking the tightwire of probabilities with an
 umbrella of facts, balancing on one foot while he tries
 to keep the other out of his mouth.
 You knew he would come, someone eager to pick up your mind to be pressed.
 And he did:

¶ SOUND: *cross-fade morse signals with:*

Commentator.   . . . and according to unofficial spokesmen and from usually reliable sources, it is reported in the Bolivian Press in a story emanating from Sweden, (where it is unconfirmed the Japanese radio yesterday admitted) semi-officially, that there was a possibility (sooner of later) there would be good reason to suspect that a bulletin allegedly issued by the Soviet news agency, Tass, and picked up by short wave in Rome, was true. . . . [*FADING*] The story reads as follows . . .
Surrealist.   You paid no attention to him for a moment.
 The great, fat, wingless moth of Earth battered on
 below you. But you could see on its body ugly red patches of mange.
 They spread too quickly for mange, you noticed, and must be fire.
 The moth was on fire, you saw, flaunting the Sun.
 What's the Sun got that it hasn't got, you asked
 yourself, given time and mad, mad people? [*PAUSE*]
Synonymous with your thoughts, you heard the Commentator again:
Commentator.   It has also been brought to our attention that the world is on fire.

¶ SOUND: *the growing crackle of flames builds under:*

Commentator.   Although this has not been definitely confirmed, there is reason to believe that it may be true.

¶ SOUND: *growing.*

Commentator.   The fact that the air is filled with smoke [*COUGHS*] probably proves something. In fact, although our wire services have been disrupted, I think it almost safe to say —

¶ SOUND: *the deep roar of flames and a crashing wall.*

Commentator.   [*OVER THE DIN*] It's finally *happened!*

¶ SOUND: *inferno up full and slowly cross-fade into tympani rumble: hold a moment: then slowly fade out to:*

Surrealist. You were alone now.
All alone.
[*PAUSE*]
Radio is unseen.
But you had seen it.
You had heard its idiot-tale, with its sound and fury,
and now it was heard no more.
[*PAUSE*]
You were not asleep.
You were not awake.
You were tired, bored, and unhappy.
[*PAUSE*]
Automatically, you reached over and turned your
radio back on again.

¶ SOUND: *click — pause — chime.*

Announcer. From Vancouver, the CBC has brought you "Brainstorm Between Opening and Closing Announcements" — an epileptic farce in seven fits — presented as Program Number Eleven of *Baker's Dozen*: a 13-week cycle of original radio diversions by the Canadian writer, Fletcher Markle. The production was under the direction of Andrew Allan. Bernard Braden was heard as the voice of the Surrealist with the voices of Alan Pearce, Clare Murray, Larry McCance, Peggy Hassard, John Bethune, Ruby Chamberlain, William Buckingham, and Fletcher Markle. The original music was composed and conducted by Laurence Wilson. Special Effects by James Gilmore and Frank Vyvyan. The author wishes to extend his thanks to Mr. Eric Nicol for his general assistance during the preparation of the script. Your announcer, John Drainie.

The Devil's Instrument

W.O. MITCHELL

Production

Producer: Andrew Allan
Music: Lucio Agostini
Sound: David Tasker
Operation: Bruce Armstrong
Announcer: Elwood Glover
Program: Stage 49, Item 26
Broadcast: March 27, 1949, 10:00–11:00 pm EST
Studio: Toronto
Network: Trans-Canada

Cast

George Barnes *as* Narrator and Preacher
William Needles *as* Jacob Schunk
Budd Knapp *as* the Devil
Lloyd Bochner *as* Darius
John Drainie *as* Peter, the Goose Boss
Toby Robins *as* Marta
Vogel Unger *as* Henry Karpus
Alan King *as* Wong, the Chinese
Jerry Sarracini *as* Jake

Alfie Scopp *as* Joe
Sandra Scott *as* Mrs. Wipf and Annie
Mavor Moore *as* the Oats and Barley Boss
and
Tommy Tweed *as* Norman the Truck Driver and Bone-Setter

•

THE DEVIL'S INSTRUMENT

Preface

Radio audiences perhaps know W.O. Mitchell best for his *Jake and the Kid* serial broadcast over CBC from 1949 to 1957. It was Harry Boyle who convinced a reluctant Mitchell to adapt the stories to radio. At the time, Mitchell was fiction editor for *Maclean's* and already known for his novels and short stories. He was neither new to the theatre nor to radio. Born in Weyburn, Saskatchewan in 1914, he worked with the Penthouse Players in Seattle, Washington, and was writing plays at the University of Alberta during the 1930s. Radio, as he said, was the only game going in the 1940s. From 1949 to 1961 Mitchell wrote sixteen original plays produced on the CBC, four of them for Andrew Allan. By his own admission, radio contributed considerably to Mitchell's development as a writer. It provided, along with his other work, sufficient income to permit him to remain in High River, Alberta as a full-time writer. Writing for radio also helped him to develop his interest in the oral tradition and his technique with dialogue, an interest which serves him well in his novels and short stories.

Mitchell is a regional writer, but not in a parochial sense. His writing is rooted in, rather than limited by, time and place, geography and culture. The universality of his work emerges from the depiction of a precise locale, seen as a microcosm. "The Devil's Instrument" is a case in point. At a superficial level, it is a simple story about the tensions internal and external to Hutterite communities on the Southern Alberta prairie. At a deeper level, the play reveals a fundamental tension between community and individual. This theme is not uncommon in Mitchell's writing. The use of a fictional Hutterite community permits an exaggeration of the dark side of community, the same dark side found in the actions of Mrs. Abercrombie in *Who Has Seen the Wind*. It is the constraint of the imperialism of church, school, and magistrate which at first prompts Jacob's hesitation in accepting brother Darius' offer of truth, beauty, and freedom. These values, from the point of view of the dominant vision of authority, can be achieved only through the devil's instrument — a child's mouth organ. Music is, after all, not wicked, we are told by Darius. The devil's instrument is *music* because it symbolizes art and instinct and sensual communication between individuals. In the end, however, what is depicted is not an escape from community to a possessive individualism, but an escape to a more open community where humanism reigns over materialism. The theme is ultimately a choice of communities; and the "new" open community is depicted as preferable, as the satirization of the Hutterite leaders makes clear.

W.O. MITCHELL

The Devil's Instrument

Announcer.   The Devil's Instrument . . .

¶ MUSIC: *title cue: up and under:*

Announcer.   *Stage* 49, Item 26 "The Devil's Instrument," a new original play by W.O. Mitchell . . . starring William Needles. Produced and directed by Andrew Allan, with an original musical score composed and conducted by Lucio Agostini. . . . "The Devil's Instrument," by W.O. Mitchell.

¶ MUSIC: *up and end.*

Narrator.   Throughout Southern Alberta there live in small colonies the Hutterite people; they are gentle souls and good farmers who live in religious and communal brotherhoods ruled by the bearded patriarchs commonly known as bosses: the chicken boss, the wine boss, the sheep boss, the wheat boss, and so on. These people are German in origin; their conventions must not be broken under risk of punishment through isolation by the rest of the colony; or worse — through that exquisite torture that comes from a conscience promising hell fire and brimstone to the sinner. To leave the colony means eternal damnation and sure doom.

¶ MUSIC: *sneak background.*

Narrator.   The Hutterite figure, in its black homespun with dark caracul hat pail-shaped, is a familiar one in many Southern Alberta towns. The casual traveller has often seen the colonies with their simple buildings, usually barn-paint red — the sleeping houses, the communal dining hall, the church, the schoolhouse. The exactness of the rank of buildings within the barbed wire fence seems a little shocking in a country where foothills lift in soft rhythm higher and higher to the jumble of Rockies, grey and abiding in the distance. [*PAUSE*]

In this story of the Hutterites all places and characters are purely fictional — with one important exception — an individual of many aliases: The Devil, Old Nick, Old Scratch, Mephistopheles . . .

¶ MUSIC: *fades out, as devil comes in continuing enumeration.*

Devil. . . . Satan, Beelzebub, Old Cloutie, take your pick. I'm a travelling man. I travel in sin. I travel in souls [*PAUSE*] wholesale souls and retail sin. Nothing flashy about my line through this country — the small novelty sort of thing goes well here: petty intolerances, lust for community power, now and again a minor carnal itch, within-the-family-tyranny, or just plain gossip — that sort of thing — quick turnover. Wholesale souls — retail sin. Recently a rather nice bit of business came my way. I've just closed a deal. Started — oh — a year ago with a Hutterite name of Jacob Schunk, male, sixteen, grand-nephew of Peter Schunk, goose boss in the hook and eye colony. They do their jackets up with hook and eye fasteners. It started with Jacob Schunk and a mouth organ the day he'd come into town with Peter, the goose boss. Peter left young Jacob off at the Palm Cafe while he went on to Doc MacCartney's to take final delivery on a set of uppers and lowers. Jacob was standing by the juke-box — a sideline I carry, by the way, find it listed in the sulphur coloured section of our catalogue under "T" — Torments, Hellish — juke boxes, that is.

¶ MUSIC: *nasal plaint of cowboy song: background for:*

Wong. What do you want? You want buyee something? You buyee — ha!
Jacob. Nothing, thank . . .
Wong. Doesn't pay me some kinda money — listen my juice box . . .
Jacob. I do not want to buy anything thank you.
Wong. You kinda Hooterite nevah buyee nothing — nevah buyee dinnah — ham and egg . . .
Joe. Costs money. Hooterites' too tight to spend . . .
Wong. . . . nevah buyee — nevah buyee ice cream — vanillah — mapoo wa'nut — nevah smoke —
Jake. Sinful. Hooterites ain't 'sposed to smoke. Them bosses —
Wong. . . . nevah buyee seegah — you like plug —
Jacob. Nothing. I would like only to . . .
Wong. You like plug — Green Eagle — you chew he some —
Jacob. I would like only to listen to the music out of the little box.

¶ SOUND: *of screen door slapping shut.*

Wong. You like music. Make music. Make your own.
Joe. He ain't even 'sposed to whistle.
Wong. Make you own. Mouth ohgan. I got lots of mouth ohgan.

44

¶ MUSIC: *record end on juke box.*

Wong.   You buyee one — make your own music — make Hooterite religion music —

Joe.   Send him straight to hell, blowin' a mouth organ. Better watch out young fella, one of them beardy bosses come in an' catch you listenin' to that juke box —

Jake.   Aw let him alone. Here — have one on me, kid.

¶ SOUND: *coin rings on counter.*

Jake.   Go on — stick it in the slot. Push that there leever down an' —

Jacob.   No thank . . .

Wong.   [TO MAN WHO HAS COME IN] What you wan'?

Jake.   Go on — won't hurt you.

Darius.   Couple of those penny matches. Package . . .

Jake.   Any of the bosses show up I'll give you a high sign. They're all over in the Royal Beer Parlour suckin' it down.

Joe.   Hooterites is so religious — won't smoke — drink tea or coffee — chew — when she comes to beer — lookout.

Jake.   Stick that nickel in.

Jacob.   No thank you.

Jake.   What's wrong? Here! First time I ever saw one a you people didn't . . .

Jacob.   No thank you. I don't . . .

Jake.   . . . jump at the chance a gettin' something' for nothing' . . .

Jacob.   Please, no . . .

Jake.   Take it!

Darius.   If he doesn't want to, he doesn't have to.

Jake.   Who the — I ain't tryin' to force nothin' on him. I just . . .

Darius.   He doesn't want it — obviously.

Jake.   I jist offered him a nickel for that juke box an' he . . .

Darius.   He's told you at least three times — he doesn't want it.

Jake.   No skin off of my . . .

Wong.   Alla time Hooterite come in — nevah buyee —

Darius.   Don't let it . . .

Wong.   Nevah buyee — nevah buyee even comb —

Joe.   Too tight.

Wong.   Ice cream comb. All he do — listen my juice box on othah peopoh nickoh —

Jake.   Then when you offer him a nickel to play . . .

Jacob.   Excuse me — I will go away outside now.

Darius.   No — no. Sit down. Will you have a dish of ice cream with me?

Jake.   Ain't gonna listen to music on my nickel — sure as heck ain't gonna eat ice cream from a tee-total stranger.

Darius. Will you — please?

Joe. He's gonna disappoint you, stranger.

Jacob. Thank you.

Jake. [*SOUND OF DISGUSTED AMAZEMENT*] Well . . .

Darius. Thank *you*. What kind? Pink? Vanilla? Chocolate?

Jake. Look at that, will you! Hooterite for you.

Joe. [*THEIR VOICES FADING*] Contrary.

Jake. Touchy as a cut calf. Some stranger from outa town . . .

Jacob. Pink.

Darius. Pink.

Wong. Pink.

  Pause.

Darius. You from the hook and eye — from the Cash River colony?

Jacob. Yes.

Darius. What is your name?

Jacob. Jacob. Jacob Schunk.

Darius. [*WITH INCREDULITY*] Jacob Schunk! Jac . . .

Wong. Ice cream.

¶ SOUND: *dishes being set down.*

Darius. Jacob Schunk!

Wong. Pink. Thirty cen'.

Darius. Oh — yes — yes — I — here.

¶ SOUND: *of coin on table.*

Darius. [*SLOWLY*] Jacob Schunk. [*LONG PAUSE*] Your father — your mother — they live in the colony?

Jacob. My father and mother are dead.

Darius. Who looks after you?

Jacob. I work and I sleep with Peter, the goose boss. He is my grand-uncle.

Darius. Goose boss! Isn't that woman's work.

Jacob. [*WITH SOME SPIRIT*] No, it is not! It is important!

Darius. And will you be a — a goose boss when you get older?

¶ SOUND: *just the clicking of Jacob's spoon.*

Darius. I should think it would be much finer to be a horse boss or the oats and barley boss — or —

Jacob. I would like to be a goose boss when I get older.

Darius. How old are you?

Jacob. Sixteen.

Darius. I see. Then — you do not go to school anymore?

Jacob. No.

Darius. For it was from the tree of knowledge that the apple came from

Adam and Eve's first sin. It was that way when I . . .

Jacob. Where are *your* father and mother?

Darius. Mine. [*PAUSE*] They are dead. Like yours.

Jacob. And have you any sisters?

Darius. One brother.

Jacob. How old is he?

Darius. He is your age.

Jacob. [*SUDDENLY*] Is it hard to blow music out of a little mouth organ?

Darius. Do you like music?

Jacob. Oh yes! No! I don't know how to — to say it. It hurts me . . .

Darius. Hurts you!

Jacob. But not bad. It — I —

Darius. How does it — hurt?

Jacob. Like when I come home — when the hills are dark — only high on top there is light there yet and I see that die — and it leaves me like — like —

Darius. Sad — Jacob?

Jacob. Like I am the only one left in the whole world. It is like I am left hanging. And it hurts — in your throat. I want to — to cry for something is lifting up in me and I want to cry.

Darius. Is it the same with music?

Jacob. I think so — the feeling. When you want something so you ache and it hurts . . .

Darius. [*KNOWINGLY*] . . . and you know it is sinful . . .

Jacob. Yes. Yes. It is the devil's music! It . . . [*SUDDENLY REALIZING THE IMPORT OF WHAT HE HAS SAID AND MAKING A NOBLE EFFORT*] I do not love — like — anything of the devil!

Darius. How do you know it is the devil's music? How can you know it isn't —

Jacob. I know.

Darius. Because the bosses tell you? Because old men with their . . .

Jacob. I know.

Darius. . . . dry old hearts — with their very ordinary hearts . . .

Jacob. I know it with my own heart.

Darius. . . . their gross materialistic hearts — tell you it is sinful.

Jacob. It *is* wicked and sinful!

Darius. Do you think the devil likes beauty!

Jacob. It would send me to everlasting burning.

Darius. Jacob — that is not true.

Jacob. I know.

Darius. It *is not true!*

Jacob. The Preacher says it is true. The chicken boss says it is true. Otto, the oats and barley boss . . .

Darius. The oats and barley boss?

Jacob. He is head boss over all the bosses. He is just like Moses.

Darius. Is he?

Jacob. Yes. His beard is black and he is not afraid of anything. He is not afraid to look into the face of the Lord. He is not afraid.

Darius. Is he not.

Jacob. John, the Blacksmith — when I was a child I used to think he looked like Christ. His beard is lovely. It is soft. His eyes are blue. He is Marta's father. Marta Schreiber. Her eyes — they are blue — too.

Darius. Are they now?

Jacob. Yes. They are blue — like a crocus — is blue. The little braids — they — do you know something?

Darius. What — Jacob?

Jacob. If you had a beard, then — then you would look a lot like John, the Blacksmith. Thank you for the ice cream.

Darius. That is nothing. About this — mouth organ?

Jacob. No thanks. I am going to be a good boy like Vogel Unger.

Darius. Is he a good boy?

Jacob. Oh yes. He is going to be the Preacher when he — He has faith.

Darius. Has he?

Jacob. He has tested it. He tested it two years ago when he was shingling the new horse barn. He laid down his shingling hatchet and he told me he said to himself when the noon bell rang for dinner: "Our Christ walked upon the waters. Why not Vogel Unger, son of the pig boss?" Do you know what he did?

Darius. No — Jacob.

Jacob. The peak of the new horse barn is seventy-five feet up in the air. That is high.

Darius. That is high.

Jacob. Vogel Unger walked off it onto the air.

Darius. To test his faith.

Jacob. He told me he started walking towards the community kitchen behind the spinning building where the women work.

Darius. I don't imagine he reached it, Jacob.

Jacob. No. The air did not hold him up. He fell. He fell fifty feet onto a load of hay Joseph Martin had just driven up.

Darius. But he is still going to be the Preacher?

Jacob. Vogel cannot say his "s"'s very well now.

Darius. Can't he?

Jacob. When he landed on the hay he bit the tip off of his tongue.

Darius. It is quite probable that Vogel will become the Preacher.

Jacob. The bosses said he was vain of his faith. They said he was setting it above his love for God.

Darius. Still — the Lord did save him. And Joseph Martin. Oh — and the load of hay.

Jacob. I am going to be a good boy. I am not going to ever blow music out of a little mouth organ.

Darius. Wanting to make music with a little mouth organ — that is not sinful. Come over to the counter with me.

¶ SOUND: *pause for scrape of chairs: footsteps.*

Darius. See them. They are very splendid — there is one taken out of its scarlet box and placed upon the lid.

Wong. [*VOICE GROWING AS HE COMES DOWN THE COUNTER*] Buyee some kin'a thing? Foh Hooterite kid? Buyee mouth ohgan — buyee foh make own music — not listen my juice box othah peopoh nickoh —

Darius. Jacob, I am going to give you something.

Jacob. Oh — no — please —

Wong. Lovely mouth ohgan.

Darius. How much are they?

Wong. Dollah fi'ty cen'.

Darius. Give me one, please. The — your bosses are not right. Jacob. Music is not wicked.

Wong. Heah. [*TOOTS MOUTH ORGAN*] You mouth ohgan. Very nice.

Darius. I want you to have this, Jacob. I want you to learn to play it. Hide it away from the bosses. Play it when you are alone. Be a good boy and do it. If there is a devil in that — if he is in it — I can tell you this — he is a little devil, Jacob — [*SOFTLY AND REGRETFULLY*] such a very — unimportant little devil.

¶ MUSIC: *bridges gently, ironically.*

Devil. It started then with Jacob — the stranger — the mouth organ — yes — and that — those rather mawkish references to — beauty — underhanded references. But this other thing — Jacob took the mouth organ, telling himself that he would never play it, you understand. He walked towards Weaver's General Store where old Peter, the goose boss, had hitched the team. He could feel the hard rectangular lump of the mouth organ giving off a special heat of its own against his thigh. To get to Weaver's from the Palm Cafe one has to cross the CPR tracks. Jacob stopped there before an empty freight car. It just happened that way. It just happened too that the door was slid open enough to let a person into the dusk within. Just happened that Jacob climbed into it. Happened he took the mouth organ from his pocket. Happened . . .

¶ MUSIC: *sound of one clear mouth organ note, pure, questioning.*

Devil He felt that to the very sole of his boots.

¶ MUSIC and SOUND: *mouth organ note at bottom of scale: high clear note again: sound of mouth being run length of mouth organ. [PAUSE] Meadow lark sings. Mouth organ manages first two notes of lark's song then discords. Sound of lark again. Orchestra takes the melody of lark up, then into cowbody air, back to meadow lark melody. Horse's hooves leisurely, creak of harness, tinkle of haltershanks, grind of wheels, clucking of Peter to the horses.*

Peter. You be a good boy, Jacob. The devil don't like good boys, so you be a good boy, Jacob.

Jacob. Yes, Uncle Peter.

Peter. The devil is a lot like a weasel. In his thirty-six inch Massey-Harris separator he threshes souls. He likes fat Hutterite souls — mixes them with others to bring the grading up. He is a lot like a weasel. You be a good boy — *not like* Darius. [PAUSE] It was not right to keep me waiting, Jacob.

Jacob. I am sorry, Uncle Peter. I thought you would be longer. I thought you would still be in the beer parl . . . at the dentist's getting your new teeth. They look nice.

Peter. His breath is hot. His eyes are red. He is pure evil.

Jacob. They shine very white. They are whiter even than your beard.

Peter. Are they? When he steps from his weasel hole, he leaves behind him footprints of drought scorching the prairie for — they pinch a little.

Jacob. They are lovely and white like an egg. After you've peeled it. Your beard is so white . . .

Peter. You be a good boy — like Vogel Unger.

Jacob. Vogel says a beard could not be so white unless there was some bluing. He says it is not right to be so vain about a beard. He says . . .

Peter. Let Vogel talk about beards when he is old enough to be married and grow one himself . . .

Jacob. . . . just a little bluing in the wash water when you wash your beard . . .

Peter. Do not listen to such talk! You are easily led in the ways of wickedness as it is. Darius was so too. Remember Darius when you are tempted.

Jacob. Yes, Uncle Peter.

Peter. Darius's soul is doomed to damnation and everlasting hell fire. Remember that!

Jacob. Yes, Uncle Peter. Do they still hurt?

Peter. The top ones — at the back. It is like a saddle sore where they rub and rub.

Jacob. Could you not take them out?

Peter. I will keep eighty-nine dollars and fifty cents in my mouth where it is safe!

Jacob. The chicken boss says he has not had any teeth at all for fifteen years.

Peter. The chicken boss is jealous!

Jacob. Just his bare gums, he said.

Peter. It was the chicken boss himself who said to send your brother Darius away to . . .

Jacob. [*WITH EVIDENT RESIGNATION*] Yes, Uncle Peter.

Peter. . . . the teacher's training school so that we could have our own teacher for our own kids. And how did he come back from the city? How — what did Sodom and Gommorrah do to him — your brother.

Jacob. He smoked.

Peter. Yes . . .

Jacob. He hanged pictures on the school house walls.

Peter. You did not see. You were not old enough to remember . . .

Jacob. But you have told me often enough, Uncle Peter.

Peter. You did not hear him teach the kids to sing songs. The devil got his finger into the colony that time. The devil will not get *your* soul, Jacob.

Jacob. No, Uncle Peter.

Peter. And there will be no more about bluing.

Jacob. [*OBEDIENTLY*] No, Uncle Peter.

Peter. In the water for washing my beard.

Jacob. No, Uncle Peter.

Peter. Or about loving my beard and my new teeth more than the Lord, my God?

Jacob. No, Uncle Peter.

Pause.

¶ SOUND: *of meadow lark.*

Peter. The devil is like a weasel — very like. And the devil is in women. He is pure evil. [*VOICE SUBSIDES TO BLURRED MURMUR*] Jezebel!

Jacob. Do they hurt now, Uncle Peter?

Peter. Yes — they do. There is no reason for them to stop. Marta is a good girl. You must be a good boy. In fall there will be marrying — no straw stacks, Jacob.

Jacob. It is not like that! It is not like that at all with — Marta — with me! We — you can't make it like that!

Peter. I am sorry. Sit down. Be a good boy, Jacob. Marta is a good girl. I know how it is. I guess you and Marta . . . [*VOICE FADES*]

¶ SOUND: *of meadow lark.*

¶ MUSIC: *such as Aaron Copeland has done with now and again a threatening of ponderous chords in minor key: to background for:*

Devil. That night, as he lay beside Peter, the goose boss, Jacob thought of the stranger. He wondered why he had given him the mouth organ — why he had questioned him — why he had given him ice cream —

pink. He wondered if the stranger might have been me — me!

Peter. [*SNORING*]

Jacob. The devil is like a weasel. [*SLEEPY TONES*] It could not have been. His breath was not hot. His eyes were not red. He was not pure evil . . .

¶ SOUND: *coyote howls outside.*

Peter. [*TURNS AND GROANS IN HIS SLEEP*] Be a good boy, Jacob — don't be — Darius.

Jacob. Oh, I will make lovely music. I will blow all the songs. I will blow all I have ever listened to. I will play tunes that have never been played before. I will play them first. They will be beautiful tunes. They will . . .

¶ MUSIC: *mouth organ and orchestra up in Jacob's dream.*

Devil. Straw stacks. There is something to make the old bosses stir in their sleep. But, of course, it was not that way with Jacob and Marta — not the thing that had begun months before on an evening in April when Jacob had stood by the door of the community kitchen, when he had looked up into the eyes of Marta, daughter of John, the Blacksmith.

Marta. Water. [*BREATHLESS: THIS GAL IS INNOCENT*]

Jacob. Huh. [*STARTLED*]

Marta. Water — hot. [*AFTERTHOUGHT*] Jacob.

Jacob. Hummmmmh.

Marta. Here is a towel too.

Jacob. Hummmmmh.

Marta. It is clean — Jacob.

Jacob. Thank you.

Marta. It is fresh for the old one — Jacob.

Jacob. I am all done.

Marta. Oh. [*SHE IS VERY SORRY THAT HE IS ALL DONE*]

Jacob. Er — except my neck. [*NOW HE'S VERY SORRY HE IS ALL DONE TOO*] I will need it for my neck. It is very very dirty — it — I will need hot water too —

Marta. Yes?

Jacob. For — for my neck — my dirty neck . . .

Marta. [*GIGGLES SELF-CONSCIOUSLY*]

¶ SOUND: *pause: sound of water being poured into a basin.*

Jacob. It gets dirty working the summer fallow . . .

Marta. Yes . . . Jacob.

Jacob. Your eyes — they — they are — they —

Marta. Yes?

Jacob. Blue. [*LONG PAUSE*] Very blue. [*PAUSE*] I should not — it wasn't right for me — I —

Marta. No? [*GIGGLES AGAIN*]

Jacob. Yes. Looking at them. It was looking at them — Marta — that — that . . .

¶ SOUND: *sudden and furious splashing and blowing through water as he buries his face in the basin.*

Marta. [*BURSTS INTO LAUGHTER*]

¶ MUSIC: *punctuates, then background.*

Devil. Jacob ate his evening meal with a half-dazed feeling of inner release. He could not free himself of Marta's look — from the clear sound of her laughter — for days. Deliberately he began to take indirect ways about his errands in the colony. By the open door of the community kitchen — the spinning room with its fifteen spinning wheels and the shrill lapping of women's voices.

¶ MUSIC: *out for:*

¶ SOUND: *spinning wheels: women's voices background.*

Marta. Oh! It is you — Jacob.

Jacob. Yes — I was — just — Uncle Peter — on my way to the — to Uncle Peter and the — the — geese.

Marta. But they are beyond the horse barn.

Jacob. Oh. Are they, are they? Yes — I should — they are . . .

Mrs. Wipf. Marta — the wool! Girl — the wool — we are waiting! [*FROM WITHIN THE SPINNING BUILDING*]

Marta. Yes! In a moment! Jacob! In a moment! Jacob — you must not do this — we will be seen — and it is not right!

Jacob. Seen!

Marta. No one speaks now to Anna or Walter!

Jacob. I know but . . .

Marta. Two weeks of isolation! She is in there now and no one dares speak to her.

Jacob. It is bad for Walter too . . .

Marta. No one dares look at her even, for it will mean as bad for them!

Jacob. Today at lunch Vogel was laughing and he saw Walter's face and he stopped right in the middle and . . .

Marta. [*IN TERRIFIED WARNING*] Jacob! Pl . . .

Oats and Barley Boss. What is this! What is this! Jacob Schunk — you are not with Peter, the goose boss.

Jacob. I — he has sent me — I came to — I was going to . . .

O and B Boss. Marta Schreiber — you are not with the women.

Marta. I came outside to . . .

53

O and B Boss.   I can see that.

Marta.   [*IN A RUSH*] And I saw Jacob pass — and I was to tell him to bring wool from the sheep.

O and B Boss.   Profit by the sight of Anna, the Preacher's daughter, and Walter, son of the wine boss. See them as they move through days that are hushed and lonely. See conversation cease at their approach. See laughter end and all eyes turn from them! For they have been gifted now with power to blight; the shadow of their sinning does travel always before them. The wrath of the Lord has descended down upon them. His angered hand lies on their smothered hearts. Now — about your work. [*MEANINGFUL PAUSE*] No — straw stacks!

¶ MUSIC: *short and out.*

Devil.   But to come back to this mouth organ business. Jacob justified his sin to himself at first, by playing only Hutterite hymns, feeling out their slow and mournful notes with his tongue.

¶ MUSIC: *mouth organ: crude efforts at above with sound of disgust from Jacob as he fails first try: then he manages recognizable hymn, like the tune which orchestra takes to background for:*

Jacob.   [*IN TONE OF REVERIE*] Ahhh — there is music from the little mouth organ and it was not so hard — it was not so hard at all — just the hymn tunes — that cannot be sinful to play the hymns only — that is not the devil's music. It cannot be wrong to feel this way — this strange feeling that is so daring and so fine and . . .

¶ MUSIC: *up in hymn-like stuff with rolling chords, which suddenly breaks and goes into Red River Valley picked up by mouth organ: orchestra breaks off to leave mouth organ alone carrying tune: mouth organ breaks off.*

Jacob.   No! No! I must not! It is wicked! That is the devil's music. I must not! I will not! I . . .

¶ MUSIC: *punctuates, to background for:*

Devil.   Simple people! Jacob was aware of his guilt. At evening worship one night he was sure the Preacher spoke only to him.

¶ MUSIC: *pauses.*

Preacher.   Return to your God, for you have fallen into iniquity. He will heal you of hurt and sin. He will love you freely. The mercy of the Lord is kind as August shade, fresh as morning dew upon the hills around.

¶ MUSIC: *a prayer, up and background.*

Jacob.   [*PRAYING*] Our Father: the stranger gave me the little mouth organ and I have used it. I blew through it and I played music. Forgive me and I will not do it again — ever — I will not blow through the wooden teeth to make songs. I will not even blow the hymns, O Lord, let alone "The Strawberry Roan" and "Goin' to Heaven on a Stream-line Train" and — and — "Where Do the Flies Go in the Winter Time." I will not. I promise. Amen — Lord.

¶ MUSIC: *amen.*

Devil. I've heard that sort of thing before, of course. My business you get so you know just how to evaluate it. For three days he kept his promise and then the choking yearning gained such strength that Jacob's resolve weakened, fainted, died away. Little by little his need built up until at last in a blaze of excitement and anticipation . . .

¶ MUSIC: *mouth organ: enthusiastic cowboy tune.*

Jacob. [*SIGHS WITH SATISFACTION*]
Devil. You see what I mean. Unresisting he allowed it to charm him away from the monotony of colony life — from:
Peter. [*SNORES*]
Devil. Peter snoring. And from:

¶ SOUND: *slurping of soup: sigh of repletion: belch (this could be an old-man belch, casual, starting out with restraint, but ending up in glory).*

Devil. The ugliness of old men at their soup, the monotony of naked floors and bare walls.
Jacob. I would like to — oh — it would be wonderful to kick the colony open — like — like — an ant pile!
Devil. He didn't, of course, for there came a day when Peter told him of a wonderful thing.

¶ SOUND: *geese: meadow lark a couple of times.*

Peter. Jacob. Jacob.
Jacob. Yes, Uncle Peter.
Peter. What is that on your face?
Jacob. On my face!
Peter. In no time at all you will be growing a beard. By fall perhaps. Marriage and a beard — they go together, Jacob.
Jacob. Marriage — a beard!
Peter. In fall there will be marrying. The devil don't like married men. Marta . . .
Jacob. We have not been . . .
Peter. There was a meeting of the bosses last night. The bosses are not blind, Jacob.
Jacob. But we had not . . .

Peter. Marta is a good girl. You could have lots of kids. In fall, Jacob. If you wish — if Marta wishes . . .

Jacob. I do — I do — she — oh — Uncle Peter . . .

¶ MUSIC: *a yearning comment.*

Devil. So — a marriage had been arranged — if not in Heaven — well, by the pig boss and the oats and barley boss and the bone-setter and the chicken boss and the sheep boss — Godly men. That night Jacob decided that no sacrifice was too great to make him worthy of Marta Schreiber, daughter of John the Blacksmith. He buried the mouth organ deep at the base of a straw stack — a straw stack well known to Anna, the Preacher's daughter and Walter, son of the wine boss. They were the two who — but I need not explain further. Some of the boys had been in the town helping to assemble new colony machinery. Among them was Vogel Unger, son of the pig boss — you will remember — he of the great faith and no tip to his tongue — who would someday be the Preacher — he came to Jacob.

Vogel. Jacob — Jacob — there was a man! Do you know — do you know — he wanted to see you!

Jacob. Man — wanted . . .

Vogel. He is not one of the people from the town. He had just come — he said. Do you know — he is staying at the hotel. Do you know he wants to see you.

Jacob. But — why? Who is he? What did he say his name . . .

Vogel. He just came where we were doing the machinery. Do you know Jacob Schunk, he said. He said — do you know whether he is coming into town. Do you . . .

Jacob. Was he tall? Did he look like John, the Blacksmith?

Vogel. He had no beard. He hadn't any at . . .

Jacob. I know — but without a beard — would he look like John, the Blacksmith? Did he?

Vogel. I couldn't tell.

Jacob. Are you going in tomorrow? Are — could you let me go in your place, Vogel?

Vogel. We are going all this week but I could not — you couldn't.

Jacob. Just tomorrow. That will be enough. Tell them — you could have a — tell them you do not feel well tomorrow.

Vogel. But — it doesn't — they — that would be lying!

Jacob. Vogel — you do not feel well at all — your head aches — your back hurts.

Vogel. It does not! They don't — at all!

Jacob. They will tomorrow. You will have to go to the bone-setter and tell him . . .

Vogel. Oh, no I won't! Do you know I never felt better?

Jacob. If you *do* feel well tomorrow, do you know, Vogel — you are going to have to go to the bone-setter anyway! [*THIS IS SAID SLOWLY AND OMINOUSLY*]

Devil. Strangely — Vogel Unger did *not* feel well the next day. And as Jacob rode into town in his place he resolved to take the first opportunity he got to see the stranger. He knew who he was. There was no doubt in his mind that it was the man who had bought him the mouth organ — who had given him a dish of ice cream — pink. Jacob went first to the back of the hotel and was greeted by the steaming smells of the kitchen and a fat woman with face flushed as she threw out the contents of a slop bucket.

¶ SOUND: *slurshsh of slop bucket: clank.*

Annie. You git away from here! Nothin' for thievin' Hooterite 'roun' here! Way you go!

Devil. Jacob did not mind; he knew that those outside the colony always accused the Hutterites of their *own* sins. He walked to the front of the hotel, had just reached the corner of the alley . . .

¶ SOUND: *traffic sounds.*

Darius. [*SLIGHTLY OFF*] Jacob, Jacob Schunk!
  Pause.

Jacob/Darius. [*IN UNISON*] I played the little mouth . . . / I have something to tell . . . [*BOTH LAUGH*]

Darius. Get in, Jacob, get into the car. [*BUSINESS OF GETTING IN THE CAR*]

¶ SOUND: *car door shuts.*

Darius. Well, how are you, Jacob?

Jacob. I played the little mouth organ.

Darius. That's nice, Jacob.

Jacob. You wanted to see me?

Darius. Yes, Jacob. Yes. I — I — I am your brother, Jacob. [*LONG PAUSE*] I am Darius.

Jacob. [*LONG PAUSE*] You — you say it like that — you are my brother?

Darius. Yes. [*PAUSE*] I was twenty when I left the colony — twenty years, Jacob, is along time to eat the bread of security — to have all your decisions made for you by the bosses. Perhaps I have not lost — all that — weakness. I have dreamed often of coming for you and taking you away with me, but when you told me who you were that day, I could not do it.

Jacob. Could you not?

Darius. I wanted to but I couldn't. When I returned to the city I cursed myself for not bringing you back with me.

Jacob. That was all right — Darius. [*HIS BROTHER'S NAME SAID WITH*

HALTING UNFAMILIARITY AND FEELING] I guess it was all right — Darius.

Darius.   Outside the city — during the war — there was a camp where prisoners of war were kept. Each morning they would take the men out in the trucks to work in the beet fields. Each night they would take them back to sleep in the shacks. And I thought of you each time I would pass the camp, Jacob. There were guards with guns instead of bearded bosses; the fence was higher, but those were slight differences. They — were — so — slight. You are not free either, Jacob . . .

Jacob.   [*PROTESTING*] But it is not like that . . .

Darius.   It is — it is — you are not free in body or in soul! You are not saved. None of you are — not even the oats and barley boss.

Jacob.   That is not right.

Darius.   None of you are! The colony is not God's way! It is wicked.

Jacob.   Not wicked, Darius!

Darius.   Freedom is light, Jacob! The way of the Lord is a shining light — the way of the wicked lies in the shade and darkness of ignorance and bondage!

Jacob.   Our people are not wicked.

Darius.   There are three things. There is truth and that is the best thing. There are freedom and beauty too, and the devil hates all these things. Truth and beauty are the same — that's all you need to know, Jacob. A poet said that and he was not a Hutterite. There are no Hutterite poets, for the colony kills what is beautiful — it will not let beauty grow — it cannot grow without freedom!

Jacob.   But — I have found —

Darius.   [*OVER-RIDING HIM: ALL STOPS OUT*] The devil wears hook and eye fasteners right down his ugly home-spun jacket! He has a long long beard and he is boss over all the bosses.

Jacob.   No — no — that is not true!

Darius.   Colony life is a profane thing! It is gross and material and wicked!

Jacob.   Please, please, Darius!

Darius.   [*LONG PAUSE*] I am sorry, Jacob.

Jacob.   You say there is no beauty in the colony. [*PAUSE*] There is Marta.

Darius.   Marta?

Jacob.   John, the Blacksmith's daughter.

Darius.   Oh.

Jacob.   The first time — in the cafe — you asked me if I was happy in the colony. [*PAUSE*] Well — I am happy — now.

Darius.   I see. [*HE DOES*]

Jacob.   I do not — not play the little mouth organ — [*PAUSE*] now.

Darius.   Did it make you unhappy?

Jacob.   Are you happy outside the colony, Darius?

Darius.   Happy! *I am free!*

Jacob.   Are you happy, Darius?

Darius.   Happiness is not everything. I must be honest with you. I am free. Anyway — I am free.

Jacob.   [*BLURTING IT*] I am going to be married. [*PAUSE*] I am going to marry Marta.

Darius.   [*SOUND OF BREATH RELEASING*] Are you? Are you, Jacob?

Jacob.   Soon.

Darius.   That is their hold — that is the bosses' strongest hold. They make that work for them too.

Jacob.   You do not understand, Darius. Last night I walked with Marta from the pump to the kitchen. We did not talk. We came to a patch of mud. We both stepped aside — in the wrong direction. She touched me, Darius. I felt her hand against the back of mine. It was lovely — it was aching lovely. I could not breathe, Darius!

Darius.   You will never leave. [*PAUSE*] After you are married. [*SIGH*] I am married now. I met her soon after I left the colony to go to the teachers' school. Women are important, Jacob. They are not weak. One takes me from the colony. Another holds you to it.

Jacob.   [*SLOWLY AND GENTLY, HIS OWN VOICE ALMOST BREAKING*] I am sorry — Darius.

¶ MUSIC: *punctuates, to background for:*

Devil.   When he returned to the colony, Jacob thought of the things that the discarded mouth organ had sharpened and made more vivid for him:

Jacob.   Stars and their cold fierceness — children in shrill tag — the old-man sound of sheep — the ring of John, the Blacksmith's anvil — telephone wires twanging through great emptiness — the summer foot-hills' stirrings — the . . .

¶ MUSIC: *pauses.*

Devil.   He sat at the wooden dining table, staring at dark figures with their black elbows up and out and he thought.

¶ SOUND: *Hutterites' eating.*

Jacob.   Crows — black — solemn crows flocking . . .

¶ MUSIC: *a comment, to background for:*

Devil.   He reached for the bowl of boiled potatoes and as he did, saw Marta standing on the other side of the table, waiting upon the horse boss.

Jacob.   Why should she serve him — why — this is the horse boss who hid five green hides behind the women's — place — then took them into town and sold them to the hide buyer so that he could have his own money for beer. Walter saw him — he is not a Godly man . . .

Devil.   Marta's steady blue eyes fired him with brief elation until he saw the other eyes fixed on him: the goose boss's fixed stare and the beautiful white beard moving gently to the rhythm of his chewing . . .

Jacob.   He *does* use bluing . . .

Devil.   The shrewd oat eyes of the chicken boss . . .

Jacob.   Why do they talk of straw stacks all the time — the chicken boss — he knows — Peter has said he once coveted the wife of the wine boss . . .

Devil.   That night as he lay beside Peter, the goose boss, Jacob thought of Darius.

Jacob.   My brother is a good man. He is *not* wicked! My brother is a good man. The face of the Lord is not turned from him. He is not — he — it is not right that — Darius — Darius see your doom — the eternal damnation of your way . . .

¶ MUSIC: *punctuation, and background for:*

Devil.   In the days that followed Jacob turned more and more to Marta; remembered her over and over — every . . .

Jacob.   Moments I have spent near her — the soft brush of her hand. The way her cheek curves and hair escaping under her polka-dot shawl. Her eyes — they are blue and laughing. . . . Darius is wrong!

Devil.   He had to reassure himself. He waited at the well where he knew she would come.

¶ MUSIC: *out.*

Jacob.   Marta — Marta — please — may I see you — alone!

Marta.   Oh, no — Jacob — We must not! We . . .

Jacob.   Tonight — the straw stack! Please!

Marta.   It is only a month now — Jacob!

Jacob.   Please, Marta. You must! You must!

Marta.   The Preacher — the sheep boss — they are coming — we will be seen.

Jacob.   I will be there, Marta! I will be there!

Marta.   No — no — go now — I won't — you shouldn't — it is not fair — yes, Jacob — Dear God — yes!

Devil.   Now this sort of thing is not limited to Hutterites, mind you. Others have — well — you know what I mean. That night Jacob stole from the side of Peter, the goose boss, past the sleeping quarters — the kitchen and the long horse barn — then he was walking through the fragrance of mown hay — the pungency of sage. The straw stack loomed before him.

Jacob.   Marta! Marta!

Marta.   Jacob! Oh, Jacob, it is wrong!

Jacob.   I had to see you — I —

Marta.   I'm afraid, Jacob — remember Anna and Walt . . .

Jacob.   It is all right, Marta. No one will know. I had to — oh, Marta — Marta! [*THEY CLINCH*]

¶ MUSIC: *up in a glory.*

Devil.   Next day Jacob sat by the goose boss — tending the geese.

¶ SOUND: *geese background.*

Peter.   The devil don't like married men. [*LONG PAUSE*] You want to marry Marta. [*THIS IS A STATEMENT*] You want to grow a beard — have kids. Be a good boy, Jacob. [*LONG PAUSE*] You were not — last night.

Jacob.   Last night!

Peter.   I do not sleep so well, Jacob. [*PAUSE*] You left.

Jacob.   Yes, Uncle Peter.

Peter.   Straw stacks?

Jacob.   Yes — no! I tell you it's not like that — it's not — I did see Marta last night — but it's not what you think — we just stood . . .

Peter.   Yes, Jacob?

Jacob.   I — we could feel the night air cooling against our cheeks — it was — the smell of hay and the wild mint — it was beautiful, Uncle Peter . . .

Peter.   Was it, Jacob?

Jacob.   It would make the spit come to your mouth.

Peter.   I had my straw stack too, Jacob. [*HE SEEMS TO UNDER-STAND*] When I was young — before I could grow a beard, the devil came to me in the city one day. He found me on the street with a bag of money in my hand. It was colony money. The devil told me to buy a new suit. [*WISTFUL NOTE*] The pants had creases in them. It was a green suit. Pretty. I wore it that day. Right out of the store. I met a woman with real red hair. She wore a blue dress like a violet. She lived with a lot of other Jezebels on the edge of the city and she called me her little geranium flower. I was going to take her away from that place, but in the Chinaman's cafe she unscrewed the top from the stool and hit the waiter over the head. She screamed very loud — long — she swore wicked too — she threw their spitoon through the whole window. [*FULL STOP*] Twenty dollars for the green suit with creases in the pants. Ten dollars for the wine. Five dollars for the Jezebel. Fifteen dollars for the window. Thirty dollars for the Chinaman. Fourteen dollars for the Judge. [*PAUSE*] Sin comes expensive, Jacob. Sinful life could run a man as high as two hundred dollars a month. [*PAUSE*] There are worse things, Jacob, than being lonely in the colony. You could be lonely outside the colony too — like your brother — Darius.

Jacob.   I know, Uncle Peter.

61

Peter.   Be a good boy, Jacob!   [*THIS IS A FIERCE PLEA*]

Jacob.   I will, Uncle Peter, I will!   [*THIS IS JUST AS FIERCE A PROMISE*]

¶ SOUND: *of a meadow lark.*

¶ MUSIC: *takes up melody of lark, then down to background for:*

Devil.   Jacob was a good boy — for two weeks. He did not see Marta after that; he did not meet her at the pump; he did not look up into her clear eyes as she served at meals; he must wait until they were married. At that thought a feeling of faintness would come over him. He would be a good boy.

¶ MUSIC: *out.*

Devil.   But there came a night when he could stand it no longer. He stole from Peter's side, the night air cool against his cheek. His steps took him to the straw stack.

¶ SOUND: *drawn howl of coyote: train whooping and the sound dissolving slowly in the night.*

Devil.   As the sound of the train dissolved slowly on the night silence, he remembered that he had hidden his mouth organ here. He placed it in his pocket and started back towards the colony. He stopped at the horse barn.

¶ SOUND: *of door opening: hoof knocks: horse nickers.*

Devil.   There in the dusk sweet with stored hay, rich with the smell of harness, he took the mouth organ from his pocket. He played it first with the slow wading quality of hymnal music — sad — sad —

¶ MUSIC: *mouth organ doing just that: breaks off: begins again.*

¶ SOUND: *of him knocking the thing against his hand.*

Devil.   He lowered his elbows, spatted the condensed saliva from its spaced teeth. His elbows rose up and out again. He closed his eyes. It was not hymn music, my friends — this was my music — my own wicked, drunken, dancing music that does not tell of Hutterite taboos.

¶ MUSIC: *has drowned out the devil momentarily: orchestra with mouth organ riding high and lyric to background.*

Devil.   This is the music of the foothills wind, of free and vital things: the hung rhythm of a blacksmith's hammer on a frosty day, a Gosh Hawk circling high with a field mouse in her claws — the wind in wheat — a lark's clear song — hoarse crows calling while a jack rabbit exuberant with life goes bouncing off across the bald prairie. Ludicrous geese lift their orange feet to fold and splay again. A fat boss

waddles and the wind takes hold and flips the skirt on a Hutterite girl
. . .

Peter.   [*CALLING*] Jacob — Jacob.

¶ MUSIC: *changes to a tremolo.*

Devil.   The ant piles open and ants do scurry round — a pigeon flaps its
. . .

Peter.   *JACOB!*

¶ MUSIC: *ends with a bump.*

Peter.   I told you. I told you, Jacob. I told you to be a good boy!
[*PAUSE*] Give me the little mouth organ!

¶ MUSIC: *a righteous bridge.*

¶ SOUND: *of men muttering.*

O and B Boss.   [*CLEARS THROAT*] Jacob Schunk — you have sinned! [*DEEP
ASSENT OF MALE VOICES IN AGREEMENT*] Peter, the goose boss, say
before us what you know and let him deny it.

Peter.   I wakened in the middle of the night. I had to go outside. I am
not a young man any more, I heard a sound. It came from the new
horse barn. I went in. I found him — *him* — he had *that* in his hands. I
called to him. He did not hear me. He was blowing into it so music
came out of it.

¶ SOUND: *clicking sounds of disapproval: preacher hawks in his throat:
sounds die down to a waiting and expectant silence: pause: rooster outside,
crows loud, clear, long, the sound stretching like an elastic band.*

O and B Boss.   Jacob Schunk, you have sinned. Let Peter say before us
again what he knows; let Jacob *deny* it.

Peter.   Four years ago he set a trap line. He caught four weasels and a
skunk. He turned in to the hide boss three weasel pelts and a skunk.
He took the weasel pelt hidden in his jacket to the hide buyer in town.
He got fifty cents for it. He bought a bag of Maple Bud candies. He
also bought five ice cream cones. From Wong, the Chinaman at the
Palm Cafe. He ate three and he gave one to Vogel Unger and another
to Otto, the sheep boss's son. Behind the livery stable.

¶ SOUND: *herd sounds of the court again: the Bone-Setter belches accusingly.*

O and B Boss.   Jacob Schunk, you have sinned. Let Peter say further
what he knows. Let Jacob *deny* it.

Peter.   [*PETER HAS BEEN WORKING HIMSELF UP INTO AN EVANGELIC FERVOR.
FOR THE FIRST TIME SINCE HIS FALL FROM GRACE WITH THE CALGARY
HOOKER OF HIS YOUTH, HE IS NOW ONE OF THE ORTHODOX FOLD. IT IS A*

WONDERFUL FEELING AND THE MOMENT OF HIS GREATEST TRIUMPH] He sneaked out in the middle of the night. He met Marta, daughter of John, the Blacksmith. It was at the straw stack in the back burnt-over forty. He kissed her on the mouth. She kissed him back. I saw them do this. I saw them.

¶ SOUND: *crowd murmurings again.*

O and B Boss. Jacob Schunk, pay attention. Three times has Peter told — three times you have not denied. [*PAUSE*]

¶ SOUND: *rooster crows (this sound both times must stand unmistakeably alone next to the name Peter and the word 'deny' so that the listener will get the relationship with the cock crowing when the Apostle Peter denied his Lord).*

O and B Boss. We are not angry with you. We want you to know that. We wish only to turn you back from the path of wickedness. To save your mortal soul from eternal damnation. Your punishment is this. You shall be apart. No one shall come near you. Everyone shall turn his eyes from you. No one shall speak to you. Or in any way make a sign to you — for — three months. To do any of these things shall be as great a sin as those you have committed. You shall not blow through the mouth organ again. John, the Blacksmith, shall place it on his anvil and he shall smash it. [*PAUSE*] Marta, daughter of John the Black-smith, shall have one month's isolation. When the fall marrying comes, she shall not marry you, Jacob Schunk. We will not lose a soul — another — soul!

Jacob. Marta! It is not fair to punish Marta . . .
O and B Boss. We will sing now the hymn.
Jacob. She had nothing to do with the mouth . . .
Preacher. [*HIS VOICE TAKES UP THE FIRST OF THE HYMN*]
Jacob. . . . organ. She — the weasel pelt —
Voices. [*TWO DEEPER VOICES JOIN THE PREACHER*]
Jacob. [*LOUDER TO MAKE HIMSELF HEARD*] It is not fair that . . . [*MORE VOICES IN THE HYMN*] she should be punished too. [*MORE VOICES IN THE CHANTING HYMN: NOW FAIRLY SCREAMING TO MAKE HIMSELF HEARD*] Listen to me — listen to me — I will not stay — if you do this to Marta, I will — Damn your black — fat — souls — I will — GO! [*HE IS LOST IN THE FULL STRENGTH OF THE MEN'S SINGING*]

¶ MUSIC: *sound of meadow lark through music which ends: pause.*

¶ SOUND: *meadow lark and country noises: truck motor labouring nearer: stops: door opens.*

Trucker. Wanta ride?
Jacob. Thank you — yes. [*OUT OF BREATH*]

Trucker.   Hooterite eh — just goin' few miles — next crossing.

¶ SOUND: *door slams.*

Trucker.   Y'ain't married.

¶ SOUND: *gears grind.*

Trucker.   No beard so you ain't married. [*SHORT BARKING LAUGH*] No beard down yer hook an' eye jacket, so you ain't. . . No offense, kid. [*PAUSE*]

¶ SOUND: *meadow lark sings.*

Trucker.   Sixteen — y'ain't old enough to git married yet — or grow a beard.

Jacob.   [*DULLY*] I am old enough.

Trucker.   Sorta keep yerselves to yerselves. Livin' in them colonies. Never was real close to you folks so I guess I don't know how to act — must have an awful holt over you folks . . .

Jacob.   Yes.

Trucker.   Real religious, ain't you. Take me — Mormon. I'd be real religious too if I — well — kinda lazy — like my beer — wimmen — that ain't right — not fer a Mormon. That's *my* faith. Mormon. Was, anyways. Married a Gentile, name of Millie Van Amburg — chambermaid at the Arlington — before I married her. Got three kids — own my own truck now. Headed for town?

Jacob.   I am going to the city.

Trucker.   [*WHISTLES INCREDULOUSLY*] That's over a hundred miles!

Jacob.   I am leaving the colony.

Trucker.   Puts us in the same boat. [*LAUGHS*] Me — I'm a jack-Mormon. Makes you a jack-Hutterite. Sort of — [*STARTS TO LAUGH BUT SEES THAT JACOB DOES NOT THINK IT IS FUNNY AND AFTER ALL HE IS A GOOD SORT OF GUY*] Won't never grow no beard now.

Jacob.   No — I will never grow a beard now. Poor Marta . . .

Trucker.   Your girl?

Jacob.   They punished her too — she would not — she could not talk to me again — she was afraid . . .

Trucker.   That why you're leavin'?

Jacob.   Yes.

Trucker.   Awful holt over you folks. Never heard of a Hooterite to git out before.

Jacob.   My brother, Darius did.

Trucker.   Why'd he leave?

Jacob.   He hanged pictures on the schoolhouse walls and he smoked cigarettes.

Trucker.   Catch you smokin'?

Jacob. No. I played some music out of a little mouth organ.

Trucker. That all! [SCANDALIZED] Jist fer blowing' a mouth organ. What you gonna do?

Jacob. I am going to my brother. [PAUSE] *He* wants me. [PAUSE] He will buy me another mouth organ.

¶ MUSIC: *mouth organ alone in a simple happy air: orchestra takes it up for a crashing and triumphant finale. Jacob may not know it but this is victory.*

Announcer. *Stage 49,* Item 26 "The Devil's Instrument," a new original radio play by W.O. Mitchell . . . was produced and directed by Andrew Allan, with a special musical score composed and conducted by Lucio Agostini. Starred in the cast were William Needles as Jacob Schunk; Budd Knapp as the Devil; Lloyd Bochner as Darius; John Drainie as Peter, the goose boss; Toby Robins as Marta; and Mavor Moore as the oats and barley boss. The others were Henry Karpus, Alan King, Tommy Tweed, George Barnes, Sandra Scott, Jerry Sarracini, and Alfie Scopp. Sound by David Tasker. Technical operation by Bruce Armstrong.

Hilda Morgan

LISTER SINCLAIR

Production

Producer: Andrew Allan
Music: Lucio Agostini
Sound: David Tasker
Operator: Bruce Armstrong
Announcer: Elwood Glover
Program: Stage 49, Item 34
Broadcast: May 22, 1949, 10:00–11:00 pm EDT
Studio: Toronto
Network: Trans-Canada

Cast

Ruth Springfield *as* Hilda Morgan
Jane Mallet *as* Mother
Pat Arthurs *as* Hilda's sister, Ruth
Budd Knapp *as* Wally Turnbull
Grace Webster *as* Mrs. Temple
John Drainie *as* David Temple
Donald Davis *as* the Policeman

•

HILDA MORGAN

Preface

"He was the centre of a coterie at U.B.C. I have never met anyone I hold to be more brilliant or more seminal of ideas." So spoke Andrew Allan of Lister Sinclair. Lister Sinclair graduated from The University of British Columbia in 1942 with a B.A. in mathematics. He moved on to Toronto, where he completed an M.A. in mathematics, and where in 1943 he became one of several writers and performers Allan chiefly depended on for the success of the *Stage* series. Sinclair had over two hundred plays produced on the CBC between 1943 and 1961; forty-six of these were produced by Andrew Allan. Sinclair of course continues his career as CBC writer, producer, and administrator.

"Hilda Morgan," while not as renowned as Sinclair's epic verse dramas like "Socrates" (which have long been in print), is nonetheless one of his best-written plays, showing Sinclair's aptitude for realistic and dramatic characterization and plot. Furthermore, it was one of the most controversial of the plays produced by Allan during the first six controversial years of *Stage*. The issue addressed in the play — the choice among the abortion of a child conceived out of wedlock, the acceptance of the child, or its surrender for adoption — shocked many listeners. Angry letters followed, directed to CBC officials, to members of Parliament, and to the Prime Minister himself. Individuals and organizations alike expressed their outrage. The rebroadcast a year later only served to increase the outrage. A reading of this correspondence suggests that those offended identified with the conservative position taken by Hilda's mother.

On the other hand, a secular humanism had penetrated the minds of the middle class following World War II. It was expressed in the push toward the welfare state, Canadian participation in international organizations, and a growing openness and honesty in interpersonal relations. These values opposed the rigidity of Victorian morality, and it is this conflict which is at the centre of "Hilda Morgan." There is also a hint at a new role for women in the world depicted in the play — a world in which women have a choice, in which the double standard is seen for what it is, and in which love dominates over concern for reputation.

A reading of the script will not quite reveal the subtleties of class and rank built into the play through the spoken language of the sound version. Wally's slang and racy style are contrasted with David's quiet manner and educated language, while Mrs. Temple's refined language contrasts with the harshness of Mrs. Morgan and Hilda's sister, Ruth. The values of secular humanism are thus associated with the educated and refined. One wonders to what degree the outrage expressed by some members of the audience was a result of their inability to identify with values remote from their level of experience. Nevertheless, "Hilda Morgan" carries an emancipatory quality, a quality shared with those of Allan's productions which he referred to as "dangerous," in contrast to those he called "bland."

LISTER SINCLAIR

Hilda Morgan

Wally. [*FAMILIAR AND LOQUACIOUS*] I had a narrow squeeze myself once, as the monkey said. Even now it's enough to make a person think when you talk about Hilda Morgan. What about her, eh? These days you can't tell by the coachwork, and I should know! After all, when a person's a Salesmanship Engineer (on the road in the wholesale end since I was eighteen), if there's one thing: well, a person certainly gets to know the girlies. One kind's worth a million dollars, and you can't buy it; and the other, why, like we always say in the business: I can get a million for you wholesale, and you take my advice; keep 'em separate. There's the kind to settle down with, and the kind to settle up with. But sometimes you never know which you've got until it's too late. If then.

¶ MUSIC: *a questioning phrase, rather dark and foreboding: then to background.*

Announcer. *Stage 49*, Item 34 . . . "Hilda Morgan," a new original play by Lister Sinclair . . . starring Ruth Springford in the title role. Produced and directed by Andrew Allan, with a special musical score composed and conducted by Lucio Agostini . . . Lister Sinclair's new play: "Hilda Morgan."

¶ MUSIC: *up for a strong punctuation: down to blues-type background: out with Wally's narration.*

Wally. Now the lay of the land was this: Thursday and Friday I used to be in Southwestern Ontario, up to and including London: that's as far as I go, as the monkey said. Friday night, I'm back in Toronto; and Saturday afternoon, I used to call on Hilda. They'd just moved near the park: 2046 Grosvenor. She lived with her mother. Very lovely person, Mrs. Morgan, we used to get on . . .

¶ MUSIC: *out with voice.*

Mrs. Morgan. [*WITH A THEATRICAL SIGH*] Wally: don't ever move. You find out how much rubbish you've accumulated during the years, and in the meantime, all your precious things are just smashed to pieces. Moving simply isn't worth it: take my advice.

Wally. I'd love to, Mrs. Morgan; but of course, I move all the time. On the road: live in a suitcase, if you get the point! Well, it's half past three, and still no sign of Hilda, eh?

Mrs. Morgan. [*SHAKING HER HEAD*] Honestly, Wally, I don't know! She said she was going to take my necklace to the jewellers. I have a beautiful pearl necklace, cultured, they say, (but I can't tell the difference, and I'm sure nobody else can); and I took it out of the case for the moving, and string must have perished, because it all broke to pieces in my hands: pearls all over everywhere, and I know some of them are lost, you can never get it back the same as it was, and that's life. And Hilda said she'd take it in, and have them look at it, but that was an hour and a half ago.

Wally. [*RATHER PLAINTIVELY*] She *knows* I always come on Saturdays.

Mrs. Morgan. [*ROGUISH*] Well, I should say so!

Wally. It's a regular date, and I brought her in some chocolates. Got 'em wholesale.

Mrs. Morgan. Oh, Wally, really you shouldn't.

Wally. Well, I behave here like I'm one of the family, so a little present does no harm. I always say you can slide further on. . . . Well, I got a four o'clock appointment. [*EMBARASSEDLY*]

Mrs. Morgan. I'm sure Hilda has so much on her mind these days, I don't know what's the matter. [*THEN ROGUISH AGAIN*] Though I have a premonition it may be love.

Wally. [*PLEASED*] Now that's a possibility. What do you think, Mrs. Morgan?

Mrs. Morgan. You're the one who'd know *that*, Wally!

Wally. A year ago, I'd have said yes. Haven't been around so much lately. [*BUT HE SOUNDS PRETTY CONFIDENT*]

Mrs. Morgan. [*WITH A NAUGHTY TWINKLE*] Haven't been around *here*, you mean.

Wally. [*DELIGHTED*] Well, if there's one thing I'm certainly sure of, all right, I'd venture to say that I pretty well know the girlies. Practice makes perfect.

Mrs. Morgan. As Hilda's mother, I shan't let you talk like that! Next thing she'll be getting jealous of me. As it is, I don't know what she'll say when she finds we've spent the afternoon alone together.

Wally. Well, it's a good sign if they get jealous: means they're getting ready for Mr. Right, if you get the point. And anyway, it's all in the family.

¶ SOUND: *doorbell slightly off.*

Mrs. Morgan.   Doorbell! That's Hilda now! Excuse me!

Wally.   [*RAISING HIS VOICE AFTER HER*] Better late than never, as the . . .

Mrs. Morgan.   [*FADING OFF A LITTLE*] Forgotten her key again. She's either crazy or she's in love, and she certainly isn't crazy.

¶ SOUND: *door opens off.*

Ruth.   [*OFF*] Hello, mother.

Mrs. Morgan.   [*OFF*] Ruth, my dear! It's my married daughter, Wally! [*CALLING BACK*]

Wally.   [*ON: CALLING FORWARD*] Well, hello, Ruth!

Ruth.   [*FADING ON*] I'm only stopping by for a moment, and if you're entertaining, I won't disturb you.

Wally.   Oh, no, no; I was just going. Got to run, you know.

Ruth.   I'm off to the shops to buy Len some new shirts. I hope you're not like my husband, Wally; of course, his position demands it, but I never knew a man so really fastidious.

Wally.   Well, I believe and hope the ladies like to see a man looking his best. So Hilda tells me.

Ruth.   [*INTEREST*] *Does* she? [*A CURIOUS LITTLE PAUSE*] You're not waiting for Hilda now? [*"OF COURSE" UNDERSTOOD*]

Wally.   Oh, I got her a few chocolates: wholesale.

Mrs. Morgan.   Hilda said she was taking my pearls in, but that was long ago.

Ruth.   Oh? The little jewellers up North Yonge?

Mrs. Morgan.   You know, Ruth, opposite the place where I get my flower transfers.

Ruth.   [*ODDLY*] Perhaps she dropped in for a cup of coffee somewhere. [*THEN WITH CURIOUS EMPHASIS*] I certainly wouldn't wait for her, if I were you, Wally.

Wally.   [*AWKWARDLY, AS THOUGH THIS HAS BEEN AN INVITATION*] Well, no, thanks very much, I'm afraid I can't. I've really got to run. Got a four o'clock appointment.

Mrs. Morgan.   Let me make you another cup of tea before you go.

Ruth.   Mother, it's not polite to try and detain guests against their will. Wally has lots of people to see, and he's very busy, and he has to fly.

Wally.   That's about the size of it. Uh . . . how if I dropped back this evening, though? [*FADING OFF A LITTLE*]

Mrs. Morgan.   Do that, Wally. I'll tell her, so she'll be sure to expect you.

Ruth.   Have you got your hat and everything?

Wally.   [*SLIGHTLY OFF*] All present and correct. Well, see you this evening, then.

¶ SOUND: *door opens off.*

Wally. Got to get away, or I'll never make my appointment. Four o'clock it's for.

Mrs. Morgan. [*OFF*] Goodbye, Wally. See you this evening!

¶ SOUND: *door shuts off.*

Ruth. [*CALLING*] Has he gone?

Mrs. Morgan. [*FADING BACK*] Now then, Ruth, what's the meaning of this? You practically hustled that poor man off the premises as if we didn't want to see him. Hilda's not going to thank you for this, you know.

Ruth. Mother: I've found out about Hilda.

Mrs. Morgan. [*IMMEDIATELY EXCITED*] Sit down, Ruth, and tell me all about it.

Ruth. She's ill. There's something the matter with her.

Mrs. Morgan. I've had an uncanny feeling that something like this was going to happen. How do you know?

Ruth. Well, I saw her on the street a couple of hours ago; that's what put me on the track.

Mrs. Morgan. How?

Ruth. I know she saw me, because she looked right at me; then she dodged into the nearest store. So I knew something was happening, and I just kept quiet, and next thing, out she came, and walked off down Bloor Street.

Mrs. Morgan. She said she was taking my broken necklace in.

Ruth. She did nothing of the sort. I was right behind her. Do you know where she went?

Mrs. Morgan. No, where?

Ruth. Into one of those old houses near the Medical Arts Building. I went up and looked at the brass plates, and it was full of surgeons.

Mrs. Morgan. What did she say when she came out?

Ruth. I didn't speak to her.

Mrs. Morgan. Why not? Didn't you wait?

Ruth. She ran into David Temple.

Mrs. Morgan. Oh, him! He was round *here* a week ago.

Ruth. So *that's* why she's been acting up.

Mrs. Morgan. I knew she was ill.

Ruth. Or thinks she is.

Mrs. Morgan. No, you can't tell me. I'm her mother. And I know what it is. I know as if some one had just spoken it in my ear. It's cancer.

Ruth. Now, mother, don't be silly! She probably got a sore throat or something.

Mrs. Morgan. They why hasn't she said a word about it? I can always tell when somebody's got a growth. I should have realized long ago.

Ruth. Don't be a fool, Mother. [*KINDLY, IF IMPATIENTLY*]

Mrs. Morgan. [*WITH IRRITATING ASSURANCE*] Your mother's not a fool, dear. I just know. What on earth shall I do, if I lose her? [*WITH MORE FEELING*]

Ruth. Oh, come on, Mother! Hilda's as strong as a horse.

Mrs. Morgan. [*CORRECTING HER*] She *looks* strong, dear; but she's been delicate ever since she grew up. I don't know *what* I'll do if they have to cut her open. [*WITH SIMPLE HOPELESSNESS*]

Ruth. [*TRYING TO PULL THINGS TOGETHER*] Mother, I only mentioned this in case you knew what was the matter. I'm sure there's nothing wrong that time won't cure.

Mrs. Morgan. [*WELL AWAY*] She's my own daughter, Ruth; *I*'ve noticed she's not been the same these last few weeks. You can't tell *me* they aren't going to cut her open. She was foolish to go to a surgeon. They're never happy till they're cutting into you. Your poor father used to get into their labs whenever he got the chance, and it was simply terrible. Cutting up dogs and all sorts of cruelty. [*HER TONE IS GETTING MORE AND MORE VICIOUS*] I'd like to cut some of them up, and see how they'd like it.

Ruth. They have to learn somehow.

Mrs. Morgan. Cruelty is cruelty. We're told to love one another, and that doesn't mean cutting up poor dumb animals. If I ever have to be cut open, I will not have it done by a surgeon, and it worries me to think what Hilda may have to go through.

Ruth. What worries *me* is who's going to pay for it?

Mrs. Morgan. If money is truly needed in a Christian spirit, it will be provided, and that we know.

Ruth. Len and I haven't the money to spend on operations.

Mrs. Morgan. Weren't you saving for a dining room suite? *I* shall have to make sacrifices too.

Ruth. In any case, there's no reason why it should have to be, well, cancer. [*WITH A TINY HESITATION ON THE DREADFUL WORD*]

Mrs. Morgan. I'm never wrong about this kind of thing, Ruth. It goes in our family. I can remember knowing about it with your Aunt Nellie, and I can remember it just started as a lump, and then she was gone almost before we realized.

Ruth. But you don't have it until you're old; and Hilda's just a girl.

Mrs. Morgan. [*RATHER SHARPLY*] Nellie was just a girl. She wasn't even fifty; she was the youngest next to me. Besides, you don't know what happened last night. My chrysanthemums burst the pot.

Ruth. It must have got cracked moving.

Mrs. Morgan. No, dear! It shattered in the middle of the night. You should have seen the mess. They outgrew the pot! I knew then it was a special warning for me!

Ruth. Such as how?

Mrs. Morgan. [*SOLEMN*] It was a warning from Providence about a growth, and now it's all come true, and what on earth will become of me if Hilda dies, and ends up losing her job, I really don't know! [*DISSOLVING INTO THE VERGE OF TEARS*]

Ruth. Come on, Mother, cheer up! I'm going to wait till I know what the doctor really said [*SHE THEN ADDS ALMOST TO HERSELF*] and why that Dave Temple was hanging around.

¶ MUSIC: *low and ominous to a restaurant background.*

¶ SOUND: *very light restaurant background.*

David. So that's it, eh Hilda?

Hilda. That's it, David.

David. You shouldn't have helped with your moving. Might have strained you.

Hilda. I'll be strained a lot more before we're through. This coffee's perfectly foul. See if you can find the waitress.

David. I've been drinking mine.

Hilda. A woman could put up with disasters but not inconveniences.

David. Is this a disaster?

Hilda. Not to me.

David. Nor me. Did he say when?

Hilda. In six months. He'll be more exact later.

David. Three months ago. Lake Simcoe.

Hilda. [*MUSING*] I suppose. The doctor's a very nice man. Teaches himself, he says. Asked me if it gave me a pain in the eyes. I told him teaching gave me a pain in the feet and a pain in the neck. He kept calling me Mrs. Temple, and both he and the nurse looked for the ring.

David. You were right about getting one then. They didn't seem to realize . . . that . . .

Hilda. [*COOLY*] That I'm not really entitled to it? Of course not, David.

David. Why of course not?

Hilda. Because I *am* entitled to it. As far as I'm concerned, we've been married ten months.

David. I still wish we'd made it legal. We should have done.

Hilda. Dollars and cents, David.

David. Dollars and cents aren't going to count now, are they?

Hilda. No, we'll *have* to afford it now. May I have a cigarette? I feel a little shaky for some reason.

David. [*SOLICITOUS*] Sure, honey; here you are.

Hilda. I'll be all right in a moment, I expect. Probably poisoned by the coffee. David: I think you're *glad* this has happened.

David.   I am glad. Because now we're going to be married; and because we're going to have a child.

Hilda.   Darling! Do you want to tell your parents about the baby? Right away, I mean?

David.   I'd like to soon; I think they'd be very happy too. Happy as I am.

Hilda.   You happy about it?

David.   Very happy.

Hilda.   Darling. OK, pick the time, and tell 'em; but while you're at it, tell 'em to keep it from Mother.

David.   Well, they're up at the cottage right now. I'll wire them we're engaged, and explain when we meet.

Hilda.   Don't you want to put it in a wire?

David.   I do not. These days telegraph companies don't send telegrams; they phone in messages, and this is no item for a rural party line.

Hilda.   I'll tell mother we're engaged tonight, after supper.

David.   I'll call for you tonight. No need to soothe your mother now.

Hilda.   I suppose. I bet Wally Turnbull called this afternoon. This is his day. I used to like him quite a lot, once; and now he's a bit of a nuisance.

David.   *He*'ll be surprised. [*QUITE PLEASANTLY*]

Hilda.   I suppose. I think I'll go home now, David. I feel a bit upset.

David.   OK, let's go. I'll get a cab.

Hilda.   Never mind about *that*; dollars and cents. And don't come with me. I want to save the row till after supper. You go and wire your parents; that'll give *you* something to do. And when you turn up this evening, be sure and ask mother to show you the new duplex. That may soothe her.

David.   Lucky you said *that*, or I'd have been off down Eglinton to the old stamping ground. Fine thing when a fellow doesn't know his wife's address.

Hilda.   [*PLEASED AT THE LITTLE JOKE*] Dear David. [*THEN FIRMLY*] But I'm going to write down the address for you.

David.   Want some paper? Better keep me on a lead, too. Might meet a new girl friend.

Hilda.   Lend me a pencil.

David.   Here. You wouldn't like *that*, would you?

Hilda.   [*ABSENT-MINDEDLY*] Like what?

David.   Me getting a new girl friend.

Hilda.   [*GOING ALONG WITH THE GAG*] Why should I care? I'd run away with Wally Turnbull. Now here you are. This is the address: 2046 Grosvenor Street; and this is the girl's name. It's Hilda. And you remember that, Master David, or I'll have something to say to you.

David.   Yes, teacher. Hilda it is; and I'm very proud of her, and very happy. So let's get the glad news circulating!

¶ MUSIC: *with a sprightly figure takes Hilda back home: and ends with a chord of expectancy.*

Mrs. Morgan. [*WATCHING OUT OF THE WINDOW*] Here she is, Ruth! She's coming up the path. Open the door, quick!

Ruth. [*OFF AT THE DOOR*] All right, Mother; I'm here!

¶ SOUND: *door opens: slightly off.*

Ruth. [*OFF*] Well, *hello*, Hilda!

Hilda. [*OFF*] You gave me quite a fright. I was just going to put the key in.

¶ SOUND: *door shuts off.*

Ruth. [*FADING ON*] Mother saw you coming, through the window.

Hilda. [*FADING ON*] I didn't expect to see *you* here, Ruth. Thought you spent this time of day cooking up hot dinners for that tyrannical man of yours. Hello, Mother. [*CASUALLY*]

Mrs. Morgan. [*QUITE EMOTIONALLY*] Oh, Hilda, Hilda, darling!

Hilda. [*ASTONISHED: BUT SOOTHING HER*] Mother, Mother, Mother. [*MRS. MORGAN CONTINUES TO CLING TO HILDA AND TO MURMUR*] What is it, dear? Ruth, what's the matter with Mother.

Mrs. Morgan. Nothing, darling; everything's going to be all right: I *know* it is.

Hilda. [*AS USUAL QUITE CALM*] What's the matter, Ruth?

Ruth. [*RATHER POINTEDLY*] We're waiting for you to tell us.

Hilda. Waiting for *me*?

Ruth. I saw you this afternoon with Dave Temple.

Hilda. [*WITH BLANK COURTESY*] Yes?

Ruth. You'd just come out of that little surgeon's building.

Mrs. Morgan. [*BURSTING OUT AGAIN*] Oh, Hilda, why didn't you *tell* me! I'm your mother; I could have comforted you; don't you realize I've been through all this before, more than once.

Hilda. [*SLOWLY*] I suppose.

Ruth. [*WITH GENTLE REMONSTRANCE*] You should have told us you were going to the doctor.

Hilda. I didn't want to say till afterwards.

Ruth. It might have put us in a very funny position.

Mrs. Morgan. [*WARMLY*] Sweetheart, *I* understand; you didn't want to worry us. Well, you're home now, Hilda, and we must all be brave together, just the three of us. That's the way people do nowadays. In our day, we made a shameful secret of it; but that was wrong, oh, quite wrong. Now tell us what the doctor said.

Hilda. He said: yes.

Mrs. Morgan. [SUDDENLY BECOMING EDGY IN SPITE OF HER APPARENT CALM] You see, Ruth? I had the premonition and the warning. It is cancer.

Hilda. [ASTOUNDED] What on earth put *that* into your head, Mother?

Mrs. Morgan. Don't be ashamed of it, dear; it runs in the family. Several cousins had it. Aunt Nellie had it.

Hilda. [PULLING HERSELF TOGETHER] Well, if that's what you were worrying about, you're wrong. It's nothing; not cancer at all. Just a — sort of stomach upset. Indigestion — overwork.

Ruth. Operation?

Hilda. No! A good rest, the doctor said, and it'll clear up eventually.

Ruth. Will it pass off naturally in due course?

Hilda. [WITH AN INWARD SMILE] Quite naturally, yes.

Ruth. Then why all the mystery? [FLINGING HER ARMS IN THE AIR]

Hilda. There's no mystery.

Ruth. You didn't tell us.

Hilda. You didn't ask. I don't like a fuss.

Mrs. Morgan. [IN A LOUD VOICE] It's not a fuss to tell your family.

Hilda. Well, I've told you.

Mrs. Morgan. And what did he say again? [JUST TOO CASUALLY]

Hilda. I thought it was overwork, and he said yes.

Mrs. Morgan. Tell me again what he *said*, dear.

Hilda. I've told you, Mother. That's all there is to it. Got a match, Ruth?

Mrs. Morgan. On the side table, dear.

Ruth. Len and I have quit smoking. Saves a lot of money.

Hilda. *I* can't smoke at school; or near the school buildings.

Ruth. Ridiculous.Old-fashioned.

Hilda. The teacher must be purer than the snows of yesteryear.

Mrs. Morgan. Well, Grandpa did say: If God had meant us to smoke . . .

Ruth & Hilda. [FINISHING IT OFF TOGETHER] We'd all been born with chimneys in our heads.

Hilda. And a girl who smokes will drink . . .

Ruth. . . . *And* a girl who drinks will do anything!

Hilda. [WITH A SMILE] Wally Turnbull used to think that was true.

Ruth. [GIGGLING] Don't be awful, Hilda! He was here this afternoon with a present for you.

Hilda. [POSITIVELY] Wally's got nothing I'm interested in.

Mrs. Morgan. [RETURNING TO THE CHARGE IN HER SWEETEST VOICE] Hilda.

Hilda. [CASUALLY] Yes, dear?

Mrs. Morgan. Hilda, look at me.

Hilda. [NOT CASUALLY] Yes?

Mrs. Morgan. Hilda: is that all you have to tell your mother about this afternoon?

Hilda. [*AFTER A PAUSE*] No, Mother, there *is* one thing.

Mrs. Morgan. [*COMPLACENTLY*] I knew it.

Hilda. He rooked me fifteen bucks for telling me I was all right.

Ruth. Fifteen. . . . What a waste of dough!

Mrs. Morgan. It's nothing to pay for peace of mind: if your mind *is* at peace.

Hilda. Why not?

Mrs. Morgan. [*WITH EXASPERATING SERENITY*] I don't know why not. I only know you're keeping something back.

Hilda. [*CAREFULLY*] I've told you what he said; that's *all*.

Mrs. Morgan. I haven't brought you up for twenty five years without knowing when there's something on your mind, and I want to know what it is. [*HARDENING A LITTLE*]

Hilda. Well, OK. There is something, yes.

Mrs.Morgan. Neither of you can ever keep anything from your mother. It only hurts me a little that you don't trust me in the first place. Out with it, dear.

Hilda. It's nothing to do with the doctor.

Mrs. Morgan. Just say what it is.

Hilda. I wanted to save it till after dinner, but you can't fool Mother. [*WITH A CURIOUS EDGE*]

Mrs. Morgan. Say what it is.

Hilda. I'm engaged.

Ruth. Hilda!

Mrs. Morgan. [*SHOCKED INTO SINCERITY*] Engaged to be *married*? Oh, my dear, Wally's a very lucky man.

Hilda. I expect he is, but I'm engaged to be married to Dave Temple.

Mrs. Morgan. [*SHOCKED AGAIN*] Dave Temple! But I hardly know him.

Hilda. Why should you? You aren't marrying him.

Ruth. It's certainly sudden enough, Hilda. [*SHE DOESN'T KNOW IF SHE LIKES IT OR NOT*]

Hilda. It may be sudden to you, but David and I have been talking it over for a long time.

Mrs. Morgan. [*GETTING BACK ON HER PEDESTAL*] In our day the girl waited till she was asked before she did any talking over.

Hilda. I waited till I was asked; otherwise he mightn't have asked me.

Mrs. Morgan. Then you've been plotting it for a long time?

Hilda. A few months.

Ruth. [*SHREWDLY*] What made you tell us now?

Hilda. We decided it was time to be getting on with it.

Mrs. Morgan. It's certainly time to talk everything over. *I* have something to say, you know.

Hilda. You didn't have anything to say when Ruth got married.

Ruth. There was still you to look after Mother. Now what happens?

Len and I certainly haven't room for her.

Mrs. Morgan. Don't think of me, Ruth. Hilda doesn't. Even though she is my baby. [ON THE VERGE OF TEARS]

Hilda. I'm twenty-five.

Mrs. Morgan. Don't try and tell your own mother how old you are.

Ruth. You might have given us a chance to make arrangements.

Hilda. [EASILY] I'm giving you a chance. This is it.

Mrs. Morgan. I only hope *you* don't feel like this when *your* little girl's taken away.

Hilda. Taken away! You see Ruth all the time.

Mrs. Morgan. Can't a mother see her daughter once in a while without endless complaints? [HILDA SIGHS] Or is it the funny old joke about the mother-in-law whose daughters haven't room for her?

Ruth. [JUST AS SHARP AS HER MOTHER] Len and I have to keep the spare room for his brothers.

Mrs. Morgan. [TURNING THE POINT] Yes, Len thinks of his family, and Wally thinks of *his* family, but I'd like to know who David and Hilda think of!

Hilda. Mostly of each other lately.

Mrs. Morgan. Selfishness never pays.

Hilda. It pays the selfish ones.

Mrs. Morgan. Oh! Ruth, did you hear that?

Ruth. What a thing to say to Mother!

Hilda. Mother's in the clear; she never has a guilty conscience.

Ruth. And I have?

Hilda. Why scratch if it isn't itching?

Ruth. Believe me, if anybody's going to have mother-in-law trouble, it's you! If you think old Mrs. Temple is going to let her darling David fly the coop into *your* back yard, you're crazy!

Hilda. Nag Len, Ruth; that's what he supports you for.

Ruth. Darling, I'm keeping clear of this whole mess, as of now! But how do you think Mother and I feel when you put us in a very funny position over this doctor, and then march in, cool as a cucumber, and tell us you're going to marry the one and only original mother's boy.

Mrs. Morgan. And what's Wally going to say? I'm sure he's more of a man than Dave Temple.

Ruth. What did you do to him? Twist his arm, or something? Or did you propose to him?

Hilda. Len hung around here for long enough before you got him on the dotted line.

Mrs. Morgan. I see we have a good deal to talk over.

Hilda. For my money, there's nothing to talk over.

Mrs. Morgan. We'll see about that, Hilda, when the time comes; tempers have become frayed, and we'll apologize. I'm sorry for anything I've said. Ruth?

Ruth. I'm sorry.

Mrs. Morgan. Hilda?

Hilda. I suppose.

Mrs. Morgan. And we'll talk about it again after supper.

Hilda. I shall be going out after supper.

Ruth. With David?

Mrs. Morgan. Is he going to show himself here?

Hilda. He is.

Mrs. Morgan. Then perhaps he can talk it over too. I don't doubt we shall all see reason by the time we're through.

¶ MUSIC: *picks up the threat and passes the time.*

Mrs. Morgan. She's taking a long time getting dressed.

Ruth: Give her a chance. She wants to hit the new fiancée.

Mrs. Morgan. I'll *hit* him. You wait. I'll make them see reason. Wally's coming round later. I'll talk them out of it.

Ruth. [NOW MORE ON HILDA'S SIDE] You didn't talk Len and me out of it.

Mrs. Morgan. [BRIDLING] My dear, never for one moment did I try!

Ruth. [OFF-HAND] Didn't you?

Mrs. Morgan. I should certainly hope not. My girls have their own lives to live. I hope I realize that. It's just my duty to advise them and make them think of someone besides themselves occasionally. And though there *was* some understanding with Wally Turnbull, please don't think I hold anything against David *personally*, no more than I did with Len.

Ruth. David isn't in the same position Len was.

Mrs. Morgan. Be fair, dear. He's in his father's business.

Ruth. There's a difference between a sales clerk and a banker.

Mrs. Morgan. Len's hardly a banker yet, is he, dear?

Ruth. He'll be an Assistant Manager in ten or fifteen years. Already we've been to the manager's house three times for bridge; so all his work *is* getting him somewhere.

Mrs. Morgan. It's up to you, of course, if you have to make your way by gambling.

Ruth. We play for fun.

Mrs. Morgan. Your father and I could never see the fun in playing cards; but things change, and people feel they must change too.

Ruth. Well, Len doesn't smoke, and he doesn't drink, and . . .

Mrs. Morgan. Ruth, our mother always told us: a gambler's worse than a drunkard. A drunkard can do no more than make a beast of himself, but a gambler can lose everything for you, and never let on till the men come to take it away. And Mother certainly knew what she was talking about.

82

Ruth. You never told me grandpa was bad about money.

Mrs. Morgan. [*PIOUSLY*] Whatever he was, dear, Mother made him repent before we grew up; and forgive and forget is the only Christian thing.

Ruth. [*AGITATED*] You might have told me this before. It might affect Len.

Mrs. Morgan. Len? How?

Ruth. Everything must be *right* in a bank, especially family background. The temptation is enormous and the salaries are rather moderate, so they have to be sure of perfect honesty, or else the insurance companies won't put up a bond.

Mrs. Morgan. [*GOING PINK*] I'm sorry if I said anything wrong.

Ruth. You should have told me sooner or not at all.

Mrs. Morgan. Then simply forget I said it.

Ruth. [*SCRUPULOUSLY*] But you *have* said it. If I had to swear on the Bible, did I know any bad blood in the family? I'd have to tell them, yes.

Hilda. [*COMING ON*] I've been pinning up that slip, and I don't think it shows now.

Mrs. Morgan. [*GLAD TO CHANGE THE SUBJECT*] Turn round, Hilda. No, that's fine.

Hilda. Stocking seams straight?

Ruth. [*SOURLY*] Oh, straight enough.

Hilda. [*PAUSING*] What's the matter now?

Ruth. Nothing *you* need to worry about. Mother's just let out that grandpa was a gambler.

Mrs. Morgan. We have no right to judge others. Forgive us our trespasses.

Ruth. I'm not thinking of myself; it's Len. [*AND IT REALLY IS, TOO*]

Hilda. Poor grandpa's wild oats aren't going to tickle Len at this late date.

Ruth. [*STUBBORNLY*] What's bred in the bone comes out in the flesh.

Mrs. Morgan. If we're talking about breeding, you're descended from your grandmother as well, and she was a lovely person almost till the day she died.

Hilda. Even if she wasn't, we have our own lives to live.

Ruth. Len's different.

Hilda. How so?

Ruth. You don't know what a strain it is; we have to think of his position at the bank every minute. Everything we say or do is taken note of, day or night.

Hilda. Dictaphone in the mattress?

Ruth. You're the coarse side of the family, Hilda. You're certainly grandpa's child.

Hilda.   What's the matter? Broken your funnybone?

Ruth.   [*HONESTLY UPSET*] There's nothing funny about the way we worry and scrape; and you'll know that when you're living off David.

Mrs. Morgan.   If it's my fault, I'll give back every cent you've given me. I only took it because I thought you wanted to help.

Ruth.   We do, but when Hilda goes, we can't do any more, and David'll have to take over his share. [*THIS IS HER REAL WORRY*]

Hilda.   [*SYMPATHETICALLY*] If that's all that's worrying you, dear, cheer up and settle down. Of course David'll take over his share.

Ruth.   [*SUSPICIOUS YET HOPEFUL*] How do you know? Are you sure?

Hilda.   We've talked it over lots of times.

Mrs. Morgan.   [*REGALLY*] Not that I mind my private and personal affairs being discussed and debated with perfect strangers, but I do think, Hilda, you might tell me.

Hilda.   I am telling you, dear.

Mrs. Morgan.   Every so often I meet Mrs. Temple in the street; and how was *I* to know they knew all our private and personal arrangements?

Hilda.   There's nothing to be ashamed of. I never care who knows the truth.

Mrs. Morgan.   I know you haven't any secrets from anybody, Hilda, but when you're as old as I am, and living off your daughters' charity . . .

Ruth.   Charity! Oh, Mother!

Mrs. Morgan.   It makes me go hot all over when I think how I'm going to face that boy when he comes in the door; and you should have thought of it before you blurted out our business to him, Hilda.

¶ SOUND: *doorbell rings off.*

Ruth.   You sit down. I'll let him in.

Hilda.   Do I look all right?

Ruth.   [*FADING OFF*] You look fine, darling.

Hilda.   I hope so. Do I look all right, Mother?

Mrs. Morgan.   You look as well as you ever do in blue, dear, even if you are a little tired. Sit still quietly and wait for him.

¶ MUSIC: *a tense figure: down to Wally's background.*

Wally.   But it wasn't him. It was just little me. I was a bit surprised, because they put me in the front room where nobody was sitting, as if I was company, and after a while, and a bit of whispering here and there, Hilda came in — in full war paint! She was always a stunner when she had her glasses off, and she had lots of the old twinkle-twinkle that night. I felt pretty flattered that she'd got all the rigging on for yours truly, for to tell the truth, I had noticed we weren't as pally as we used to be, if you get the point. Even so, I did notice she didn't quite seem to have her eye on the scoreboard.

¶ MUSIC: *out with Wally.*

Hilda.   Hello, Wally. This *is* a surprise seeing you.

Wally.   Oh, I can tell better than that! [*WITH GREAT COYNESS*] Don't tell *me* you weren't expecting somebody!

Hilda.   [*RATHER ILL AT EASE*] Well, yes, Wally, I was expecting somebody. You see . . .

Wally.   I just brought in a little package for the duchess of Grosvenor Street, eh? Look as if you'd stepped straight out of the silver screen.

Hilda.   Do you really like it, Wally?

Wally.   [*SMILING HAPPILY*] I like the packaging, and I like the product. I like the nice blue dress: I like what it hides, and I like what it shows.

Hilda.   [*SMILING*] Wally. And how nice of you to bring me something.

Wally.   [*HOPEFULLY*] No real need to open it right away.

Hilda.   [*MISSING THE POINT: BRIGHTLY*] All right, I'll put it over here.

Wally.   [*DISAPPOINTED*] It's just something a fellow in the line was able to get me specially. You can't get those sort in the regular way, you know. It's a special sort of chocolates.

Hilda.   Oh, how nice of you, Wally; but I'm afraid it'll spoil my figure.

Wally.   [*EXPANSIVELY*] No, no, no: there can't be too much of you to please me. I think it's *wonderful* you're putting on weight.

Hilda.   [*ALERT AT ONCE*] Oh. Is it . . . very noticeable?

Wally.   [*NOTICING HER TENSION*] No offence intended. I just think the smile looks brighter when the cheeks are plumper.

Hilda.   [*RELAXING*] Oh yes, I have put a little weight on my face.

Wally.   And it makes perfection even more dandy. You know, when I see you with your hair that way, like the monkey says, where have you been all my life?

Hilda.   It's sweet of you, Wally, to think of all these nice things, because, frankly, this is a special occasion for me.

Wally.   And the same goes for me, doubled in spades.

Hilda.   You see, I'm so fond of you Wally, I wanted you to be the first to know. I'm going to be married.

Wally.   [*AFTER A PAUSE*] You're going to be married?

Hilda.   Dave Temple asked me this afternoon, and I said yes, and he's coming round this evening to see Mother. He should be here any minute.

Wally.   [*AFTER A PAUSE*] Dave's fond of blue, is he?

Hilda.   So he says.

Wally.   [*AFTER ANOTHER PAUSE: GETTING UP*] Well, OK, then. Does he like hard centres.

Hilda.   Well, I certainly do.

Wally.   Then, I guessed wrong again. The candy's all soft centres, I'm afraid. Don't bother opening it right now, though. There's a couple of fellows I've got to see, and I only had time to drop in for a moment. And congratulations, Hilda — no, I'm a liar — that's wrong. Congratulations for the Mister: *best wishes* for the Mrs. Best wishes, Hildy.

Hilda. Thank you.

Wally. I'll save the congratulations till the family comes along; never do to let you have 'em now, would it? But for what they're worth you got my best wishes such as they are; and if there's ever anything you need, this makes no difference to me, you know. Just give me a ring, and I'll be right on over.

Hilda. I'll remember that, Wally.

¶ SOUND: *doorbell off.*

Wally. Here's the lucky guy now. I'll slip out the back way. [*HE ADDS WISTFULLY*] Might make him jealous.

Hilda. [*TOO HEARTILY*] Of course not! [*WALLY SADLY MURMURS: NO*] I'm not going to give up *all* my boy-friends just because I'm marrying one of them.

¶ SOUND: *door opens off.*

Mrs. Morgan. [*OFF*] Oh! Good evening.

Police. [*OFF*] Good evening, madam.

Hilda. [*ON*] *That's* not him.

Police. We're from the City Police. This 2046 Grosvenor?

Mrs. Morgan. [*OFF*] Yes. 2046 Grosvenor is certainly the address.

Hilda. Where'd you park your car?

Wally. [*ON*] Caught a cab.

Mrs. Morgan. [*OFF*] We have nothing to do with the police; unless you're selling tickets?

Police. [*OFF*] No, madam; we want to know if there's anybody here by the name of Hilda.

Wally. [*ON*] They want you.

Mrs. Morgan. I'm sure Hilda hasn't done anything I wouldn't do. I'm her mother, so you can take my word for it. You see, she's a schoolteacher, and she lives right here with me.

Hilda. I'll go and see. [*RAISING HER VOICE*] All right, Mother, I'll talk to him! Just a moment! [*FADING OFF*]

¶ SOUND: *brisk footsteps fading off then on.*

Hilda. [*ON*] My name is Hilda Morgan, officer. Can I help you?

Police. [*ON*] Do you happen to know a man, aged twenty five to thirty; height five foot ten; weight a hundred and forty five; brown hair; blue eyes; complexion fair, clear shaven, small scar on right wrist.

Hilda. [*RATHER LOUDLY*] It isn't David . . . !

Police.   [*INQUIRINGLY*] David?

Hilda.   [*CONTROLLED AGAIN*] David Temple.

Police.   Do you know him well?

Mrs. Morgan.   [*ON*] Hardly at all.

Hilda.   We're going to be married.

Ruth.   [*OFF*] What's the matter?

Hilda.   [*ON*] What's happened?

Police.   Perhaps I'd better come inside a moment.

Mrs. Morgan.   [*A GASP*] Oh dear!

Wally.   [*FADING ON*] Anything I can do?

Police.   The fact of the matter is, you see, there's been a traffic accident. [*WITH A DEFINITE FALL TO THE VOICE*]

Hilda.   [*AFTER A MOMENT'S PAUSE*] He's dead.

Police.   Well . . . yes, miss, I'm afraid he is. We went to his home address but the people are away, and we like to get identification and there was your name on a piece of paper in his pocket . . .

Mrs. Morgan.   [*EVER CURIOUS*] What was that doing there?

Ruth.   [*QUICKLY AND QUIETLY*] Never *mind*, Mother!

Hilda.   [*FIRMLY*] Please tell me what to do.

Police.   We wondered if you'd have any objection to giving us an identification.

Mrs. Morgan.   My daughter doesn't have to do anything!

Hilda.   You mean go and look at him?

Wally.   Does she *have* to do it?

Police.   Certainly not, but you see . . .

Hilda.   I don't mind looking at him . . .

Wally.   He may be all mashed . . . uh, you know . . . [*HE TRIES TO CATCH HIMSELF*]

Hilda.   [*EMPHASIS*] I don't mind looking at him. I shan't be seeing him again.

Wally.   OK, then, let me go with you!

Mrs. Morgan.   Oh, Wally, I wish you would!

Hilda.   [*CUTTING THEM OFF*] I shall go alone, please.

Police.   We can wait outside while you get ready.

Hilda.   I'm quite ready. My coat's right here. I was expecting to go out in a few minutes anyway. Goodbye, Mother. Bye, Ruth; Wally.

Mrs. Morgan.   Oh, Hilda, isn't there anything we can do?

Hilda.   [*FLATLY*] Well, is there? Goodbye.

¶ MUSIC: *firm and melancholy: under Wally as background with a vaguely ecclesiastical flavour.*

Wally.   [*VERY EARNESTLY*] We all have to go some day, of course, but even when it's the other fellow's turn to meet the grim reaper, it makes you think. After all, you can't take it with you, and it sure lets you know that poker games and the Casino's all right for a while, but a man's got to build up something solid by clean living and square dealing, and going to church regular Christmas and Easter, and of course for weddings and funerals. [*THE SERMON OVER HE TAKES UP HIS LAST IDEA IN EASIER VEIN*] I was at David's funeral myself; slipped in the back quietly. Hilda was there, naturally. Didn't wear black; didn't cry; didn't even speak to David's mom and dad much, except on the way out I saw her talking to Mrs. Temple, while the organist was finishing things off. Most people thought the girl-friend and the mother were exchanging condolences: but, how does it go? most people are wrong, and as it turned out, they certainly were this time:

¶ MUSIC: *during the last few lines of Wally's speech has gradually cross faded to very distant church organ playing "Abide with Me."*

Mrs. Temple.   Please forgive me, Hilda, for taking you aside like this.
Hilda.   Quite all right, Mrs. Temple.
Mrs. Temple.   [*WHO, THROUGHOUT, HAS A KIND OF FEEBLE PERSISTENCE THAT IS QUITE IRRESISTIBLE*] All during the ceremony, I thought I simply *must* speak to you, Hilda, no matter what you say.
Hilda.   Please, Mrs. Temple, anything at all.
Mrs. Temple.   You see, you have your mother and sister to comfort you. Father and I have nobody.
Hilda.   You have each other. [*WITH A SLIGHT EMPHASIS ON THE "YOU"*]
Mrs. Temple.   We have each other for memories: but no hopes, Hilda.
Hilda.   [*SLOWLY*] No hopes, no.
Mrs. Temple.   No hopes at all: he was everything, you know, for us.
Hilda.   I know he was.
Mrs. Temple.   Now he's gone and there's nothing left. It's as if he'd never lived.
Hilda.   [*WITH GREAT SINCERITY*] Oh, Mrs. Temple, please, no it *isn't.*
Mrs. Temple.   It is for Father and me; all we can do is wait our turn.
Hilda.   [*NERVOUS*] I'm sorry . . . we're both upset. I don't know what to say to you.
Mrs. Temple.   Father doesn't know I'm speaking to you, you understand. [*THIS POINT SEEMS VERY IMPORTANT TO HER*] Look, he's over there, talking to the minister. Father knows nothing about it. But he was so glad when we heard that you two were engaged, and I was so glad too, though I had quite a good cry over it. Do you know, I didn't cry at all when I found out he was dead?

¶ MUSIC: *the organ has stopped by now.*

Hilda.   Neither did I.
Mrs. Temple.   [*DREAMILY*] Though I used to cry a lot as a girl, when I wasn't allowed to go to all the dances I thought I should . . .

[*SUDDENLY*] Well, I'm going to say it, Hilda, and you can think what you like of me. We haven't any other hope. Were you and David secretly married?

Hilda. [*LONG PAUSE*] He told you in the telegram we were engaged. That's all.

Mrs. Temple. I had hopes (Father doesn't know) there might be a child.

Hilda. A child?

Mrs. Temple. Even if he were dead, he might have had a child. [*A QUERY SEEMS TO RUN THROUGH MANY OF THESE REMARKS*] Then you see . . . I think he was fond of children. But of course you weren't married.

Hilda. No, we weren't.

Mrs. Temple. [*NODDING*] No. David saw you the day he was killed?

Hilda. Yes: we saw each other in the afternoon.

Mrs. Temple. And then you decided to get married?

Hilda. [*GENTLY REJECTING THE IMPLIED INFERENCE*] We'd decided *before*.

Mrs. Temple. But you decided to *tell* us then?

Hilda. Yes, we thought we'd tell you.

Mrs. Temple. Why?

Hilda. We just thought you should know.

Mrs. Temple. [*GOING STRAIGHT ON AS IF SHE HADN'T CHANGED THE SUBJECT*] Your sister tells me you went to see the doctor.

Hilda. [*EDGY*] I'd been having a lot of indigestion.

Mrs. Temple. You went to see the doctor the same afternoon?

Hilda. Yes, I did.

Mrs. Temple. [*GENTLY BRINGING HER ARGUMENT TO ITS CLIMAX*] And did you send the telegram to say you were engaged *before* you saw the doctor — or *after*? [*THERE IS A LONG PAUSE AND WHEN THE CONVERSATION RESUMES IT SEEMS AS IF THEY HAVE MADE AN UNSPOKEN UNDERSTANDING*]

Hilda. I don't remember — just now.

Mrs. Temple. I believe it's rather important.

Hilda. If you really believe so . . .

Mrs. Temple. Indeed I do.

Hilda. Then I'll think it over very carefully; and let you know at once, if I should happen to remember.

Mrs. Temple. I do so hope you will.

Hilda. [*WITH ABSOLUTE ASSURANCE AND GENTLENESS*] You can trust me. I will.

Mrs. Temple. [*BREAKING THE MOOD AND RETURNING TO HER FEATHER-BRAINED REPETITIOUSNESS*] But then of course, you have your mother and sister to comfort you. Father and I have nobody.

¶ MUSIC: *a sad feeble phrase ends the scene: background under Wally.*

Wally. I saw them finish their talk, but I didn't offer to see Hilda home. Bad taste: fellow shouldn't look as if he's gloating. Felt pretty low myself, so I took in a movie instead. Hamlet. When a fellow's up against it, there's nothing like the classics to make you feel things aren't all that bad, and better cheer up if I was to do Hilda any good. So thought I'd drop around in the evening. But by the time, *I* showed up, the shooting was almost over. I gather the fun had started with Ruth.

¶ MUSIC: *out with Wally.*

Hilda. [*RATHER TENSE AND ON HER NERVES DURING THIS SCENE IN SPITE OF HER USUAL AIR OF ASSURANCE AND STRENGTH*] Hello, Ruth. Mother in?

Ruth. Ladies Auxiliary. Were you at the ceremony?

Hilda. Yes, I was at the funeral.

Ruth. Nice ceremony?

Hilda. Oh, as nice as you'd expect when they're burying the man you're engaged to. [*THEN SEEING RUTH MEANT WELL*] But it was a lovely funeral, really; lots of flowers — music.

Ruth. That's consolation in a way, really.

Hilda. I suppose.

Ruth. You sit down and rest; I'll get you a cup of coffee.

Hilda. No thanks. [*OUT IT COMES*] Ruth, I guess I might as well start with you.

Ruth. [*NO MORE THAN MILD INTEREST*] Oh?

Hilda. I'm going to have a baby.

Ruth. [*AFTER A PAUSE*] *Oh! You fool!* Are you sure?

Hilda. Doctor says so.

Ruth. I always was suspicious about that doctor business. Were you married to David?

Hilda. No. Not legally.

Ruth. Couldn't you *think*? Couldn't you remember Len's in a *bank*? The least breath of scandal. . . . Well, we'll have to do something, that's certain, and argue about it afterwards. Got any ideas?

Hilda. I want to get leave of absence from the school — telling them why. Have the baby; hire a nurse for it; and go back to work.

Ruth. You can't support Mother as well.

Hilda. She'll have to go to work too.

Ruth. Perhaps *we* shan't have to chip in either. It's an ill wind. Did he know?

Hilda. Yes. He was very pleased.

Ruth. Well, we've got to think of the living. This'll finish Mother off.

Hilda. I doubt it.

Ruth. [*CONCEDING THE POINT*] Well. Probably Len's career will be finished on the spot.

Hilda. David's was.

Ruth. [*MISSING THE POINT*] Well, of course. He was *killed*, wasn't he?

Well, I'm not going to preach at you. We've got to help you for our own sake as much as yours.

Hilda. If you don't want to, you don't have to.

Ruth. I know I don't *have* to, but I'm going to all the same. [THEN SOFTER] Oh, Hilda, honey, why did it have to be *you*? How much money have you got?

Hilda. About three hundred dollars.

Ruth. It's not enough. Well, we haven't much, but we've some.

Hilda. It's very kind of you, Ruth . . .

Ruth. Forget it. Lucky I've been a miser. We were going to get a new dining suite. . . . Well, who the hell cares? If I hurry I can get to the bank before three o'clock. You wait here. Mother should be back any minute. Don't say a word to her till I get back!

¶ MUSIC: *excited: ending with a suggestion of Mrs. Morgan.*

¶ SOUND: *the door shutting off.*

Hilda. [RAISING HER VOICE] That you, Ruth?

Mrs. Morgan. [OFF: FADING ON] No, it's me. So you're home, are you, Hilda?

Hilda. Yes. The funeral was over later than I thought, and I spoke to David's mother afterwards . . .

Mrs. Morgan. Well, I don't think you should have gone.

Hilda. Oh?

Mrs. Morgan. I don't like to intrude on people's grief.

Hilda. [ALMOST WITH A SECRET SMILE] I don't think it was an intrusion. I don't think Ruth does, either.

Mrs. Morgan. You weren't married to the lad; you weren't even engaged.

Hilda. Oh, yes, we were.

Mrs. Morgan. Nothing was announced. Nothing was discussed with the parents. So there's no reason to assume things had gone very far.

Hilda. Isn't there? I'm going to have a baby.

Mrs. Morgan. [AFTER A SCANDALIZED PAUSE] A baby!

Hilda. When I went to the doctor on Saturday, he said David and I were going to have a baby.

Mrs. Morgan. I had a premonition you and David had gone and got married regardless.

Hilda. We were not married.

Mrs. Morgan. Not married!

Hilda. Not legally.

Mrs. Morgan. [ASHAMED WHISPER] I can't believe this, Hilda. If somebody'd said you'd do a thing like this to me, I'd never have believed it. I don't know what to say. Ruth won't know what to say.

Hilda. [*FULL OF HER SECRET CONFIDENCE*] I think she will.

Mrs. Morgan. [*FLATLY*] You've broken your mother's heart.

Hilda. Yours isn't the only broken heart, Mother. I don't make much fuss as a rule, but this is it. I need your help.

Mrs. Morgan. I've worked and slaved over you girls, and then for you to do a thing like this to me!

Hilda. I'm not as sure about things as you are.

Mrs. Morgan. It's not me that's sure. *Providence* has spoken, Hilda, and that we know.

Hilda. [*HARDENING*] What do you mean?

Mrs. Morgan. The wages of sin is death.

Hilda. Are you trying to tell me David was killed as a punishment for sin?

Mrs. Morgan. Don't try and blame it on *him!*

Hilda. [*SCORNFULLY*] I wouldn't dream of it! We were both responsible.

Mrs. Morgan. I'm well aware of *that*, thank you; why couldn't you wait till you were married?

Hilda. We were in love.

Mrs. Morgan. Your father and I didn't call that *love*. That's not the word I'd use.

Hilda. It's the right word.

Mrs. Morgan. Why didn't you get married?

Hilda. We couldn't. We wanted to be able to support you as well.

Mrs. Morgan. [*FLYING UP IN A CONVULSION OF IRONY*] So that's it! I'm to take the blame, am I? Poor little innocent thing, didn't know what she was doing; it was all her mother's fault.

Hilda. Perhaps it *was* your fault.

Mrs. Morgan. [*STRIKING HOME*] Because my children didn't bring me up properly? That's the modern idea, and it's certainly ruined you. And if it's any consolation to you, you can't come crawling to your family. I wash my hands of the whole thing.

Hilda. You aren't all my family.

Mrs. Morgan. [*NOT REALLY LISTENING*] You've had a good Christian home, my girl, and I'm through if this is what you make of a good Christian upbringing.

Hilda. Perhaps *you* should have had it instead of me.

Mrs. Morgan. What do you mean?

Hilda. If this is a good Christian home you're running, how about some good Christian forgiveness?

Mrs. Morgan. I can't forgive people who sin deliberately. [*THEN WITH REAL EMOTION*] Don't you know you've told me the most dreadful thing a mother can hear? I'd rather I'd heard you were dead.

Hilda. [*RESPONDING TO THE HONEST NOTE*] I'm afraid I'm still alive, mother; and I do need your help badly.

Mrs. Morgan. [*RECOVERING FROM HER MOMENTARY WEAKNESS*] Punishment before forgiveness. You've sinned and you must suffer for it.

Hilda. I loved him, and he's dead, and I'm going to have his baby, and we aren't married. Don't you think I'm suffering enough?

Mrs. Morgan. [*RELENTING*] I'm sure you must deserve it.

Hilda. Is that all? Am I to expect no help from you at all? [*SHE IS INCREDULOUS*] Very well then.

Mrs.Morgan. Come back, Hilda. I know my duty, if you don't know yours.

Hilda. [*COLDLY*] What is your duty?

Mrs. Morgan. It's my duty to smuggle you away somewhere to have your baby, and find a place to put it so that you can go back to work again. And I'll do it; but if you think I shall forgive you dragging me through this, then you're very much mistaken. Is that clear?

Hilda. If that's your damned dirty duty, I don't want it. I want your love, if you've got any. I want somebody to say they understand and they're sorry for me, and they love me.

Mrs. Morgan. Do what you like and then say you're sorry!

Hilda. I don't say I'm sorry, because I'm not sorry to have David's baby!

¶ SOUND: *door opens off.*

Mrs. Morgan. This may be *your* idea of something to be proud of, but it isn't mine, and it isn't Ruth's!

Ruth. [*OFF*] Mother!

Hilda. Ruth knows me better than to try and put me off with talk about duty.

Mrs. Morgan. [*RAISING HER VOICE EVEN MORE*] Never mind about that! You're going to find out before you're very much older . . .

Ruth. [*FADING ON: CUTTING HER OFF*] Mother, don't shout so! They can hear you in the street!

Mrs. Morgan. They'll all know soon enough. Tell her what you've done, Hilda, if you aren't ashamed, though why should you be ashamed to tell it when you weren't ashamed to do it?

Hilda. [*TRIUMPHANTLY*] I *have* told her, Mother, and do you know what she's done? She's gone to the bank to get some money to help me.

Ruth. And I don't know what Len'll say.

Mrs. Morgan. [*RATHER TAKEN BACK*] She's doing no more than I am. I shall do my duty too.

Hilda. Ruth isn't doing her duty. She isn't doing the wisest thing, or the most moral thing, or the most dutiful thing. She's doing the *kindest* thing; she's helping me because she loves me.

Ruth. Somebody has to do something, and Hilda's had bad luck ever since she grew up, eh kid?

Mrs. Morgan.   I don't see what this has to do with luck.

Hilda.   Don't you?

Ruth.   Well, it has.

Mrs. Morgan.   You needn't look at me like that, you girls. I know there's sin in this world, and not all of it found out in *this* life.

Ruth.   [*INDIGNANTLY*] And there's human nature too, Mother.

Mrs. Morgan.   That's no reason to encourage wickedness. We aren't put into this world to glorify human nature. It's a vale of tears for the sinner, and we do wrong to make it anything else.

Hilda.   No need to defend yourself, Mother.

Ruth.   *You* haven't anything to be ashamed of.

Hilda.   And neither have I.

Ruth.   Well, whatever you did, I'm sure there were reasons. Now about the money.

Mrs. Morgan.   [*GOING DOWN FIGHTING*] I hope you're not going to squander Len's money on *her*.

Ruth.   It's my money as much as his. He earned it, and I saved it; and I don't call this squandering. How much did you say you had?

Hilda.   About three hundred.

Ruth.   All right. Now I got out another three.

Mrs. Morgan.   That was for your dining suite.

Ruth.   It isn't now. That'll give you six hundred dollars.

Mrs. Morgan.   [*WITH A NASTY SMILE*] The price of sin is very high today.

Ruth.   [*ANGRY*] Very high, Mother, yes.

Mrs. Morgan.   [*STERNLY*] Well, it's even higher than you think.

Ruth.   Moralize later, Mother. For the moment, we have to be sensible, haven't we, Hilda?

Mrs. Morgan.   You be sensible about wickedness, if you can. This is no time for being sensible, as you call it.

Ruth.   Look at it this way, Mother. If it gets out about Hilda's baby, she's through at the school. Marg Patterson was fired because she went to beer parlours.

Mrs. Morgan.   They know that one thing leads to another.

Ruth.   [*IGNORING THIS*] Second, if it gets out about Hilda's baby, your name will be mud. You know how the old harridans'll take *this* juicy item.

Mrs. Morgan.   Why should the sins of the children be visited on the fathers?

Ruth.   I don't know why, but they will be. And thirdly, if it gets out about Hilda's baby, Len's career at the bank will be through: we'll wait for a million years and not get anywhere.

Mrs. Morgan.   [*RELUCTANTLY*] So?

Ruth.   So it mustn't get out about Hilda's baby. It's as easy as that. And the only way to be sure is if she doesn't have it.

Hilda.   I don't understand.

Ruth.   I'm just explaining why you need so much money. You see, she isn't going to go through with it, Mother.

Mrs. Morgan.   I won't hear of it, Ruth! It's murder.

Ruth.   It's no more murder than, well, than anything else.

Hilda.   Some people think so.

Ruth.   Some people can afford to think so.

Hilda.   [*POSITIVELY*] No use, Ruth. It won't do.

Ruth.   Why not? Nobody else knows.

Hilda.   Not yet.

Ruth.   I'll look after you, and you'll have a hundred over for expenses. It costs five hundred dollars.

Hilda.   How do *you* know?

Ruth.   From Norah Campbell.

Mrs. Morgan.   That Campbell girl! I *knew* . . .

Ruth.   Her sister had it done.

Hilda.   Is *that* what killed her?

Ruth.   Well, there is a risk. You can't call a doctor afterwards, because he has to report it. But you'll be all right. Mother and I'll be backing you up.

Hilda.   [*BEGINNING TO STRIKE HARDER*] Is *this* your idea of backing me up? Was this your only idea of sympathy? Taking David's child from him?

Ruth.   Don't let's get sentimental. We've got to be practical in this world.

Hilda.   Now I *am* ashamed. Horrible! [*WITH A SHUDDER OF DISGUST*]

Ruth.   It's not only for you; it's for Mother and Len and me as well.

Hilda.   [*SCORNFULLY*] *Daren't* you say it's for David too?

Ruth.   Well, it certainly is for David. [*ELOQUENTLY*] Would *he* want you to disgrace your family? Would he want you to suffer miseries knowing there's no one else you can turn to?

Hilda.   Don't be too sure.

Ruth.   Don't you be too sure! No one else would give you their savings for a thing like this!

Hilda.   Probably not. [*WITH INWARD REVULSION*]

Ruth.   Then be sensible while you can. Now here's the money. I got it in twenties . . .

Mrs. Morgan.   [*SUDDENLY*] Put it away! Don't let *me* see it! I don't want to know anything about it! I'm going straight to my room and lock the door! Do whatever you decide, the pair of you, and God forgive you, but don't tell me about it!

Hilda.   No need for you to leave, Mother. I'm the one that's out of place here. I'm getting out right now. I may be back. If I'm not don't be surprised.

95

Ruth. But Hilda, *please . . .*

Hilda. [IN DISGUST] Don't try to follow me, Ruth, or I'll knock you down. [PAUSE] Goodbye, you two.

¶ SOUND: *door shuts.*

Mrs. Morgan. Ruth, she's going to do something dreadful. You've gone too far.

Ruth. She's just being stubborn.

Mrs. Morgan. If she walks out on us, there's nowhere for her to go. I can feel she's going to do something dreadful. [RISING INTENSITY] We've lost her, Ruth, we've lost her!

Ruth. Don't be silly, Mother; she's tougher than you are.

Mrs. Morgan. I don't know what you mean.

Ruth. You're the one that's gone too far; you and your moralizing!

Mrs. Morgan. We're told we must speak out, and I've done it!

Ruth. Well, I'm going after her.

Mrs. Morgan. Do you think you should?

Ruth. What else should I do?

Mrs. Morgan. She's made up her mind; do you think it's right to stop her?

Ruth. I don't think you care what happens to her.

Mrs. Morgan. Well, if she's taken, we must bow our heads to Providence, and remember it's all for the best. I told her I'd rather I'd been told she was dead than . . . [SHE IS FALTERING]

Ruth. [HORRIFIED] Mother!

Mrs. Morgan. [BREAKING DOWN] I don't know, I don't know! I'll think of something! Go and find her, and bring her back, and I'll think of something. But I can feel it's too late; I've an awful feeling we've lost her!

¶ MUSIC: *turbulent and gloomy: time passes: change to a mood of waiting.*

¶ SOUND: *a little clock chimes three quarters: a pause: then the door opens and shuts off.*

Mrs. Morgan. [CALLING] Hello, Ruth, I'm in here. [NO ANSWER] I'm in here, Ruth. [STILL NO ANSWER] Ruth!

¶ SOUND: *footsteps have been approaching and stop.*

Hilda. [QUITE NEAR AND IMMEDIATELY FADING RIGHT ON] Why are you sitting in the dark, Mother?

Mrs. Morgan. [IN TEARS] Oh, Hilda, Hilda, darling, it's you! I was afraid we'd lost you!

Hilda. [WHO SEEMS TO HAVE SOME KIND OF SECRET TRIUMPH] Were you, Mother?

Mrs. Morgan.   I had a feeling you were going to do something irrevocable.

Hilda.   Everything is irrevocable.

Mrs. Morgan.   If you'd done something terrible, people would have blamed us.

Hilda.   It depends what you call terrible.

Mrs. Morgan.   Oh, you're young; you're not afraid of death. Wait till you're my age; then you'll wish you'd lived a better life.

Hilda.   Do you wish you'd lived a better life? [*SEARCHINGLY*]

Mrs. Morgan.   You won't shrug off dying when you're as old as me.

Hilda.   Did you think I had some idea of killing myself? As though I were ashamed of David's baby? If I were going to kill myself (which I'm not) I'd wait. My life is David's life for the next six months.

Mrs. Morgan.   Hilda, I've been thinking what to do. I feel responsible, in a way. I can't forgive myself. [*THIS IS A PAINFUL CONFESSION*]

Hilda.   That's because you can't forgive me.

Mrs. Morgan.   You talk as if *I* were in the wrong. If you were in the right, you wouldn't need forgiving.

Hilda.   Now you're near it, Mother. Only the guilty need forgiving; and it's only the guilty you can't forgive. [*FADING OFF SLIGHTLY*]

Mrs. Morgan.   Come back, Hilda! Where are you going?

Hilda.   To pack. I'm leaving.

Mrs. Morgan.   To disgrace us all.

Hilda.   Do you want me to take Ruth's advice and die discretely in a back bedroom?

Mrs. Morgan.   Very few die.

Hilda.   You're forgetting something. This child is *wanted*.

Mrs. Morgan.   Then take my advice.

Hilda.   [*A PAUSE: SLIGHTLY SURPRISED*] What is it?

Mrs. Morgan.   Even if you go away and have it, you'll ruin us when you come back with it.

Hilda.   So I must have it adopted?

Mrs. Morgan.   I know you won't do *that*.

Hilda.   Then what must I do?

Mrs. Morgan.   You must bring back a husband too.

Hilda.   My husband has just been killed.

Mrs. Morgan.   Wally Turnbull likes you. He's a bit wild, but what man isn't? You could make him settle down.

Hilda.   [*WITH FATAL MILDNESS*] If David and I had been legally married, would you have dared throw me at somebody else before I'd been a widow a week?

Mrs. Morgan.   [*MAKING HER POINT*] But you *weren't* married.

Hilda.   [*AS IF SEEING THAT THIS MADE ALL THE DIFFERENCE*] Ah! Of course not.

Mrs. Morgan. All I want is for you to be happy and do the right thing.

Hilda. Very well, Mother; tell me what the right thing is.

Mrs. Morgan. We're all sinners, and that we know; but there is such a thing as repenting.

Hilda. By marrying Wally Turnbull?

Mrs. Morgan. [*ARTFULLY*] No. You're wrong there. That's what you *thought*; but you were wrong. *Not* by marrying him at all; unless you want to.

Hilda. Go on.

Mrs. Morgan. All I'm asking is that you don't let yourself be worried by out-worn conventions.

Hilda. [*ALMOST SPEECHLESS*] Oh?

Mrs. Morgan. In other words, dear; *if* . . . I say only, *if* . . . you found you were beginning to like him as much as he likes you; or even half as much. Or less.

Hilda. A quarter as much?

Mrs. Morgan. Even a little bit, then all I ask is that you remember two things. David is dead now. And your sister and I . . . and yourself . . . are all alive. Well, you know the world's ways Hilda. If Wally and you *happened* to become interested in each other; well, there'd be short memories after the baby was born.

Hilda. Thank you, Mother. You make everything very clear. You've been doing some hard thinking since I went out.

Mrs. Morgan. I hope you've done the same.

Hilda. Oh, indeed, I have.

Mrs. Morgan. My father would have turned any of us out of doors lock stock and barrel.

Hilda. I'm sure he would.

¶ SOUND: *the doorbell off.*

Mrs. Morgan. Pretend we're not in; I'll peep through the curtain and see . . . who [*REALLY ASTONISHED*] Hilda! It's Wally!

Hilda. [*HARD*] Wally! Did you invite him?

Mrs. Morgan. How could I have done? I didn't know you were coming back. You might have been floating in the lake for all I knew. That's why Ruth's out looking for you.

Hilda. You gave me a good start first.

¶ SOUND: *doorbell again.*

Mrs. Morgan. Providence has given you one terrible lesson, Hilda. This is another. I hope you can take it. You open the door, and talk to him. I'll keep out of the way. [*AS AN AFTER THOUGHT*] I worried about you, Hilda; while you were out. I thought we'd lost you, and . . . oh, well, please hurry up and let him in! [*SHE SOUNDS QUITE EXCITED*]

98

¶ MUSIC: *echoes the excitement: excited background for Wally.*

Wally. When I finally called round, I had to ring a couple of times. After a while, the door opened and there was Hilda. She looked a bit pale, but there was a funny gleam in her eye. She said her mother was lying down. I was pleased I'd decided to drop round, because she seemed quite glad to see me!

¶ MUSIC: *background out with Wally.*

Hilda. [RATHER EXCITED: IN REALITY SHE IS SEETHING WITH RAGE AND INDIGNATION AT HER MOTHER AND DELIGHTED AT THE PROSPECT OF GETTING OUT PERMANENTLY] I'm glad you called, Wally. I'm going away soon, and Mother thought I should see you, before I went.

Wally. I don't want to bother you, Hildy. Just wanted to say, I'll always be waiting. I know how you're feeling. Must be an awful disappointment for you.

Hilda. Even disappointments can sometimes be lightened a little.

Wally. Sure, you weren't actually married to him, were you?

Hilda. Even so, I have certain compensations. Wally: do you understand that David and I were in love with each other?

Wally. [AMUSED AT THIS SELF-EVIDENT REMARK] Well, of course! You were going to marry him.

Hilda. And do you understand it'll be a very long time before I can fall in love with anybody else.

Wally. Sure, I understand all that; it'll take months to get over it.

Hilda. Even so, would you marry me in a week or two from now. If I asked you.

Wally. [SIMPLY] Yes, I would, Hilda. I'm no angel; never have been. Played around a bit in my time, but if we got married, that'd be out. It'd just be you as far as I'm concerned; and I'd marry you like a shot; supposing you wanted it.

Hilda. Mother wants it.

Wally. [WARMLY] She's the right sort; lovely person, your mother. I really admire her. Always right in there with the good word.

Hilda. There's just one thing. I gather you've had something to do with other women.

Wally. Honest to God, Hildy, that's right out, from now on. The past is the past; the future's what counts.

Hilda. I'm glad to hear you say that. Because there's something Mother doesn't expect me to tell you. I'm going to have a baby.

Wally. [AFTER AN IMMENSE PAUSE: WITH FORCED CASUALNESS] Oh?

Hilda. I thought that'd change your mind. Thanks very much, Wally, anyhow.

Wally. [MOISTENING HIS LIPS] Wait a minute, wait a minute; take it easy.

Whose is it? David's?

Hilda. Yes.

Wally. That's why you got engaged, eh?

Hilda. He wanted to marry me for a long time. I wouldn't let him. [*WITH A LITTLE LAUGH*] I thought I had a duty to Mother.

Wally. It's a shock, Hildy; no use kidding. I . . . I don't know what to say. I didn't really think you were the kind of girl who'd . . .

Hilda. Play with fire? Or get burnt? Which?

Wally. [*THINKING*] If we got married now, the baby'd be early, but that'll happen. If we watched the arithmetic every time the wedding bells rang, there'd be a lot of surprises. It shouldn't happen, but it seems to. Lots of couples cheat a little on the deadline, so I guess we might get away with it. [*ANNOUNCING HIS DECISION*] I'm willing, Hildy, if you are.

Hilda. Are you willing because you think I was doing right, or just because it happens all the time?

Hilda. [*REASONABLY*] Same thing. If everybody does it, sooner or later it's all right. Look at the pyramid clubs. You know, Dave Temple was pretty much my colouring. We could get away with it. It'd be a lot better than adopting a kid.

Hilda. Thank you, Wally, it's very kind of you. [*A REFUSAL*]

Wally. I'm willing.

Hilda. Because your friends'd just think you'd been cheating a little on the deadline; might make you a bit of a Casanova? [*SMILING*]

Wally. [*PLEASED*] Oh, I wouldn't say that.

Hilda. [*WITH THE SAME LIGHT SMILE SOMEHOW HARDENING*] Just as it makes me a bit of a light woman; or would if we weren't married. [*THE QUALIFICATION IS A LITTLE OVERDONE PERHAPS*]

Wally. Well, a girl isn't like men, you know.

Hilda. [*THE LIGHT SMILE SUDDENLY VANISHING*] No, the girl's the one that's caught with the evidence. But every time a man wants to be a Casanova, a girl has to help him do it, and take all the blame into the bargain. Well, if she takes the blame, she's going to take the credit.

Wally. [*OUT OF HIS DEPTH*] I don't understand.

Hilda. David wanted a child. I shall give him one. Would you marry me a year from now, after I'd had the baby; after everyone knew that I'd had David's child? [*A LONG PAUSE: NO REPLY*] I'm not ashamed of it, but I should be if I pretended it was yours.

Wally. But what are people going to say? You can't just think of yourself, Hilda.

Hilda. [*HONESTLY*] I must, Wally; and I must think of David. Everybody else thinks of duty and morality and neighbours, until the human beings are covered up with noble abstractions. And when the human beings are covered up, people can be as cruel and thoughtless as they like without hurting their consciences. Well, I can't help them; I can't play fair. I can only think of the people: David, and Mrs. Temple, and me, and the baby. Judge not that ye be not judged. If they want to judge me, I shall judge them, and be jury and executioner into the bargain. [*SHE IS BEGINNING TO BLAZE*]

Wally.   What do you mean?

Hilda.   When I go away, Mother's going to be ripped apart by the neighbours; and serve her right. If she thought more of me, she might think less of them.

Wally.   Well, no one could accuse you of being soft, Hilda.

Hilda.   Only a man ever thinks a woman's soft. Don't be misled, Wally. Women are as hard as rocks; that's why they find it so difficult to live together. We're only the weaker sex when it comes to weight-lifting; and even then, you mightn't like to wring out half-a-dozen blankets.

Wally.   But what are you going to *do*? You got to have somewhere to *go*.

Hilda.   When I found my family didn't support me, I went to see Mrs. Temple. I've just got back. I told her everything, and I shall live with them until it's all over. Then we shall see.

Wally.   You told Mrs. *Temple*? That frail old lady?

Hilda.   She's no more frail than I am; she knows what she has to do.

Wally.   She doesn't have any prejudice?

Hilda.   All she had was a son. Being hard is our virtue as well as our vice. Goodbye, Wally.

¶ MUSIC: *a short figure: scarcely more than a take: down to background.*

Wally.   Maybe she was joking, only girls don't have a sense of humour. And if it was a joke it was a practical one. Maybe I should have taken her up. Course I'm married now to a real sweet little girl, and what she doesn't know won't hurt her, I mean about the others. Like I say, there's the ones to settle down with, and the ones to settle up with. But you never know which is which till it's too late. If then.

¶ MUSIC: *finale.*

Announcer.   *Stage* 49, Item 34 . . . "Hilda Morgan," a new play by Lister Sinclair . . . was produced and directed by Andrew Allan, with a musical score composed and conducted by Lucio Agostini. Ruth Springford starred as Hilda Morgan; Jane Mallet as her Mother, Pat Arthurs as Hilda's sister, Ruth; Budd Knapp as Wally Turnbull; Grace Webster as Mrs. Temple; John Drainie as David Temple; and Donald Davis as the Policeman. Sound by David Tasker. Technical operations by Bruce Armstrong.

The Macdonalds of Oak Valley

HARRY J. BOYLE

Production

Producer: Andrew Allan
Music: Lucio Agostini
Sound: David Tasker
Operator: Bruce Armstrong
Announcer: Elwood Glover
Program: Stage 49
Broadcast: May 29, 1949, 10:00–11:00 pm EDT
Studio: Toronto
Network: Trans-Canada

Cast

Frank Peddie *as* Grandfather Macdonald
John Drainie *as* the Narrator
Bruce Stevens *as* Billy
Budd Knapp *as* Jim
Mona O'Hearn *as* Mary Henderson
Robert Christie *as* Alex
Beth Lockerbie *as* Annie

Tommy Tweed *as* Red Sandy Macrae
with
Pat Sheppard, Peter Mews, and Herb Gott

•

THE MACDONALDS OF OAK VALLEY

Preface

Harry Boyle's first job with the CBC was in the Farm Broadcasts division. The principal objective of the farm programs, whether educational productions such as "Farm Forum" or dramatic productions such as Dean Hughes' "The Craigs," was to convert farmers from the old to modern ways. From a farm community, Boyle not only was familiar with the struggle, he was one of the principal advocates of the new ways. But while "The Craigs" takes progress for granted, Boyle's play "The Macdonalds of Oak Valley" honestly portrays the agonizing ambiguity of sacrificing the past for the future.

The transformation of farming from agriculture to agribusiness and agronomy and thus from the family to the industrial farm had been a long process. There had been a reduction in the number of family farms in Canada following the depression of the 1930s, and the process continued after the war. It entailed the introduction of new technology, a consequential increase in the debt held by farmers, a shift in control to financial institutions, and the transformation of farmers from independent commodity producers to a labouring class. In "The Macdonalds of Oak Valley," grandfather Macdonald, working a farm inherited from his father, a Scottish immigrant, uses the nineteenth-century technology of a steam-driven threshing machine and equipment powered by horses; and he drives an automobile. His resistance to tractors and to new varieties of grain seed is not simply an old man's refusal to accept new ways of doing things, but an objection to a dimly-perceived threat to a long established way of life. This is not a play which simply romanticizes rural life in opposition to its urban counterpart; nor is it strictly a play addressing the old question of intergenerational conflict. It is also an even-handed consideration of the effects on the family and the individual of changing modes of rural social organization. On the one hand, there is a lament, not only for a lost time, but for the defeat of culture by technology. And on the other hand, there is, almost in a McLuhanesque

105

sense, a celebration of the human potential of technology.

From 1943 to 1961, some forty of Harry Boyle's were produced on CBC, twelve of them by Andrew Allan, but some by every major CBC producer. At the time this play was produced, Boyle had moved to CBC Arts programming as an administrator, becoming one of Andrew Allan's bosses. In this new capacity, Boyle was one of the best of arts administrators: not only did he continue to write plays, but he was instrumental in the creation of the flagship arts-and-drama series, *CBC Wednesday Night*, in 1947. His subsequent career, on CBC radio and television, as a novelist, and as head of the CRTC, is too well known to need rehearsing here.

HARRY J. BOYLE

The Macdonalds of Oak Valley

¶ SOUND: *clap of thunder.*

Narrator. Every time I hear thunder I think of my grandfather. Gramp always liked storms. Maybe they matched something inside him and yet I remember one night when it stormed . . . Gramp was a great man in his day . . . six foot one in his stocking feet and as straight as the white ash tree in the east meadow. His face was leathery and wrinkled. Gramp had a moustache with a full and majestic sweep, and his hair was bushy and grizzled with grey. Everybody knew Jack Macdonald, because the Macdonalds were the first to settle in Oak Valley.

¶ MUSIC: *title cue up to background.*

Announcer. *Stage* 49, Item 35 . . . "The Macdonalds of Oak Valley," a new play by Harry J. Boyle . . . starring Frank Peddie and John Drainie. Produced and directed by Andrew Allan, with an original musical score composed and conducted by Lucio Agostini . . . "The Macdonalds of Oak Valley" by Harry J. Boyle.

¶ MUSIC: *up nostalgically to background.*

Old Timer. The Macdonalds? Of course I know them. First there was Black Angus from out of the Highlands, Jack's father. I remember him telling about starting out from Toronto with a team of oxen and a wagon and a few tools, looking for a new home . . .

¶ MUSIC: *pleasant and pastoral: hold in background.*

Narrator. Gramp loved to talk about his father. We would be riding in to Lochalsh with a load of grist for the mill and when we got to the rim of the valley Gramp would pull up on the horses and look back . . .

¶ MUSIC: *out here.*

Gramp. Aye Billy, my father was a real man. He took one look at this valley and he said, "This will be the new home of the Macdonalds." There's hills here and great trees and rich soil. When the Creator rolls up the face of the earth and counts his flock, he'll find the Macdonalds here . . . right here in Oak Valley." Chk . . . Chkkkkk . . . get up . . .

¶ SOUND: *of team and wagon in background.*

Gramp. He was a powerful man, lad. I remember when I was eighteen and feeling my oats one day and I sassed him because I was getting on and wanted to be on my own. He just nodded to me and I followed him over behind the milkhouse. He threw me three times in a row until I had enough, and he was going on fifty six at the time. He was a man, lad. He loved this land, and the last thing he said to me before he died was, "Jock, look after it. Take care of it until you die."

¶ SOUND: *out into:*

¶ MUSIC: *background.*

Narrator. I started thinking about my grandfather today, I can't seem to get him out of my mind. Sitting in the Union Station I couldn't help overhear a man and a woman who were talking . . .

¶ MUSIC: *out.*

¶ SOUND: *bring in background of station.*

Man. But dear, we can't get married now.
Woman. But I can't understand why?
Man. Milly, my father is a well-off farmer. You know that. He's been running the farm for so long that he simply can't give up.
Woman. That's a fine thing. Surely, he must appreciate the fact that you've been working on that farm for six years without wages.
Man. Milly, it's awful hard to explain. He thinks he's doing right. One of these days he'll hand the place over to me.
Woman. Why don't you just tell him that you want to get married and that he has to help you?
Man. But Milly, my dad is a good man. He thinks he's doing the right thing.
Woman. Well I think it's completely silly. You're a grown man now. I can't see this nonsense at all.

¶ MUSIC: *up full and them down to background.*

Narrator. Listening, I thought of Gramp and Oak Valley, my home until I was eighteen. Away off down there at the far end where the Oak River is only a tinsel ribbon, is where the MacNabbs live. The place with the red barns and the white house belongs to Jock Fraser and on this side

108

there is the McGillivray homestead. The untidy place belongs to Red Sandy MacRae, known always as an easy fellow with more hankering for playing his fiddle at the dances in the schoolhouse than for working his land. That's the kirk, the white brick building where the Reverend Duncan MacPherson thundered out the uncompromising Presbyterian word of God.

¶ MUSIC: *up briefly and down as background.*

Narrator. And over it all stood the farm buildings of the Macdonald place, and in my day, grandfather was the acknowledged and inflexible ruler . . .

¶ MUSIC: *up sharply and out.*

Gramp. There's a matter Jim that you and I have to discuss.

Jim. [*JUST A TRIFLE SULLEN*] What's that?

Gramp. I am not one to interfere in what you might call the "romantic side" of your life, but there is the matter of yon school teacher.

Jim. What about her?

Gramp. You've been spending a great deal of time with her of late.

Jim. Well?

Gramp. I have nothing against the lass, mind ye that, but ye cannot sit up half the night and work the next day.

Jim. I'm not sitting up half the night.

Gramp. Mind your tongue lad. I happened to look at my watch when ye came in this morning and it read ten past one.

Jim. Good heavens that's not late.

Gramp. It was late in my time. No decent girl would be caught with a beau after ten.

Jim. Oh heavens. Times have changed a lot since then.

Gramp. What's decent is decent with no reference to times.

Jim. You just don't like her that's all.

Gramp. We have discussed the matter as fully as I care to go into it. I have nothing against the lass, I told ye that. She's a town girl, and not cut out to be a farmer's wife.

Jim. Well, I don't care.

Gramp. [*HARSHLY*] Ye'll mind my word while ye take shelter under my roof. Hitch the black mare, I'm going in to Lochalsh.

¶ MUSIC: *sharp angry chord.*

Narrator. I stood still in the box stall where Gramp couldn't see me. When he walked away I heard my uncle Jim muttering to himself, and I had a strange and uneasy feeling that I couldn't quite identify.

¶ MUSIC: *foreboding and out.*

109

Narrator. Growing up was fun even if I had to work hard. There was Gramp and Alex my dad and Uncle Jim and mother and my younger sisters, Jessie and Jean. I can still remember mealtime when everybody sat around the plain table with the white oilcloth in the big kitchen. From the window you could look down to the barn and out across the valley. There was a big sideboard with some fancy plates on it, and a sampler on the wall with the embroidered words GOD BLESS OUR HAPPY HOME, and a picture of Edinburgh Castle that grandmother had cut from a magazine and framed. On the east wall, Gramp had a binder twine calendar with big figures, where he could write down the intimate statistics on the family relationships of all the female stock on the farm. The kitchen was plain but comfortable with a good smell of cooking about it. The food was always placed on the table and then Gramp would take the chair at the head and sit down.

¶ SOUND: *chair scraping.*

Gramp. Time to eat.

¶ SOUND: *background of chairs scraping.*

Gramp. [*IN GAELIC*] Bless us oh Lord for these thy gifts which we are about to receive from thy bounty Oh Christ our Lord Amen.
Chorus. AMEN

¶ SOUND: *meal sounds.*

Gramp. Pass the meat Annie.
Annie. Yes pa.
Alex. Jock Fraser says he's going to try those new oats from the Agricultural College.
Jim. 'sposed to stand off rust better than the ordinary kind.
Gramp. Hmmmm! Can't see how they grow better oats at a place like that than we have right here in the valley.
Alex. They do a lot of experimenting there in Guelph. I was readin' about them in the *Farmers' Advocate* the other day.
Gramp. Where's he puttin' them?
Alex. In the big field behind the barn.
Gramp. Suit him better if he'd pull those barberry bushes out, than tryin' to beat the rust with fancy oats.
Jim. He was pullin' them out with the tractor yesterday.
Alex. I see McNabbs bought a tractor. At least that's what Red Sandy told me.
Annie. It's a caution the way Red Sandy knows everything that's going on in the community!
Alex. He told me the other day that Jessie Simpson is expectin' this fall.
Jim. There's nothing Red Sandy would rather do than talk, unless it's

playin' the fiddle.

Pause.

Gramp.   Pass the gravy Jim!

Alex.   A lot of people seem to be gettin' tractors this year. The implement dealer in Lochalsh was tellin' me that he has more orders than he can fill.

Pause.

Annie.   Jessie don't slop your food like that.

Gramp.   I tell you a lot of people buyin' tractors now will be darn glad to go back to horses one of these days. You can't fertilize a farm with tractor fumes and smoke.

Jim.   I don't know but I think a tractor is a pretty good thing to have around a farm. Just think of the amount of work a person can get through with one. Dan Cameron plowed that west field of his in one day.

Alex.   They were demonstrating one up at McIntyres the other day, and they tell me they had over a hundred farmers there.

Annie.   Marg McGillvray said her husband went up to see it and all he can talk now is tractor.

Gramp.   Destroy the land, that's all they do. Rip across the field and burn up oil and put nothing back in to the soil. Where are these fellows going to get their manure!

Alex.   Getting a tractor won't stop them from having stock Dad.

Jim.   I think it's the modern way of farming, tho'.

Gramp.   Modern be damned! They're just a *fad*. Gobbling up fuel fastern they work.

Jim.   You can still get a lot of work done and with the price of stuff the way it is now, it seems like the time to make money.

Alex.   It's a cinch that prices won't stay up this way for too long.

Gramp.   [FINALITY] Mark my words, tractors will be the ruination of farming if people all start buying them. I'll take that team of Percherons any day and stand up to a tractor — Not much salt left in that cellar Annie.

¶ SOUND: *chair scraping.*

Annie.   I'll get some more, Pa.

Jim.   [SARCASTIC] Pass the applesauce Alex.

¶ MUSIC: *trace of sarcasm in it: to background.*

Narrator.   That was the second spring after dad came back from the war. He wasn't feeling too well and didn't seem to mind about Gramp running everything but Jim resented it. I was pretty young at the time, but I gradually felt that there was a tension around the place. I remember on a Saturday afternoon before we went to town and Gramp was sitting at the kitchen table with the black scribbler that he kept the accounts in. Mother was putting braids in my sister Jeannie's hair. Jim was at the washstand off the pantry, shaving. My dad was sitting in the rocker beside the window smoking his pipe.

¶ MUSIC: *out.*

Annie.   [*OFF*] Hold still child, I can't put these braids in if you're going to fidget all over the place.

Gramp.   Here's the grocery money Annie. How much was that last cream chock?

Annie.   [*OFF*] Ten twenty two. Hmm! Down from the week before. Here Alex, you get those drill attachments at the shop.

Alex.   If they're ready. Danny told me the other day he'd do his best.

Gramp.   Yes. Hmm. You want some spendin' money, Jim? [*PAUSE*] You hear me, Jim?

Jim.   [*COMING ON*] Yes, I heard you, but I'd hate to be a drag on the family resources.
Pause.

Narrator.   Gramp looked up as Jim came away from the washstand with flecks of shaving soap around his ears. They stared at each other and the sound of the clock in the kitchen seemed like gun shots. Finally Gramp put some money out on the table and looked back at his book. Jim stood there looking as if he were going to say something and then he grabbed up the money and walked back to the basin at the cistern pump and started washing his face. I felt just as if somebody had squeezed my insides real hard.

¶ MUSIC: *up in full break.*

¶ SOUND: *descriptive background to following.*

Narrator.   Only a man born and bred in the country can appreciate the thrill of going to town on Saturday night as a boy. When the Model T. rounded the corner at the Presbyterian church and hit the main drag, Jack Phillips, the hardware man was busy measuring gasoline out in gallon cans for a waiting line of cars, still considered a novelty because the Anglican church shed was jammed with buggies, democrats, and even a few wagons. There was a buzz of conversation in the air, and gossip flew up and down the street like shivers on an old maid's spine. The bigger boys, decked out in unaccustomed good clothes, were hanging around Alten Adam's Drug Store, and Tim Murphy's General Store was packed with people. On this particular occasion we were all in the car waiting . . . Jessie and Jennie asleep with their heads in mother's lap . . . my dad at the wheel of the car and Gramp standing on the sidewalk. We were waiting for Jim when a neighbour passed by . . .

Neighbour.   Waitin' for Jim?

Gramp.   Yes, as a matter of fact we are.

Neighbour.   [*CHUCKLING*] He's doin' a little hell raisin' up at the China-man's Cafe [*CAYFE*].

Gramp.   What?

Neighbour.   Just thought I better tell you. He got a bottle of swamp some place and the last I heard he had thrown out the Chinaman.

Gramp.   We'll see about this. Where is he now?

Neighbour.   Just up the street there next to Pinkney's Veterinery Stable . . .

Gramp.   [*GOING OFF*] Headstrong young fool. Been on the verge of breaking out for days. Confound that bootlegger anyhow.

Neighbour.   [*OFF*] They say he broke a chair over George Tim's head and he's a fightin' fool.

¶ SOUND: *car door slams.*

Annie.   Billy you come back. Let your father and grandpa go. [*FADING*] Billy did you hear me. You come back here.

¶ SOUND: *bring in background of crowd.*

Jim.   [*THICKLY OFF*] Step right up folksh. Everything' on the house! Gonna have me a fried Chinaman sandwich. Ooh Hopalong . . . where is he. Threw him out . . . that's what I did.

¶ SOUND: *laughter up: suddenly cut for Gramp.*

Gramp.   Jim, come out from behind that counter!

Jim.   Whaaa . . . what'ell you doin'?

Gramp.   [*CONTROLLED TEMPER*] Jim, are you coming home?

Jim.   Whafor? To live on your charity? Me, I'm gonna buy out tha Shinaman.

Gramp.   Get hold of yourself.

Jim.   Whafor?

Gramp.   Are you coming, or do I have to take you?

Jim.   Jush try it?

¶ SOUND: *gasps of astonishment.*

Alex.   Come on Jim.

Jim.   Take your hands off me.

Gramp.   Are you coming?

¶ SOUND: *crowd astonishment.*

Narrator.   Jim took a swing at Gramp. Gramp just seemed to grab him then by the back of the neck and the seat of the pants. He marched him down to the car. I think the meanest thing of all happened just as they left the cafe.

¶ SOUND: *bring in laughter.*

¶ MUSIC: *start on laughter motif and up: then down for:*

Narrator.   Drunk or sober, I don't think Jim ever forgot that humiliating moment when the crowd laughed.

¶ MUSIC: *up full to end.*

Narrator.   I heard my uncle being sick during the night. Dad went in to him. Next morning nothing was said about it at the breakfast table. In fact nothing at all was said at the breakfast table, or all day Sunday. [*PAUSE*] On Monday morning Gramp walked down to the barn. I slipped up on the barn floor beside the place we put the bedding down and I heard all the conversation when Jim came into the stable . . .

¶ SOUND: *background of some stock: suggest voices have a slight echo.*

Gramp.   I didn't mean to be rough with you last night lad.
Jim.   Oh, guess I deserved it.
Gramp.   Jim, I'm not a harsh man about liquor, but either hold it or leave it alone. What were you drinkin'?
Jim.   I bought a bottle swamp from Bill Jenkins at the livery table.
Gramp.   It's rotgut. Enough to poison a man.
Jim.   You're tellin' me. I've never been so damn sick in my life before. [*PAUSE*] I guess I better work up that patch of ground for Annie. She's getting anxious about a garden.
Gramp.   Yes. Take the bay team. I'll take the blacks.

¶ SOUND: *trace chains and sound of picking up harness: horses stamp and blow a bit.*

Gramp.   I take ye're not too satisfied with the way things are around here.
Jim.   [*HE FEELS LIKE HELL*] Oh, I get sort of fed up.
Gramp.   Do you think I'm being unfair with ye lad?
Jim.   It's just that a fellow likes to get out on his own.
Gramp.   But this place will belong to you and Alex when I die.
Jim.   Well, I . . . I look around and I see other fellows my age working for themselves.
Gramp.   You don't have to do that lad. My father turned this place over to me when he died. It's a better farm now than it ever has been.
Jim.   That may be. But there's Alex now. I know he doesn't feel the same way I do, but I blame the war for that. I get ideas about farming that I want to try out.

Gramp.   Well, try them out here Jim. The benefit will go to you two. Lord knows I don't waste anything.

Jim.   I know that, but I can't seem to explain the feeling that a fellow has for independence.

Gramp.   A man is only independent when he's standing on land with a clear title and no debts pressing him down.

Jim.   [*DISGUSTED*] Oh never mind.

Gramp.   I remember what my father said to me. "Jack," he said, "the place is yours. Take good care of it and hand it over to your sons and let them carry on. There must always be Macdonalds in Oak Valley."

Jim.   That's old stuff Dad. That was all right back in the Old Country in the day of the clans, but out here it's different. You made an awful fool out of me last night by draggin' me out of that place.

Gramp.   [*SUDDENLY STIFFENS*] No more of a fool than you made of yourself by gettin' in that disgraceful condition — [*GOING OFF*] You better work that land for the garden.

¶ MUSIC: *sneak background.*

Narrator.   For a few minutes I thought they were going to get along, but that was the way with Gramp and Uncle Jim. They were like strange dogs that would behave for a little while and then go at it again almost for no reason at all. I beat it out of the barn and cut across the fields to school.

¶ MUSIC: *up full to end.*

¶ SOUND: *descriptive under following:*

Narrator.   There's no place for grudges and spites on a farm. The ground was drying up and the creek in the west pasture was swollen but chuckling. I started slipping away to try and catch the odd fish. The days had a warm smell of early summer about them and the trees flashed into leaf. Staying in school was a real hardship when you could feel the soft wind brushing in and hear the sounds of work all around you in the valley. Our teacher was Mary Henderson, and I knew Jim was a bit soft on her, but I didn't realize how much until she asked me to stay after school one day . . .

Mary.   Don't look so worried, Billy. I didn't ask you to stay because I wanted to punish you.

Billy.   Gosh, Miss Henderson I've been trying to figure out something I did that was bad.

Mary.   [*PLEASANT LAUGH*] Well, you stop worrying. I . . . I . . . don't know how to ask you this, and I don't want you to mention it to anyone.

Billy.   I won't Miss Henderson.

Mary. You know that your uncle Jim . . . Mr. Macdonald and I have been seeing each other quite a lot.

Billy. Well . . . yes . . . I guess so.

Mary. I don't want you to misunderstand what I have to say now Billy, but is your grandfather . . . that is, is he very hard to get along with?

Billy. Gosh no! Gramp's a real man Miss Henderson. He's good to all of us.

Mary. I know but . . . well, is he . . . will he retire from the farm?

Billy. No, I don't think so. He told me that his dad, that was my great grandfather Black Angus Macdonald, told him to keep the place and give it over to his family when he died.

Mary. [*STRICKEN A BIT*] Oh . . . I . . . ah see.

Billy. Is there something wrong Miss Henderson?

Mary. No . . . I . . . I'm all right. I'm sorry to keep you so late Billy. You better go now. Please don't mention this to anyone.

Billy. I . . . I . . . I . . . Goodnight Miss Henderson.

¶ SOUND: *hurrying from room and door slam: not too hard.*

¶ MUSIC: *background.*

Narrator. I cut across the fields and the edge of McRory's swamp before it hit me. She had started to cry and I felt gawky and miserable. She was beautiful with hair that was a sort of combination of lemon and gold and I could feel her soft eyes right down in my heart. Somehow Gramp was mixed up with her unhappiness and it made me feel helpless because I couldn't think of anything to do to help her. I guess that was my first love affair because I couldn't go to sleep all right for thinking about her. The next day was Saturday and I had to work.

¶ MUSIC: *out.*

¶ SOUND: *cackling hens.*

Billy. Get out of the road you darned old cacklers.

¶ SOUND: *scraping sound of hoe on boards.*

Billy. Shooo, get out of there before I cut your heads off.

Jim. What's the matter Billy. Are you in bad humour or something?

Billy. Hello Uncle Jim.

Jim. What are you chasing the hens for Billy. They won't lay if you do that.

Billy. I don't care.

Jim. Well, I must admit that cleaning out the henhouse on a day like this certainly isn't a very attractive job. Did your dad send you out here?

Billy. No it was Gramp.

Jim. Gramp. Why he never comes near the henhouse.

Billy. I know, but he caught me cheating when I was planting those Dutch setts for ma this morning, and he said I had to clean out the henhouse as punishment.

Jim. [*LAUGHING*] What did you do? Put them all in a bunch or something.

Billy. Well, my back was hurting and I was almost at the end of the row anyhow. Shucks, we planted twenty rows of the darn things.

Jim. Well, never you mind. Mark my words, you get all the experience you can around hens. There's going to be real money in hens some day.

Billy. What do you mean Uncle Jim?

Jim. I've gotta hunch that most farmers are missing a bet that they don't keep more hens and look after them better. You take the average farm and the hens are running all over and people just keep them to get a few eggs and have the odd chicken for Sunday dinner or when the preacher comes.

Billy. [*PUZZLED*] Yes, I guess so.

Jim. City people like chicken meat and they like eggs too, and they would be willing to pay for good stuff. A fellow with a big bunch of hens could make himself some easy money.

Billy. Gosh, do you really think so?

Jim. I certainly do. A fellow was written up in the paper that has a place near the city and he does nothing but raise chickens and eggs for one of the big hotels.

Billy. Why don't you mention it to Gramp. He'd be interested.

Jim. Humph! [*DERISIVE*] Gramp. I did and he told me to stop dreaming. He says chickens are just for women to putter around with on the farm.

¶ MUSIC: *snorting: to background.*

Narrator. Dad and Jim had been working the Percherons and the bay team, and then one night the coughing started. It terrified me to hear my dad cough and cough as if he was going to explode inside with the force. Next morning Gramp started working the Percherons and Dad stayed in bed. His face had a dusty look about it and when I looked in the room he didn't even seem to have the strength to lift his hand. It was the gas bothering his lungs again. Things like that changed everything around the place and I noticed that Gramp and Jim seemed to be getting along pretty well with each other.

¶ MUSIC: *settled: back to background.*

Narrator. Then the off horse in the Percheron team took sick. The vet came but he couldn't do very much for him. We were getting behind with the work. Gramp was worried and after everybody was in bed I could smell the smoke from his pipe come wafting up through my bedroom window. I slipped down and went out the back door and came around to the veranda.

¶ MUSIC: *out.*

¶ SOUND: *night noises of late spring.*

Gramp. Who's that?

Billy. It's me.

Gramp. What are you doin' up at this hour?

Billy. Had to go out?

Gramp. Sit down boy. Don't talk loud now or your ma will hear you.
Pause.

Billy. It's a great night, isn't it Gramp.

Gramp. If the good Lord intended man to toil by day and rest by night, why did he make the night so wonderful.

Billy. I never thought of it that way before. [*PAUSE*] Does Doc Dinkney think the horse will get better Gramp?

Gramp. I don't know lad . . . I don't know. Doc wouldn't say much.

Billy. I think the McNabbs are through with their seeding. When I was coming home from school today, they were harrowing the front field.

Gramp. Aye.

Billy. I guess the tractor helps a lot.

Gramp. Aye, I guess it does lad.

Billy. You don't like tractors do you Gramp?

Gramp. I have nothing personal against machines, but somehow it doesn't seem right.

Billy. How Gramp?

Gramp. That's a bit hard to say Billy. Sitting here now with the soft sound of things growin' all around, takes me back a good many years.

Billy. To when you were a boy?

Gramp. In a way of speaking it does lad. My father had the finest horses in Oak Valley. They could outdraw or outpull or outwork anything in these parts. Spirited they were too. My father was a good hand with horses and he brought me up with the touch for them.

Billy. I like horses Gramp.

Gramp. I can tell that Billy. Your dad was a hand with horses too, but since he's come back from the war he hasn't the spirit.

Billy. Dad's pretty sick isn't he?

Gramp. He's not a well man.

Billy. But Uncle Jim likes horses Gramp.

Gramp. Aye, but as far as Jim is concerned, he likes them on Fall Fair day with the noise and the crowd and the feeling of winning first

118

prize. Your uncle Jim is like a lot of young fellows now. He's got the everlasting bite on his tail to hurry about everything.

Billy. Like with the work.

Gramp. That's right lad. The world is moving too fast. Some day it'll have to slow down and catch up with what it's missing. [*PAUSE . . . THE BOY DOESN'T UNDERSTAND.*] Sometimes I think I'm getting old Billy. Things press in hard. We're having trouble now, but there'll always be trouble. Jim now, he wants to take the bull by the horns and go out and wrestle with it. Maybe he's right. I can't see it. We've had a good life here and we've prospered. Things are fine now. The land's clear and there's a tidy bit in the bank and a few mortgages out earning good interest.

Billy. Maybe Jim wants to get married.

Gramp. That's natural. When I married I came back here with your grandmother and we all lived together with never a harsh word. That was a family, and that's the way God wanted it to be. Now, Jim wants to start up on his own. He's a good boy and he's worked hard. I like to think that when I pass on he'll be better fixed than any man his age in this valley, but he admits that and still he wants things different. I don't know lad. Life can be a puzzling thing at times. [*PAUSE*] Better go along to bed now Billy. Have to get up in the morning you know.

Billy. You coming to bed Gramp?

Gramp. By and by. Finish my pipe and then I'll go and take a look at the horse.

Billy. Goodnight Gramp.

Gramp. Goodnight lad.

¶ MUSIC: *gentle to background.*

Narrator. Gramp could be like that . . . when he lost the ramrod in his back and started worrying a little. Next morning it was all changed when we were sitting around the breakfast table . . .

¶ MUSIC: *out.*

¶ SOUND: *sound of meal.*

Annie. More tea Jim?

Jim. Just a little.

Annie. Jessie stop pushing the food off your plate. Eat it up.

Gramp. How's Alex this morning, Annie?

Annie. Well the cough seems to have stopped and he got quite a bit of rest. He was determined to get up this morning but I made him stay in bed.

Jim. Keep him there Annie. Do himself more harm than good getting up now.

Gramp.   That's right Annie. Make him stay in bed.

Annie.   How's the horse Pa?

Gramp.   Seems to have taken a turn for the better. When I went in the stable this morning, he tried to get up.

Annie.   That's good . . . I hope he'll be bet . . .

¶ SOUND: *tractor in distance: coming up laneway.*

Gramp.   What's that confounded racket?

Jim.   It must be McNabb with his tractor.

Gramp.   What's he coming here for?

Jim.   I saw him last night and he offered to come over and help us with the seeding.

Gramp.   We don't need that machine around here. I'm going to borrow a horse from McGillvray.

Jim.   [*JUST A TRACE OF HEAT*] Well he offered to come and I could hardly turn him down.

Annie.   [*TRIFLE HELPLESS*] It was good of him to offer to come.

Gramp.   You sure this isn't some scheme of yours to get a tractor on the farm?

¶ SOUND: *chair scraping.*

Jim.   Of course it isn't. I'm not going to sit around and let the work all go to pot just because of a sick horse.

¶ SOUND: *footsteps: screen door slamming.*

Annie.   [*A TRIFLE HELPLESS*] Hurry up Billy and finish your breakfast or you'll be late for school.

¶ MUSIC: *background.*

Narrator.   Gramp sat staring into his teacup for long minutes. Then he got up and took his straw hat from where it was hanging on the mouthpiece of the wall telephone and went outside.

¶ MUSIC: *up full to background.*

Narrator.   Spring swelled into summer and the bare face of the new seeding sprouted a whisker of green. Dad was up and around again. Gramp never mentioned the tractor and neither did Jim.

¶ MUSIC: *briefly.*

Jim.   Annie, there's something I'd like to have you do for me.

Annie.   Yes Jim, what is it? [*PAUSE*] What did you want me to do for you Jim?

Jim.   Well, school's almost over for the year, and . . . I was just wonderin' if maybe you might ask the teacher to come and stay the weekend.

Annie. Of course I will. As a matter of fact it's been careless of me not to ask her before, but when Alex's ailin' it's hard to have somebody around.

Jim. I appreciate this a lot Annie.

Annie. Don't bother your head about it. I'll send a note with Billy to school and ask her if she would come along on Friday night.

Jim. I kinda think maybe we'll be gettin' married in June.

Annie. Now that's wonderful. [SUDDENLY THE LIGHT STRIKES] But where are you going to live.

Jim. I wish I knew. I don't suppose there's the chance of a snowball for us to get the old man to let me take over the Heather farm.

Annie. Dear me, but your father's so set in his ways.

Jim. Every time I try to talk to him, it ends up in a row of some kind.

Annie. Maybe, Mary wouldn't mind living here for a little while and then later on . . . when . . .

Jim. I've talked to her about it, but she says that only leads to trouble.

Annie. She's perfectly welcome as far as I'm concerned.

Jim. I know that Annie. You have enough patience for twenty people. There wouldn't be trouble between you two.

Annie. If you tell Gramp you intend to get married, I think things will work out.

Jim. I hope so, because I've got a hunch that if they don't, Mary won't marry me.

Annie. We'll see. I've heard that she's a very nice girl. Let me see, I think I'll give her the front room and move . . .

¶ MUSIC: *fade out of voice into transition music.*

Narrator. Conversation was stiff on Friday night but by Saturday it had warmed up a lot. I knew that my mother liked Mary Henderson. Grandpa didn't change much but he was polite and he told a couple of stories that made everybody laugh. Sunday afternoon we had a big supper with roast chicken and mashed potatoes and two different kinds of pie.

¶ SOUND: *meal sounds.*

Gramp. By godfrey Annie, that was a wonderful meal.

Mary. It certainly was. I don't think I've ever tasted dressing that I liked better.

Annie. Some people don't like dressing with that much spice, but Pa here complains bitterly if it hasn't enough sage.

Gramp. Sage is a herb that people don't use enough of. I remember that German family . . . Hoffstedders I think they were that used to make the country sausage. They used sage and it was certainly tasty.

Alex. Annie, pass the teach . . . I mean Miss Henderson another piece of pie.

Mary. Oh for heavens sake, I couldn't eat another mouthful if I were paid for it.

Jim. You know Annie, Mary here's quite a good cook too.

Mary. Go on with your blarney Jim. My dad says he can cook better than I can.

Jim. He'd have to be pretty darn good then.

Mary. My mother was an excellent cook and Dad wasn't actually too bad.

Annie. Do you like cooking Mary?

Mary. Yes . . . I think I do. I get a kick out of just puttering around the kitchen and trying new things.

Alex. Better watch out Jim, if she tries experimenting too much.

Jim. Say that's right.

Annie. Now don't be teasing her. The first month we were married I could have served Alex old socks boiled and he'd have eaten them.

Alex. The first good dose of indigestion you get will be enough to cure that.

Annie. Pa, I guess you better get that new suit you've been talking about for the past three years.

Gramp. Eh . . . ah what for?

Annie. Now, can't you guess?

Gramp. No, I can't say that I can.

Annie. I guess I shouldn't be the one to spill this but I think before too long you're going to have a new daughter-in-law.

Gramp. [SHAKES HIM] Well, and when does this take place.

Jim. I've been meaning to speak to you before this, but Mary and I have been talking about getting married when the school year finishes.

Gramp. Well . . . *well* . . . hmm . . . guess we'll have to get a new teacher eh?

Mary. [TESTY] Yes, I guess you will.
  Pause.

¶ SOUND: *small and nervous shuffle of chairs.*

Annie. [TRYING TO BREAK IT UP] Will anybody have more tea?

¶ MUSIC: *up full to background.*

Narrator. I think everybody felt a strange feeling at the table. Uncle Jim and the teacher went for a walk back through the fields and Gramp sat on the front veranda and smoked. Usually he took a sleep on Sunday afternoon. It was one of those hot Sundays when the flies buzz around in a monotonous way and all the sounds like . . . the screak of the windmill and the window blind flapping in the hot breeze add up to boredom for a ten year old boy. I was playing with the pup on the shady side of the house when I heard Jim and Mary come up . . .

¶ MUSIC: *out.*

Gramp. [*OFF*] Have a good walk?

Jim. Pretty good. There's a bad spot in the fence around the oats that we'll have to fix tomorrow.

Gramp. Yes, I noticed it last night when I was coming up the lane. Well Miss Henderson, what do you think of the Macdonald farm?

Mary. It's wonderful. It's so . . . sort of clean and all.

Gramp. Yes, my father always prided himself on having a clean farm. I can't stand the sight of fence bottoms growing up with weeds. It takes work tho'.

Mary. Yes, I would think so. I suppose farming is actually getting easier with new implements like tractors and such like . . .

Gramp. We have no tractor.

Jim. [*TRYING TO PASS IT OFF*] Yes, that's a matter of long standing between Dad and myself.

Gramp. Jim here, thinks that I'm just an old fogey who doesn't know enough to catch up with modern ways of doing things.

Mary. With no intention of being disrespectful Mr. Macdonald, I do think the world wouldn't have got very far if everyone had disregarded progress. After all you use a binder in place of a reaper.

Jim. Atta girl!

Gramp. [*SLOWLY*] My father came into this valley and cleared the first of our farms. He built this valley, sending back to Scotland for my mother to come out and for other relatives. He loved it dearly. When he died I took over. It's a heritage. I know that the world is moving on and that there are new things like tractors and all that, but mark me . . . those are the things that will destroy the good world we have here. Why, do you know I heard in Lochalsh the other day that the bakery is going to start a wagon peddling bread to farmers?

Mary. Why not Mr. Macdonald?

Gramp. Well, it's a . . . it's just that we've always baked our own bread. Bakeshop bread is for town folks and some of them would be better off makin' it for themselves in place of running up bills.

Jim. I know Dad, but I don't think you can hold the world up like that.

Gramp. When a man's right . . . he's right. As long as your conscience tells you.

Narrator. Just then my dad showed around the corner of the back kitchen and I had to pretend to be busy so that I couldn't listen. He made me move. I think he wanted to listen himself. Next day the teacher looked tired and she was snappish with everyone in the class.

¶ MUSIC: *up briefly to background.*

Narrator. McGillvray bought a tractor and put his sorrel team up for

123

sale. Gramp didn't say a word one morning when he took the car out of the driving shed and drove up the valley road but I heard Jim say to my father . . .

¶ MUSIC: *out.*

Jim. [*FADING UP*] I wonder where the old man's going?
Alex. I can guess.
Jim. He's going to McGillvrays to buy that sorrel team.
Alex. That's right. I don't know whether he wants the team or else it's because he hates the idea of so many tractors coming into the valley.
Jim. [*SAD LAUGH*] Do you know what I heard him say to Annie yesterday, and you know how he prides himself on never going to the doctor.
Alex. Yah. What did he say?
Jim. [*MUSED*] Thought he'd go to see the doctor. His lungs were bothering him. He wondered if the gasoline fumes in the valley didn't have something to do with it.
Alex. Good Heavens — that's a laugh.
Jim. It's not funny for me. Mary won't say finally whether she'll marry me or not, until this situation is straightened out here.
Alex. I mentioned to him the other day about fixing up the house on the Heather farm for you and Mary but I didn't get any place with him.
Jim. Well Alex, I've got to have a showdown real soon. I've only got a week and a half before school is over.
Annie. [*OFF*] Billy . . . Billy come and pump some water for me.

¶ MUSIC: *in and under.*

Narrator. I had to go then and pump water for Ma. My dad went to the driving shed to sharpen the mower knife and Jim was puttering around the barnyard. I was kind of worried because everybody said the sorrel team were a pair of bad actors and McGillvray hadn't been working them much after he bought the tractor. I had to bring some wood in from the back woodshed for the box behind the kitchen range. I heard ma yelling in the kitchen and she ran out the door towards the driving shed . . .

¶ MUSIC: *out.*

Annie. [*OFF*] Alex . . . Jim . . . Alex . . . look down the road . . .

¶ SOUND: *screen door slamming.*

Narrator. I ran out in the back yard. There was a great cloud of dust rolling up behind a team and wagon on the valley road. We all started running towards the front gate. It was Gramp and he had the sorrel team hitched to a democrat and they were running away.
Jim. [*RUNNING . . . OFF*] He'll be killed . . . for the love of heavens why

doesn't he jump . . .

Annie. [*RUNNING . . . OFF*] Oh dear oh dear . . . do something.

Alex. I hope he doesn't try to turn in the gateway.

Jim. If he'd let them run he could tire them out.

Narrator. His hat was off and he was standing up in the wagon pulling on the lines. The team were racing like mad and when they came close to the gateway I saw he was going to try and turn them . . .

¶ SOUND: *yells of the people: clatter of light wagon: horses hooves.*

Jim. [*LOUD*] Let them go . . . let them go . . .

Gramp. [*LOUD OFF*] Whoa . . . whoa . . . hold up there . . . hold up there . . .

Narrator. He turned them but the off wheel caught the post [*CRASH*] and to this day I can see Gramp hurtling through the air. He seemed to sort of bounce against the post and then he lay still . . . very still . . . the team ran on into the barnyard and stopped by the water trough with the wreckage of the democrat dangling behind them.

¶ MUSIC: *tragic to background.*

Narrator. The accident sort of settled things around our place for a time. Gramp broke his arm and sprained his hip and he was put to bed in the spare bedroom off the sitting room. Mary Henderson came to visit us before she went home to Belleville, and they got along very well. On Sundays the place was jammed with visitors. People took care not to mention the sorrel team. Gramp moved out to the front veranda and school was over. Harvest came in with a rush and I knew that Gramp was itching to get out in the field. One day, there was a special delivery letter for Jim. I knew it was from the teacher because it was postmarked Belleville. I took the letter back to the field where he was cutting wheat. He looked at the letter, shoved his straw hat back on the top of his head, mopped the beads of sweat from his brow with the back of his tanned and freckled hand, and said:

¶ MUSIC: *out.*

¶ SOUND: *background of outdoors and horses.*

Jim. Billy, this is it!

Billy. What's what?

Jim. Here hold the lines for me.

¶ SOUND: *paper tearing.*

Jim. I wrote and told her that Dad had agreed to make some arrangements this fall.

Billy. Did he really? You mean the Heather place?

Jim. Yes . . . hmmm . . . [*SUDDENLY*] Boy Billy . . . you've got an aunt
. . . she says yes . . . Billy . . . you drive the team around a couple of
rounds. I'm going up to the house. . . . Yippee . . .

¶ MUSIC: *jubilant: hold as background.*

Narrator. A wedding in the country is a great event. That's doubly true
when it comes right between the threshing of the wheat in the field
and the attack on the ripened oats and barley. Some said that Jim
should have waited until fall and the work was over, but my Uncle Jim
was a happy and determined young man in love. He walked out of the
wheat threshing into a bath and a new suit of clothes, picked up the
touring he had rented from Joe Taylors Auto Sales in the village, and
set out for Belleville and his wedding to Mary Henderson.

¶ MUSIC: *up into final sharp and ominous chord.*

¶ SOUND: *thunder in the air.*

Narrator. Gramp always enjoyed thunder storms. He sat calmly on the
back veranda and watched the black clouds rolling up over the sky-
line. There were always those first puffs of wind that swirled dust in
the laneway and sent curtains and blinds flapping in every room in
the house. Ma always scurried through the house pulling out the
screens and slamming down the windows. The smoke from Gramp's
pipe curled up and escaped through the spot in the veranda where the
bricks from the chimney, when it was hit by lightning, had made a
permanent dent. Grandfather had just moved his chair over to escape
the drip when Jim's rented car turned in the laneway from his honey-
moon.

¶ MUSIC: *moody: up and out.*

Narrator. There was a lot of confusion that night and Ma put Jim and
his bride to sleep upstairs in the room where Gramp had slept before
his accident. . . . Next morning . . .

¶ SOUND: *meal sounds.*

Annie. You certainly look like a bride this morning dear.
Jim. Isn't she wonderful?
Alex. By George I believe she's better looking now than when she was
teaching school. Look at Billy there staring at her.
Mary. He just doesn't have to be afraid of the old ogre of a teacher.
Gramp. Pass the cream.
Annie. Here you are Pa. One thing, Billy always stuck up for you as a
teacher anyhow.
Mary. That was sweet of you Billy. He was always, I must confess, one

of my favorite pupils.

Alex. Now look at the sunburn on him. He looks like a pickled beet.

Jim. Stop teasing him.

Annie. That's what I say Billy.

Gramp. Pass the sugar.

Annie. Here Pa.

Mary. And how are you feeling Mr. Macdonald?

Gramp. Couldn't sleep all night.

Alex. Shoulder bothering you again, Dad?

Gramp. Some. I'll move back upstairs tonight Annie and you can give Jim and his wife the front room.

Annie. But Pa . . . you said . . .

Gramp. Slept in that room for over thirty four years and I can't get a rest any place else.
   Pause.

Alex. Pass me the salt Billy.

¶ MUSIC: *sharply and out.*

Narrator. Mother was horrified because she had put new wallpaper on the room and painted the floor and placed some scatter mats around and I knew she was proud of it. That was just the start. There always seemed to be some minor friction. Like the morning Ma was sick and Mary got the breakfast . . . and Gramp was in bad humour anyhow . . .

¶ SOUND: *fade up on meal sounds.*

Alex. Better watch out this morning with a new cook.

Mary. You certainly better. I just realize that I've got to get in practice.

Jim. Don't worry dear. You'll do fine.

Gramp. Where's the cream?

Mary. Oh dear. I guess I forgot it.

Alex. I left a jar of it after separating on the shelf in the pantry.

¶ SOUND: *chair scraping: footsteps away: then back.*

Mary. [COMING ON] Here you are Mr. Macdonald.

Alex. Did you notice any rust in that field next to the creek, Jim?

Jim. Yes, there's one spot that's pretty bad.

Alex. Jock says those oats he got from the Agricultural College are as clean as a whistle.

Gramp. Hmph! What's wrong with this porridge?

Jim. [GENTLE] No salt in it Mary.

Gramp. Tastes flat.

Mary. Oh it does. Well . . . well . . . [TEARS] well . . . [CHAIR MOVING] Damn the porridge anyhow . . . [SOUND OF FOOTSTEPS AND DOOR

SLAMMING]

Gramp. What's wrong with her?

Jim. For the love of Pete will you stop picking on her?

　Pause.

Alex. Here you kids, eat up your breakfast.

Jessie. This porridge tastes funny.

Alex. [*ANGRY*] Eat it and be quiet.

　Pause.

Narrator. Gramp sat and stared at his plate without eating. Then he got up and took his hat down from the peg on the back of the door and went out to the barn.

¶ MUSIC: *up and then hold as background.*

Narrator. Harvest time is the peak for everything on the farm. The sun casts a golden haze over the valley and you can hear the whirring and clacking of the binders, knifing through the golden stalks of grain . . . and the pam-pam-pam of the steam engines as the noisy separators take the grain and cast the straw aside. It was good weather and everybody was busy. Ma and Mary went picking berries on the slash and they were busy putting down pickles. The kitchen had that nose tingling smell of vinegar and pickling spice. The chores were over and Gramp was reading the newspaper. Ma put the kids to bed and I was trying to remain unobserved in a dark corner of the kitchen when Mary spoke to Jim.

¶ MUSIC: *out.*

Mary. How do you like the pickles Jim?

Jim. They look wonderful. I hope you put down some of those ones with the cinnamon in them.

Mary. [*LAUGHING*] There'll be plenty of time to put those down. Annie warned me about you. She said if you had your way you'd eat a jar of pickles at a meal.

Jim. I sure like pickles.

Mary. And remember when you start fixing up that house on the other place I want you to be sure and put some cupboards in down cellar for preserves.

Jim. Gosh how much stuff are you going to have?

Mary. The ones on this side of the table belong to us. I do wish Annie would have let me pay for part of the vinegar and spices.

Jim. We'll get back at her for that.

Narrator. [*GENTLY AS IF OFFSTAGE*] I saw Gramp look up over the edge of the paper and then go on as if reading but I knew he was hearing every word.

Mary. When are we going to start work on it Jim?

Jim. Have to wait until the harvest is over now.

Mary. Aren't you almost finished with the harvesting?

Jim. There's quite a bit yet.

Mary. Mother wrote me again wanting to know when she should have the furniture shipped . . .

¶ SOUND: *footsteps on outside veranda and rapping.*

Sandy. [*OFF: LITTLE ECHOING: VERY SCOTCH*] Are ye thair?

Gramp. Who's that?

Sandy. It's me . . . Red Sandy Macrae.

Gramp. Come in Sandy, the latch is up.

Sandy. It's a grand night tha'night. [*HE COMES IN AND CLOSES THE DOOR*]

Jim. Hello Sandy.

Sandy. It's gude to see you and you Mrs. Macdonald and yon's Billy lad. [*ACKNOWLEDGEMENT OF GREETINGS*]

Gramp. What brings you this way, Red Sandy?

Sandy. I'm on my way to weave a carpet of melody for the twinkletoes of the dancers at the schoolhouse.

Jim. [*LAUGHING*] Gosh, that's right, I forgot all about it.

Sandy. Seeing your light, I thought I would bide a wee while with you.

Gramp. How's your crop?

Sandy. It's no so bad, but my rheumatism has been bothering me lately and I haven't been able to keep up with the work.

Gramp. [*AMUSED*] You wouldn't have been taking some medicine for it tonight would you?

Sandy. As me old father said to me: "Sandy he says, a wee drop between friends loosens the chords of the heart, and so long as it doesn't loosen the chords o' the tongue over much, it'll bide ye well."

¶ SOUND: *general amusement.*

Sandy. Jim, I wanted tae put a word in for my brother-in-law Dugald Patterson. He's no worked this past while and he's a handy man with tools and I thought when you started fixin' the Heather place ye might keep him in mind.

Jim. [*EMBARRASSED*] Yes . . . ah . . . well, we won't be starting on it for a while yet.

Sandy. Well, just so long as you keep him in mind that's all I ask.

¶ SOUND: *fiddle tuning.*

Gramp. Play us something Red Sandy.

Sandy. Aye and I know what ye want.

¶ MUSIC: *solo fiddle on "Flowers of Edinburgh."*

Gramp. Aye, it's a bonny tune.

Jim.   Mary, how be we go to the dance.
Sandy.   Yes, by all means . . . come along . . .
Mary.   Oh Jim — I . . . I . . .
Jim.   We can be ready in no time and there'll be no dance until Red
Sandy gets there.
Mary.   All right . . . I'll get ready as quick as I can.
Sandy.   That's the way . . .

¶ MUSIC: *solo fiddle up into orchestral bridge using same theme and then background for narrator:*

Narrator.   Gramp never had much use for Red Sandy but he certainly
was glad to see him that night. I think my uncle Jim was too, in a way,
because he had been putting off facing up to Gramp about taking over
the Heather place.

¶ MUSIC: *up full and out.*

Narrator.   It was hot when I went up to my room. Even the night breeze
had a searing quality to it and the sheets felt warm to touch. The
freight going across the far end of the valley screamed and a cat
yowled, sharp and harsh. The sky had a strange look about it and the
full harvest moon was a globule of white heat in the night. I could hear
the springs on Gramp's bed whining as he turned from side to side
and I knew that there was more than the oppressive heat of the night
bothering him. The jagged splotches of heat lightning seemed like
unearthly spirits gleefully waiting for the trouble that was bound to
come.

¶ MUSIC: *weird to background.*

Narrator.   The heat kept up steady and unrelenting all weekend. We
finished harvesting on Monday, except of course for the buckwheat.
The earth was drying up and Ma kept me busy carrying water for the
cucumber patch. I was at the pump at the end of the veranda when
Jim and Mary came out the door. They were going to town. Gramp
was sitting on the veranda smoking . . .

¶ MUSIC: *out.*

Gramp.   When you're in town would you get me two plugs of smoking.
Jim.   Yes. Is there anything else?
Gramp.   Do you need any money?
Narrator.   There was a dead silence. Jim turned red in the face. I could
see the lines around Mary's mouth sort of tighten up and then it
happened . . .
Mary.   Yes Mr. Macdonald, enough money to fix up the Heather place.
Gramp.   . . . I don't quite understand.

Mary. Well I do. If Jim hasn't gumption in him to tell you I will. When are we going to fix up that place?

Gramp. You're happy here aren't you?

Mary. Oh . . . I . . . [*RAGE*] Look, I don't want to be unkind about this. Annie has been wonderful to me. So has Alex and the children. I'm not complaining about that. Just the same, I want a home of my own. That was what Jim promised me before I came here.

Jim. Dad, Mary's right.

Gramp. I see. I'm not capable of running things any more.

Jim. It's not that. It's just that . . .

Mary. That he's tired of being treated like a child and given so much money to spend.

Gramp. But the money I have will go to all of you when I die.

Mary. Oh . . . how . . . why can't you understand it Mr. Macdonald. We've got a life to lead. We're just . . . just dependents here.

Gramp. [*NOT UNDERSTANDING*] There's six hundred acres of the best valley land here. It's the Macdonald farm. We've worked together to make it the best place this side of Toronto.

Mary. We're not asking for anything but the chance to make a life for ourselves . . .

Gramp. [*NOT HEARING HER*] It seems like breaking up everything that my father and myself have worked for. I want to be square with you and Alex. You're my sons. This place is ours. When I'm gone it will go on to your children. I remember something my father told me: "There'll always be a Macdonald in the valley until the day the Creator calls everybody back . . . "

Mary. [*GENTLY BUT FIRMLY*] I know how you feel. You love this place and I can understand that, but do you realize that you're killing Jim. He wants to make a life and to go on and prove that he can. If he doesn't do it now, he . . . well, he won't be able to.

Jim. You and I differ on a lot of things Dad. I think there's a new way of farming and I want to try it.

Gramp. Yes . . . yes, I know.

Pause.

Mary. This is Annie's house and her home. She has been simply wonderful to me, but I can't go on this way. [*VERGE OF TEARS*] If you don't want to let Jim have a chance, then I'm going to go. [*VOICE RISING*] I can't stand it. I simply can't. I'm leaving and you have to make up your mind now Jim, whether you come or stay here.

¶ SOUND: *screen door slams.*

Pause.

Jim. I'm going.

Gramp. Where?

Jim.   I don't know. To get a job I guess.

Narrator.   Gramp stood up then and looked down across the valley as if he were seeing it for the last time. His voice had a strange but commanding note to it when he spoke.

Gramp.   Go and tell your father to come here Billy. We're going in to town to see MacDougall the lawyer. Jim, you come too.

¶ MUSIC: *up full.*

Narrator.   Gramp and my dad and Uncle Jim drove off to town. There was a strange stiffness about them as they sat in the car. I heard Mary crying in her room and my mother went up to speak to her. That was the longest afternoon I've ever put in. When they were getting the supper ready, my mother kept talking to Mary. The heat seemed to be building up even worse than before.

¶ SOUND: *the two women are moving around the kitchen.*

Annie.   I wouldn't take on about it Mary. Before Alex went away to war he had the same fight with his father, and when he came back and he wasn't feeling well, I think he just sort of accepted things.

Mary.   Sometimes I think I would have been better to have just gone away myself and not said anything.

Annie.   Now don't say that Mary. They'll get it fixed up.

Billy.   Maw, there's the car coming up the road now.

Annie.   Oh dear, and here we are with meat to fry yet. Mary, would you take a look at those potatoes?

Mary.   All right . . . dear me I hope things are settled.

¶ MUSIC: *up briefly and out.*

Narrator.   The three of them came into the kitchen. Gramp went upstairs to change his clothes. Dad said in a voice that was just above a whisper . . .

Alex.   He signed this place over to us and the Heather place to Jim. He gave Jim the money to start up for himself. The three of us will work the other four hundred acres on shares . . .

Jim.   Sssh.

¶ SOUND: *coming down the stairs.*

Gramp.   Will we eat now or after the chores Annie?

Annie.   Supper's all ready except to put it on the table.

¶ SOUND: *footsteps and chair being pulled out.*

Annie.   But Gramp, this is your place up here.

Gramp.   No . . . that's Alex's place.
   Pause.

Alex. Oh come on Dad.

Gramp. No Alex. Better eat now because I think there's a storm blowing up from the west.

¶ SOUND: *shuffle of chairs and then silence.*

Alex. [*NERVOUSLY*] Bless us oh Lord for these thy gifts which we are about to receive through thy bounty oh Christ our Lord Amen.

¶ MUSIC: *amen.*

¶ SOUND: *thunder in the air.*

Narrator. The sky darkened and a whisper of breeze ran through the valley. The heat lightning flashed on and off and then the thunder started and the heavens seemed to crack open. We just got in from the barn when the first big, splattering drops of rain fell on the parched ground. Then a deluge followed. Gramp hung his hat on the peg and walked over to the stairway.

Gramp. Think I'll turn in.

Mary. I . . . I . . . I'm sorry if I said anything that . . .

Gramp. It's perfectly all right lass. What must be done must be done . . .

Narrator. There wasn't much conversation. Jessie and Jean cried because they were afraid of the storm. Mother went up to them. Dad sat on the back veranda smoking and staring out into the storm. Jim and Mary went to bed. I went up the stairs and when I came to Gramp's room, something made me open the door. . .

¶ SOUND: *click of latch: rain and storm in background: low.*

Narrator. A flash of lightning burned that scene into my memory so that I shall never forget it. Gramp was sitting on the side of the bed with his head in his hands and there was a strange slope to his shoulders. There was only the washstand with the white crockery and the rocking chair and the rugs on the floor and the picture of my grandmother that seemed to be staring down the wall at him.

Billy. Goodn . . . goodnight Gramp.

Pause.

Gramp. [*JUST A TRACE OF A SOB*] Goo . . . goodnight my boy.

¶ SOUND: *click of the latch.*

¶ MUSIC: *sneaks background.*

Narrator. I went to my room and I knew then that the sound of a man crying is a lonely and fearful thing. Tears come to women as naturally as life, but when a man cries it has a different sound. There are tears of passion and tears of sorrow but the sound of an old man crying in the night has in it the whole meaning of life and the death that yawns ahead . . . dark . . . lonely . . . and unknown.

¶ MUSIC: *slowly builds to climax.*

Announcer. *Stage* 49 . . . the thirty-fifth and concluding item . . . was "The Macdonalds of Oak Valley," a new play by Harry J. Boyle . . . produced and directed by Andrew Allan, with an original musical score composed and conducted by Lucio Agostini. Frank Peddie starred as Grandfather Macdonald; John Drainie as the Narrator; Bruce Stevens as Billy; Budd Knapp as Jim; Mona O'Hearn as Mary Henderson; Robert Christie as Alex; Beth Lockerbie as Annie; Tommy Tweed as Red Sandy Macrae. The others were Pat Sheppard, Peter Mews, and Herb Gott. Sound by David Tasker. Technical operation by Bruce Armstrong.

Man With a Bucket of Ashes

LEN PETERSON

Production

Producer: Andrew Allan
Music: Lucio Agostini
Sound: David Tasker
Operator: Bruce Armstrong
Program: Stage 52
Broadcast: May 4, 1952, 9:00–10:00 pm EST
Studio: Toronto
Network: Trans-Canada

Cast

Frank Peddie *as* Dave Clough
Ruth Springford *as* Mrs. Clough
Billie Richards *as* Michael
Tommy Tweed *as* Lundquist
Beth Lockerbie *as* Mrs. Ennis
Alan King *as* Fred Ennis
Alice Hill *as* Sadie Gillen
Budd Knapp *as* Kurt Balla
with
Hugh Webster, Larry McCance, Alan Pearce, Paul Kligman,
Gerard Sarracini, *and* Douglas Master

MAN WITH A BUCKET OF ASHES

Preface

If the *Baker's Dozen* series written by Fletcher Markle in 1942 firmly established for Andrew Allan a dramatic technique unique to radio, then it was Len Peterson's plays which for Allan accomplished the combination of this new technique with a contemporary social and moral message, and with a new high seriousness. The first three plays in Allan's new 1944 *Stage* series were Markle's; but the next three were by Peterson, whose work and whose discussions with Allan in 1943 (as Allan insists) were the most important single stimulus to Allan's creation of a Canadian national theatre.

Len Peterson was born and received his early education in Regina. He studied mathematics and science at Northwestern University in 1938, and was stimulated — among other things, by the excitement of American radio drama — to begin writing radio plays. In 1939 he moved to Toronto, where he began selling plays to the CBC; Allan was among their earliest producers. Peterson served in the army in Ottawa during the war, writing war documentaries but meanwhile continuing to supply plays to the CBC, especially to Allan. Peterson was one of the major contributors of plays to Allan and other drama producers during the Golden Age. Allan produced 37 of his scripts, the vast majority originals, as many as 25 of these on the *Stage* series. In all, Peterson has written (on his own count) some 1,200 radio scripts, 40 television scripts, and numerous film scripts for the NFB, as well as nine stage plays and several novels. His career as a radio dramatist continues to the present.

Peterson's plays are among the most experimental technically, though because of his sense of colloquial reality, they speak to a wide audience. Because of what Allan calls Peterson's "ruthless honesty . . . his daring in tackling forbidden subjects," Peterson's plays were among the most controversial of those produced on *Stage*. Many of his scripts angered both audiences and CBC officials — and indeed Parliament itself — because they dared to discuss topics such as racism, social inequality, and the loss of religious faith in the post-war world. Peterson's best serious play — "Man with a Bucket of Ashes" — provoked one of the worst crises with the CBC "brass." "Man with a Bucket of Ashes" is an existential tragedy of the loss of faith in God's love and forgiveness. The image here is of the Old Testament Lord of anger and revenge: the major archetypes are of Abraham sacrificing his son Isaac and of the life-destroying Flood. What converts the play from sheer epic fantasy to a play with which the audience cannot help but identify is its strong realistic and psychological levels, reinforced by Peterson's achievement of a convincing colloquial language. The protagonist may possibly be God's messenger of warning and punishment or he may be a homicidal maniac in a world devoid of meaning. And this is the modern, existential level of the play, reflecting our alienation from God, our uncertainty about God's very existence.

This play is at the other end of the spectrum from Allan's own early wartime play on the same theme, "All the Bright Company." At the end of that equally serious and violent 1942 play, Allan comforts us with a vision of an ultimately benign God of Nature, or, at the very least, a conscious and caring God, carrying out a necessary apocalyptic purification prior to a new post-war beginning. The violence in Peterson's play is identified, through many clear references, with the senseless carnage of the war and brutalization of victor and victim alike. And there is no optimism, nor any comfort; for Peterson in 1952 is writing in the shadow of the failure of that bright early-post-war-time hope for a new beginning, with the growing polarization of East and West, the beginning of yet another war — the Korean conflagration in which Canadians were fighting — and the fear of an atomic apocalypse.

LEN PETERSON

Man With a Bucket of Ashes

¶ MUSIC: *title cue . . . up and background.*

Announcer. *Stage* 52 . . . Item 31 . . . "Man with a Bucket of Ashes," a new play by Len Peterson. Produced by Andrew Allan, with music composed and conducted by Lucio Agostini. Starring Frank Peddie and Ruth Springford . . . "Man with a Bucket of Ashes," by Len Peterson.

¶ MUSIC: *suggesting beautiful spring weather, but with the threat of a flood.*

Michael. [*FIVE, LIVELY, HUSKY: IMITATING THE MOTOR OF A BULLDOZER AND CHANGING TONE WHENEVER HE MEETS RESISTANCE*]

Clough. [*SEVENTY-FOUR, FADING IN*] Huh, what you doin', Michael?

Michael. It's a bulldozer, Daddy. See? I made it out of wood. [*THERE IS A PLEASANT RELATION BETWEEN THE TWO, THOUGH OCCASIONALLY A TOUCH OF APPREHENSION SHOWS IN THE BOY*]

Clough. Huh, you oughta be in the implement business, workin' for Massey-Harris.

Michael. [*SOUNDS HIS MOTOR AGAIN FOR A MOMENT*] I been shorin' up earth 'gainst the dike.

Clough. Water ain't broke through anywhere 'long here yet?

Michael. Nope.

Clough. Don't forget: if it does you run and tell somebody, Michael.

Michael. [*PROTESTING WITH A TOUCH OF PRIDE*] I did that other time, didn't I?

Clough. [*HE IS TIRED AND SHOWS IT*] Yeah, guess you did.

Michael. [*FADING SLIGHTLY*] River's up another row a bags. [*HE HAS CAUGHT THE CONCERN OF THE ADULTS*] See?

Clough. Yeah.

Michael. Come and look.

Clough. You're not the only one's noticed. [*HE IS SICK AND WEARY OF DIKES*] Be needin' to raise the dike 'long here too.

Michael. Daddy, come and see.

Clough. You stay down off there or your mamma'll be givin' you a hidin'.

Michael. [*FADING IN*] Won't fall in.

Clough. It might reach up and grab you.

Michael. Oh, river can't do that.

Clough. River these days, kid, do anything.

Michael. [*SCOFFING*] Reach up and grab me?

Clough. Yeah, like this. [*PICKING HIM UP AND SHAKING HIM*] How you like that, eh?

Michael. [*LAUGHING*] Do it some more!

Clough. Maybe a big fir tree'll come floatin' down the river from the mountain . . . knockin' out bridges, dams, dikes . . . reach out its branches and grab you!

Michael. [*DODGES AND FADES LAUGHING*] Hah, missed me!

¶ MUSIC: *sneaks into background, accompanying the old man's fantasy.*

Clough. Tree'll upend to get you then! [*LUNGES*]

Michael. [*ENJOYING BEING FRIGHTENED*] It's not a very good tree! Hah, ha!

Clough. [*GROWLS*] Then it'll spin. [*CLAPS HIS HANDS TOGETHER*] And fly through the air! Hah, got you! [*PICKING UP THE BOY*] The devil tree'll fling you into the devil river. [*SWINGING HIM AROUND WITH THE BOY LAUGHING*] The water'll swirl you round and round, and you gaspin' for air — and gulpin' water — round 'n' round — nothin' to grab hold of . . . !

Michael. [*HIS LAUGHTER HAS TURNED TO A FRIGHTENED APPEAL*] Daddy, let me down!

Clough. It's the devil river and the devil tree!

Michael. Daddy! Stop! Daddy!

Clough. Nobody can help you! It's . . .

Michael. [*SCREAMS PROTESTINGLY*]

¶ SOUND: *the old man stumbles.*

Clough. Oo!

¶ SOUND: *and the boy hits against a tree.*

¶ MUSIC: *cut.*

Michael. [*LETS OUT A YELL THEN BEGINS TO CRY*]

Clough. [CONSOLINGLY] Oh, Daddy was clumsy, bad fellah. There, don't cry. Nothin' like that's gonna happen. [AS THOUGH FACING A REALITY] I won't let it.

Michael. When'll the — the d-devil tree and — and the devil river get me?

Clough. Never. Never get you. No sir! The devil tree and the devil river better leave you alone. God'll see they do!

Michael. Daddy, don't hurt me.

¶ SOUND: *screen door slightly off, pushed open.*

Mrs. Clough. [FIFTY-TWO, DISAPPOINTED WITH WHAT LIFE HAS GIVEN HER, OR HAS NOT GIVEN HER . . . SLIGHTLY OFF] Michael, [CALLING AUTOMATICALLY WITHOUT REALLY LOOKING FOR THE BOY] How many times do I gotta tell you to come in and get your breakfast? Oh, these flies around this door.

Clough. Go on in, Michael.

Mrs. Clough. So, Dave, you've finally turned up. Where you been all night?

Clough. On the big dike. Where you think I been?

Mrs. Clough. Wasn't your shift.

Clough. Dike saggin'. They grabbed me when I was in McBirney's gettin' some tobacco. Just took everybody they could find.

Mrs. Clough. So you ain't had any sleep. What about your shift?

Clough. Laid down a pile of gunny sacks for a while, waitin' for the trucks to bring sand.

Mrs. Clough. Michael, what you been cryin' about?

Clough. We were playin'; he hit against the tree.

Mrs. Clough. Well, get in here for breakfast. Both of you. Michael.

Michael. [FADING] Yeah.

¶ SOUND: *screen door slams.*

Clough. Don't feel hungry. [WEARILY] Better sit 'fore I fall.

Mrs. Clough. [FADING IN] Go in and go to bed then.

Clough. Sit here on the saw horse. [SIGHS] Turned out a nice day.

Mrs. Clough. Will the people around here 'preciate your work after the flood?

Clough. Everybody's in the same boat.

Mrs. Clough. Anybody give you a job?

Clough. Not much work around here 'cept loggin'.

Mrs. Clough. First time we've been really settled; nice easy job for you ...

Clough. Whistle punk?

Mrs. Clough. Yes, whistle punk. If that was hard work — all you had to do, sit on a stump and press a button now and again, signal the donkey engineer to pull in the logs for loading. But you had to keep fallin' asleep.

Clough. It was them hot days.

Mrs. Clough. Easiest job in the world and you couldn't hang on to it. Live on the old age pension from now on, I suppose. Suit you fine. Sit all day on that saw horse, leanin' against the woodshed.

Clough. I'll get another job. Ain't I always managed? Three hundred jobs at least I've got various times . . .

Mrs. Clough. Somethin' to brag about, three hundred jobs, fired three hundred times.

Clough. Most of'm I quit.

Mrs. Clough. Got fired.

Clough. When I got fired it was 'cause I was too independent for'm. Told'm what's what.

Mrs. Clough. Big talk, do nothin'.

Clough. [DROWSILY] My life ain't over yet.

Mrs. Clough. If you're gonna fall asleep get in the house.

Clough. Do somethin' yet, surprise you.

Mrs. Clough. What, discover an oil well on your seventy-fifth birthday?

Clough. [DROPPING OFF TO SLEEP] Unjust world made for . . .

Mrs. Clough. Thought I was gonna have you help me with the washin', but you'll be snorin' all day. Wake up.

Clough. [COMING TO] What? One a these days . . .

Mrs. Clough. Yes, Mr. Big Plans, I believed in your talk once, that blather. Your life is over, David Clough.

Clough. You like feedin' the worms inside me, don't you?

Mrs. Clough. Kids workin' as whistle punks, but you couldn't do the job. So we move again.

Clough. If the hot spell keeps on and melts all that snow on the mountains everybody'll have to move. River up another foot 'n' a half last night, and the bridge's gone.

Mrs. Clough. The bridge gone? No.

Clough. We'll have to climb the cliff behind the village if the worst comes.

Mrs. Clough. What're the reports up the river?

Clough. Nobody's sayin' anymore when the crest'll come.

¶ SOUND: *screen door opened.*

Mrs. Clough. They be addin' more to the dike here?

Clough. If the big dike holds.

¶ SOUND: *screen door slammed.*

Michael. [WITH HIS MOUTH STUFFED, FADING IN] Timber, timber . . .

Mrs. Clough. Michael, go back in the house till you've finished your breakfast.

Clough. He's shakin' his food down so he can get more in, ain'tcha,

Michael?

Michael. Sure. [*SKIPPING*]
> A whiskey jack
> Will take and snap
> The food right outa your big mouth, Mac,
> Timber, timber . . .

Michael. Michael, you heard me.

Clough. Edna, bread'n' jam tastes better outdoors.

Mrs. Clough. Michael . . .

Michael. [*IMPISHLY*] There, it's all gone. Hah!

¶ SOUND: *a slap.*

Michael. [*SMOLDERING*] You old cow.

Mrs. Clough. Dave, you gonna let him talk to his mother like that?

Clough. [*JUST A FORMALITY*] Michael, don't swear at your momma. You know what we need for this bulldozer? The narrow chisel to carve it out a bit.

Michael. Yeah, okay.

Clough. It's in the box on the front verandah.

Michael. [*FADING*]
> A whiskey jack
> Will take and snap . . .

Mrs. Clough. All right, don't punish him, let him say whatever he likes to me.

Clough. Lost faith in punishment long time ago; sometimes wish God went in for less. But guess he looks down and says to himself: "Human beings: hatin' and destroyin'. Well, if 'at's what they want, I can show'm. Drown'm out!"

Mrs. Clough. Oh, sure, you got a direct line to God.

Clough. Anybody has if they wanta use it.

Mrs. Clough. You and Sadie Gillen.

Clough. Agh! She's a ranter, worships a dead god, worships words.

Mrs. Clough. You sound like her sometimes.

Clough. Her god ain't the god who created man.

Mrs. Clough. I'd like to meet the god who created you, give him a piece of my mind.

Clough. You approved, one time.

Mrs. Clough. Yeah, imagine. Well, I got Michael now, when he ain't under your influence.

Clough. You didn't want him.

Mrs. Clough. No, I'd already made up my mind to leave you: after puttin' up with you for twelve years.

Clough. You still wanna go? I'll look after Michael.

Mrs. Clough. You know I'd never leave him.

Michael. [FADING IN] Here's the chisel! We'll gouge out a seat for the driver.

Mrs. Clough. Don't run with that, Michael! You'll fall and cut yourself.

Michael. Gonna be the strongest bulldozer around here! Shape the blade in front first, Daddy.

Clough. Okay. Ah, that's a nice sun.

Michael. Yeah, probably be real corker 'safternoon.

Mrs. Clough. Who's this coming?

Michael. [ENTHUSIASTICALLY] Oh, guys gonna work on the dike here! I'll get my shovel. [FADING] Help'm fill the sand bags!

Mrs. Clough. What're they carrying? [WITH SHOCKED CONCERN] Oh, no . . . !

Clough. Lundquist . . .

Lundquist. [SOLEMN BUT EASY-GOING, HUSKY, MIDDLE-AGED LOGGER] We found her up the river, me and McKinnon.

McKinnon. [TOUCH OF SCOTTISH ACCENT, FORTY, FAIRLY EASY-GOING LOGGER] Wedged in between a rock and stump.

Clough. It's the Reneau girl.

Mrs. Clough. Cecile.

Lundquist. Cecile Reneau, that's who we thought.

McKinnon. Worked on her, but she was in the water too long. We were inspectin' the top end of the dike; Lundquist spotted her.

Michael. Is she dead?

Mrs. Clough. [FADING SLIGHTLY] Michael, you come here with Mamma.

Michael. [FADING] I ain't doin' nothin'.

Mrs. Clough. [SLIGHTLY OFF] Oh, hello, Vi. Look.

Mrs. Ennis. [FADING IN] Yes, I just happened to glance out my kitchen window and saw. It's Cecile Reneau.

Mrs. Clough. Yes.

Clough. Reneau was sayin' last night they'd moved outa their house into the village.

Mrs. Ennis. Stayin' with the Harrisons.

Clough. What she doin' up the river?

Mrs. Ennis. Maybe she went back for her kitten they left behind. She was makin' a fuss about it last night. I was over at the Harrisons.

McKinnon. Just about old enough to start havin' a boy friend.

Michael. The devil river get her?

Clough. Yeah, the devil river.

Mrs. Clough. [FADING] Michael, this's nothing for you. Come in the house with Mamma.

Lundquist. How're you, Dave? Get another job yet?

Clough. Yeah, Lundquist, on the dike.

McKinnon. Everybody's job now, eh?

Lundquist.   No pay.

McKinnon.   Lundquist, let's get on our way 'n' get this over with. [*FADING*] The sooner the better.

Lundquist.   [*FADING*] Good lookin' kid.

Clough.   [*WITH A TOUCH OF PROTEST*] Reneau's got four left.

Mrs. Ennis.   Oh, here comes Sadie Gillen. She don't miss much.

Sadie.   [*FADING IN, EXCITEDLY*] Oh, Mrs. Ennis, have you heard about the oldest Reneau girl?

Mrs. Ennis.   Yes, her they're carryin' past the woodshed.

Sadie.   Oh, dear! The ways of God . . .

Mrs. Ennis.   I suppose, Sadie, you'll be takin' some of your religious tracts to the Reneau's now.

Sadie.   Our bereavement one. Maybe it's all for the best. God has His plan. You never know what mighta happened to her, poor girl. She mighta ended up disgraced or something. God in His infinite mercy . . .

Clough.   Kills children. [*SARDONICALLY*] Yeah, kills children.

Sadie.   Mr. Clough, don't you believe in God's will?

Clough.   Yeah, in my god's will, not yours.

Sadie.   There is only one god. Suffer little children to come unto Me, and forbid them not. For such is the Kingdom of Heaven . . .

Clough.   Words, words, stop spoutin' words, woman. What do you know about God?

Sadie.   I know everything about God and my Master who suffered infinite pain for us.

Mrs. Ennis.   I'm sure, Sadie. Well, I think I better get cleaned up and go see Mrs. Reneau, [*FADING*] see what I can do for her.

Clough.   Nobody can do much, Mrs. Ennis.

Sadie.   O taste and see that the Lord is good; blessed is the man that trusteth in Him.

Clough.   Your god is a paper god, Sadie, nothin' but paper.

Sadie.   The Lord is my light and my salvation; whom shall I fear? The Lord is the strength of my life; of whom shall I be afraid?

Balla.   [*FADING IN*] You can be afraid of me, Sadie, if you wanta.

Sadie.   [*SNIPPY*] I'm not afraid of you, Mr. Kurt Balla. [*FADING*] The Lord God is my shield.

Balla.   Then what're you runnin' away for? [*LAUGHS*] I know what she needs, Clough. Sometimes that type's all right too.

Clough.   She wouldn't know how to handle a living god.

Balla.   Or a living man. With a shortage of women around the camp, that's what we find in Baldock.

Clough.   How come you ain't married yet, Balla?

Balla.   Am.

Mrs. Clough.   [*OFF*] Dave, I don't suppose I can expect any help with the washin' from you!

¶ SOUND: *window slammed down.*

Clough.   Huh, Balla, didn't know you were married.

Balla.   [*SLIGHTLY AMUSED*] Your wife sounds a bit put out.

Clough.   You have it like this?

Balla.   Oh, no, my wife and me hardly ever fight.

Clough.   Huh, no?

Balla.   She lives on the east coast and I live here in the west.

Clough.   One solution.

Balla.   Miss her sometimes. One a these days send her a telegram and tell her to come back. She ran away; she was scared I was gonna leave her so she ran away. She's livin' alone at Campbellton, and I'm livin' alone here — 'less you can call sleepin' with a buncha loggers in a bunkhouse some kinda family life.

Clough.   You caught here in the village when the bridge went out?

Balla.   Yeah, 'bout ten of us in boozin', Lundquist, McKinnon, the kid Lukasik, Moberg. . . . You movin' on to 'nother camp when the water goes down, Clough?

Clough.   Don't know what I'm gonna do.

Balla.   Plenty a work around here cleanin' up the mess after the flood. See that barn go by early this mornin'?

Clough.   Reneau lost a girl.

Balla.   Yeah, I was with Lundquist and McKinnon when they found her. Reneau just lost his father last month.

Clough.   One two: what's one two? I lost my whole family in one night. We was livin' in a shack. I came home from work: the bedsteads and the stove all that was left. Tess and three of the youngsters burned to . . . Second oldest girl got out, but she died later.

Balla.   This is your second wife then.

Clough.   I drifted for a long time after that. Edna thinks I'm still driftin'.

Balla.   We're all driftin'.

Clough.   You're not driftin', Balla. A high-rigger, you're at the top at the heap. You'll end up bull o' the woods. I can't even hold a job at the bottom of the heap: whistle punk.

Balla.   [*WITH A LAUGH*] All I need's one slip toppin' a spar tree and I'll be at the bottom of the heap.

Clough.   The only way it made sense, the fire: God was testin' me.

Balla.   Naw, it's a joke; life, death, marriage, and taxes.

Clough.   If I thought that, Balla — I'm seventy-four — I'd be inclined to . . .

¶ SOUND: *screen door pushed open.*

Michael.   [*SLIGHTLY OFF*] Daddy, the light fuse's blown and Mama wants you to put in a new one.

Clough.   What she want the lights for?

Michael.   She don't. It's for the washing machine.

Clough.   [*WITH A SIGH*] Yeah, okay, I'll come in and . . .

Balla.   Ain't the fuse, Dave. Power lines knocked out last night same time's the bridge.

Clough.   Tell your mamma the power's cut, Michael. It's not the fuse.

Michael.   No 'lectricity?

Clough.   No.

¶ SOUND: *screen door slammed.*

Balla.   That your grandson?

Clough.   No, son.

Balla.   Son? Clough, you're a better man'n I thought, havin'a kid that young.

Clough.   Didn't look like we was gonna have any kids. And then this fellah came along. All them years in between Michael and my other kids, they went by and I didn't notice.

Balla.   I'm s'posed to be roundin' up a gang from this end of the village to fill more sandbags.

Clough.   You want me now?

Balla.   [*FADING*] Naw, you worked all night. I'll get anough other guys. See you later, eh?

¶ SOUND: *screen door opened.*

Clough.   Yeah, Balla.

¶ SOUND: *screen door banged.*

Michael.   [*FADING IN*] Where's he goin', Daddy?

Clough.   Work on the dike.

Michael.   We gonna fix my bulldozer now?

Clough.   Yeah, okay. Where's that chisel?

Michael.   Fell on the ground. Here.

Clough.   Round this off a bit here . . .

Michael.   Don't take too much off.

Clough.   Don't worry, I'm the best woodcarver in British Columbia. Taught the Indians how to carve totem poles.

Michael.   [*LAUGHS*] Did not. You gonna put tracks on my bulldozer?

Clough.   We'll tack a coupla small pieces of wood on each side and shape them like tracks, eh?

Michael.   Sure! And put an exhaust pipe on top there.

Clough.   Oo! Keep your hands away; you lose a finger.

Michael.   Don't forget a seat for the driver.

Clough.   You gonna drive one of these when you grow up?

Michael.   Sure, and be a high rigger too.

Clough. That fellow, Balla, who just left's a high rigger.

Michael. Is he? Go up the spar tree?

Clough. Yep. One a the best high riggers around. Pretty dangerous job, Michael. You wanna do that?

Michael. I ain't scared.

Clough. Anything happened to you, I wouldn't believe in God no more, no kinda god. No god'd be worth prayin' to who'd go on snatching everything away!

Michael. Daddy, don't hold my arm so tight, you're hurtin' me.

Clough. Most a my life, driftin', runnin' away from something, lookin' for something . . . failin' at everything . . . starin' out at the horizon, starin' into the dark, starin' into the past, starin' into myself . . . gettin' used to emptiness, gettin' used to horror sweepin' over everthing like a flood.

Michael. Daddy, I don't wanta play that devil river game no more.

Clough. For sufferin' God ga'me you.

Michael. [*DEFENSIVELY PROTESTING*] I haven't done nothin'.

Clough. But if I gotta give you up . . .

Michael. Daddy, don't hurt me! Lemme go . . .

Clough. If God, the god we've made terrible again, demanded you, I'd stand up to him, put you behind me and defy him. Even if he said, "I'll not destroy Baldock if Dave Clough will give up his son," I'd say, "No!" [*FALLING OFF TO SLEEP*] I'd say — say uh . . . that . . . the uh . . .

¶ MUSIC: *sneaks into background: yearning and threatening.*

Michael. Daddy, you're leaning on me. Hey, Daddy, don't go to sleep. You're falling off the sawhorse. Daddy! Daddy, wake up. Carve this. Make my bulldozer — Daddy . . . !

¶ MUSIC: *snaps sharply, but not too loudly, and ends.*

Clough. [*JERKING UP, STARTLED*] Uh! Where — who — where uh . . . ?

Michael. What's wrong?

Clough. Oh, Michael . . .

Michael. Carve my bulldozer with the chisel. Come on, Daddy, you promised.

Clough. I dreamt something' was happen' to you. [*TRYING TO RECALL*] And I was told to go up along the river. Some threat — some — We should go right away. Come along. Michael!

Michael. Where?

Clough. Come along! We'll go the way that . . .

Michael. Wait, I wanna take my bulldozer!

Clough. All right, bring it.

¶ MUSIC: *sneaks into background: yearning and threatening.*

Clough. [*DRIVEN: FADING*] Don't know what we're s'posed to do, but we gotta go's far's we can up along the river to a rock — salvation . . . !

¶ MUSIC: *up into subtle salvation: levelling off and out.*

Mrs. Ennis. [*FADING IN*] Oh, you've got your washing done already, Edna.

Mrs. Clough. Gettin' there, Vi. It'll dry fast in this sun.

Mrs. Ennis. Wonderful day, except for the flood. Isn't it? Terrible day for the Reneaus though.

Mrs. Clough. You're dressed up. You been or just goin' to see them?

Mrs. Ennis. Been. They're takin' it very hard.

Mrs. Clough. I'll go along late this afternoon.

Mrs. Ennis. They laid Cecile out on a couch and fixed her hair. She looks beautiful.

Mrs. Clough. How's Mrs. Reneau?

Mrs. Ennis. They didn't know what they were gonna do with her for awhile; and no gettin' a doctor from town with the bridge out. They gave her a big glass of whiskey to dull her.

Mrs. Clough. And what about Mr. Reneau?

Mrs. Ennis. He just sits.

Mrs. Clough. Hand me a couple more of them clothes pins, Vi, will you?

Mrs. Ennis. I offered to take the children; the Harrisons'll have enough on their hands with Mr. and Mrs. Reneau. And then Mrs. Howard stepped in and said she'd take them. Isn't that like her? Didn't say a thing till I suggested it.

Mrs. Clough. Course she's just a few doors away from Harrisons.

Mrs. Ennis. Yeah, but why'n't she think of it first? A great one though for takin' the credit. Mrs. High Muckynuck! But what was she before she married George Howard? — a waitress in a Chinese cafe in Vancouver!

Mrs. Clough. Anything I can take the Reneaus?

Mrs. Ennis. I brought the kids some candy. Don't know what else we can do just now.

Mrs. Clough. Not much even you can . . .

Clough. [*AGGRESSIVELY, STARING WILDLY*] Agh!

¶ SOUND: *the snapping and ripping of a sheet on a line pulled sharply aside.*

Mrs. Ennis. [*GIVES A LITTLE STARTLED SHRIEK*] Oh! — Oh, Mr. Clough, you scared me.

Mrs. Clough. Dave, what's this nonsense, sneaking up like that and then scaring us, jerking one a the sheets aside like — ? And you've ripped it!

Clough. [*WILDLY*] Yeah, go ahead and say what you've got to say, Edna! But what you know about it?

Mrs. Clough. About what?

Clough. You'll never understand.

Mrs. Clough. Understand what?

Clough. He chose me. I stood up under his trial, I did his deed. But now I ain't big enough to go on, all I want' to lie in the woodshed and close the door.

Mrs. Clough. What you talkin' about?

Clough. Been lyin' in a hole under the roots of a tree blown down, but the sun come in.

Mrs. Clough. That's just fine for your arthritis. I told you to go in the house and go to bed. Now you'll be groanin' for a month.

Clough. The rest a my life.

Mrs. Clough. And serve you right.

Clough. [*LAUGHS*] Told you I'd do somethin' important someday.

Mrs. Clough. What's got into you?

Clough. Told you I was cut out for more'n — [*VAGUE AND GLAZED*] more than — more . . .

Mrs. Ennis. You haven't caught a fever, Mr. Clough?

Clough. [*STARING AT HER WITH GREAT CONCENTRATION*] Mrs. Ennis, you'd be in a fever too if you'd been commanded to commit the terriblest deed any man's committed since the Lord created the earth.

Mrs. Clough. [*EXASPERATED AND WEARY*] Oh, dear, another one of his religious spells. You've been in the presence of God again, I suppose.

Clough. I know now, Edna, I wasn't those other times.

Mrs. Clough. [*GIVES A DISGUSTED SIGH*] You see, Vi, what I have to put up with? Thank heaven this's the first spell since we moved here.

Clough. Only my imagination before when I felt his presence. Oh, but this — God was there beside me, big, higher'n the trees. Air was still, surrounded by a cyclone. The sun on the leaves stopped shimmering. And I felt joy and dread. There was God, come for me.

Mrs. Clough. Yeah, you're his special favorite.

Clough. I thought I was gonna die. A pain in my chest, and I felt I was the lowest, miserablest cuss that ever — God was more real than you now, though I couldn't see him.

Mrs. Clough. Stop it, Dave. What will Vi Ennis think?

Clough. And I said, "Lord God, I don't wanna die, I ain't done nothin' yet. Gimme more time, a little. There's more to me than just a whistle punk's spirit!" He didn't move.

Mrs. Clough. So you came home.

Clough. Michael pulled my arm and wanted to know who I was talkin' to.

Mrs. Clough. Dave, you're not gonna fill that boy with your crazy ideas.

Clough. [FADING] No. No . . .

Mrs. Clough. First thing you'll start acting like a Doukhobor, and wanna burn the house down.

Clough. [FADING IN AGAIN] Edna, don't make fun of the living god. You understand nothing, you understand nothing.

Mrs. Clough. Well, if you're silly enough to have God dropping in on you, you're silly enough to burn the house down.

Clough. [FADING] When God comes there's nothin' silly about it, Edna. The most awful . . .

¶ SOUND: *woodshed door creaks.*

Mrs. Clough. What're you goin' in the woodshed for?

Clough. [SLIGHLY OFF] To lie down and sleep.

Mrs. Clough. Are you completely out of your head? Go in the house.

Clough. I'm too humble now.

¶ SOUND: *woodshed door creaks shut.*

Mrs. Clough. Well, Vi, what you make of that? This's the wildest he's ever been about the god business.

Mrs. Ennis. S'pose it's losin' his job — and the flood.

Mrs. Clough. I've had seventeen years of it.

Mrs. Ennis. But he never goes to church.

Mrs. Clough. I don't encourage him. If the minister says something he don't agree with, he gets up and starts an argument. I had that twice just after we were married, and no more, thank you.

Ennis. [OFF] Vi! Vi!

Mrs. Ennis. Oh, that husband of mine now.

Ennis. [FADING IN] When're you gonna start gettin' a meal ready? [HE IS LETHARGIC AND ADENOIDAL] I got the water on, and the table's set. When're we gonna eat? You know I gotta be on dike duty by four.

Mrs. Ennis. Yes, I'll be right along, Fred. Just came from Harrisons.

Ennis. How's Reneau and his wife?

Mrs. Ennis. You can imagine.

Ennis. If we don't keep the dikes holdin' there'll be lotta other people in the same state.

Mrs. Ennis. Where're the children, Fred?

Ennis. Over in the lot playin'.

Mrs. Ennis. You go get them, and I'll have food ready in a jiffy.

Mrs. Clough. Is Michael with them?

Ennis. Michael? No, don't think so.

Mrs. Clough. Oh, yes, [FADING] he was with Dave.

151

¶ SOUND: *woodshed door opened.*

Mrs. Clough. Dave, where'd you leave Michael?
Clough. Leave me alone! Shut the door!

¶ SOUND: *firewood hitting the door frame.*

Mrs. Clough. What're you throwin' firewood at me for?
Clough. Don't wanna speak to nobody!

¶ SOUND: *a couple more pieces of firewood hit the door frame.*

Clough. I said shut the door!
Ennis. What's eatin' Dave?
Mrs. Clough. [*FADING IN AGAIN*] God.
Ennis. God?
Mrs. Clough. [*CALLING OUT*] David, be sensible. Do you know where Michael is?
Clough. Michael? God knows.
Ennis. What's this god stuff?
Mrs. Clough. Michael was with you, David. Why'n't you look after him? Wandering all over and the river the way it is.
Clough. I'm tryna imagine where he might be.
Mrs. Clough. And what you mean by that nonsense?
Clough. [*FADING IN*] Do I talk nonsense? Am I silly? Is God playin' with me, makin' a fool outa me?
Mrs. Clough. I'm thinkin' of what happened to Cecile Reneau. Where's Michael? He was with you last.
Clough. God said, "Dave Clough, take your son and lift him up on this white rock." I did. And God said, "You are fond of the boy?" And I said, "Yes, Lord, I love him above everything." "Above your God?" I was afraid then.
Mrs. Ennis. Where is Michael now?
Clough. God said, "Lay the boy down, Dave Clough." I didn't budge. "Do you fear your God, Dave Clough?" "I do, Lord God." "Then lay the boy down, so I can be a living god again." "Will this save Baldock from the flood, Lord God?" "Lay the boy down, Dave Clough." God was all around. I took hold of Michael and laid him on the rock, and he said, "Daddy, what you gonna do?" And God said, "Offer him up," and the chisel was in my hand. I flung it out into the river, but it hit a branch and bounced back on the rock beside me. God said, "Dave Clough, you must sacrifice your son if I'm to be a god among men!" I picked up the chisel, and Michael shouted, "Daddy, Daddy!" and I killed him.
Mrs. Clough. If that's your idea of a story, Dave — but what the purpose is, I . . .

152

Clough.   An act to prove my faith. But God didn't hold back my hand like he did Abraham's, and catch a ram by the horns for me. He took my son.

Ennis.   [NOT SURE WHAT TO THINK] Dave, get off the pitch. Your wife'll . . .

Clough.   Then God went away. I called out to him, "God, come back! Gimme back my son! What you need him for? Gimme him back! You've taken all my kids!" He didn't come back.

Mrs. Clough.   David, where is Michael?

Clough.   His husk is on the rock.

Mrs. Ennis.   He's imagining it, Edna. Something's happened to him, but he wouldn't do that.

Ennis.   The boy's off somewhere playin' by himself. He'll . . .

Mrs. Clough.   [DISTRACTEDLY] Oh, God, he's all right, he's all right, he's all right, but we've got to find him.

Ennis.   Dave, where's this rock?

Clough.   The white rock, at the sharp bend up the river.

Ennis.   Near where that old stone chimney stands?

Clough.   [VAGUELY] Chimney? Yeah, a chimney there.

Ennis.   Used to be a cabin. Burnt down.

Mrs. Clough.   [GROANS] Oh . . .

Mrs. Ennis.   Edna. Nothing to worry about.

Mrs. Clough.   Why you doin' this, Dave?

Ennis.   Mrs. Clough, I'll go up the river and take a look.

Mrs. Clough.   I'm going too.

Mrs. Ennis.   No, you say here, Edna. Let Fred go. I'm sure there's nothing to this, but he'll check. Go on, Fred.

Mrs. Clough.   I can't stay here.

Ennis.   [FADING] I won't be long.

Mrs. Clough.   [BESEECHINGLY] David, tell me the truth . . .

Clough.   Tess, I thought I could save you and the kids this way.

Mrs. Clough.   I am not Tess.

Clough.   I'm tryna find the meanin' . . .

Mrs. Clough.   [PLEADING] Speak to me sensibly, tell me what you've done.

Clough.   Nothing more to worry about, [LAUGHS] what else can happen? We're free of God now, Tess, a terrible god without mercy or meaning.

Mrs. Clough.   He don't know me.

Clough.   If I wanna speak to Tess and pretend you're her, why can't I? There a law?

Balla.   [CALLING OFF] Here's 'nother place we oughta raise the dike, guys.

Sankey.   [ALSO OFF: MIDDLE FORTIES: HE HAS A NARROW, VINDICTIVE

PERSONALITY] Yeah, Balla.

Craig. [*ALSO OFF: MIDDLE THIRTIES: PLEASANT, SOMETIMES DIDACTIC*] Be over the top here in no time if we don't get at it.

Mrs. Clough. Vi, they don't need to know.

Mrs. Ennis. Maybe they've run into Fred.

Balla. [*FADING IN, BUT NOT COMING RIGHT UP*] Well . . . s'pose you won't mind us puttin'a bit more to the dike here?

Mrs. Clough. [*WITH COLD CALM*] No, go ahead.

¶ SOUND: *working sounds occasionally.*

Balla. Clough, you've had a chance to get some shuteye. You give us a hand now? Rise in the last coupla hours don't look good. Up where the old tradin' post used to be she's broke through.

Moberg. [*SLIGHTLY OFF: FAT AND WITH BULLYING TENDENCIES*] Flooded right back to the cliff.

Balla. Ridge a rock only thing kept it from comin' this way.

Sankey. Saw your husband, Mrs. Ennis, goin' up that way on the road when we were comin' down along the dike. What's up there?

Balla. Ennis, he's s'posed to be with this gang.

Mrs. Ennis. He'll be back soon.

Balla. Get much worse we'll be callin' out the women to lend a hand on the dikes.

Lukasik. [*SLIGHLY OFF: BULL GANG KID, ZOOTY*] The dames get called out, Balla, I know one I'd like ta get in our gang.

Moberg. Yeah, we know, Lukasik. Out in the woods all you ever talk about is dames, but get you in town with the dames: all you talk about is logs.

Lukasik. Yeah, and all you talk about, Moberg, is trucks.

Craig. [*FADING IN*] Hey, Clough, we use your wheelbarrow to bring the bags a sand up here?

Clough. Take it, take it, take everything. You think it'll do you any good? Take my clothes if you want them. There's my coat.

Craig. What do I want your coat for?

Clough. And you can have my shirt too [*STRUGGLING WITH IT*] if I can get it — it . . .

Mrs. Clough. Dave, what you doing? You've made enough fuss already. For heaven's sake, behave. I can't stand any more.

Clough. I know what I'm doin'.

Mrs. Clough. David!

Mrs. Ennis. Mr. Clough.

Sankey. [*LAUGHS*] What's he gonna do, a striptease?

Clough. [*FLOWERING WITH ANGRY CONTEMPT*] Sankey, tryna be humble is something' filthy to you.

Sankey. You think you can give me a thrill?

Balla. Take it easy, Sankey. [*FADING IN*] What's wrong, Dave?

Clough. I just done something.

Mrs. Ennis. Edna, don't you think we should take him into the house?

Clough. God's meaning ain't always clear at first. We gotta puzzle it out.

Mrs. Ennis. Why don't you go in the house, Mr. Clough?

Clough. No, that house is too good for me.

Balla. What is it, Clough?

Clough. Balla, you're the only one around here with a head on your shoulders. Not Craig, the school teacher, and not Sankey, the junk dealer, and . . .

Sankey. I'm not a junk dealer. I'm hardware.

Clough. Rusty hardware. Balla, I just killed my boy Michael. You saw him. God come and told me to do it and I did.

Mrs. Ennis. He's imagining it. He's . . .

Clough. [*FURIOUS*] I'm not! Stabbed him with the chisel! But why'd God want that? Abraham's trial was nothin' . . .

Balla. Clough, you still whacked out from last night. Walkin' around havin' nightmares. Go lie down.

Lukasik. The old boy off his rocker?

Mrs. Clough. If he's hurt the boy I'll kill him.

Mrs. Ennis. That's not true. Fred'll be back soon.

Balla. He very fond of the kid, eh?

Clough. Ain't no more bad things can happen to me.

Sankey. Balla, you're the guy gets fussed up about us not keepin' at it, and there you are gassin' away . . .

Balla. Aw, don't get your shirt in a knot, Sankey. Clough, take it easy, eh? [*FADING*] Okay, guys, bear down! Everybody at it!

Lukasik. Aw, no different from bein' on the bull gang up at the camp. Even same boss barkin'.

Balla. [*LAUGHS*] Only ain't no pay for gettin' pushed around here, Lukasik. Fill your shovel up or you'll never get that bag filled.

Clough. When I was a little boy there was a god in the world. I tried to bring him back.

Mrs. Clough. [*DESPERATELY*] I can't stand it! [*FADING*] Have to find Michael. Maybe the other kids'll know something.

Mrs. Ennis. [*FADING*] Edna, where you goin'?

Clough. [*RELAXED WITH EYES CLOSED*] God ain't around now. Why'n't he stay and explain? Mum after the fire too. Bodies like charred roots of trees. And god silent. Blood curling down the rocks streaking the water. Lord God, you spared Isaac, but you took my son. You guys, what I done, does it make you believe in God, in a living god?

Lukasik. No, in fairies.

Clough.   God ordered me to do it to shock you. Did it in His name.

Craig.   Birds of a feather, Clough. I bombed cities in His name. Padre even came along once.

Clough.   I had enough faith to offer up my only son.

Lukasik.   Hallelujah!

Clough.   There's the deed to prove my faith! The Lord God commanded! I obeyed.

Moberg.   Glory hallelujah!

Balla.   Break up the revival meeting and get this dike built.

Clough.   Building it up ain't an act of faith, Balla.

Balla.   Come on, hurry up with them bags.

Moberg.   Aw, stuff it, Balla, we ain't in the army.

Balla.   Moberg, I wished I'da had you in my platoon.

Moberg.   Next war maybe you in mine.

Balla.   Next war I'm gonna be a civilian.

Sankey.   [*STRAINING*] If I ain't got a rupture I'll get one 'fore we finish with this flood.

Lukasik.   Huh, lookut the old whistle punk droppin' off to sleep in a wink just like he used to on the job.

Balla.   Bring some more bags over here.

Craig.   Oh, here comes Fred Ennis back.

Sankey.   Wet to the waist.

Balla.   Pack in around them bags.

Sankey.   What happened to you, Ennis?

Ennis.   [*FADING IN*] Got cut off, water shot in behind me. This dike ain't gonna be high enough for very long.

Balla.   What you find out about Clough's kids?

Ennis.   Nothin'. The rock where he was s'posed to be's under a foot a water now.

Balla.   Yet get close? Any sign of the kid?

Ennis.   No, and I don't think Clough'd do a thing like that.

Craig.   Oh, here come the women back.

Mrs. Ennis.   [*FADING IN*] Fred, we saw you comin' long the dike. What'd you find out?

Ennis.   He wasn't there.

Mrs. Clough.   Oh, thank God, thank God . . .

Mrs. Ennis.   But you haven't found him?

Ennis.   No.

Mrs. Clough.   Where is Dave?

Ennis.   Over there on his saw horse. Dozed off.

Mrs. Ennis.   I'm sure he made it all up.

Mrs. Clough.   Boastin' and lyin'. Only one who knows anything, and look at him, biggest failure in Baldock. Be a tramp if I didn't keep at him. Made him a home and — but I'm just about at the end of my tether.

Clough. [*SLIGHTLY OFF: GRUNTS A COUPLE OF TIMES IN HIS SLEEP*]
Mrs. Clough. Lookut the old fool.
Ennis. He's gonna fall off the saw horse. I better prop him up.

¶ SOUND: *fade in rattling fenders of a bicycle.*

Mrs. Clough. No, leave him, Fred. Let'm fall. Do him good.

¶ SOUND: *bicycle bell.*

Mrs. Ennis. Oh, Mr. McBirney, them my groceries?
McBirney. [*STILL A BIT OFF*] Yes, Mrs. Ennis.
Mrs. Ennis. What you doin' delivering on the bicycle? Where's your boy Ken?
McBirney. [*FADING IN*] He was just ready to leave with them when — uh — So I thought I better come myself. So I hopped on Ken's bike. Mrs. Clough . . .

¶ SOUND: *out.*

Mrs. Clough. Yes?
McBirney. I hate to be the one who . . .
Mrs. Clough. [*SHE KNOWS ALREADY*] Michael.
McBirney. Yeah. Some kids found him washed up just the other side of the big dike.
Mrs. Clough. [*TRYING TO DEADEN HER FEELINGS*] No . . . some other . . . no, not Michael . . .
Mrs. Ennis. Drowned?
McBirney. Stabbed half a dozen times.
Mrs. Clough. [*SCREAMS*] David!
Clough. [*GIVES A CONFUSED AND STARTLED GRUNT*]

¶ SOUND: *saw horse overturning with some clatter: all sound of working has ceased.*

Clough. [*LETS OUT A LITTLE CRY AND THEN GROANS*] Wh-what? Wh-what happened?
Mrs. Clough. It's true!
Clough. What? [*STRAINING*] Help me up. What's true?
Mrs. Clough. You've killed Michael! [*SHE GOES OFF INTO HYSTERICAL CRYING*]
Clough. You believe me now.
Ennis. Dave what kind of a . . . ?
Sankey. [*A BIT OFF*] The dirty, filthy, jerkin' son of a so and so . . .
Clough. [*CONSOLINGLY*] Edna . . .
Mrs. Clough. No!
Clough. I feel as bad, Edna. I struggled against God, I tried to turn the chisel in on myself.

Mrs. Clough. [*WHIMPERING*] Michael, my baby, my boy . . . he was my life and now he's my death.

Clough. And mine, Edna.

Mrs. Clough. Murderer!

Clough. No, No . . .

Sankey. [*FADING IN*] What you call it, Clough?

Clough. God's will.

Moberg. [*FADING IN*] That the alibi you're gonna use in court?

Clough. You think you can try God in a court?

Lukasik. [*FADING IN*] You God now?

Clough. I am a warning from him, to remind you, all of you, that he is a living and terrible god.

Mrs. Clough. [*SHUDDERING*] Oh, I can't stand his voice. Make him stop, make him — ! My Michael, my . . .

Mrs. Ennis. Catch her!

McBirney. Oh, dear!

Mrs. Ennis. She's fainted. Can you carry her into the house?

McBirney. Yes, Mrs. Ennis. [*FADING*] You go ahead and open the door.

Clough. [*FADING*] I'll do it.

Ennis. No, you'd better stay out here, Dave.

Clough. [*IN AGAIN*] She's my wife.

¶ SOUND: *screen door opened off.*

Ennis. Don't think she wants to see you just now.

Clough. Why not?

Moberg. [*HOOTS*] Hah, why not!

¶ SOUND: *screen door closed.*

Clough. [*WITH A TOUCH OF ANGER*] Yes, why not?

Sankey. Man, you just murdered her kid, ain't you?

Clough. 'Zat what you believe? 'Zat what you all believe?

Balla. Who's this coming?

Lukasik. Looks like Lundquist and McKinnon. — Yeah, 'tis.

Moberg. And Sadie Gillen.

Lundquist. [*OFF*] Where's Clough?

Craig. [*OFF*] There.

Lundquist. [*FADING IN*] McBirney from the store's been here and told you, eh? Who you think done it?

Sadie. [*FADING IN*] Oh dear, where's poor Mrs. Clough?

McKinnon. [*FADING IN*] We'll string the rat up for you, Clough, when we find him.

Sankey. Clough did it himself.

McKinnon. Oh, you've caught the guy! Where is he?

Balla. Clough killed his own son.

McKinnon. What you mean?

Clough. Stabbed the boy with a chisel.

Lundquist. You wouldn't do that, Dave.

Clough. Lemme go to my wife.

Sankey. Maybe he wants to stab her too. Hey, see if he's still got the chisel on him.

Clough. Don't know what I did with it . . .

Lukasik. No, nothin' on him.

Moberg. What's this?

Clough. [DEEPLY CONCERNED] No, don't take that, Michael made that. Gimme it!

Moberg. Yeah? What's it s'posed to be?

Clough. Bulldozer.

Balla. Give it back to him, Moberg.

Moberg. A bulldozer . . . ?

Clough. Give it to me. It's my boy's.

Moberg. Okay . . .

Sankey. No, I'll take it. Why we care what he wants? — a killer. Take his little keepsake and . . .

¶ SOUND: *stamping on wooden toy on rock to smash it.*

Sankey. . . . smash it!

Clough. [BEYOND HIMSELF] Sankey! You do that to Michael's toy? [TUSSLING] Broke it! What you do that for? Gimme that bulldozer! Gimme it!

Balla. Easy, Dave, easy.

Clough. Sankey, gimme that bulldozer!

Sankey. Okay, go fetch it outa the river.

¶ SOUND: *slight splash.*

Moberg. Why'n' we throw Clough in too?

Lukasik. Yeah, why don't we?

Sankey. Yeah, into the river with him!

Lundquist. Hold on, you guys, it ain't up to us, it's up to the police.

Balla. Yeah, lay off, Moberg.

Moberg. Why?

Balla. Any punishment, up to the courts.

Clough. The courts, they'll find me guilty, I know they will.

Moberg. Well, then?

Clough. Courts don't believe in God.

Craig. Make you swear by him.

Clough. Their laws don't reckon with a living god, who demands uh — God is fed up with us! I've faced the worst, but you guys still got your worst ahead a you. God is fed up with people everywhere, that's why he sent this flood.

McKinnon. Flood ain't everywhere.

Clough. Other places God'll have other ways.

Sadie. Yes, God speaks in many ways. We're all sinners with our evil thoughts and evil deeds! Now He's coming down the river to destroy us.

Balla. Dave, you've converted Sadie Gillen anyway.

Moberg. Aw, she's always had God in her gullet.

Sadie. We've strayed far from Thee! Take us, take us in Your arms, take us, we are Thine, oh God!

Moberg. [*GRINNING*] Yeah, I know what she wants.

Sadie. Oh, God, forgive us our evil deeds and thoughts. Forgive Mr. Clough for killing his boy . . .

Clough. Shut up, you ranter, Sadie! What had God to forgive? It was his will!

Lukasik. [*LAUGHS*] Hah! Mix it up you two.

Balla. Guys, what about the dike? The flood ain't stoppin' for this.

Craig. What do we do with Clough?

McKinnon. Lock him up somewheres.

Sankey. Don't know why we need wait for the police — or the courts — to take care of him.

Moberg. Neither do I!

Lukasik. Me neither!

Clough. You don't believe me. Don't none of you people? I did it to help. You gotta believe me: God has come back among us. I was in his presence — his glorious, terrible presence! — and he took my son.

Moberg. Shut up!

Clough. You shouldn't be judging me, but listening to God. Maybe he took my son to — we are too numb to notice anything less horrible — so you'd notice him.

Sankey. Stop tryna hide behind God.

Clough. I'm not trying to — to . . .

Moberg. You are!

Lukasik. Murder a kid!

Clough. I tell ya, I'm more horrified than any of you. Oh, my son, Michael! I don't feel saved, I don't feel blessed, only a great emptiness and weight. But there must be a meaning. Why did God — ? I been tussling with it all this — it just gets heavier — thicker — a fog I can't grab hold of anything in.

¶ MUSIC: *sneaks in: suggesting the boys closing in menacingly to the end of the scene.*

Sankey. Maybe we can clear things up for you.

Moberg. Yeah, we'll fix you up, Clough. You'll know the score when we're finished with you.
Craig. Killin' his own kid . . .
Lundquist. Guys, guys, don't hurt him.
Lukasik. Well, Clough . . .
Moberg. Guys . . . ?
Sankey. Yeah, grab him!

¶ MUSIC: *up into the grabbing: level off and out.*

¶ SOUND: *suddenly: angry pounding on a shed door.*

Clough. [ANGRY, SLIGHTLY MUFFLED] Open this damn door or I'll break it down! Open it! Open it!
Lundquist. [COMPLAINING IN A FRIENDLY WAY] Aw, for Moses' sake, Dave, you were quiet and slept when Lukasik and Ennis were here, but ever since I came on guard you been yellin' and pounding.
Clough. Well, lemme out, Lundquist, and I'll be quiet! Locked up in my own woodshed!
Lundquist. Better'n bein' strung up like some of the boys wanted, ain't it?
Clough. Lemme out, Lundquist.
Lundquist. I can't!
Clough. Why can'tcha?
Lundquist. Go to sleep. Still dark out. They hauled a couch in there for you. More'n your guards got. Just this sawhorse to sit on.

¶ SOUND: *pounding becomes more violent.*

Clough. I'll get out! I'll break the door down!
Lundquist. [FRIENDLY] Dave, I don't wanta get tough with you.
Clough. Get tough! You bloody Swede! Open the door and come in and get tough!
Lundquist. I got a rifle here, you know.
Clough. Then use it!

¶ SOUND: *more furious pounding.*

Lundquist. Clough! Clough!
Clough. Shoot! Fire away! Kill me!
Lundquist. The way you behave, maybe you are off your rocker. That's why I can't let you out.

¶ SOUND: *pounding stops.*

Clough. Off my rocker? How?
Lundquist. That's what the others say. Senile.
Clough. And you say it too, don't you, or you'd let me out. Off my

rocker 'cause I believe in a god who cares about us.

Lundquist. I think you're awright, Clough, but I don't know why you
. . .

¶ SOUND: *furious pounding again.*

Lundquist. You'll have that door off if you don't stop.

Clough. Lemme out! Lundquist! Lemme out!

Lundquist. Okay, okay, I'll open up. Take it easy.

¶ SOUND: *catch pulled back: pounding stops: woodshed door creaks open.*

Clough. 'Bout time.

Lundquist. Putthat hunk a firewood down. I don't wanta have to tie
you up.

Clough. Like a criminal or a madman?

Lundquist. Yeah.

¶ SOUND: *piece of wood dropped.*

Clough. Sky's lighting up a bit.

Lundquist. Clough, if you'll stay inside the doorway I'll leave it open
for you.

Clough. I wanna go and see Michael.

Lundquist. They haven't brought him here.

Clough. Why not?

Lundquist. Thought it'd be too hard on your wife. Woman next door's
stayin' the night with her.

Clough. Mrs. Ennis?

Lundquist. Yeah.

Clough. So where is he?

Lundquist. They've got him in a root cellar behind the empty house on
Siwash Street.

Clough. He ain't a turnip.

Lundquist. It's cool. They can't bury him till the police've seen him.

Clough. So I'm a criminal — Oh, dike's had another coupla rows of
bags added to it. River still risin'?

¶ SOUND: *screen door slaps shut.*

Lundquist. That you, Mrs. Ennis?

Mrs. Clough. [FADING IN] No. It's me.

Clough. Oh, Edna. How you feeling, dear?

Mrs. Clough. You are very considerate to ask, David . . .

Clough. I was . . .

Mrs. Clough. After killing my child and me.

Clough. I loved Michael as much as you. I did it, Edna, to help the
people here in Baldock — in the whole world.

162

Mrs. Clough. What a kind and considerate monster.

Clough. A monster, me? How can you . . . ?

Mrs. Clough. There ain't been many fathers who could kill their children.

Clough. No, there been more mothers.

Mrs. Clough. When their men been cruel to them.

Clough. The man's always to blame, eh?

Mrs. Clough. It's his world. Ain't I followed you around, makin' do with what you provided, puttin' up with your dreamin' and gassin' about peace and god and mankind and one world . . . ? 'N' this's how it ends.

Clough. Edna, I've thought and thought about the sacrifice you and me've . . .

Mrs. Clough. Whistle punk thoughts.

Clough. Don't sneer, Edna.

Mrs. Clough. [ALMOST OUT OF HER MIND] Don't kill children, David!

Lundquist. Don'tcha think you'd better go inside again, Mrs. Clough?

Mrs. Clough. My boy isn't in there.

Lundquist. Go on back in. Dave upsets you too much.

Clough. 'At's what God wants. When you gonna get upset, Lundquist, you cold, dumb Swede? Even God in his despair had to nail his son on a cross to — to get the . . .

Mrs. Clough. You and God. You and . . . [LAUGHS PAINFULLY]

Clough. God is with us as much now as he was in Moses' time, and Abraham's, and . . .

Mrs. Clough. You and the devil. I shoulda known after killing off your first family you'd turn on Michael and me someday.

Clough. Killing them? How can you say that?

Mrs. Clough. What about the bucket of ashes?

Clough. What bucket of ashes?

Mrs. Clough. That you left on the back stoop and the wind fanned up.

Clough. Wunt no bucket of ashes.

Mrs. Clough. You told me about them one night.

Clough. No, never.

Mrs. Clough. [SADISTICALLY NICE] You couldn't remember where you'd left the ashes when you cleaned out the stove before you went to work. You thought maybe you'd left them on the back stoop . . .

Clough. Never worried about no bucket. Always dumped the ashes in the snow and covered them up.

Mrs. Clough. But not that time.

Clough. There was no bucket after the fire.

Mrs. Clough. You looked for it, didn't you? You were afraid you didn't dump the ashes in the snow that night, that night . . .

Clough. If I left them on the stoop and set fire to the shack, Edna, how could I a gone on living?

Mrs. Clough. Yes, how could you? How can you now?

Clough. I ain't been draggin' a bucket a ashes around all these years — hah, but it's been like that. I had a lotta hope once, even studied arithmetic at home on my own. I was in line for a foreman's job at the factory — and then the fire. Slowed me right down. Nothin' but failure ever since, 'n' things being destroyed; almost as if I was draggin' a bucket of ashes around with me everywhere. Thought Michael got me free of all that. Sure, was free! Wanted to do something, wanted to help mankind . . . !

¶ SOUND: *rifle cocked.*

Lundquist. Mrs. Clough . . . what're you doing with that rifle? Give it to me.

Mrs. Clough. No.

Clough. Edna, what's that for?

Mrs. Clough. Michael.

Lundquist. Mrs. Clough, give me the rifle.

Clough. Edna, don't.

Mrs. Clough. It's not so good to die, is it?

Clough. I'm not afraid, Edna, but I got a mission.

Mrs. Clough. You took mine.

¶ SOUND: *rifle shot.*

Lundquist. [*LUNGING*] Gimme that rifle!

Clough. [*HOLDING HIS OWN AFTER THE SHOCK*] I told you, dear, I got a mission.

Lundquist. You're not hit, Dave?

Clough. God pushed the bullet aside.

Mrs. Clough. [*BREAKS DOWN AND WEEPS UNCONTROLLABLY*]

Balla. [*FADING IN*] What's up?

Lundquist. Nothin', Balla.

Balla. Somebody just fire a shot.

Lundquist. Yeah, I did, accidently. Mrs. Clough, won't you go back in the house?

Mrs. Clough. Why is he still alive?

Lundquist. [*FADING*] Come along.

¶ SOUND: *screen door opened.*

Mrs. Ennis. [*SLIGHTLY OFF*] Oh, Edna, how did you get out here? I heard a shot. What was it?

Lundquist. [*SLIGHTLY OFF*] Nothing, Mrs. Ennis. My rifle went off accidently. Will you take Mrs. Clough in?

Mrs. Ennis. Yes. How'd you get out on me?

Clough. [*CALLING AFTER HIS WIFE KINDLY*] Edna, I'm sorry we didn't do better together.

Mrs. Clough. [*OFF SLIGHTLY*] What kinda god is it who protects you, but not your kids?

¶ SOUND: *screen door slaps shut, then door is closed.*

Balla. An accident? Then why's everybody actin' kinda peculiar?

Lundquist. [*FADING IN*] What we got to shoot at, Balla?

Balla. What's Clough runnin' around loose for?

Lundquist. Just to quiet him down. Makin' a fuss in the shack. Woulda broke the door down.

Balla. What his wife want?

Clough. [*FADING*] She'll never understand.

Lundquist. Hey, where you goin', Clough?

Clough. [*SLIGHTLY OFF*] Sit on this rock.

Balla. You can go, Lundquist. I'll take over.

Lundquist. River ain't risin' quite so fast now.

Balla. Almost levelled off. But I'm still worried about the big dike, the pressure on her.

Lundquist. They add any more to her during the night?

Balla. Crew workin' when I came by just now. She might hold, she might go.

Clough. God is waitin' for you people to make up your minds. You gonna go on in your old ways?

Balla. Clough, the Catholic Church, the United Church, the Seventh Day Adventists, the Salvation Army and Youth for Christ, they all worked this territory. You think you be any more successful?

Lundquist. Guess I should clean the barrel of that rifle.

Balla. I'll do it, Lundquist. There a pull-through in this butt?

¶ SOUND: *a click.*

Balla. Yeah.

Lundquist. I'll push off then.

Balla. Who takes over from me?

Lundquist. [*FADING*] McKinnon, I think. 'Night.

Balla. Well, Dave . . .

Clough. [*FADING IN*] What is well?

Balla. Oh, I d'know. Just tryna be sociable.

Clough. Did you say the river's levelled off?

Balla. Yeah, ain't gone up more'n an inch in the last six, eight hours. Go over to the dike and look.

Clough. Don't wanna look.

165

Balla. [*WITH A GRIN*] No, what good news for everybody else's bad news for you. Soon's we make contact with the other side again — then . . .

Clough. The stupid police and the godless courts.

Balla. Wish I could help you, Clough.

Clough. No, you don't believe I'm God's instrument.

Balla. Sadie Gillen believes you are. You got one convert.

Clough. For you, Balla, everything is a joke.

Balla. Only way to survive maybe.

Clough. My deed is a joke?

Balla. Yeah, when I don't think of the little boy. I seen too many smashed-up kids in the war to feel the same's a lotta people in this village're feeling about your deed. The people in Baldock've killed a good many kids, and they're gettin' ready to kill a lot more. But they do it second hand, so they sleep okay in their beds, snoring. They send the young fellahs out to do the killin'. People in enemy villages do the same, and sleep just as peacefully. Their fancy reasons for killing often ain't any bettern'n yours, Dave. Tell you what: I'll give you a sportin' chance, if you wanna fly to coop, vamoose.

Clough. Fly the coop how? We're cut off.

Balla. Make a dash for it while I'm cleanin' this rifle. I'll say, didn't have the chance to take a pot shot at him. Get a log to hang on to and push out into the river.

Clough. I'm too old, you know that. Why do you play with me?

Balla. Sure, water's cold, or you might get smashed against a rock, but there's a chance to might make the other side.

Clough. I got a mission, I can't run away.

Balla. They'll find you insane or guilty of murder.

Clough. No, I gotta convince them!

Balla. [*LAUGHS*] Yeah, I can see all the professionals in the god business comin' to your support, and then all their flocks . . .

Clough. Balla, why'n't' you believe I stood in the presence of God?

Balla. I'm slow in the head. I used to believe everything I was told, but now I'm slow in the head. Go on, into the river before I get this gun cleaned and have to fire at you.

Clough. Well, maybe it would — if I — no, I gotta stay. My mission. Gotta persuade — try — if I can't persuade them . . .

Balla. Would be a joke, Clough, if you started a religious revival. The whistle punk of Baldock. "I was around the day he had his vision." But what I know a religious revivals you can have'm. The elect killin' off all the mudheads like me.

Clough. Gettin' light, the stars're goin'. Maybe the stars are God's thoughts.

Balla. Yeah, can't stand up to the light a day.

166

Clough.   Balla, if you'd let God speak to you . . .

Balla.   Any time he feels like it, but what little I know a him I think we'd disagree.

Clough.   [*PUZZLED, BUT QUIETLY*] Blood on my — my front all over blood. Where'd it . . . ?

Balla.   So you were shot? Who did it? Why you been hiding it?

Clough.   Didn't feel it before. My stomach.

Balla.   Lemme see.

Clough.   Gonna die without persuadin' anybody. Why's God doin' this?

Balla.   Easy, take it easy, sit down. Mmm, neat hole.

Clough.   What's Michael died for?

Balla.   I've seen too many knocked off; I stopped asking why.

Clough.   Wasn't for nothing.

Balla.   Why not?

Clough.   You gonna have your fun with me now?

Balla.   No.

¶ SOUND: *cloth ripping.*

Balla.   Make a plug outa the bottom of your shirt, try'n' stop the bleeding.

Clough.   Maybe it's good I'm gonna die.

Balla.   Maybe. Here, hold that wad there with your hand.

Clough.   If I offered Michael up for nothing — if I killed him . . .

Balla.   Like dyin' on the battlefield, Clough, wonderin' what you're fightin' for.

Clough.   What if Edna's right and it was the devil I met by the river? What if I have been draggin' a bucket of ashes around all these years? — still got hold of it. Maybe there's nothing to me, Balla, but destruction and failure.

Balla.   Maybe.

Clough.   I murdered the boy. Take this wad! Lemme go. Bleed.

Balla.   Dave!

Clough.   No, I'm fine.

Balla.   Don't stand up!

Clough.   Why not, why not?

McKinnon.   [*FADING IN*] Hey, what's up, Balla, you havin' trouble with Clough?

Balla.   No, McKinnon. He's been shot.

McKinnon.   Who did it?

Clough.   I did it.

Mrs. Clough.   [*OFF*] No, I shot him.

Clough.   No, Edna, let it be that I did it myself.

Mrs. Clough.   [*FADING IN*] Why should I hide I shot you?

167

Clough. If there's no living god, then you did right, Edna. McKinnon, how's the river?

McKinnon. Droppin'. Ain't you looked? Dropped six inches during the night.

Balla. When'd this start?

Clough. Dropped. Balla, I wanna see. Gimme a hand.

Balla. No, sit down.

Clough. McKinnon, you gimme a hand then, lemme lean on you. Hurry!

Balla. Okay, we'll both help you over.

McKinnon. Guess the crest is passed.

Clough. Down six inches . . .

McKinnon. See the high water mark there above the . . .

Balla. More'n six inches.

Clough. 'N' where's God?

Mrs. Clough. Sorry the water's goin' down, David? You'd like to see us all destroyed.

Clough. No, Edna, no. I was afraid God was gonna punish us for all the — but looks like he don't give a hoot.

Balla. So we go right on. Maybe your god's dead.

Clough. No. But so far away . . .

Balla. Good's dead, eh?

Clough. Bella, McKinnon, don't let'm do anything to Edna. It was all my doing. Mine, not God's, *mine*. We're on our own. Alone. And the way of God is — is . . .

Mrs. Clough Some fool idea thought up by fools like you. [*BITTERLY*] God's way, the only way.

Clough. Edna, I'm a man with a bucket of ashes, and that's all, eh?

¶ SOUND: *a splash.*

Balla. Thrown himself in!

McKinnon. Grab him! Can you?

¶ SOUND: *minor splashing.*

Balla. Ah, got him. . . . He's dead.

¶ MUSIC: *summing up: the climb, the plunge.*

Announcer. Stage 52 . . . Item 31 . . . "Man with a Bucket of Ashes," a new play by Len Peterson . . . was produced by Andrew Allan, with music composed and conducted by Lucio Agostini. In the cast were Frank Peddie as Dave Clough; Ruth Springford as Mrs. Clough; Billie Richards as Michael; Tommy Tweed as Lundquist; Beth Lockerbie as Mrs. Ennis; Alan King as Fred Ennis; Alice Hill as Sadie Gillen; and Budd Knapp as Kurt Balla. The others were Hugh Webster, Larry

McCance, Alan Pearce, Paul Kligman, Gerard Sarracini, and Douglas Master. Sound effects by David Tasker. Technical operation by Bruce Armstrong.

Mother Is Watching

PATRICIA JOUDRY

Production

Producer: Andrew Allan
Music: Lucio Agostini
Sound: David Tasker
Operator: Bruce Armstrong
Program: Stage 53
Broadcast: November 23, 1952, 9:00–10:00 pm EST
Studio: Toronto
Network: Trans-Canada

Cast

Ruth Springford *as* Virginia
Patricia Joudry *as* Mary
Roxana Bond *as* Harriet
Bud Knapp *as* Henry
William Needles *as* Calvin
Michele Landsberg *as* Sally
Donald Saunders *as* Jimmy
Howard Milsom *as* Mr Haskins

Barbara Cummings *as* Mrs Haskins
Marjorie Lecte *as* Mrs Wilshaw
with
Frosia Gregory, Jean Keller, Claude Rae,
Paul Kligman, *and* Jane Mallet

•

MOTHER IS WATCHING

Preface

"To become myself I must become everybody, and eventually with everybody touch the source. From that Source has come the drive, the energy, the sense of purpose and the will which has propelled me in my unrelenting endeavours to achieve." So says Patricia Joudry about herself. Radio, television, and stage dramatist, novelist, champion of children's rights, and mystic, Patricia Joudry was one of the handful of women writing for Andrew Allan. Born in Spirit River, Alberta, she began her radio career with CBC in 1939, acting and writing in Montreal. A year later she moved to Toronto, where she continued her work with the CBC.

During the early 1940s, she worked in the United States writing, among other plays, the scripts for the popular radio series, *The Adrich Family*. From 1951 to 1958, now back in Canada, she wrote nineteen original plays for the CBC, five of them for Andrew Allan. Her stage play "Teach Me How to Cry" was not only the first all-Canadian production to play in London's west end but was also adapted to radio, television, and film. In 1957, she and Gabrielle Roy were named Canada's outstanding women in literature and the arts.

"Mother is Watching" spoke with bitterness and hope to the many young women trapped in the post-war suburbs which had sprung up on the outskirts of Canada's metropolitan centres. It was in these new middle class communities that the struggle between consumerism and culture and between individualism and community expressed itself. The play is at once a commentary on the contradictory values of the new middle classes of the 1950s and on the profound effects of the new life styles on women, effects which, in retrospect, sowed the seeds for the feminist movement of the last two decades. Neither the theme of feminine emancipation nor the critique of suburban life styles was uncommon in the plays produced on *Stage* during the 1950s. "Mother is Watching" is an especially penetrating example of the genre.

173

PATRICIA JOUDRY

Mother Is Watching

¶ MUSIC: *title cue up and under:*

Announcer.   Stage 53 . . . Item nine . . . "Mother is Watching" . . . a new play by Patricia Joudry . . . starring Ruth Springford . . . produced by Andrew Allan, with music composed and conducted by Lucio Agostini. . . "Mother is Watching," by Patricia Joudry.

¶ MUSIC: *up and end.*

¶ SOUND: *restaurant background.*

Virginia.   Well, let's see, what'll we have Mary? How about a cocktail to start?
Mary.   That'd be *lovely.*
Virginia.   Martini?
Mary.   Yes, all right.
Virginia.   Well, this is nice. This is very very nice. You're looking well, Mary. My, I'm glad to see you looking so well.
Mary.   Thank you, Virginia.
Virginia.   I worry about you sometimes, dear.
Mary.   Why?
Virginia.   Oh — no reason especially — you seem far away sometimes. Where's the waiter?
Mary.   Aren't we going to wait for Harriet?
Virginia.   We'll wait lunch if you want, though heaven knows how long she'll be. We might as well have our drink, though. You know Harriet. Dear Harriet. I always thought she made a mistake about that.
Mary.   It doesn't matter.
Virginia.   Perhaps not. Waiter! Two martinis, please. *Dry.*
Waiter.   [*SLIGHTLY OFF*] Yes, Mrs. Harrison.
Mary.   They know you, Virginia.
Virginia.   Since Henry got this restaurant, we've been coming here.

174

Henry says it's on its way up.

Mary. Up where?

Virginia. [*LAUGHS POLITELY*]

Mary. No, I mean, are they going to improve the food or what?

Virginia. The food's all right. They're going to get the people in. Look around, Mary — and this is only *Monday.* They hardly got a soul here, lunchtimes, before Henry got the account.

Mary. How is Henry?

Virginia. Working like a mad fool. I keep telling him he should slow down. Please Henry, I say, please darling, for your own good — Oh, here comes Harriet. [*LOWERING HER VOICE*] Mary, can't we do something about her clothes? Look at her. It's a shame.

Harriet. [*FADING IN: WORRIED, SHE'S ALWAYS WORRIED*] I'm sorry I'm late, Virginia. I don't know where the time went — I just thought I'd tidy up a little — Mr. Haskins' desk, it gets in such a mess . . .

Virginia. Sit here, Harriet, and don't fuss, dear.

Harriet. I'm sorry if I kept you waiting.

Virginia. I know you're sorry, Harriet. You don't have to be sorry, dear, it doesn't really matter. But it would be so much easier on you if you'd make just a little effort to be punctual — then it wouldn't be so hard on you.

Mary. Oh, leave her alone, Virginia.

Harriet. Hello, Mary.

Mary. Hi.

Harriet. How are you? How's Calvin?

Mary. We're both fine.

Waiter. Madame.

Virginia. Oh, here we are. Well — cheers. You'll forgive us, Harriet.

Harriet. Why, certainly. It's just that I don't — I don't care for them . . .

Virginia. Mother wouldn't have minded, you know.

Harriet. I know.

Virginia. Not if you'd stood up to her. But after that awful row . . .

Harriet. I never had a row with Mother, Virginia. I never in my life had a row with Mother!

Mary. How — how *is* Mr. Haskins, Harriet?

Harriet. Mr. Haskins? He's worried about the war.

Virginia. Well, you tell dear old Mr. Haskins not to worry. Henry says there isn't a chance of war.

Harriet. Well, Mr. Haskins says . . .

Virginia. Mary, what does Calvin say? Calvin's the smart one. Isn't Calvin the smart one?

Mary. The way you say that.

Virginia. The way I say what?

Mary. About Calvin being smart. As though you disapprove.

Virginia. Disapprove! Why, you dear child! Listen, Harriet, Mary's going to get psychological now.

Harriet. I — I'm so glad you arranged this, Virginia. I keep thinking perhaps you'll forget, but you never forget. It's lovely, meeting for lunch like this, once a month. I wonder if Mother knows, wherever she is.

Virginia. Oh, Harriet, really.

Mary. Do you doubt where she is, Harriet?

Harriet. Of course not. I just meant . . .

Virginia. Well, let's order. What do you want, Mary? Don't look at the right side now, this is my treat. Harriet, the salads are very good here. Did you know that one can lose five pounds in a week by sticking to salads?

Harriet. Yes — all right, Virginia.

Virginia. That suit is very becoming, Harriet.

Harriet. Thank you.

Virginia. Chicken salad?

Harriet. . . . Yes. Yes, Please.

Virginia. I think you'd like the baked ham, Mary. It's very good.

Mary. Fine.

Waiter. Yes, Mrs. Harrison.

Virginia. Two baked ham and one chicken salad. And coffee later, please. And may we have an ashtray?

Waiter. [SLIGHT FADE] Certainly.

Virginia. Oh, wait'll you hear about Jimmy. He's gone into business.

Mary. Not really.

Virginia. Really and truly, he's the cutest thing. Lemonade. He wanted a paper route, but the hours! He's got a little stand out front — Henry helped him with some posters — and he's selling lemonade right and left. It's terrible lemonade, he insists on making it himself — I've been phoning my friends and having them send their children around to buy it — and then I'd doctor the stuff up on the Q.T. so they won't get poisoned.

Harriet. Are you going to eat your butter, Mary?

Virginia. If you gave up butter, Harriet, it would be easier to give up bread.

Mary. Is Sally helping with the lemonade?

Virginia. Sally's developed a selfish streak. She wants to go to boarding school. That's all I hear any more, boarding school, boarding school, boarding — honestly, I'm nearly driven to the point of sending her.

Mary. Why not send her, Virginia?

Virginia. To boarding school? Why, she's just a baby!

Mary. She's twelve.

Harriet. Mother called me a baby until . . . [SHE STOPS]

Virginia. That's right, and you the oldest. There you are, Mary. Why did Mother call Harriet her baby, and Harriet the oldest?

Mary. Why ask me?

Virginia. You're the psychologist.

Mary. I'm not a psychologist, don't be silly.

Harriet. Mary just knows about children.

Virginia. I've often thought, Mary, that that was an awful waste. Mother was right. All those years studying child psychology, and then you never had any children.

Mary. No, not yet.

Virginia. I mean, when you consider — [*SHE STOPS*] What do you mean, not yet?

Harriet. Mary, you look funny.

Mary. [*SMILING*] Do I?

Virginia. Mary! You're not!

Mary. Well, don't look so horrified, Virginia. I'm not going to have it now, right here.

Harriet. Oh, Mary, do you mean it, really?

Virginia. Why on earth didn't you tell us?

Mary. [*LAUGHS*] Oh you're wonderful, both of you! Why, you're making more fuss than Calvin, and he . . .

Virginia. Well, just imagine. Harriet, just imagine! Isn't that simply wonderful! Mary, I'm so happy. Wait'll I tell Henry, he'll die!

Harriet. [*WORRIED*] How are you feeling, Mary?

Mary. I'm feeling wonderful. I wish you'd both stop looking as though it were illegal. I'm only thirty-two.

Virginia. Mary, I hope you're not telling your age around like that.

Mary. You sound like Mother. Did any of us ever find out how old Mother was?

Harriet. Sixty-eight. Or nine. Under seventy anyway when she — passed away.

Virginia. [*ANGRILY*] Died, Harriet! For heavens sake, died!

Mary. Virginia . . .

Virginia. I can't remember a single conversation with Harriet, not a single conversation, when Mother doesn't pass away or pass on or go to her reward! [*VICIOUSLY*] Mother DIED! And do we have to keep talking about it?

Mary. [*SLIGHT PAUSE: QUIET: TENSE*] Harriet, don't cry. Please don't cry.

Harriet. I'm leaving.

Mary. Don't be silly. You haven't had your lunch. Virginia didn't — didn't mean . . .

Virginia. Harriet, darling, I apologize. I'm sorry, Harriet. I'm very very sorry. I didn't mean it. [*PAUSE*] Harriet?

Harriet. That's all right Virginia.

Virginia. Friends?

Harriet. Friends.

Virginia. Now then, Mary. Tell us all about the baby.

Mary. Well — he's tall — and kind of skinny, and he's got blondish hair that won't stay put — and he's got long slim beautiful hands and kind blue eyes . . .

Harriet. Why, that's Calvin!

Mary. Harriet, you're a genius.

Virginia. Mary, really, you're in love with Calvin, it's disgusting.

Harriet. What if it's a girl?

Mary. I'll keep it anyway.

Virginia. Imagine you and Calvin with a baby!

Mary. I think we'll look fine with a baby.

Harriet. You're lucky, Mary. Mary, if it's a boy — are you going to call it — Peter?

Mary. [BEAT] No, Harriet.

Virginia. Harriet, don't start that.

Harriet. I'm not — I just . . .

Virginia. [SINCERELY] Mary, you must take very good care of yourself. It's terribly important. Doctor Palsson is the very best, there's no one like him. You can *talk* to him. And he stays right with you the whole time. He stresses diet, diet is very important, and exercise.

Mary. Virginia, I've got a doctor.

Virginia. Well, is he a good doctor?

Mary. Yes, I think so. One of the clinic doctors.

Virginia. Clinic!

Mary. They're all very good, they're all specialists.

Virginia. Oh come now, Mary. You don't have to go to extremes. Clinic! If you give that a little thought, you'll realize . . .

Mary. I've given it a little thought, Virginia. It's all settled, so . . .

Virginia. Do you mean to honestly say that you're going to a *clinic* — where they treat you like riff raff . . .

Mary. They treat you beautifully.

Virginia. A charity!

Mary. It's not charity. You pay what you can afford. Don't be ridiculous, Virginia.

Virginia. You're the one who's being — you must have lost your mind — you don't know what it's like, having a baby — and to put yourself in the hands of some incompetent — Mary, listen to me!

Harriet. Virginia, don't you think — I mean, people are listening.

Virginia. Harriet, I'm proud of you, I must say! Your own sister is contemplating suicide and all you can think about is people are listening!

Harriet.   Well, leave her alone, Virginia. Just — leave her alone!
Virginia.   I . . .
Harriet.   Mary, make her leave you alone. From start to finish. This is
   your baby — you're the mother — and Mother's the one to decide!

¶ MUSIC: *bridge.*

Henry.   Well, what do you know about that! Isn't that great news!
Virginia.   Didn't you hear what I said, Henry? She's going to a clinic!
Henry.   What for?
Virginia.   She's doing it to be stubborn.
Henry.   Why would she want to be stubborn? And what's so terrible
   about a clinic?
Virginia.   Why, anything can happen! Henry, you don't seem to realize
   — she's my sister!
Henry.   I realize that.
Virginia.   Mary needs decent care. We've always had trouble having
   babies, all of us.
Harriet.   You're the only one of the bunch that's had any babies,
   Virginia.
Virginia.   Look at Mother. She had a terrible time with all of us. And
   then she lost David. She never got over David. Why, if she knew what
   Mary was doing, she'd die!
Henry.   She's already dead.
Virginia.   Henry, are you — are you trying to be funny?
Henry.   I don't think so. I don't think that's very funny.
Virginia.   Neither do I.
Henry.   Then we're agreed. Let's have dinner.
Virginia.   Dinner isn't ready yet. Martha had one of her spells this after-
   noon, and I've been too upset to do anything about her.
Henry.   You have been upset.
Virginia.   What — what do you mean?
Henry.   Nothing.
Virginia.   Henry, what's got into you lately?
Henry.   Has something to into me?
Virginia.   There — that kind of thing. Repeating my questions. Every-
   thing I say . . .
Henry.   Okay, I'm sorry. Where were we? Oh, yes, the clinic.
Virginia.   It isn't just that. It's the whole way they live. I've been
   worried about it, Henry — I can't tell you how it's been worrying me.
   Every time I see that dreadful little apartment — the way Mary has to
   scrimp and save — her clothes, for instance . . .
Henry.   She usually looks pretty good.
Virginia.   That's because I give her things. And tell her how to alter
   things. But how are they going to raise a child?

Henry.   Maybe they've thought of that.

Virginia.   What it boils down to is it's time Calvin stopped fooling around with dead civilizations and got a decent job.

Henry.   Have you told Calvin?

Virginia.   [*BEAT*] Have I told Calvin what?

Henry.   There. You're doing it.

Virginia.   Henry, I don't understand you any more. You don't seem to take anything seriously any more.

Henry.   What is it you want me to do, Virginia. Just tell me what you want me to do.

Virginia.   [*SENSING FOR A MOMENT THAT SOMETHING IS WRONG: HER LIPS TREMBLES JUST A LITTLE*] I'd like you to try to understand — why I'm concerned about my sister — how much she means to me . . .

Henry.   [*TIRED BUT KIND*] All right, Virginia. You tell me. And I'll try to understand.

Virginia.   It's something that — that we've always felt — our whole family. We don't talk about it very much. But we're very close, we've always been very close. Some people don't realize just how important a family is. But we were taught the importance — how to help each other and care for each other.

Henry.   Most families care about each other.

Virginia.   Yes, but that's when they're together. We're apart now — now that Mother's gone. And someone has to carry on for her. I owe it to her, Henry. She gave up everything for us.

Henry.   What did she give up?

Virginia.   Why . . . [*SHE IS STARTLED AND HESITATES*]

¶ SOUND: *a sudden violent crash of thunder.*

Virginia.   [*PANICKED*] The children!

Henry.   Virginia . . .

Virginia.   There's going to be a storm. The children aren't back yet. Henry — they'll be caught in it . . .

Henry.   Hey, now, take it easy. They're all right.

Virginia.   [*FADING A LITTLE AS SHE GOES TO THE WINDOW*] I told them, I told them, I gave them explicit instructions to be home by six!

Henry.   It's not six yet. Only five to. A little rain won't hurt them.

¶ SOUND: *thunder rumbles.*

Virginia.   [*COMING BACK ON*] Henry, get the car out. They're over at Barlows — perhaps you can get them before they leave . . .

Henry.   That's only a block away. Virginia, why do you go all to pieces over a little rain?

Virginia.   You always say that! *I don't like storms!* Don't TALK about it — get the children!

180

¶ SOUND: *door bangs off.*

Virginia. [*ALMOST SIMULTANEOUSLY*] Jimmy!
Jimmy. [*OFF*] Yes, Mom.
Virginia. Is Sally with you?
Sally. [*CLOSER*] Are we late, Mother?
Virginia. [*CALLING: LOWERING HER VOICE AS SHE GOES TO THEM*] No, darling, you're right on time. I was afraid you'd be caught in the storm — I was so worried — bless you — oh, darling . . .
Sally. [*FADING*] I have to wash my hands.
Virginia. [*HUGGING HIM*] Jimmy.
Jimmy. Gee, Mom. [*A LITTLE MUFFLED*] You're hurting me, Mom. I — I have to get my coat off.
Virginia. Did you have a nice time at the Barlows?
Jimmy. It was all right.
Virginia. Did Sally have a good time too?
Jimmy. Sure. Frank Barlow slugged her.
Virginia. What?
Jimmy. She's crazy about him.
Virginia. I'll have to speak to Mrs. Barlow.
Jimmy. [*SLIGHT FADE*] What about?
Virginia. Jimmy, don't take your coat upstairs. Your coat goes here in the closet.
Jimmy. [*SLIGHTLY OFF*] I like having it in my room. I got stuff in my pockets I need.
Virginia. Take the things out of your pockets, dear, and hang your coat downstairs. This closet is the place for coats.
Jimmy. [*FURTHER OFF*] Aw gee, Mom.
Virginia. And don't lean over the railing like that. You'll fall.
Jimmy. No I won't.
Henry. [*SLIGHTLY OFF*] Virginia . . .
Virginia. [*CALLING*] Tell Sally to comb her hair for supper. Oh and Jimmy . . .
Henry. [*ON: QUIETLY*] Don't take every step for them. Give them a little room to breathe. Try, Ginny. Try.
Virginia. [*A SLIGHT PAUSE: SHE SOBS SUDDENLY, QUIETLY*]
Henry. I'm sorry . . .
Virginia. No — you just — Henry, you haven't called me Ginny — for such a long time.

¶ MUSIC: *bridge.*

¶ SOUND: *rain falling steadily outside.*

Calvin. You listening?
Mary. Yes.

Calvin. [*A LITTLE PAUSE*] With all his honours on,
  he sighed for one
Who, say astonished critics, lived at home;
Did little jobs about the house with skill
And nothing else; could whistle; would sit still
Or potter round the garden; answered some
Of his long marvelous letters but kept none.
[*PAUSE*] No you're not.

Mary. I guess not. But you read so beautifully, darling.

Calvin. Well I'll read you some more beautifully, and you listen to the rain.

Mary. All right.

Calvin. What's the matter?

Mary. I'm not just sure, Calvin. Something . . .

Calvin. How've you been feeling today? In the middle, I mean.

Mary. Haven't been feeling anything.

Calvin. Maybe the little fellow's gone. Not there. Maybe it was all a mistake.

Mary. [*SMILING*] It was a mistake all right.

Calvin. And about time. I was thinking about it today. How many babies would be born if everyone waited till they could afford it?

Mary. Not many, I guess. Not ours.

Calvin. You worried about the money, darling?

Mary. I never worry about money, you know that.

Calvin. Well, you should. One of us should worry.

Mary. We'll let the baby worry about it. He'll have time on his hands.

Calvin. [*SLIGHT PAUSE: SERIOUSLY*] A child — shouldn't have to think about . . .

Mary. [*QUICKLY*] Oh, darling, I was only joking. Of course he won't have to — we'll manage, Calvin. We'll manage just fine.

Calvin. We'd manage better if we had some money.

Mary. Did something bring this on? Something special? You don't usually — I thought we had it all decided.

Calvin. [*A LITTLE PAUSE: SUDDENLY*] Stillman called me into his office today. About the expedition — [*THE STORY COMES OUT IN JERKS*] he's got it financed finally — he wants me to go — next summer — he says he can replace me at the Museum — Oh, Mary . . .

Mary. [*CLOSE*] Put your arms around me, darling. [*MUFFLED: CLOSE TO HIM*] Why didn't you tell me?

Calvin. I just told you.

Mary. As soon as you got home. You've wanted it — you've been years wanting it — and you waited all this time to tell me.

Calvin. I intended to — I was going to phone you from the Museum and something stopped me. I thought I should run all the way home

— I wondered why I didn't want to run — and when I got home I
didn't want to tell you.

Mary. Why?

Calvin. You — you seemed preoccupied . . .

Mary. That isn't why.

Calvin. [PAUSE] I don't want to go.

Mary. Of course you want to go. Don't talk crazy!

Calvin. Mary, a whole year!

Mary. We've talked about it — we knew it would be a year . . .

Calvin. We didn't know there'd be a baby.

Mary. The baby — will keep me company.

Calvin. Let's not talk about it.

Mary. What?

Calvin. I don't want to talk about it. It's going too fast — you can't
decide things this fast. We're getting excited and when you get excited
you decide things quickly, you say things and then foolishly think you
meant them when you didn't.

Mary. You're not making sense.

Calvin. That's why I say we should stop talking about it.

Mary. Calvin . . .

Calvin. Mary, please. Just for a little while. The idea seems so different
from the way I thought — please, Mary. I want to get used to it before
— before we . . .

Mary. Of course, darling. Oh darling, of course. [PAUSE] Listen to the
rain. I love it, I love the rain. I love you, Calvin. It'll be all right.

Calvin. Funny you liking the rain. The way your sisters carry on. Did
your mother teach them to be afraid of storms?

Mary. Yes.

Calvin. [REALIZING] This is Monday. First Monday — that's why you've
been feeling low. You had lunch with them today.

Mary. Yes.

Calvin. Was it bad?

Mary. No worse than usual. Calvin, I wish I could like them. I feel so
dishonest.

Calvin. It's not disliking them that makes you feel dishonest. It's seeing
them carrying on with it. Why do you see them?

Mary. It's easier to give in to Virginia.

Calvin. Did you tell them about the baby?

Mary. Yes. That was when I felt so sorry for Harriet. She loved somebody once.

Calvin. What was he like?

Mary. I don't know. None of us ever saw him. She hadn't dared bring
him home, and then one night she walked in and said she was going
to get married. Virginia was married by then — I was still in high

school. Mother put her arms around Harriet and kissed her and said she was happy. She said we must celebrate Harriet's engagement and she started down cellar to get a bottle of brandy. That was when she fell.

Calvin. You haven't told me this before.

Mary. I didn't like to think about it.

Calvin. Brandy? I thought she was opposed to . . .

Mary. She was. But she left Father's supply there so she could talk about it.

Calvin. What happened when she fell?

Mary. Nothing. The doctor said nothing. He did at first. But when she never got out of bed again, they decided — oh, we never did get it straight. A lot of talk. Internal injuries. Harriet nursed her for seven years.

Calvin. What about her man?

Mary. He was never mentioned. She went on working for her Mr. Haskins. He's all she's got now. That and Mother. She's still got Mother.

¶ MUSIC: *bridge.*

¶ SOUND: *rapid typing: it stops: a door opens slightly off: a sheet is pulled from the typewriter.*

Mr. Haskins. [*SLIGHTLY OFF*] Well well, does that mean you're finished?

Harriet. Yes, Mr. Haskins, just this minute. If you'll check it over now and sign the letter, I think you'll get home in time.

Mr. Haskins. [*FADING IN*] It's good of you to work so late on this, Harriet. Very good of you indeed.

Harriet. Oh, it's not late. I'll be able to get the brief in the mail before eight — here's the pen . . .

Mr. Haskins. Thank you.

Harriet. . . . and they'll get it tomorrow.

¶ SOUND: *he signs.*

Harriet. There's an erasure in Paragraph Three. I'm very sorry. I'd do it over, but we promised Mr. Bingham he could take it into Court tomorrow.

Mr. Haskins. It doesn't matter in the least. There we are. Now then. My coat . . .

Harriet. Here it is, Mr. Haskins. I got it out for you. And your umbrella — the rain seems to have stopped, thank goodness, but it might start again.

Mr. Haskins. Yes, the rains are unpredictable this time of year.

Harriet. Yes.

Mr. Haskins. Now, then. Come along, Harriet. Where can I drop you?

Harriet. Oh no, I — I'm going to tidy up a bit. Your desk — Mr. Powell is going to be here at nine tomorrow — I want to get his file in order.

Mr. Haskins. Won't you change your mind about coming up to the house?

Harriet. I'd like to. But I'm afraid I've made a previous engagement. Thank you, though.

Mr. Haskins. Well, then, I'd better run along. [*FADING*] Good night, Harriet.

Harriet. Good night, Mr. Haskins.

¶ SOUND: *door opens and closes: telephone receiver up: dialing, phone rings on filter, click.*

Mrs. Haskins. [*FILTER*] Hello?

Harriet. Hello, Mrs. Haskins.

Mrs. Haskins. Oh, Harriet, is that you?

Harriet. Yes. Mr. Haskins has just left the office. I thought you might like to know.

Mrs. Haskins. Oh, isn't that thoughtful of you.

Harriet. He should be home in twenty minutes.

Mrs. Haskins. I'm very disappointed, Harriet, that you're not coming this evening. It's a very small party — I do wish you could be with us.

Harriet. I wish I could too, Mrs. Haskins. And thank you for inviting me. But unfortunately, I have — I have other plans . . .

Mrs. Haskins. Well, I won't press you. I appreciate your calling me, Harriet. You're so efficient.

Harriet. I hope you have a very nice time.

Mrs. Haskins. You too, Harriet.

Harriet. Thank you.

Mrs. Haskins. Good-bye.

Harriet. Good-bye.

¶ SOUND: *receiver down: at the same time, the sound of a key rattling in the lock, slightly off.*

Harriet. [*CALLING NERVOUSLY*] Who is it? *Who is it?*

¶ SOUND: *door opens slightly off.*

Harriet. Oh.

Mrs. Wilshaw. [*SLIGHLY OFF*] Oh, you're still here, Miss Sutherland.

¶ SOUND: *door closes.*

Mrs. Wilshaw. [*FADING IN*] And how are you this evening?

Harriet. I'm very well, thank you, Mrs. Wilshaw. How are you?

Mrs. Wilshaw.   In the pink, dear. Now don't let me disturb you one bit. You carry right on with your work and I'll carry on with mine and I'm sure we can work around each other neat as can be.

¶ SOUND: *a pail goes down with a thump, and a scrub brush.*

Harriet.   I won't be long.

Mrs. Wilshaw.   To tell you the truth, Miss Sutherland, neither will I. I'm just giving these offices a lick and promise tonight. The fact is, it's my birthday, today is.

Harriet.   Oh. Many happy returns, Mrs. Wilshaw.

Mrs. Wilshaw.   Thank you, dear, that's real sweet of you. I'm not usually one for laying down on the job, but my girls and my boy are giving me a surprise party tonight and I don't want to be late.

Harriet.   A — a surprise party?

Mrs. Wilshaw.   Yes, ma'am. I take them in every year. Every year they give me a surprise party, and I act so surprised they think they put it over, bless them. Lands, will you look at those windows. I'd better give them a swish, birthday or no birthday.

Harriet.   Are your daughters married, Mrs. Wilshaw?

Mrs. Wilshaw.   That they are, married and raising families. My boy too.

Harriet.   It must be lonely for you.

Mrs. Wilshaw.   Lonely? Bless you, no. I'm a grandmother five times over. Why, it seems like I get busier every year. There, that looks better, don't you think? I'll give the floor a quick going over . . .

Harriet.   I'll be out of your way in a minute.

¶ SOUND: *receiver up.*

Harriet.   I just want to make a phone call.

Mrs. Wilshaw.   Go right ahead, Miss Sutherland, dear, I can work around you.

¶ SOUND: *dialing over above.*

Mrs. Wilshaw.   I don't have to change my clothes or anything. If I got dressed up, they might think I knew they were doing something for me. That's the whole fun of it, you see, me not expecting anything.

Girl.   [ON FILTER] Good evening, Rialto Theatre.

Harriet.   Oh — good evening. I wonder if you could tell me, please, what the feature picture is this evening?

¶ MUSIC: *bridge.*

¶ SOUND: *a small crowd: casual.*

Doorman.   [ANNOUNCING IN A SOMEWHAT CONFIDENTIAL MANNER, ONLY TO THE IMMEDIATE GROUP] Seats available in the loges and front rows.

Last complete show starting in three minutes. [*SLIGHT FADE*] Seats available in the loges and . . .

Romantic Very Young Man. [*COMING IN OVER ABOVE FADE*] Haven't you got any at the back, Miss?

Ticket girl. Sorry, loges and front seats.

R. V. Y. M. [*WORRIED*] The only trouble with loges is . . .

Girl. I don't care, Johnny. We can sit at the front and move back later.

R. V. Y. M. Well . . .

Ticket girl. Two?

Girl. Yes, please.

R. V. Y. M. Thanks. [*FADING*] Do you want some popcorn?

Man. [*FADING IN OVER LAST LINE*] Uh — I'd like three tickets. In the front I guess.

Woman. [*TIRED*] Oh, Fred, in the front?

Man. Mother can't see at the back.

Ticket girl. Three. Next please.

Calvin. Two loges, please. Thanks.

Mary. Oh, Calvin, you're so cute . . .

Ticket girl. [*FADING*] Next please, step right up.

Mary. [*OVER LAST WORDS*] . . . When it's a picture you really want to see, you economize.

Calvin. Makes sense. Nothing wrong with cheap seats when you're going to enjoy the picture.

¶ SOUND: *the box office crowd moves away, over above, as they go in: now a heavy door opens.*

Calvin. Go ahead, darling.

Mary. I still remember the movie we saw when you were trying to decide whether to propose to me or not.

¶ SOUND: *door closes.*

Calvin. That's nonsense. I decided the moment I saw you.

Mary. You heard that line in a movie.

¶ MUSIC: *bridge.*

¶ SOUND: *phone rings several times: door opens slightly off.*

Mary. [*SLIGHTLY OFF*] I think it's going to rain again.

Calvin. [*SAME*] Stuffy in here.

¶ SOUND: *door closes.*

Calvin. [*CLOSER*] Phone's ringing.

Mary. Um — hum.

Calvin. Anyone you want to talk to?

Calvin. [PHONE HAS STOPPED] Come and sit over here.

Mary. You're a funny darling. You and your movies.

Calvin. They're so wonderfully unreal. For me, they — they mix up with the unrealities — or the unimportant issues in my own life — and carry them away. The things that have got too close, and taken on the wrong proportion. You comfy?

Mary. Yes. I'm listening.

Calvin. Well — it's easier to see where I'm at. What's important. You know?

Mary. Yes. I don't need that — not with you. With me, maybe. But not with you. I can see you better. I've seen you planning this expedition — I've seen it important — nothing getting mixed up with it.

Calvin. What do you think then?

Mary. I think you should go.

Calvin. Why?

Mary. Because it's your work. Your work isn't just a job, Calvin. It's one of the reasons for your being.

Calvin. It's why we're poor.

Mary. It's why you're you. And what you are — is what I love. That's all.

Calvin. [PAUSE] Go on.

Mary. That's all, Calvin.

Calvin. No. Tell me. Tell me what you think.

Mary. It shouldn't be a big decision, darling. We made the big decision five years ago. That was when we took a good look at it, at the money, the struggle, and decided that you should continue with the work that is so important to you — and to me now. Because we've been happy. That proves it.

Calvin. Proof doesn't remain conclusive if circumstances change.

Mary. What can change? Just the geography. You'll be one place for a while, and I'll be someplace else. Does that change loving each other and understanding each other? You'll be *you*, Calvin, not changing yourself or sacrificing yourself for me.

Calvin. Did you see Harriet tonight at the movie?

Mary. Yes.

Calvin. Have you ever been lonely, Mary?

Mary. [THINKING] Maybe. I don't remember. I don't seem to remember, so that I can really feel it, anything much before I loved you. I haven't been lonely since, that's all I know.

Calvin. We've been growing together for five years.

Mary. But not growing into one person, Calvin! Standing apart — two people — with respect for each other and for each other's rights. We decided that, early. So that we could grow *up* and not together leaning on each other or robbing each other.

Calvin. All right. [*LEANING FORWARD*] Now look. You just — can you reach the lamp?

¶ SOUND: *light switch.*

Calvin. . . . you just drew a picture — two people, side by side, growing up. That's fine. Not leaning on each other. All right. Like two trees . . . eh?

Mary. If you want . . .

Calvin. Well, now there's something new. There's a third one. Mary, a baby doesn't grow up without leaning. It leans and demands and takes — but that's all right because it brings its own love with it. But the two tall ones, on either side, have to join hands somewhere near the top, and stay joined, forming a secure shelter. All of a sudden the picture changes. It isn't separate any more — it's a unit. The unit has to be the more important — for a long time — or the individuals won't grow properly.

Mary. Oh, Calvin . . .

Calvin. Our baby needs security. We have to give him that from the day he's born — from right now. My work is part of me, sure, but I'm more important than it is, and the three of us are more important than any of it.

Mary. [*BREATHLESS*] There's more money if you go . . .

Calvin. And maybe advancement at the Museum if I stay. It'll even out. I'll go on with my work. But our life is short and it's for us. We'll stay together.

¶ SOUND: *phone starts to ring during above speech (or earlier) & rings uninterrupted till end of scene.*

Mary. Oh, Calvin — I didn't want you to go!

Calvin. That was apparent. You presented a perfectly lousy argument.

Mary. [*LAUGHS, AND THE LAUGH CHANGES TO A SOB*]

¶ MUSIC: *bridge: out.*

¶ SOUND: *phone is ringing: receiver up.*

Harriet. Hello?

Virginia. [*FILTER*] Harriet, where have you been?

Harriet. I've been to a movie, Virginia. I just got home.

Virginia. I've been phoning you and phoning you!

Harriet. I didn't come straight home, I dropped in at the Drug Store to have a dish of ice cream.

Virginia. Harriet, really, you know what ice cream does to your figure. [*PAUSE*] Harriet? Are you there?

Harriet. Yes, Virginia.

Virginia. Well that isn't what I phoned about. I've been frantic — I even tried Mary's — I thought you might be there . . .

Harriet. I hardly ever visit Mary and Calvin.

Virginia. They should invite you more often. You're lonely, Harriet. They should be more considerate. Anyway, they're not at home tonight.

Harriet. Oh. [*SHE IS BLANK: HER THOUGHT PROCESSES STOP WHEN SHE IS OUT OF THE OFFICE, AND ESPECIALLY WITH VIRGINIA: ONLY HER EMOTIONS ARE CAPABLE OF FUNCTIONING AND THESE SHE KEEPS UNDER CONTROL*]

Virginia. Harriet, we have to do something about them.

Harriet. Why?

Virginia. You know why, you know very well. I've been thinking about it all evening. Henry's going to help and I need you too.

Harriet. Why do you need me?

Virginia. Please don't keep asking me "why," like a child. I'm not your mother, Harriet!

Harriet. [*BEWILDERED*] No — no — you're not . . .

Virginia. Now I want to arrange it for next week — one night next week. Wednesday of next week, as you know, is the twenty-sixth.

Harriet. [*LITTLE PAUSE: TENSE*] Yes.

Virginia. Now, Harriet, I don't want to start anything. I don't want you to get upset, dear. That's why I'm talking about it on the *phone*. I'm sorry to talk about it at all, Harriet, but I must know in advance what night. Do you understand, dear?

Harriet. [*A BREATH*] Yes.

Virginia. All right. Now just think for a moment and tell me when you'll be feeling best. Before the twenty-sixth, or afterwards. [*PAUSE*] Would it help if I went out to the cemetery *with* you, dear? Maybe Mary will go too. Would that help?

Harriet. I don't know . . .

Virginia. Well don't you think you'd better decide? Myself, I think it's criminal the way you torture yourself. It isn't your fault Mother died. You'd almost think it was your fault, the way you act. I think you'll feel better the day before — Tuesday. Don't you think you'll feel better Tuesday? Then if you're going to break down — see what I mean? Doesn't that make sense, Harriet?

Harriet. [*A SIGH*] Yes, Virginia. If you say it makes sense . . . yes, Virginia.

¶ MUSIC: *bridge.*

Virginia. Mary, dear, I'm glad I caught you at home. How are you?

Mary. [*FILTER*] I'm fine, Virginia.

Virginia. Oh, I'm glad. And how's Calvin, dear?

Mary. He's all right. He's fine too.

Virginia.   Mary, are you and Calvin doing anything Tuesday evening?

Mary.   Well — [*CAUTIOUSLY*] not that I — I'm not sure if Calvin . . .

Virginia.   Why don't you both come up for the evening? We've got something very exciting!

Mary.   Really?

Virginia.   A new television set, Mary.

Mary.   Another one?

Virginia.   With a twenty inch screen. We've put the little one in Sally's room. Mary, it's terribly exciting, you must come.

Mary.   Well, Virginia — we'd like to . . .

Virginia.   Good!

Mary.   But I'll have to ask Calvin.

Virginia.   Why, dear?

Mary.   He might — he sometimes works in the evenings . . .

Virginia.   Well, don't let him work Tuesday evening. They're running a film on his subject — it's British, and very good — he'll be fascinated!

Mary.   Oh. Well, that sounds . . .

Virginia.   They're only playing it one night, and I don't think Calvin should miss it. Now say you'll come.

Mary.   All right. Yes — all right, Virginia. And thank you.

Virginia.   Henry will pick you up at eight-thirty.

Mary.   Oh, he doesn't have to do that. We can take the street car.

Virginia.   Nonsense. You shouldn't be bouncing around on street cars in your condition.

Mary.   Oh, Virginia, they don't bounce. And I ride them all the time anyway . . .

Virginia.   Mary dear, don't argue. If you take street cars all the time, that's all the more reason you should ride in a car when you can. Now it's all arranged.

Mary.   Yes. I guess it is.

¶ MUSIC: *bridge.*

¶ SOUND: *footsteps up cement walk.*

Henry.   [*SLIGHTLY OFF, CALLING TO THEM*] I'll just put the buggy away. You folks go on in.

¶ SOUND: *car pulls away.*

Mary.   All right, Henry.

Calvin.   Nice buggy.

Mary.   Yes, isn't it fancy? Henry looks right in it. And yet he doesn't look right in it. Do you know what I mean?

Calvin.   No, honey.

¶ SOUND: *door is thrown open slightly off.*

Virginia. [*SLIGHTLY OFF*] Hello, darlings!

Calvin. [*LOW*] But Virginia looks right in that doorway.

Mary. [*UP*] Hello. We're a bit late . . .

Virginia. [*FADING IN, AS THEY GO UP THE STEPS*] Not at all, you're right on time. Calvin, how nice to see you. Mary, you're looking wonderful. Come in, come in.

Calvin. Thanks, Virginia. You're looking beautiful as always.

Virginia. Aren't you sweet.

¶ SOUND: *door closes.*

Women. [*A WHISPERED AD LIB, OFF, WHICH DIES DOWN*]

Mary. Oh, are you having a party?

Harriet. [*NOT QUITE OFF*] Shhh! She's here . . .

Mary. Why, there's Harriet.

Harriet. [*FADING IN*] I'm sorry, Virginia, they wouldn't keep quiet . . .

Virginia. [*CALLING*] It's all right, girls. She's here!

Harriet. Mary, darling . . .

Women. [*MOVE IN*] Surprise! Surprise, Mary! [*ETC.*]

Mary. Good heavens. Virginia . . .

Virginia. It's a shower, Mary! Surprise and congratulations, darling. Now come on into the living room.

Henry. [*OFF: OVER BABBLE*] Calvin! Calvin, you there?

Calvin. I think so.

Henry. [*FADING IN*] Looks like the fun's started.

Women. [*FADE CHATTERING*]

Calvin. Yes. What about the television program?

Henry. Just a gag. We've got the new set though — you must come up some other evening.

Calvin. Yes.

Henry. [*AWKWARDLY*] Well.

Calvin. Well, that was a bit of a surprise. Very kind of Virginia.

Henry. Virginia is very kind.

Calvin. I hope it wasn't too much of a — Mary looked a little stunned. I suppose it's too early though to do any harm.

Henry. Harm?

Calvin. You're supposed to avoid sudden — well, I guess it's pretty standard routine, isn't it, a shower?

Henry. Yes. Pretty standard. They get a lot of stuff. Comes in handy sometimes. [*SLIGHT PAUSE*] Well — Calvin — looks as if we're on our own.

Calvin. Yes.

Henry. What do you say we go downstairs — mix ourselves a little drink.

Calvin. Fine.

Henry. Come on then. We've just redecorated the rumpus room. It's very gay.

¶ MUSIC: *bridge.*

Henry. So that's the way it goes. Quite a business, advertising. Stimulating — you'd be surprised, Calvin. Keeps you on your toes. Fascinating business. Drink?
Calvin. I'll nurse this one thanks.
Henry. Suit yourself.

¶ SOUND: *Henry pours himself a drink, a long one, with no mixer.*

Henry. Well, tell me about yourself, Cal. I've been doing all the talking. Got kind of keyed up to-day, for no reason. I always talk too much when I — Tell me about yourself. You been working hard?
Calvin. Pretty hard, yes.
Henry. You work long hours, don't you, Calvin?
Calvin. It depends. This — this is very attractive. Good big room.
Henry. The kids use it more than we do. Don't know what they'd do without it. It's important for kids to have room to stretch out in.
Calvin. Yes, I guess so.
Henry. Say, that brings me to the subject of the evening! Speaking of kids. "Children," Virginia keeps telling me, not kids. [*HE LAUGHS*] Congratulations, Calvin.
Calvin. Oh — thanks.
Henry. My heartiest congratulations!
Calvin. Anybody can do it.
Henry. Yes, it's easy to have children. You're right, anybody can do it. Bringing them up, of course, is another matter.
Calvin. Mary's had pretty good grounding for that.
Henry. Yes, so I understand. It isn't all a Mother's job though. You need something more concrete. It's a fine thing, raising children properly. A great responsibility. [*AS THOUGH SEARCHING*] Great . . . responsibility. Woop . . .
Calvin. [*AS HENRY SPILLS HIS DRINK*] Oh . . .
Henry. It's all right . . . didn't spill much . . . it'll dry. Guess I'm getting old.

¶ SOUND: *he pours some more.*

Henry. [*GOING RIGHT ON, AFTER TAKING A DEEP BREATH. HE'S ONLY PARTLY TIGHT: MORE TENSE AND EXCITED*] It's a terrific feeling. A baby. A baby's coming. The first — wonderful — realization — the excitement and the planning — I'll never forget it. What you're going through now, Calvin, you and Mary. You picture it. Your own baby — little and helpless — all you're going to do for it. All it's going to be. Maybe it'll grow up to solve the world's problems, who knows?

Calvin.   Yes, that's it.

Henry.   You say to each other, isn't it going to be fun? You get a bassinet and some diapers and bottles and nighties. Pink or blue, that's the big question. A childlike thing, planning for a baby. Like a little kid — like when you wanted a pup and your mother said, "You'll have to look after it," and you said, "I'll look after it all right. Boy, wait'll you see how I can look after it." Something like that, isn't it, Calvin?

Calvin.   I hadn't thought of that.

Henry.   Well, it's something like that. Only better.

Calvin.   I suppose so.

Henry.   And the money. You buy the stuff for the baby, and it comes to practically nothing . . . especially with showers like upstairs . . . and if you happen to have a little medical insurance. It's a breeze. Nothing to it. You say, what's everybody talking about, it costs a lot to have a baby. Why, it's a breeze!

Calvin.   [WITH A LITTLE LAUGH] Have another drink, Henry, you're doing fine.

Henry.   I'm right though. Isn't that about the way it is? You listen to me, because I'm right. Yeah, I'll have another drink. How about you?

Calvin.   A small one, thanks.

Henry.   Isn't that about the way it is?

¶ SOUND: *he pours the drinks.*

Calvin.   Just about — yes.

Henry.   How much do you make a year as an archaeologist?

Calvin.   [A SMALL STARTLED PAUSE] Twenty-six hundred.

Henry.   Twenty-six hundred. Do you know how much I've spent on Jimmy's teeth? Just straightening them. How much? Guess?

Calvin.   I can't imagine . . .

Henry.   Fourteen hundred dollars.

Calvin.   Is that so?

Henry.   You don't think about that, why should you, a baby hasn't got any teeth. A baby's no trouble. It just lies there and sleeps. Summer vacation. You gaily give that idea up, for the first year, maybe even the second and third. What do you and Mary do in the summer?

Calvin.   This year we went on a camping trip.

Henry.   Yes, that's right. A tent and a lot of cans of beans and you're all set. Then first thing you know your kid's four or five — pardon me, child — and all the other children are going to summer cottages. Or camp. Do you know what camp costs?

Calvin.   I — I haven't looked into it . . .

Henry.   How about nursery school. Have you looked into that? How about the price of bicycles, piano lessons, broken legs, winter overcoats, corrective shoes, insurance, automobiles, television sets — a house they're not going to be ashamed to bring their friends to — university . . .

Calvin. No — no — I haven't thought of those things . . .

Henry. Well, you'll think of them, boy. You'll think of them because they'll be right on top of you, ploughing you under, you and Mary both, and both of you scrapping and wondering where it all went wrong.

Calvin. Hold on — What's this all about?

Henry. This is facts, Henry. This is our way of life. If you don't face it now you've got to face it later. Twenty-six hundred dollars for the study of ancient man. Ancient man was cheap. Modern man is expensive.

Calvin. What's this leading up to, Henry?

Henry. I'll put my cards on the table.

Calvin. I'd appreciate it.

Henry. There's an opening with the agency. A job you could fill nicely, with your education. Six thousand a year, to start.

Calvin. That's a lot of money.

Henry. You're going to need a lot of money.

Calvin. What does this job consist of?

Henry. Using your head, that's all, Calvin. A certain amount of writing ability — you've got that — and some ideas.

Calvin. What kind of ideas?

Henry. You know — selling.

Calvin. [*A PAUSE: HE STARES AT HIS DRINK AND SPEAKS THOUGHTFULLY AND QUIETLY*] What did you have in mind for me to sell, Henry?

Henry. Well . . .

Calvin. I could — uh — I could sell television sets and automobiles, I suppose, and gadgets — All the gadgets to go in the house that my children can bring their friends to and not be ashamed. I could do that. Just in case the rest of you don't quite manage to make those things important to my children. I can pitch in and make sure the demand continues. And get paid for it. Get paid enough to buy all the gadgets. It works out pretty neatly.

Henry. You owe something to your children, Calvin.

Calvin. I agree. But if I assume that what I owe my children is to give up my life for them, turn my back on my own honesty — I'm not paying a debt. I'm putting them in my debt. Every day of their lives then I can remind them of what I gave up for them. I would too, Henry. We all do. We say, "Look, my children, look at what you owe me." It turns around on you, Henry. Everybody winds up in debt to everybody else.

Henry. [*PAUSE*] Have another drink.

Calvin. Thanks, though, Henry. And maybe you're partly right. It'll be bumpy in spots. But Mary and I — Mary and I think we can give our children something that doesn't need so much advertising — or doesn't get so much advertising — it should.

Henry. Such as what?

Calvin. Oh — well . . .

Henry. Go on, Calvin, what? I'd like to know.

Calvin. Security, mainly. Not the security of a big house and car and money in the bank. But the kind that comes with real love and affection and understanding. And freedom. Freedom to grow into whole people, utilizing all their forces, being truly whatever they have the capacity to be. Whether they want to study ancient man or fly rockets to the moon, whatever it is, that's what they'll do. It'll take some teaching and guiding. Helping. But not pushing. If Mary and I start pushing ourselves or each other around, we might not know where to stop. [*SLIGHT PAUSE*] That's part of it.

Henry. [*PAUSE*] I guess I made a hash of that. I'm glad. Sorry too, in a way. I wanted to do a good job. Because it's the last job I'm doing for Virginia.

Calvin. How do you mean?

Henry. [*HE'S SOBER NOW*] I'm leaving her. A week from Friday.

Calvin. What?

Henry. Sally's birthday is next Thursday. I don't want to spoil it. I'm leaving Friday.

Calvin. Henry — for God's sake . . .

Henry. What you said about pushing each other around. It happens slowly — so gradually you don't realize it's happening. And then one day you're a stranger. You've been pushed into somebody — entirely different. It doesn't do any good to push back. The kids get in the middle and they get pushed all out of shape too. All you can do is go away and hunt and dig — not for bones and relics of the past like you, Cal — but for the live individual that was there before the stranger.

Calvin. Henry, Listen . . .

Henry. I've been listening for fourteen years. I can't hear any more — not from the outside I can't hear. Don't tell Mary.

¶ MUSIC: *bridge.*

¶ SOUND: *typing: it is interrupted by a buzz: then a click.*

Harriet. Yes?

Mr. Haskins. [*FILTER*] Will you come in a minute, please, Harriet?

Harriet. Yes, Mr. Haskins.

¶ SOUND: *click: chair goes back: footsteps: door opens.*

Mr. Haskins. [*SLIGHTLY OFF*] Powell just phoned. I have to be in court in half an hour . . .

Harriet.   Then I'll cancel your lunch with Mr. Evans. And I'd better phone the Trust Company, in case you run over.

Mr. Haskins.   Yes, do that, will you? Oh and Harriet, I'd almost forgotten this is the twenty-sixth. Check the florist first thing will you please — you ordered the flowers Saturday, didn't you?

Harriet.   Yes.

Mr. Haskins.   Well, I won't have time to go in and write the card. Too bad, but she'll understand. Give it to them by phone. Here's the message, I scribbled it out for you.

Harriet.   Thank you.

Mr. Haskins.   Now run along. I want to collect my data on this case.

¶ SOUND: *footsteps.*

Mr. Haskins.   [*SLIGHT FADE*] Give me a buzz in twenty minutes. That'll give me ten to get there . . . should be plenty.

¶ SOUND: *door closes: couple more footsteps: phone up & dialing.*

Florist.   Green Leaf Flower Shop, good morning.

Harriet.   This is Miss Sutherland, calling for Mr. Edward Haskins. I'd like to check on the roses that were ordered for Mrs. Haskins.

Florist.   Three dozen roses — American Beauty — long stem — to be delivered November 26th. I have the order right here. They'll be delivered this afternoon.

Harriet.   And would you enclose a card, please.

Florist.   Certainly. What is the message?

Harriet.   "With love to Frances on our eighth wedding anniversary." Signed, Edward.

Florist.   Right. That's Miss Sutherland, isn't it?

Harriet.   Yes.

Florist.   I have your flowers ready too, Miss Sutherland. The wreath?

Harriet.   Oh. Good.

¶ SOUND: *door opens slightly off.*

Florist.   Would you like it sent to the cemetery? Or will you . . .

Harriet.   [*WITH COMPLETE CONTROL*] No thank you. I'll be taking it to the cemetery myself. I'll pick it up at four o'clock.

Florist.   Right, Miss Sutherland.

Harriet.   Thank you very much. Goodbye.

¶ SOUND: *receiver down.*

Mr. Haskins.   Harriet, I'm very sorry. I'm extremely sorry. That was thoughtless of me.

Harriet.   I don't think I know what you mean, Mr. Haskins.

Mr. Haskins. You must forgive me. Fortunately you have understanding of a business man . . . a man who can nearly forget his wedding anniversary . . . Harriet, I should have remembered that you have an anniversary today too. Not just such a happy one.

Harriet. You'll be late . . .

Mr. Haskins. When you asked to leave early today I should have thought. You never ask for time off, Harriet. Just this one day each year.

Harriet. You have no reason to apologize, Mr. Haskins.

Mr. Haskins. Perhaps I have. Perhaps I haven't told you sufficiently I may not have told you at all — how much I have appreciated — and needed — your help and loyalty. Your selflessness . . .

Harriet. Mr. Haskins . . .

Mr. Haskins. Mr. Haskins, Mr. Haskins! Harriet, that never seemed right . . . not that you should build that wall between us. Can't there be friendship?

Harriet. You said you would never talk of it.

Mr. Haskins. Fifteen years, and to meet like strangers every day. Harriet, forgive me, you know me well enough to understand that I'm not — that I'm not trying . . .

Harriet. You just have time to get to court.

Mr. Haskins. Yes. Yes, I suppose you're right. [*FADING*] Goodbye. Leave as early as you wish.

¶ SOUND: *door opens and closes.*

Harriet. [*AFTER A PAUSE: SAYS HIS NAME, AS THOUGH LISTENING TO THE SOUND OF IT: HER VOICE IS FILLED WITH LOVE AND WE KNOW SHE HAS SAID IT TO HERSELF A THOUSAND TIMES*] Edward. Edward.

¶ MUSIC: *bridge.*

Virginia. I can't believe it.

Mary. Virginia . . .

Virginia. I simply can't believe it, Mary, that's all. After all the trouble Henry went to to line that job up for Calvin. And then for Calvin to turn it down, on the spot, without so much as a moment's consideration . . .

Mary. He considered it.

Virginia. You simply have no idea how much trouble Henry went to. It worried him terribly. He's been very upset. Did you say Calvin considered it?

Mary. Not that job. But he's given a great deal of consideration to what he shall work at, and why. Henry's talk just strengthened his conviction, that's all.

Virginia. Then Henry didn't handle it right. Mary, let me put in to you.

Look around you. Look at this apartment. And look at what we're used to. We're used to having things nice . . .

Mary. Virginia, please. It won't do any good.

Virginia. Well, there you are! That's the whole trouble, you close your mind. You and Calvin both!

Mary. We haven't closed our minds.

Virginia. Then listen to me. If Calvin won't listen to common sense, it's your duty, as his wife, and as a mother . . .

Mary. Don't talk about duty, Virginia! You sound like Mother! There's only one duty, and that's to ourselves.

Virginia. That's an utterly selfish attitude, Mary. You say I sound like Mother — well, Mother was right when she said we should be unselfish. Look at me. Do you think it matters to me, personally, if you want to live in poverty? I'm acting purely in your own interest.

Mary. Mother would be proud of you.

Virginia. Mother knew what unselfishness meant. Look at all she gave up for us!

Mary. She gave up her whole life.

Virginia. That's right.

Mary. And asked our lives in return.

Virginia. Mary, I won't listen to this. I refuse to talk about Mother with you. The things you say . . . the terrible sacrilegious things you say . . . and Harriet out at the cemetery this very minute.

Mary. What's Harriet got to do with it?

Virginia. Harriet is a dutiful daughter. She loved Mother and respected her the way a daughter should.

Mary. You said you didn't want to talk about it, Virginia.

Virginia. That's right, I don't. We're talking about Calvin. Mary, I have this one last thing to say, and then I'll give up. It's a wife's duty to help her husband.

Mary. I agree that wife should help her husband.

Virginia. Then why don't you open Calvin's eyes?

Mary. They're already open.

Virginia. I mean about this job, and you know it. Mary, you've heard about the woman behind the man. You've just been pampering Calvin, letting him play along with this silly business of digging up old skeletons because it's fun. If Calvin has no sense of responsibility, you should teach it to him. Look at Henry.

Mary. Henry?

Virginia. He used to have some silly ideas about drawing — drawing buildings or painting pictures or something. He needed my helping hand in getting started at a job that was worth while. He decided to settle down to something respectable, and paint his pictures in his spare time.

Mary.   Did he ever paint them?

Virginia.   No. He didn't have time, and he soon gave the whole idea up anyway. And he's thanked me for it ever since.

Mary.   [PITYINGLY] Oh, Virginia, Virginia . . . I wish I could tell you . . . so that you could see . . .

Virginia.   Tell me what?

Mary.   It's like — it's like the time I wanted to build a house in the tree — and I tried to explain to Mother why I wanted it. It was more than just the novelty of a tree house. There were so many reasons why I wanted to be off the ground. Such an important long story . . .

Virginia.   [IMPATIENTLY] It *is* a long story, Mary. I can't stay all afternoon, dear, I have to shop for Sally's birthday party.

Mary.   It was about like that. Mother didn't have time to listen.

Virginia.   We're not talking abou tree houses. We're talking about Cálvin.

Mary.   [REMEMBERING] We're not talking about tree houses, Mary. We're talking about being ladylike.

Virginia.   What?

Mary.   I was just thinking how very like Mother you are. You *are* Mother, aren't you?

Virginia.   I don't know what you're talking about.

Mary.   No. That's why it wouldn't do any good to — to tell you . . .

Virginia.   Now there. You're accusing me of the very thing . . . why, just a minute ago when I tried explaining things to you you said, "Virginia, it won't do any good."

Mary.   That's true, I did. I guess we all close our minds when we think we're right. I can't blame you, Virginia. I'm doing the same thing, in my own way. No one can blame you.

¶ MUSIC: *bridge: into gay birthday.*

Children.   [SINGING] Happy birthday to you, Happy birthday to you, Happy birthday, dear Sally, happy birthday to you.

¶ MUSIC: *up and into Friday and Henry's leaving.*

Virginia.   [IN A DEAD VOICE] He told me. He didn't write me a letter. He told me. Words . . . thousands and thousands of words. And he cried. And then he left.

Harriet.   You shouldn't sit in the dark, Virginia. Let me put the light on.

Virginia.   No. Leave it dark.

Harriet.   Can I make you a cup of tea? [SLIGHT PAUSE] Virginia? [NO ANSWER]

Sally.   [OFF, IS HEARD CRYING]

Harriet.   [LOW] Mary, does Sally know?

Virginia.   I didn't tell her.

Mary. She's just crying.

Harriet. But why? If she doesn't know, what's she crying for? Maybe she's hurt.

Virginia. The children. I said, Henry what about the children. He said — I don't remember what he said.

Harriet. Virginia, he doesn't mean it. He'll be back.

Mary. Don't, Harriet.

Harriet. But, Mary . . .

Mary. Don't!

Virginia. Don't be cross with Harriet, Mary. Harriet doesn't know what it's like to love a husband, do you, Harriet?

Harriet. No.

Virginia. Harriet just knows Mr. Haskins, and he's very kind. A man is kind when he's not your husband. He asks her to parties. Mr. Haskins asked you to a party just last week, didn't he, Harriet?

Harriet. Yes.

Virginia. [GETTING EXCITED] An anniversary party. We have anniversary parties too, Henry and I, every anniversary. And birthday parties. Sally had a birthday party yesterday. I wish she'd stop crying. Isn't it funny about Mr. Haskins.

Mary. [GENTLY] What about Mr. Haskins, Virginia.

Virginia. About his anniversary. About him getting married the same day Mother died. It wasn't very thoughtful of him to get married the same day Mother died. But Mother didn't die until night, did she? I'm talking and talking. Henry talked and talked.

Harriet. Oh, Virginia, poor dear Virginia. Henry's a brute! He's heartless! Tell us what else he said.

Virginia. What did Father say to Mother?

Harriet. What?

Virginia. [DREAMILY] When he left. What did Father say when he left?

Mary. We don't know what he said.

Virginia. She told us, didn't she? Sitting in the dark. Like this. She said, he's heartless — [WITH SURPRISE] why, Harriet just said . . .

Mary. Never mind, don't talk, Virginia. Don't talk yet. Cry if you can.

Virginia. Mother didn't cry. [PLAINTIVELY] I can't remember! I can't remember what Henry looks like! He looks like Father. I can just see Father and I want Henry back I want Henry back I want . . .

Harriet. Oh, why doesn't the doctor come.

Mary. I'll phone him again.

Virginia. [UP] And tell Sally to stop crying! I can't stand it!

Mary. [A LITTLE OFF] All right, Virginia.

¶ SOUND: *door opens and closes, off, gently.*

Virginia. Harriet. Come over here.

Harriet. Yes, dear.

Virginia. Sit here. Sit here beside me, Harriet.

Harriet. Of course, Virginia.

Virginia. There. You'll stay with me tonight, won't you, Harriet? Don't let go — don't let go — take my hand! You won't leave me, will you, Harriet? You'll stay with me.

Harriet. [SHARPLY] No!

Virginia. I'm alone.

Harriet. I won't stay!

Virginia. You can't leave me alone. Harriet, if you leave me alone, I'll die.

Harriet. You'll die! Yes, you'll die! But not if I go — if I go, you'll be all right — you'll be safe, Mother. [CRYING FOR A SECOND] Oh, Mother, darling you'll be safe.

Virginia. You called me Mother. What are you doing with that pillow?

Harriet. I'm putting it behind your back. Leave it behind your back. Not on your face. Don't let anyone put it on your face. You're weak, and you can't struggle very long. I'm going, because I can't stay with you any longer. I have to go. I'll remember — I'll remember the pillow behind your back. [CALLING] Leave it there now, so that I can remember it.

Virginia. [SLIGHTLY OFF] You're all going! Where's Mary? Harriet, come back. Mary! Henry? Henry, come back.

¶ SOUND: *door opens on and closes.*

Mary. [SLIGHTLY OFF] Thank you, Doctor, I'd appreciate it if you would. Good-bye.

¶ SOUND: *receiver down.*

Mary. Oh, Harriet.

Harriet. I'm going home now. I have some typing [FADING A LITTLE] that I must do for Mr. Haskins.

Sally. [ALMOST ON, IN A LITTLE VOICE] Aunt Mary.

Mary. Sally . . .

Sally. [ON] What's the matter?

¶ SOUND: door opens slightly off.

Sally. Where's my Daddy?

Virginia. [COMING ON] Everything's all right, Sally. It's all right, baby. Mother is here.

¶ MUSIC: *closing.*

Mr. Arcularis

GERALD NOXON

Production

Producer: Andrew Allan
Music: Lucio Agostini
Sound: David Tasker
Operator: Bruce Armstrong
Announcer: Lamont Tilden
Program: Stage 53
Broadcast: November 28, 1948
Rebroadcast: January 25, 1953
Studio: Toronto
Network: Trans-Canada

Cast

John Drainie *as* Mr. Arcularis
Donald Harron *and* Herb Gott *as* Medical Students
Mora O'Hearn *as* Miss Hoyle, Clarice, and Mother
Howard Milsom *as* Dr. Mitchell and Reverend Mr. Mordant
Bud Knapp *as* Dr. Venner and the Ship's Captain
Patrick Macnee *and* Alan King *as* the Stewards
Alan Pearce *as* the Ship's Officer
Richard Gilbert *as* Uncle David

•

MR. ARCULARIS

Preface

When "Mr. Arcularis," Gerald Noxon's most famous play — and perhaps also Andrew Allan's — was first broadcast, it caused a sensation among the listening audience. It has turned out to be the one play from the *Stage* series best remembered (in our experience) by the many people who recall Allan's work. It is for this reason, and because the play has a special symbolic relevance in defining our national character, that "Mr. Arcularis" was chosen, the only adaptation among the plays in this anthology.

Gerald Noxon was born in Toronto in 1910. He attended school in Montreal and England, and completed his undergraduate degree at Trinity College, Cambridge. He then did graduate work at the Sorbonne and at Regia University, Perugia. His earliest radio work was mainly script-writing, for the BBC, for NBC and CBS, as well as for the private 'offshore' English stations: Poste Parisienne, Radio Luxembourg, and Radio Normandie. He returned to Canada at the start of World War II to write drama, variety, and documentary shows for CBC. Noxon, whose other main interest has always been film, began a career in the teaching of film, radio, and television writing and production at Boston University in 1947; he has been Professor of Film and Dramaturgy there since 1952.

The relationship between Conrad Aiken's story "Mr. Arcularis" and Noxon's play is fascinating. Noxon, an acquaintance of Aiken's, wrote the play during the summer of 1948 at Aiken's Cape Cod home. Andrew Allan was also there, writing an adaptation of Joseph Conrad's "Heart of Darkness," also for *Stage*. As Allan hints in his autobiography, the atmosphere was supercharged while Noxon laboured over the translation of the narrative to the radio-drama medium, with Aiken's and Allan's encouragement and support. There had been previous attempt at dramatizing the story; Diana Hamilton wrote the adaptation for a 1946 touring production in England, culminating on the London stage. Aiken was called in to do desperate rewrites as the play toured the

205

provinces. Unhappy with the liberties taken by Hamilton with the story, he never did achieve a satisfactory rewrite at that time. Aiken discusses all this in the introduction to his own (the third!) version of the play, published five years after the CBC Noxon production. Noxon's "Mr. Arcularis" is the most satisfying of the three dramatizations: the most dramatic, and the most faithful of all to the spirit and substance of Aiken's original story.

GERALD NOXON

Mr. Arcularis

Andrew Allan.   Good evening, this is Andrew Allan. Tonight with Item 18 of *Stage* 53, we observe the ninth anniversary of the Sunday Night *Stages*, and begin our tenth year of broadcasting. To mark this occasion we are doing a revival performance of what is perhaps the most popular play we have presented in these nine years . . . "Mr. Arcularis."

¶ MUSIC: *title cue up: to background.*

Announcer.   *Stage* 53 . . . Item 18 . . . "Mr. Arcularis," a story by Conrad Aiken, adapted for radio by Gerald Noxon. Starring John Drainie in the title role. Produced and directed by Andrew Allan, with an original musical score composed and conducted by Lucio Agostini. Conrad Aiken's "Mr. Arcularis."

¶ MUSIC: *up and finish.*

¶ SOUND: *lecture theatre chatter sneaks into background and remains.*

Kurt.   [*COMING ON*] Hello, John . . .
John.   Hello, there, Kurt, I . . .
Kurt.   Thanks for saving my seat.
John.   I nearly let it go . . . thought you might not be coming.
Kurt.   Matter of fact, I didn't intend to, not till I heard what old man Venner had up his sleeve for today.
John.   Something special?
Kurt.   You haven't heard? You . . . the perfect student?
John.   No. What's up?
Kurt.   The illustrious surgeon, Robert D. Venner, is going to operate on a case of advanced disease of the Mitral valve for our edification.
John.   But that's hopeless, Kurt.
Kurt.   Venner's pulled it off several times, you know.
John.   It's one chance in a hundred. Whoever the patient is, he's

207

practically signing his own death warrant. Some poor devil who
doesn't know what it's all about, I suppose?

Kurt.   On the contrary, my friend, today's guinea pig is neither poor,
nor ignorant.

John.   You mean he's not a charity case?

Kurt.   Far from it.

John.   Then he must be crazy. What's his name?

Kurt.   His name is Arcularis.

John.   What?

Kurt.   Ar — cu — lar — is. Mr. Arcularis.

John.   That's a rum sort of a name.

Kurt.   Yes. And I gather he's a rum sort of a fellow . . . all kinds of
money . . . no wife . . . family . . . all alone in the world.

John.   I see. By the way, how come you're so well informed on the subject of today's victim?

Kurt.   I've been taking an interest in the girl who's been nursing him
. . . little Miss Hoyle . . .

John.   Oh . . .

Kurt.   And, I may say, I've been getting precisely nowhere with her.

John.   You must be slipping, Kurt. She's no beauty.

Kurt.   That's debatable. Anyway, she doesn't seem to have much time
for yours truly. She's far too wrapped up in her patient . . . her dear,
precious Mr. Arcularis.

¶ MUSIC: *short Arcularis statement up.*

Miss Hoyle.   There, Mr. Arcularis . . . you'll feel better in a moment . . .
when the injection begins to take effect.

Arcularis.   Thank you, Miss Hoyle, you're very kind to me . . . and
patient. I don't know why I feel so restless.

Miss Hoyle.   It's only natural, Mr. Arcularis, after all . . .

Arcularis.   You mean on account of the operation? I'm quite prepared
for it, Miss Hoyle . . . quite prepared, only . . .

Miss Hoyle.   Yes . . . ?

Arcularis.   [DROWSILY] Only, I haven't been sleeping very well lately. I
don't usually dream much, but lately I've had dreams . . . all kinds of
dreams . . .

Miss Hoyle.   I know.
   Pause.

Arcularis.   Will . . . will they be coming for me soon?

Miss Hoyle.   Very soon.

Arcularis.   [TRYING TO ROUSE HIMSELF] Miss Hoyle . . .

Miss Hoyle.   Yes.

Arcularis.   You won't leave me, will you?

Miss Hoyle.   Of course not, Mr. Arcularis.

208

Arcularis. Stay with me. Take my hand and stay with me. Please stay with me . . . I . . . [SIGHS AND FALLS ASLEEP]

¶ MUSIC: *a sigh.*

¶ SOUND: *chatter background: in lecture theatre.*

Mitchell. [SOTTO VOCE, CLOSE ON] How's your patient, Miss Hoyle?

Miss Hoyle. [SOTTO VOCE, CLOSE ON] He's been very restless, Doctor Mitchell, but he's all right now . . . sleeping quietly. Do you want to wheel him in?

Mitchell. No, not yet, nurse . . . not till Doctor Venner gets here. Besides, I have something to say to the students first. [PROJECTING] Gentlemen . . . gentlemen . . .

¶ SOUND: *chatter dies down.*

Mitchell. Your attention, please. . . . Today we are going to have the privilege of witnessing an operation of truly remarkable interest, performed by one of our finest surgeons . . . Doctor Robert D. Venner. Doctor Venner will operate on a case of advanced disease of the Mitral valve of the heart. As you know, such cases are not common and the operation is one of the greatest delicacy, requiring the utmost skill and judgement on the part of the surgeon. You will understand that I do not exaggerate in this particular when I tell you that in the course of this operation you will see the patient's living heart, completely exposed in Doctor Venner's hand . . .

¶ SOUND: *excited murmur from students.*

Mitchell. Our thanks are due today, not only to Doctor Venner for coming here, but to the patient who has, in the interest of medical science, consented to allow the operation to take place here in the lecture theatre. Gentlemen, I shall expect your undivided attention during the operation. And afterwards I trust that each of you will present a precise and exhaustive analysis of it.

¶ SOUND: *reaction from students which subsides into quiet.*

Miss Hoyle. [SOTTO VOCE, CLOSE ON] Here's Doctor Venner, sir.

Mitchell. Good. Ask them to wheel in the patient, nurse.

Venner. Ah, good day, Mitchell. You're going to act as my anaesthetist, I presume?

Mitchell. Yes, Doctor Venner.

Venner. Is the patient ready?

Mitchell. They're bringing him now, doctor.

Venner. All right, let's have a look at him.

Arcularis. [MURMURING UNINTELLIGIBLY] Mmmmm . . . errr . . . mmmm . . .

Venner.   Ah . . . he seems very restless.
Mitchell.   Yes. Miss Hoyle, I thought you said the patient was quiet?
Miss Hoyle.   He was, Doctor, for a while, but . . .
Venner.   He's had an injection, of course?
Miss Hoyle.   Yes, Doctor.
Venner.   All right. I'll try to quiet him. [*WHISPERING CLOSE ON*]

¶ MUSIC: *faint sneak background of nightmare theme.*

Venner.   [*STRAIGHT ON*] Mr. Arcularis . . . listen to me. Mr. Arcularis. You're going to be all right. You're going to be perfectly all right. So don't worry . . . don't worry . . . don't worry. [*PAUSE: IN NORMAL VOICE*] Check on him please, Mitchell.

¶ MUSIC: *out.*

Mitchell.   Seems all right.
Venner.   Pulse?
Mitchell.   Ninety.
Venner.   Blood Pressure?
Mitchell.   One forty over eighty-three.
Arcularis.   [*MURMURING AGAIN*] Mmmm . . . errr . . . mmmmm . . .
Miss Hoyle.   [*WHISPERING*] There, Mr. Arcularis, there . . . I haven't left you. I'm right here beside you. Everything's going to be all right. There's nothing to be afraid of, nothing at all . . .
Mitchell.   [*IN ANGRY WHISPER*] Miss Hoyle, what are you doing? What *on earth* are you doing? Let go of the patient's hand.
Miss Hoyle.   I . . .
Mitchell.   Let go of it, you idiot. Put it back under the sheet.
Miss Hoyle.   I . . . I can't . . .
Mitchell.   What?
Miss Hoyle.   I can't. He's holding on too tight, I . . .
Mitchell.   Oh, you fool. . . . Let me see. There . . . now stand back.
Miss Hoyle.   Yes, Doctor.
Mitchell.   [*IN NORMAL VOICE*] He's ready now, Doctor Venner.
Venner.   Pulse?
Mitchell.   Still ninety.
Venner.   Good enough. Time, nurse?
Miss Hoyle.   Eleven fifty-nine.
Venner.   All right. Let's go.

¶ MUSIC: *dramatic bridge introducing nightmare sleepwalking theme: up: then transition to something tender and familiar.*

Mitchell.   Good morning, Miss Hoyle.
Miss Hoyle.   Good morning Doctor Mitchell.
Mitchell.   Where's your patient?

Miss Hoyle.   Mr. Arcularis is in the bathroom, Doctor . . . dressing himself.

Mitchell.   Getting dressed on his own, eh? He must be feeling pretty
well.

Miss Hoyle.   He's still very weak, Doctor.

Mitchell.   That's to be expected. It's rather a pity he has to set off on this
trip alone.

Miss Hoyle.   I wish . . . I wish *I* were going with him.

Arcularis.   [*COMING IN*] Good morning Doctor.

Mitchell.   Good morning, Mr. Arcularis. And how do you feel this
morning?

Arcularis.   Not too bad, considering . . . a trifle unsteady on my pins
and bit fuzzy in the head.

Mitchell.   The ocean voyage is just what you need to fix you up. I don't
mind telling you now that the operation was a close thing.

Arcularis.   And I don't mind telling *you* now that I was absolutely sure I
was going to die there on the operating table. I remember faces
leaning over me, just before it started, I suppose it was, and . . .

Mitchell.   The anaesthetic does have a strange effect on people sometimes . . .

Arcularis.   And I could hear voices, coming out of a cloud. I was
reminded somehow of my mother.

Mitchell.   Your mother!

Arcularis.   Yes, my very pretty and very wicked mother who died
young. I . . .

Mitchell.   Perhaps you'd better sit down, Mr. Arcularis. You're feeling
faint, aren't you?

Arcularis.   Yes, just a trifle.

Mitchell.   Perhaps I'd better drive down to the dock with you, Mr.
Arcularis?

Arcularis.   Thank you, but it won't be necessary. An old friend of mine
is calling for me. He's going to drive me down in his car and see me
safely on board.

Mitchell.   You must take it easy.

Arcularis.   I will, Doctor, I promise you. Any other advice for the
departing traveller?

Mitchell.   Not too many latitudes with the young ladies, Mr. Arcularis.

Arcularis.   Oh, no latitudes at all, Doctor. I'll leave the latitudes to the
ship.

Mitchell.   That's right, that's right. Goodbye, Mr. Arcularis, and bon
voyage.

¶ MUSIC: *tender familiar theme as bridge.*

Arcularis.   How strange and vivid the world looks from my window,

Miss Hoyle.

Miss Hoyle.   It must, to you, today.

Arcularis.   It looks ... it looks as if it had been made freshly for me, I ...

¶ MUSIC: *itinerant band in street below playing finale from Cavelleria Rusticana: violin, harp and flute.*

Arcularis.   Ah, so our musician friends are back.

Miss Hoyle.   How nice of them. They've come to give you a final serenade.

Arcularis.   I must say, I'd rather they hadn't.

Miss Hoyle.   Why, Mr. Arcularis, I thought you liked their music?

Arcularis.   Not this tune, Miss Hoyle, not this tune. Still, they do *look* rather nice standing down there on the wet sidewalk. Oh, it's *all* so wonderful after the shower. The innumerable green fresh leaves, blowing and turning and flashing in the wind . . . and the sky, strung with rain like a harp . . . every raindrop sparkling . . .

Miss Hoyle.   And the robins in the wet trees.

Arcularis.   Even the streetcars are bright and beautiful . . . just as they looked when I was a child. It's all so dear and familiar.

Miss Hoyle.   I'm sure it is, Mr. Arcularis.

Arcularis.   I feel I don't want to leave it. I don't want to go.

Miss Hoyle.   But think of all the wonderful things you're going to see when you're abroad. Think of the sea and the sunshine.

Arcularis.   Yes, Miss Hoyle, I suppose you're right. It's silly of me to get emotional, especially now when everything is over.

Miss Hoyle.   It's probably because it *is* over that you feel emotional, Mr. Arcularis.

Arcularis.   [*TRYING TO CONVINCE HIMSELF*] After all, what could be more delightful? A sea voyage . . . Paris . . . Switzerland . . . a long time since I've seen them. And it's June with the best of the year to come. Yet somehow I'm homesick already, homesick without having left home.

Miss Hoyle.   Is that, perhaps, because you are going alone?

Arcularis.   Yes, perhaps it is.

Miss Hoyle.   I do think you should have someone with you.

Arcularis.   You, for instance?

Miss Hoyle.   Oh, Mr. Arcularis . . .

Arcularis.   Dear me, I'm used to being alone.

¶ MUSIC: *street musicians finished by now.*

¶ SOUND: *knocking on door.*

Miss Hoyle.   There, that must be your friend. I'll let him in.

¶ SOUND: *door opens.*

Arcularis. Harry!

Harry. Well, if it isn't good old Ark! How are you, feller? You look swell.

Arcularis. Fine thanks, Harry. Good of you to come.

Miss Hoyle. I'll get a porter for your bags, Mr. Arcularis.

Arcularis. Thank you, Miss Hoyle.

Harry. Well, *well* . . . how does it feel to be back on your feet again, you old sinner?

Arcularis. Wonderful, Harry, simply wonderful. Just take a look out there . . . the whole world with a new coat of paint on it.

Harry. Yes. I bet it sure looks good to you.

Arcularis. Words fail me.

Harry. Just wait till you get out there on the briny. Gosh, man, how we all envy you. What a time you're going to have! And how we're going to miss you at the club.

Arcularis. I'll miss you, Harry, and the club, too.

Harry. The bar won't be the same without you.

Arcularis. Perhaps, but let there be no moaning at the bar when I put out to sea . . .

Harry. Ha . . . ha. . . . It's the same good Old Ark.

Arcularis. [*SUDDENLY WEAK*] Not quite . . . I'm afraid . . .

Harry. Whoa there, feller, what's wrong?

Arcularis. Nothing much. It's just that every now and then things seem to swim and dissolve around me. The houses out there suddenly began to lean their heads together . . . disconcerting rather. . . and there was sort of a humming noise, rising and falling . . .

Harry. Say, are you sure you're really up to this trip? I mean . . .

Arcularis. Oh, absolutely. I've been checked out by the doctors. Hadn't we better go?

Harry. I guess so. If you're sure you're all right.

Arcularis. Right as rain now. Be a good chap and get my coat out of the closet, will you? Ah, Miss Hoyle . . .

Miss Hoyle. I'll get your coat, Mr. Arcularis.

Arcularis. Thank you, Miss Hoyle. I hate being cold.

Harry. [*MOVING OFF*] We're off because we're off, because we're off, because we're off . . .

¶ MUSIC: *bridge crossfading to:*

¶ SOUND: *harbour background with gulls, tugs, etc: faintly and murmur of conversation.*

Harry. We're here because we're here, because we're here . . .

Arcularis. Because we're here.

Harry. And now for a drink. [*CALLING OUT*] Steward . . . Steward . . .

1st Steward.   Yes, sir . . . coming, sir.

Harry.   Steward . . . two double whiskies.

1st Steward.   Right away, sir.

Harry.   Ah, as I always say, there's no bar like a ship's bar.

Arcularis.   But it's too cold in here . . . I can hardly keep my teeth from chattering.

Harry.   Cold? We'll soon fix that, eh, Steward?

1st Steward.   Yes, sir. Certainly. Your whiskey, sir.

Harry.   There. Drink it down, Ark. That'll soon chase the chill out of you.

Arcularis.   I hope so. I can't think how it can be so cold in June.

Harry.   It's the East wind, feller. And don't forget you've just come out of that stuffy, overheated hospital.

Arcularis.   Yes, that's true, but still . . . I say, Harry . . .

Harry.   What is it? Something wrong?

Arcularis.   No. It's just . . . just that girl at the table over there by the door.

Harry.   What about her?

Arcularis.   Look at her carefully.

Harry.   She's very pretty . . . almost beautiful.

Arcularis.   Doesn't she remind you of someone?

Harry.   Hummmm . . . Now you come to mention it, yes. She looks rather like that little nurse who was looking after you at the hospital.

Arcularis.   She doesn't remind you of anyone else?

Harry.   No.

Arcularis.   You never saw my mother, did you, Harry?

Harry.   Why, no . . .

Arcularis.   You couldn't have. She died so young.

Harry.   Look . . . we've embarrassed the poor girl with our staring. She's getting up to leave.

Arcularis.   [*WHISPERING*] I think not. She isn't going to leave.

Harry.   [*WHISPERING*] You're right. She's coming our way. This is bad.

Clarice.   Pardon me, gentlemen, but you have been looking at me as if you recognized me and . . .

Harry.   Please accept our humblest apologies, Madam.

Arcularis.   Our behavior has been inexcusable . . .

Clarice.   Oh, no, please don't apologize. You see, well, I have such a poor memory for names and I was afraid you might think me rude.

Arcularis.   You mean . . . ?

Clarice.   I mean that I am almost certain that I have met you somewhere before, but I have to admit that I can't remember your name.

Arcularis.   My name is Arcularis.

Clarice.   [*WITHOUT RECOGNITION*] Arcularis.

Arcularis.   Yes. And my friend here is Harry Freeman.

Clarice. I'm Clarice Dean.

Arcularis. Miss Dean.

Harry. Won't you have a drink with us?

Clarice. Thank you, but we're due to sail any minute now, you know, and I must go down to my cabin.

Arcularis. Then perhaps we can get together later on, Miss Dean?

Clarice. That would be nice. Goodbye, gentlemen.

Arcularis. Goodbye.

Harry. Well, if that isn't the strangest thing, I . . .

¶ SOUND: *ship's siren blowing the "all ashore."*

2nd Steward. [*COMING ON AND GOING OFF AGAIN*] All ashore that's going ashore! All ashore that's going ashore! All ashore that's going ashore!

Harry. Well, that's it, feller. Time for me to go.

Arcularis. Oh, Harry, do you . . . do you have to . . .

Harry. Do I have to? I'll say I have to. Can't all have your luck, you know, flitting off on trips to Europe. Goodbye, old fellow, and take care of yourself. Bring me back a spray of edelweiss from the Alps. And send me a picture post card from the Absolute, won't you?

Arcularis. All right, Harry. Will you have it finite or infinite?

Harry. Oh, infinite. But with your signature on it. Cheerio.

Arcularis. Goodbye, Harry . . . Goodbye . . .

¶ SOUND: *blast of the ship's siren cross fading with:*

¶ MUSIC: *bridge: cross fading with:*

¶ SOUND: *rhythmic thumping of ship's engines, up to establish then to background and retained.*

¶ SOUND: *knock on cabin door.*

Arcularis. Come in.

¶ SOUND: *door opens.*

2nd Steward. You rang, sir?

Arcularis. Yes. It's terribly cold in here. Would you mind closing the porthole.

2nd Steward. Certainly, sir. But I'm afraid I'll have to switch the light on, so as I can see what I'm about.

Arcularis. Yes, of course. [*LIGHT SWITCH*] When I came down here it was still light. I must have fallen asleep. Where are we?

2nd Steward. Oh, we're well on our way, sir, out of sight of land for several hours now.

Arcularis. What time is it?

215

2nd Steward. Getting on for eight, sir. [*PORTHOLE CLOSES*] They'll be sounding the bugle for second service any minute. [*PORTHOLE CLAMPS*]

Arcularis. Then I must get up and dress. But I'm so cold. Steward, why is it so cold in this cabin?

2nd Steward. It doesn't feel particularly cold to me, sir. But I understand you've been ill, sir . . .

Arcularis. Yes, very ill. I've just come out of hospital.

2nd Steward. Then that probably accounts for it.

Arcularis. Yes, probably . . .

2nd Steward. Anyway, it'll soon warm up in here now.

Arcularis. Yes, thank you, Steward.

2nd Steward. If you should ever want anything, sir, you've only to touch the bell, you know.

Arcularis. Want anything? What could I want?

2nd Steward. Oh, a drink, or a book, or a snack between meals. I've the run of the kitchens, you know, and keys to everything. Whatever you fancy, I can get it for you. If you don't feel like going up to the dining saloon, I can pick you out a prime piece of steak from the freezer and have it grilled just to your taste, sir.

Arcularis. That's very kind of you, Steward.

2nd Steward. Oh, that's what I'm here for, sir. And when a gentleman's been ill, like you have, sir, he needs some pampering, if you ask me.

¶ MUSIC: *dinner bugle in distance: fading into bridge: dining saloon.*

Arcularis. So we meet again, Miss Dean.

Clarice. Yes, Mr. Arcularis, we meet again.

Arcularis. It was thoughtful of them to seat us together at the Captain's table, wasn't it?

Clarice. Yes, indeed, but . . . but where is your friend?

Arcularis. Oh, he's not on board. You see, he just came down to see me off.

Clarice. Then you are alone?

Arcularis. Yes, quite alone. And you?

Clarice. Yes, I'm on my own, too.

1st Steward. Pardon me, sir. Your order, sir?

Arcularis. I'll take the thick soup to start with.

1st Steward. No hors d'oeuvres, sir?

Arcularis. I think not. They might kill me.

1st Steward. Beg your pardon, sir?

Arcularis. Nothing. The thick soup, please.

1st Steward. Yes, sir.

Clarice. I'm afraid you shocked him.

Arcularis. Impossible. These stewards are dead souls. How could they

216

be stewards otherwise?

Clarice.   It must be a dreadful sort of life.

Arcularis.   Of course it has its compensations.

Clarice.   Such as?

Arcularis.   Oh, they have the run of the lower decks. They can go everywhere and they've got keys to everything. They're regular little lords in their own domains.

Clarice.   Even so . . .

Arcularis.   Yes, even so, it is, as you say, a dreadful sort of life. It's because they're dead that they accept it.

Clarice.   Do you think so?

Arcularis.   I'm enough of a dead soul myself to know the signs.

Clarice.   Well, I'm sure I don't know what you mean by that.

Arcularis.   I'm just out of hospital after an operation. I was given up for dead. For six months I'd given *myself* up for dead. If you've ever been seriously ill you know the feeling . . .

Clarice.   Yes?

Arcularis.   You have a sort of posthumous feeling . . . a mild cynical tolerance for everything and everyone. What is there that you haven't seen or done or understood? Nothing.

Clarice.   I wish I could understand you, but I've never been ill in my life.

Arcularis.   Never?

Clarice.   Never.

Arcularis.   Good heavens.

Clarice.   I'm sorry.

Arcularis.   No, don't be sorry. And don't pay any attention to invalids like myself, or they'll drag you to the hospital.

Clarice.   You don't *look* like an invalid.

Arcularis.   [PLEASED] You mean that, really?

Clarice.   Of course.

1st Steward.   Your soup, sir.

Arcularis.   Ah, thank you.

Mordant.   If you will pardon the intrusion, sir, I will take the liberty of passing you the salt.

Arcularis.   Thank you, sir.

Mordant.   The Reverend Edosius Mordant, at your service, sir.

Arcularis.   My name is Arcularis and this is Miss Dean.

Mordant.   Madam, sir, I am honoured.

Clarice.   Do you think we'll have a good voyage, Steward?

1st Steward.   Well, madam, I don't like to be a Jeremiah, but . . .

Mordant.   Oh, come, I hope we have no Jeremiahs amongst us.

Clarice.   What do you mean?

¶ MUSIC: *a sinister nightmare background (on cue "Ireland" below).*

1st Steward. Well, maybe I shouldn't say it, but there's a corpse on board going to Ireland; and I never yet knew a voyage with a corpse on board that we didn't have bad weather.

Clarice. Why, Steward, you're just superstitious. What nonsense.

Arcularis. That's a very ancient superstition. I've heard it many times. Maybe it's true. Maybe we'll be wrecked. And what does it matter after all?

Mordant. What does it matter? Come, come, Mr. Arcularis.

Arcularis. With a corpse in the hold, or wherever they carry corpses, perhaps some disaster may befall us. We may run into fog or icebergs. Remember the *Titanic* with the band playing "Nearer My God to Thee" on the after-deck while she went down.

Clarice. Oh, Mr. Arcularis, please . . .

Arcularis. And the *Empress of Ireland* with all those poor people trapped in the smoking-room, with only one door between themselves and life, and that door locked for the night by the deck steward and the deck steward missing. Ah . . .

¶ MUSIC: *out.*

Mordant. I fear, sir, that you are suffering from some unduly morbid delusions this evening.

Arcularis. Delusions? Yes, strange delusions. I wonder how such thoughts arise in the mind.

Mordant. From nothing but fear, sir. Nothing on earth but fear.

Clarice. [REFLECTIVELY] How strange! [BRIGHTLY] If you gentlemen will excuse me, I'll leave you now.

Arcularis. I'm sorry. I've bored you with my foolish talk.

Clarice. No, no, it's not that.

Arcularis. Then I will see you in the lounge later on?

Clarice. Of course.

Mordant. A very charming girl, if I may say so, Mr. Arcularis.

Arcularis. Yes, isn't she delightful, so warm, so friendly and so pretty, almost beautiful.

Mordant. May I ask if you have known her long?

¶ MUSIC: *tender, familiar theme background.*

Arcularis. Yes . . . no . . . that is, I can hardly say. Tell me, Reverend Mordant, does she remind you of someone?

Mordant. Remind me of someone? Why, no I . . .

Arcularis. You see, she and I are only shipboard acquaintances, but she looks like someone I know and I feel that I knew her somewhere long ago. It wasn't at Portsmouth where I lived as a child, nor at Salem, nor in the rose garden at Aunt Julia's, nor at Cambridge where I went to school. Where do you suppose it could have been, Reverend Mordant?

¶ MUSIC: *pauses.*

Mordant. That, sir, is a question to which I feel myself totally incapable of supplying an answer.

¶ MUSIC: *resumes as bridge: nightmare: ship's engines.*

2nd Steward. Mr. Arcularis . . . Mr. Arcularis . . .
Arcularis. Yes . . . yes . . . what? Where am I?
2nd Steward. You're safe in bed in your cabin, sir. It's morning and I've brought you your tea.
Arcularis. Morning, yes. But what morning, Steward, that's the important thing. What morning . . . Monday, Tuesday, Wednesday, Thursday?
2nd Steward. It's Tuesday morning, sir.
Arcularis. Tuesday . . . and still as cold as ever.
2nd Steward. There's a bit of a mist this morning . . . a bit of a sea fog with a chill in it.
Arcularis. I'm so cold, I feel numb all over.
2nd Steward. You need more covers on your bunk, sir. I'll get you another blanket for tonight.
Arcularis. Thank you, Steward.
2nd Steward. By the way, sir, I suppose you haven't come across a bunch of keys here in your cabin?
Arcularis. Keys? No. Why?
2nd Steward. Mine are missing, sir . . . the ones that open the kitchen cupboards, and the pantries and the freezers. I must have laid them down somewhere and forgot to pick them up again.
Arcularis. I see.
2nd Steward. It's funny because I'm not one to mislay things as a rule.
Arcularis. I'm sorry, but I'm afraid I haven't seen them, Steward.
2nd Steward. Oh, I really didn't suppose you had, sir, only I thought it wouldn't do any harm to ask.
Arcularis. Of course not. And I do hope you'll find them.
2nd Steward. Oh, they'll turn up sooner or later, sir, never fear.

¶ MUSIC: *sinister, cold, nightmare bridge: gulls: bow-wave.*

Arcularis. Have you ever done any sleep-walking, Miss Dean?
Clarice. No, I never have.
Arcularis. That's the funny part of it. I never had either until last night. Never in my life. Why, I hardly ever even dream. So this really rather frightens me.
Clarice. Tell me about it, Mr. Arcularis.

¶ MUSIC: *sneaks: thin, arctic.*

Arcularis. I dreamed at first that I was walking alone, in a wide plain covered with snow. It was growing dark, I was very cold, my feet were frozen and numb and I was lost. I came then to a signpost . . . at first it seemed to me there was nothing on it. Nothing but ice. Just before it grew finally dark, however, I made out on it the one word . . . "Polaris."
Clarice. The Pole Star.
Arcularis. Yes . . . and you see, I didn't myself know that. I looked it up only this morning. I suppose I must have seen it somewhere. And of course it rhymes with my name.
Clarice. Polaris . . . Arcularis. Why, so it does.
Arcularis. Anyway, it gave me . . . in the dream, I mean . . . an awful feeling of despair, and then the dream changed. This time I dreamed I was standing outside my stateroom in the little dark corridor, or *cul-de-sac*, and trying to find the door handle to let myself in. I was in my pyjamas and again I was very cold. And at that point I woke up.

¶ MUSIC: *pauses.*

Clarice. Yes?
Arcularis. The extraordinary thing is that's exactly where I was.

¶ MUSIC: *resumes: darker.*

Clarice. Good heavens. How very strange.
Arcularis. Yes, and now the question is . . . where had I been? I was frightened when I came to . . . not unnaturally. For among other things I did have, quite definitely, the feeling that I had been somewhere. Somewhere where it was very cold. It doesn't sound very proper, does it? Suppose I had been seen.

¶ MUSIC: *ends background.*

Clarice. That might have been very awkward.
Arcularis. It's very singular. I've never done such a thing before. Altogether it's the kind of thing that reminds one . . . rather wholesomely, perhaps, don't you think? . . . how extraordinarily little we know about the workings of our own minds or souls.
Clarice. Do you think, Mr. Arcularis, that we might go into the lounge now? I find the darkness here on deck a little depressing.
Arcularis. Why, of course, Miss Dean. We'll go in and listen to the ship's orchestra. [*BOARD FADE*] We'll listen to the orchestra in the lounge.

¶ MUSIC: *fade in ship's orchestra playing the finale to Cavelleria Rusticana rather badly: continues background.*

Arcularis. Good heavens, can I never escape from that horrible sentimental tune. It's the last thing I heard in America and the last thing I want to hear.

Clarice. But don't you like it?

Arcularis. When I heard it at the hospital . . . when was that? . . . it made me feel like crying. Three old Italians tootling it there in the rain. I suppose like most people I'm afraid of my feelings.

Clarice. Are they so dangerous?

Arcularis. Now then, young woman. Are you trying to pull my leg?

Officer. Pardon me interrupting, sir, but I thought perhaps the young lady might care to dance.

Arcularis. That's all right, officer. How about it, Miss Dean? Would you like to dance?

Clarice. Would you mind very much if I did, Mr. Arcularis?

Arcularis. Not at all, not at all. You are young. You must enjoy yourself.

Clarice. Are you quite sure you won't mind?

Arcularis. Absolutely. And besides, it's my bedtime. I'm going to turn in.

Clarice. Goodnight, Mr. Arcularis. And sleep tight tonight.

Officer. Goodnight, sir.

Arcularis. Goodnight . . . goodnight.

¶ MUSIC: *bridge indicating nightmare segues out of ship's orchestra: continues graphically to end up:*

¶ SOUND: *ship's engines.*

Doctor. I'm only a ship's doctor, Mr. Arcularis, and I don't pretend to know much about the workings of the human mind, but if you'll tell me about your dream, I think it may help to relieve your anxiety.

¶ MUSIC: *sneaks background: engine rhythm at first: then thinly descriptive.*

Arcularis. Last night was the second night in succession. It started with the engines. The rhythm of the engines became positively a persecution. It gave me no rest, it followed me like the Hound of Heaven, it drove me out into space and across the Milky Way and then back home by way of Betelgeuse. It was cold there. I sparkled with frost. I felt like a Christmas tree. I was barefoot. There were icicles on my fingers and my toes. Snowflakes and tinsel blew past me. And always the perpetual throbbing, the iteration of sound, like a pain, those circles and repetitions of light . . . the feeling as of everything coiling inward to a centre of misery . . .

Doctor. Go on, Mr. Arcularis.

Arcularis. Suddenly it was dark and I was lost. I was groping, I touched the cold, white slippery woodwork with my fingernails hunting for the electric light switch. The throbbing was again the throbbing of the ship's engines. And I was almost home, almost home. Another corner to round, a door to be opened, and there I'd be. Safe and sound. Safe in my father's home.

Doctor.   And that was the end of your dream?

Arcularis.   Yes. It was at that moment I woke up. I was in the corridor that leads to the dining saloon and I was seized with such a pure terror as I have never known. My heart felt as if it would stop beating. My back was towards the dining saloon; so aparently I had just come from it. I was in my pyjamas. The corridor was dim. . . only two lights had been left on for the night . . . and thank heavens it was deserted. Not a soul, not a sound, but the engines. I was only fifty yards from my stateroom. I felt that with luck I could get to it unseen. I held to the rail that ran along the wall and crept my way forward. I felt weak, very dizzy and my thoughts refused to concentrate. I thought I was in the hospital, then I knew I was on the ship. And then I was in my room with the door safely shut behind me. I broke into a cold sweat and crept shivering into my bunk. A few moments later I heard the night watchman pass. I lay there thinking . . . where have I been?

¶ MUSIC: *ends.*

Doctor.   A nasty experience, no doubt, Mr. Arcularis, but . . .

Arcularis.   You don't think it's anything serious, do you?

Doctor.   No, I'm sure it's nothing serious.

Arcularis.   I knew you'd think that. But just the same . . .

Doctor.   Sleepwalking is by no means an uncommon manifestation of mental unrest. The condition results from worry. Are you worried . . . do you mind telling me? . . . about something. Just try to think.

Arcularis.   Worried? No. There's nothing . . . nothing at all.

Doctor.   Well, it's all very strange.

Arcularis.   Strange! I should say so. I've come to sea for a rest, not for a nightmare. What about a bromide for tonight?

Doctor.   Well, I can give you a bromide, Mr. Arcularis, but . . .

Arcularis.   Then please, if you don't mind, give me one.

¶ MUSIC: *bridge.*

Mordant.   These things always come from a sense of guilt, you know. You feel guilty about something. If you could rid yourself of the sense of guilt . . .

Arcularis.   What do you mean Reverend Mordant? What are you accusing me of? I have no guilt.

Mordant.   Oh, come, come, Mr. Arcularis, we're all of us guilty in some way or another. We're all hiding wickedness in ourselves.

Arcularis.   The wickedness was not mine. It was his, and hers, too.

Mordant.   Of course, if you would care to confide in me, I . . .

Arcularis.   What? What did I say. I didn't know what I was saying. Why must you pester me like this?

Mordant. My dear Mr. Arcularis, I don't want to pester you, I merely said . . .

Arcularis. Then let me go . . . do you hear? Let me go. I've got to find her. I've simply got to find her.

¶ MUSIC: *bridge.*

Arcularis. [OUT OF BREATH] Miss Dean . . . Clarice . . . please may I call you, Clarice?

Clarice. Of course you may, Mr. Arcularis.

Arcularis. Clarice . . . it happened again . . . it happened again last night.

Clarice. I know.

Arcularis. What? How do you know? Who told you?

Clarice. No one told me.

Arcularis. Then . . . ?

Clarice. I saw you myself.

Arcularis. You saw me?

Clarice. Yes. You see, last night after the dance was over, I was worried about you. It was very late, but I went to your cabin, just to make sure you were all right. I found you weren't there and I was very alarmed. I waited in the shadows near the door of your cabin. I saw you come back safely and I thought it better not to interfere. I've heard it's dangerous to interfere with sleepwalkers . . .

Arcularis. Ah, Clarice, if you could understand how I felt at that moment . . .

Clarice. When you had gone back into your cabin and shut the door I waited for a while longer and then came away. Just as I came to the corner of the corridor near the stairs I noticed something on the floor. It seemed to me that you had dropped it, for I had heard a curious sound.

Arcularis. What . . . what was it that you found?

Clarice. I have it here. Look . . .

¶ SOUND: *keys.*

Arcularis. A bunch of keys. No . . . no . . . NO.

¶ MUSIC: *bridge: terrified.*

2nd Steward. You sent for me, Captain?

Captain. Ah, yes, Smith. I understand that you've lost some keys.

2nd Steward. I don't know as I'd say they were lost really, sir, more mislaid like, if you see what I mean.

Captain. I have reason to believe they are being used to no good purpose.

223

2nd Steward.   You mean someone's been using my keys to get into the storeroom and pantries, sir?

Captain.   Yes, it looks rather that way, Smith.

2nd Steward.   They've been stealing stuff?

Captain.   No. That's the funny part. As far as we can discover nothing has been taken. But someone has certainly been rummaging around the kitchens and storerooms at night. And as yours are the only keys that are known to be missing, we presume that they're being used. What I want to know is whether you have any idea at all as to who might have got hold of them?

2nd Steward.   Well, sir, I did have a sort of idea I might have put them down in one of the staterooms, but . . .

Captain.   Which stateroom?

2nd Steward.   Number twenty-seven on E deck, sir. But I must have been mistaken because I looked for them in there and the gentleman said he hadn't seen them.

Captain.   I see. Who is the gentleman in question?

2nd Steward.   Mr. Arcularis, sir.

Captain.   Mr. Arcularis. Ah, yes, he's at my table.

2nd Steward.   He's been very ill, sir.

Captain.   Yes. I'll tell you what, Smith, I think it might be a good idea for you to keep an eye on that stateroom tonight.

2nd Steward.   But, sir, surely you don't think that Mr. Arcularis . . .

Captain.   You never know, Smith. Respectable gentlemen like Mr. Arcularis sometimes have strange habits.

2nd Steward.   Why would he want to go rummaging round the kitchens in the middle of the night?

Captain.   I don't know . . . but I want you to watch his door tonight. If he comes out, don't interfere with him, just follow him and find out what he does.

¶ MUSIC: *punctuation up: to background as ship's orchestra playing Cavalleria Rusticana theme.*

Arcularis.   They're playing that thing again, Clarice. How can they do it to me. As if I hadn't enough to bear with my sleep-walking . . . and the cold . . . and the keys . . .

Clarice.   Hush, Mr. Arcularis. You really shouldn't let your mind dwell on your troubles, you know.

Arcularis.   How can I help it when every time I look at you I think of her?

Clarice.   Of whom? Of whom do I remind you?

Arcularis.   Of my mother . . . my very pretty and very wicked mother who died young.

Clarice.   And whom you loved very much, no doubt.

224

Arcularis. To tell the truth I don't quite know. I have every reason to hate her. She made us so unhappy. That's why I can't bear this tune . . . it brings back all the dreadful misery, of those days. And yet she was probably the most fascinating person I've ever known.

Clarice. She's been dead a long time?

Arcularis. Yes, practially my lifetime.

Clarice. And she was unhappy?

Arcularis. Unhappy? Now what on earth made you say that?

Clarice. Why? Is there anything so extraordinary about it?

Arcularis. Yes, because somehow that had never occurred to me before that *she* was unhappy. I've always thought of it the other way round . . . that she made *us* so unhappy . . . father and me.

Clarice. Oh, I see . . .

Arcularis. She and my Uncle David . . . my father's own younger brother. Of course I found out about them, as children always do. I was nine that summer and I was always spying on them. One hot July morning he came to her through the garden playing that tune on his mouth organ.

¶ MUSIC: *ship's orchestra fades and mouth organ takes over theme which remains in background.*

Arcularis. [HIS VOICE FADING VERY SLOWLY] When she heard the song of his playing, she came out on the balcony . . .

¶ MUSIC: *stops abruptly in the middle of a phrase.*

Mother. David!

David. It is the morn and Juliet is its sun. Hi, up there. Aren't you ready yet? The mosquitos are simply awful down here. Let's get a move on. The tide turns in half an hour.

Mother. Romeo, Romeo, wherefore art thou Romeo? It's a wonder you don't learn a new tune on that thing, David. Don't you get tired of it . . . over and over again?

David. No, I like it.

Mother. Besides it's so early you'll wake everybody up. Why don't you go on down to the boathouse. I'll join you as soon as I've finished putting up my hair.

David. Why bother?

Mother. Oh, David, I'm sure I don't know why I like you.

David. Shall I tell you?

Mother. Later perhaps. Have you got some food on board . . . and something to drink?

David. Beer, cheese, pretzels and . . . oh, ouch. These darned mosquitos. Not a breath of air to keep them on the move. The whole bay's like glass. I think we may get a storm.

Mother.   Oh, nonsense. It's a lovely morning. Blow the dew out of your mouth organ and go on ahead. I'll just take a peek at the children and . . .

David.   Hush, methinks we are observed. A rat behind the arras . . . at least, not a rat, but a child's head dodging behind a rosebush.

Mother.   What are you talking about?

David.   We have a shy visitor. If I'm not mistaken it's little Mr. Arcularis.

Mother.   No. Surely he's still in bed . . .

David.   I think not. In fact, I'm sure I saw him. Very curious how he always turns up just where *we* happen to be. He couldn't be following us around, by any chance, could he? That wouldn't be very nice.

Mother.   Oh, no, David . . .

David.   Remember yesterday at the boat house?

Mother.   That's not fair. It was only be chance he happened to be there. He was pulling up his boat.

David.   Perhaps.

Mother.   Do run along now, David. I'll be with you in just a minute.

David.   Very well. [*RAISING HIS VOICE*] Bye-bye little Mr. Arcularis wherever you are. Bye-bye. Off I go, rose crowned into the darkness. Don't be long, my pet.

¶ MUSIC: *mouth organ takes up theme again which then crossfades with ship's orchestra which remains in background.*

Arcularis.   After that Uncle David was certain that I knew and that sooner or later I would tell.

Clarice.   And you were only nine.

Arcularis.   It was one of those things that stain the mind for ever. My mother's face with love in her eyes, the scene in the garden, the tune . . . they've haunted me all my life. All my life I've been trying to make some sense of it. Sometimes I want to remember and sometimes I want to forget.

Clarice.   Poor Mister Arcularis.

Arcularis.   Queer how things get twisted. It's almost as if I were to blame, as if I were guilty. The sin was hers and his, but the furies pursue me.

¶ MUSIC: *ship's orchestra finishes.*

Clarice.   But you're not . . . you're not to blame. Don't you see it's simply because you loved her.

Arcularis.   How simple you make it sound, Clarice. And how wonderfully understanding you are. Who but you would have thought that *she* was unhappy? You know, Clarice, I'm years older than you .. . centuries older, but is it possible that we're falling in love?

Clarice.   Yes, I think it is, Mr. Arcularis.

Arcularis.   Take my hand, Clarice. Feel how cold it is.
Clarice.   Yes, poor thing.
Arcularis.   Warm it. It's been to Polaris and back, you know.
Clarice.   I'll try.

¶ MUSIC: *bridge: tender, familiar.*

¶ SOUND: *ship's engines.*

2nd Steward.   There, Mr. Arcularis . . . that makes three extra blankets. I don't think you'll be cold tonight.
Arcularis.   I hope not, Steward. I hope not.
2nd Steward.   Is there anything else you'd fancy, sir, before you go to sleep . . . a nice, hot drink, perhaps?
Arcularis.   No thanks, Steward. Hot drinks don't seem to warm me any more. There's nothing you can do for me, except perhaps . . .
2nd Steward.   Yes, sir?
Arcularis.   Were you happy as a child, Steward? I mean, when you were nine or ten . . .
2nd Steward.   Happy? Yes, sir, I daresay I was happy enough.
Arcularis.   And you had a mother?
2nd Steward.   Well, yes, sir, of course I did.
Arcularis.   Did she . . . did she die young?
2nd Steward.   Why, no sir. You see my mother's still alive . . . going on ninety she is now, and sharp as a needle.
Arcularis.   I see.
2nd Steward.   Will that be all, sir?
Arcularis.   Yes, that will be all . . . and quite enough too. Good night, Steward.
2nd Steward.   Goodnight, sir.
Arcularis.   Oh, there's just one thing . . . about your keys. I don't suppose you've found them, have you?
2nd Steward.   No sir, I haven't.
Arcularis.   Don't worry about them. They'll turn up all right. I'm certain they'll turn up.
2nd Steward.   So am I, sir.

¶ MUSIC: *dream music up for long bridge and out.*

Arcularis.   Clarice . . .
Clarice.   Why, Mr. Arcularis, how you startled me!
Arcularis.   What's wrong? Why are you staring at me like that?
Clarice.   I don't know.
Arcularis.   Tell me.
Clarice.   It's nothing. It just occurred to me that perhaps you weren't looking quite so well this morning.

Arcularis.   It's true, I do feel astonishingly weak . . .

Clarice.   But it's not just that, I'm sure. Tell me, last night did you . . . ?

Arcularis.   Clarice . . . it's killing me, it's ghastly! Yes, I did.

Clarice.   I knew it. Somehow, the moment I saw you, I knew. Tell me about it.

Arcularis.   It was the same . . . the same dream of going round a star, Polaris. Betelgeuse. The same terrible coldness and helplessness. And that awful whistling curve . . .

Clarice.   And when you woke up? Where were you when you woke up? Don't be afraid.

¶ SOUND: *sneak ship's engines: building.*

Arcularis.   I was at the bottom of the stairway that leads down from the pantries to the hold, past the refrigerating plant. It was dark and I was crawling on my hands and kness . . . crawling on my hands and knees . . .

¶ SOUND: *out sharply.*

Clarice.   Oh! Oh, do you think . . . ?

Arcularis.   I know. And so do you. Once more and I'll be looking down into it. And there I will see . . . myself.

¶ MUSIC: *very short bridge, sinister.*

2nd Steward.   . . . and there he was, sir, on his hands and knees beside it, trying to open it. I tell you, sir, it gives me a real turn and no mistake. I . . .

Captain.   Just a minute, Steward, let me try to get this straight. You kept watch outside his cabin . . .

2nd Steward.   Yes, sir, just like you told me to. I hadn't been there more than half an hour before he came out . . . wearing just his pyjamas . . . and headed for the stairs . . .

Captain.   Which stairs?

2nd Steward.   The flight leading down to F deck, sir, to the dining saloon.

Captain.   I see.

¶ MUSIC: *sneak thin, arctic background: growing more sinister.*

2nd Steward.   I followed him across the saloon and when he got to the door leading through to the kitchens, he unlocked it with my keys.

Captain.   Yes, and then?

2nd Steward.   Then he went straight through the kitchens and sculleries and into the corridor where the storerooms and pantries are, and down the stairs that lead to the hold and the freezers.

Captain.   And all this time he was walking upright?

2nd Steward.   Yes, sir. When he got to the door of the biggest freezer room, he unlocked it and went in. Of course the light inside went on . . . it does that automatically . . . so I could see what he was up to. He made straight for the coffin.

¶ MUSIC: *the realization: up: out.*

2nd Steward.   He got down on his knees beside the coffin. Then he started to beat on it with his fists, sir.
Captain.   How long did that go on?

¶ MUSIC: *resumes low background.*

2nd Steward.   Only a few moments, sir. He turned round and started back for the door, crawling on his hands and knees. He managed to close it behind him and then went on along the corridor . . .
Captain.   Still on his hands and knees?
2nd Steward.   Yes, sir, but not for long. He was about twenty feet from the freezer door when he seemed to wake-up like. He staggered to his feet and stood there for a few moments without moving. Then he stumbled to the stairs and began to climb them . . .

¶ MUSIC: *out.*

Captain.   And you followed him back to his cabin?
2nd Steward.   Yes, sir.
Captain.   Well, I must say, it's a most extraordinary business, Smith.
2nd Steward.   That's putting it mildly, sir. Fair gave me the creeps, I can tell you.
Captain.   Hum . . . I don't doubt it. I hope you haven't said anything about this to anyone other than myself?
2nd Steward.   No, sir, not a word.
Captain.   Good. Keep it to yourself, Smith.
2nd Steward.   Certainly, sir. But if you don't mind my asking, sir, what are you going to do about it?
Captain.   Well, I think the best thing would be for me to have a word with Mr. Arcularis myself.

¶ MUSIC: *very short bridge: realization again.*

Clarice.   No. No . . . it can't be . . .
Arcularis.   It is, Clarice. It is.
Clarice.   But how do you know? How do you know where the . . .
Arcularis.   Don't be afraid to say it, my dear. You mean the coffin?
Clarice.   How could you know where it is?
Arcularis.   I don't need to, I suppose. You see, I'm already almost there.

¶ MUSIC: *short bridge.*

Captain. Ah, yes, Mr. Arcularis . . . so good of you to come . . .

Arcularis. What do you want with me?

Captain. A few words . . . just a quiet little chat, that's all. Please sit down and make yourself comfortable.

Arcularis. No . . . no . . .

Captain. Why, you're shivering, Mr. Arcularis. You've been ill. Is there something wrong?

Arcularis. It's so cold in here.

Captain. Is it, really? Of course, I've got the port open. I'll shut it at once. Thoughtless of me, but I'm afraid I don't feel the cold much . . . [PORTHOLE CLOSES] I've been at sea too long for that. [PORTHOLE CLAMPED]

Arcularis. What do you want with me?

Captain. Well, there's a certain matter that I feel I really must discuss with you, Mr. Arcularis . . . for your own good, of course, as well as . . .

Arcularis. What do you mean? What is it?

Captain. Mr. Arcularis, have you been sleeping well since you've been aboard this ship?

Arcularis. What are you driving at? Tell me, what are you driving at?

Captain. If you'll please answer my question, I'll explain.

Arcularis. No. I've a right to know what you're accusing me of.

Captain.. But, my dear Mr. Arcularis, I'm not accusing you of anything. I'm simply trying . . .

Arcularis. Oh, yes, you are. You *are* accusing me of something. And I know what it is. I know what you're thinking . . .

Captain. But my dear sir, I assure you . . .

Arcularis. You think it was my fault. You think my spying drove them to it. You think I was to blame for what happened.

Captain. Mr. Arcularis, you're entirely mistaken, I . . .

Arcularis. It's no good. You can't fool me. I know what the charge is and I'm ready to answer it. YES. I'M READY. DO YOU HEAR?

¶ MUSIC: *nightmare background.*

Captain. Good heavens, man, what . . .

Arcularis. I'll tell you exactly what happened . . . every single thing. It was the morning after he came to her through the garden playing his mouth organ. It was the morning after the hurricane. It was just before daybreak and the bay was calm again. I went out in my dingy. I rowed up the marsh channel towards Pulpit Rock. I knew that mother and Uncle David had sailed that way in the yacht. I'd rowed about half way up the channel, when I saw the yacht's tender . . . it was in the middle of the channel and I thought it was anchored. But it wasn't. It was still tied to the yacht. The yacht was sunk there, lying a little on her port side, with the roof of the cabin about two feet under water. I

230

could see it all quite plainly. The cabin door was shut. I sculled round to the starboard side where I could look in through the forward port-hole. Inside I could see something pink, floating close to the glass. I knew it was mother's dress, the dress she'd worn the day before. And that's all, sir . . . I didn't touch anything sir . . . I left everything just as it was . . . everything . . .
Pause.

¶ MUSIC: *out.*

Captain.   [*VERY QUIETLY*] Mr. Arcularis . . .
Arcularis.   Yes.
Captain.   I'm afraid you're not quite yourself this morning.
Arcularis.   That's right. I do feel very weak and I have a pain around my heart.
Captain.   You've been very ill and we must take care of you. The fact is, Mr. Arcularis, that you haven't been getting your proper rest at nights.
Arcularis.   No, that's true.
Captain.   To put it bluntly, you've been walking in your sleep.
Arcularis.   Yes, I told the doctor. He told me not to worry about it.
Captain.   It may not happen again, but if it does, I'm afraid we'll have to ask you to sleep in the ship's hospital where there'll be a night nurse on duty to look after you.
Arcularis.   Yes, that's right.
Captain.   And in the meantime, I think it would be better if you were to give me the keys, Mr. Arcularis.
Arcularis.   But I can't. I don't know where they are.
Captain.   I see. Well, perhaps we'll be able to locate them.
Arcularis.   I must hide them somewhere, but . . .
Captain.   No doubt, but don't worry about them. It really doesn't matter. Don't worry about anything, Mr. Arcularis. We'll take care of you. You're going to be all right. You're going to be perfectly all right. So don't worry . . . don't worry . . . don't worry . . .

¶ MUSIC: *short bridge.*

Arcularis.   He told me not to worry, Clarice.
Clarice.   I'm sure he was right.
Mordant.   Absolutely, Mr. Arcularis. There's nothing to worry about, nothing at all . . .
Arcularis.   Of course. We must be gay. Reverend Mordant, have a drink with us, won't you?
Mordant.   Thank you, thank you, but I think not.
Arcularis.   A soft drink then perhaps?
Mordant.   Thank you, but I must leave you. It's time for me to retire.

Arcularis. Ah, well, some other day. Pleasant dreams, Reverend Mordant, pleasant dreams.

Mordant. Goodnight.

Arcularis. Yes, my dear Clarice, above all we must make it gay. What would you say to some champagne?

Clarice. That would be wonderful.

Arcularis. Steward . . . Steward . . . champagne . . . champagne. Bring us champagne. [TO CLARICE IN A LOW TONE] Perhaps even now, my dear, it will all turn out to be nothing more than a nightmare from which we will both awake.

Clarice. If only that could be so.

Arcularis. Even at the worst, that little star I've set my sights on is still so far away. Champagne now, my dear . . ..

Clarice. Oh, *yes* . . .

Arcularis. And bromide later.

Clarice. Be a good boy and take your bromide.

Arcularis. Yes, Mother, I'll take my medicine.

¶ MUSIC: *dream music up to establish, then to background behind speech.*

Arcularis. The same as before . . . just the same . . . the long, magnificent delirious swoop of dizziness . . . the Great Circle . . . the swift pathway to Arcturus. All as before but now infinitely more rapid. Never have I had such speed. Beyond the moon and past the North Star in a twinkling, swooping in a long bright curve round the Pleiades . . . hello there, old Betelgeuse, I'm off to the little blue star that points the way to the unknown. Forward into the untrodden. Courage old man. In no time we'll be back to Clarice, back to Mother. If only I don't wake . . . if only I needn't wake . . . if only I don't wake in that . . . in that . . . time and space . . . somewhere or nowhere . . . cold and dark . . . that music sobbing among the palms; if a lonely . . . if only . . . the coffers of the poor . . . not coffers, not coffers, but light, delight, supreme white and brightness, and above all whirling lightness, whirling lightness above all . . . and freezing . . . freezing . . . freezing . . .

¶ MUSIC: *stab through to bridge as at beginning of operation.*

Mitchell. He's gone, Doctor Venner.

Venner. I know. [PROJECTING] I'm sorry, gentlemen. The patient is dead.

¶ SOUND: *murmured reaction of students.*

Mitchell. [PROJECTING] Gentlemen, you have had the privilege of watching Doctor Venner attempt, for your instruction and edification, one of the most delicate and exacting operations in all surgery. You have seen the patient's living heart completely exposed in Doctor Venner's hand. Unfortunately the patient was unable to support the strain imposed by the administration of the anaesthetic for a period long enough to enable Doctor Venner to complete the operation. I should add that it is only rarely that this operation meets with success. In most cases, as in this case today, the outcome is death. That will be all for today, gentlemen.

¶ SOUND: *buzz of converstion from students.*

Mitchell. [*SOTTO VOCE CLOSE ON*] Miss Hoyle, what under the sun is wrong with you?

Miss Hoyle. I'm sorry, Doctor . . . [*SOBBING*] I just can't help it . . . Oh, why . . . why did he have to die . . . ?

Mitchell. Really, nurse, you must learn to control your emotions . . .

Miss Hoyle. The way he held on to my hand . . . I . . .

Mitchell. That's enough of that. Come on, let me get you out of here before you make a complete fool of yourself.

¶ SOUND: *student conversation up to form bridge: then to background.*

Kurt. Well, that's that, my friend.

John. Yes. And I daresay you're not sorry, Kurt.

Kurt. Not sorry? What do you mean?

John. Your rival is out of the picture for good. You'll have little Miss Hoyle all to yourself now . . .

Kurt. That's right, but somehow I don't think it'll do me much good.

John Maybe not. Anyway, it was just as I said. An advanced Mitral is practically hopeless, Venner or no Venner.

Kurt. Nonsense. He's pulled it off successfully before. But you've got to have luck with a thing like that, and today the old maestro was out of luck, that's all.

John. So was the patient. What was his name again?

Kurt. Arcularis.

John. Poor devil.

Kurt. What do you mean, poor devil? We've all got it coming to us, haven't we? He was lucky. He died under anaesthetic. He didn't feel a thing.

John. Didn't he? I wonder.

¶ MUSIC: *up to curtain.*

Announcer. *Stage* 53 . . . Item 18 . . . the Ninth Birthday production of the Sunday-night *Stages* . . . was "Mr. Arcularis," adapted by Gerald Noxon from the story by Conrad Aiken. It was produced and directed by Andrew Allan, with original music composed and conducted by Lucio Agostini. Starring in the cast were John Drainie as Mr.

Arcularis; Donald Harron and Herb Gott as Medical Students; Mona O'Hearn as the Woman; Howard Milsom as Dr. Mitchell & the Reverend Mr. Mordant; Budd Knapp as Dr. Venner & the Ship's Captain; Robert Christie as Harry Freeman; Patrick Macnee and Alan King as the Stewards; Alan Pearce as the Ship's Officer; Richard Gilbert as Uncle David. Sound effects by David Tasker. Technical operation by Bruce Armstrong.

The Investigator

REUBEN SHIP

Production

Producer: Andrew Allan
Music: Lucio Agostini
Sound: David Tasker
Operator: Andrew Stewart
Announcer: Lamont Tilden
Program: Stage 54
Broadcast: May 30, 1954, 9:00–10:00 pm EST
Studio: Toronto
Network: Trans-Canada

Cast

John Drainie *as* The Investigator
with
Linda Ballantyne, Larry McCance, Fred Diehl, Eric Christmas,
James Doohan, Barry Morse, Alan King, Tommy Tweed,
Frank Peddie, Richard Gilbert, Budd Knapp, Howard Milsom,
Gerard Sarracini, John Colicos, *and* Paul Kligman

•

THE INVESTIGATOR

Preface

Reuben Ship's "The Investigator" is a bitter and hilarious satire on the activities of Wisconsin Republican Senator Joseph R. McCarthy. To appreciate the irony and force of the play, it is necessary to recall McCarthy's history. He was elected to the United States Senate in 1946, and in 1950 delivered the well-remembered speech in which he accused the State Department of employing proven communists. He was appointed in 1953 as Chairman of the Senate Government Operations Committee and of its permanent Sub-Committee on Investigations. He proceeded to attack what he maintained was a massive communist conspiracy in the country.

To appreciate fully McCarthy's attitude, one must remember the atmosphere of "cold war" which had developed between the Soviet Union and the West in the early 1950s. This was spurred by Russia's theft of the plans for the atom bomb with the help of American sympathizers, and exacerbated by a world-wide expansion of socialist ideologies, the establishment of the People's Republic of China in 1948, and the outbreak of war in 1950 between North and South Korea. This war, in which the U.S.A., Canada, and other Western nations very soon became embroiled, lasted until mid-1953. The effect in the West was a growing conservatism, which all but ended the liberal hopes of those who had, like Andrew Allan, seen World War II as a watershed for social change.

Reuben Ship himself was one of the victims of McCarthy's Committee. Ship was a Canadian author who had achieved a successful writing career in the U.S.A. He was, among other things, a writer on the popular and clever radio-comedy series, *The Life of Riley*. Having come under suspicion of McCarthy's Committee, he could no longer find writing work in the States and he was forced to leave and seek a living in Canada. It was during this time, from 1953 to 1955, that he wrote four plays for the CBC. The two original ones, "The Man Who Liked Christmas" and "The Investigator," were produced by Andrew Allan on the *Stage* series.

237

Ship soon left Canada for Britain, where he re-established his writing career.

"The Investigator" turns on a simple satiric displacement: the nameless Investigator, the chairman of an American committee very much like that of McCarthy, is killed in an airplane crash and lands in heaven. Ship asked himself what such a person would do in these circumstances, and the answer is hilarious — and frightening. This is Ship's just literary revenge, a prime example of the power of satire to comment on forbidden subjects, and one of the most compelling calls to action against Senator McCarthy.

When Ship was writing "The Investigator" at the beginning of 1954, McCarthy, though under fire, was still in full stride. Allan's reaction to the first draft of Ship' play was that "Reuben had both telegraphed his punches and loaded the dice." Ship's revised version, subtly but devastatingly satirizing McCarthy and his style, was a bombshell. What little conservative witch-hunting there was in Canada had been far more subtle and less public than in the States, but people could still appreciate the delicious satire and the accurate revelations about the Senator. Indeed, that such a program was even possible in Canada attests to the relative freedom Allan enjoyed in expressing sometimes-unpopular opinions on current issues. In America, where McCarthy had effectively muzzled criticism in most of the media, "The Investigator" was a real revelation. It became so well-known that a pirated record of the broadcast was made for sale. An American academic, who was a young liberal at the time, says that the record was a symbol and rallying cry for liberals who disagreed with McCarthy. One can surmise that it played an underground role in changing American public opinion about the Senator and in expediting his resignation.

REUBEN SHIP

The Investigator

Announcer. *Stage* 54 . . . Item 35 . . . "The Investigator," a new play by
Reuben Ship. Starring John Drainie. Produced and directed by
Andrew Allan, with music composed and conducted by Lucio
Agostini. The concluding broadcast of *Stage* 54 . . . "The Investigator,"
by Reuben Ship.

¶ SOUND: *phone rings: pick up phone.*

Investigator. [*THE VOICE OF A MAN IN A VIGOROUS MIDDLE AGE*] Hello.
Garson. [*ON FILTER: URGENTLY*] Hello, this is Mike Garson. I've got to
talk to you.
Investigator. Mike, my plane leaves in thirty minutes.
Garson. I'm in the lobby.
Investigator. Mike, we went all over it this afternoon.
Garson. Just give me five minutes.
Investigator. It's no use, Mike. I'm going through with it. I thought I
made that pretty clear.
Garson. I met with the Committee after I left you.
Investigator. [*FLATLY*] Oh.
Garson. They asked me to see you again.
Investigator. It won't do any good. Goodbye, Mike.
Garson. Wait, don't hang up. Look, we can't talk over the phone. Let
me come up.
Investigator. I'm leaving for the airport.
Garson. I'll ride out there with you.
Investigator. Mike, what's the use? I — [*RELUCTANTLY*] Oh, all right.
Meet me out front.

¶ MUSIC: *brief transition.*

¶ SOUND: *fade in car.*

Garson. [*DESPERATELY*] You've got to call off the hearings.

Investigator. It's too late now. Even if I wanted to. You saw the spread it got in the papers.

Garson. You can dream up an excuse! You're an expert at it. A postponement . . . illness . . . anything!

Investigator. Save your breath, Mike.

Garson. You realize what'll happen if you get yourself out on a limb.

Investigator. I've been out there before — way out. [*CHUCKLES*]

Garson. This time the Committee won't go along with you.

Investigator. I run the Committee. It doesn't run me.

Garson. Do you run the party too? One more error and they'll let you have it.

Investigator. You're a smart politician, Mike, but you've guessed wrong before.

Garson. I'm not guessing. I'm warning you. I'm speaking for the party now. You're going too far!

Investigator. [*LAUGHS*] I've heard that before.

Garson. This time it isn't just some crackpot college pinko or some lousy departmental assistant. This man is too big!

Investigator. [*HEATEDLY*] No one is too big! [*MAKING A SPEECH*] There's no one so high or so low as to make him immune to investigation where there is the slightest trace of evidence that his actions or beliefs are detrimental to the interests of this country.

Garson. That kind of talk is all right for the press, but . . .

Investigator. I'm not just talking, Mike. I'm going ahead with this. You can't stop me. The Committee can't stop me. The whole party can't stop me. Nothing can stop me!

¶ MUSIC: *transition: dramatic.*

¶ SOUND: *fade in plane in flight.*

Investigator. Oh stewardess.

Stewardess. [*FADING IN*] I'll be with you in a moment, sir. [*FADING*] Fasten your safety belts please. Fasten your safety belts.

Captain. [*ON FILTER*] Your attention please. This is Captain Jarvis, chief pilot speaking. We have developed some trouble in one of our starboard motors, but there is no cause for alarm. I repeat there is no cause for alarm.

Cast. [*AD LIB: REACTING TO THIS*]

Captain. However, we are bucking severe headwinds and having difficulty maintaining altitude. I have decided to turn back rather than continue with one motor not functioning. We regret the delay but arrangements are being made for you to board another plane upon landing. Thank you.

Cast.   [*COMMENTING ON THIS*]

Investigator.   Oh Miss.

Stewardess.   [*FADING IN*] Yes sir?

Investigator.   How long will it take us to get back?

Stewardess.   About four hours, sir.

Investigator.   That means we'll be delayed almost eight. *I must send a wire.*

Stewardess.   You'll have time to do that at the terminal, sir.

Investigator.   That'll be too late. I'll write out my message, and you ask the pilot to radio it back to the terminal and ask them to send it.

Stewardess.   I'm afraid that's impossible.

Investigator.   [*BRUSQUELY*] You ask the pilot.

Stewardess.   I'm sorry sir. It's against all regulations. No personal messages . . .

Investigator.   [*SNAPPING*] Do you know who I am?

Stewardess.   [*NERVOUSLY*] Yes, sir, but no exceptions can be made . . .

Investigator.   [*A KIND OF MENACE*] What is your name?

Stewardess.   I'm Miss Davidson.

Investigator.   Miss Davidson, this message concerns an investigation I am conducting. It is of the utmost urgency.

Stewardess.   I don't doubt that, sir, but . . .

Investigator.   You acknowledge the importance of my message and yet you refuse to convey my request to the pilot?

Stewardess.   [*NERVOUSLY*] It won't do any good sir . . .

Investigator.   You realize that only one interpretation can be put upon your refusal, Miss Davidson?

Stewardess.   I'm very sorry, sir, but . . .

Investigator.   It seems to me that you are deliberately obstructing an official investigation that is of vital concern to every loyal citizen of this country.

Stewardess.   [*WITH A HINT OF TEARS*] No sir. . . . But the regulations . . .

Investigator.   Miss Davidson, I'm aware that you won't be the first individual who has hidden behind so-called regulations and used them as a device to further interests directly opposed to those of the majority of loyal citizens of our country. Your unco-operative attitude can only cast the gravest doubts on your own loyalty, Miss Davidson.

Stewardess.   I'm only doing my job. I'll speak to the pilot, if you wish, but . . .

A man.   We're on fire!!

Cast.   [*REACTING*]

A woman.   [*SCREAMS*]

¶ SOUND: *an explosion: the wings breaking in half: the plane falling in a screeching dive.*

¶ MUSIC: *comes in strong over this: drowns it out in a fierce crashing crescendo: pause: then a celestial theme in softly.*

Martin. [*MILD-MANNERED, YOUNG*] Good day, sir. My name is Martin. Inspector Martin of the Immigration Service.

Investigator. [*DAZED*] Immigration? I don't understand. Where am I?

Martin. It's quite all right. You're safe now. [*FADES SLIGHTLY*] Will you follow me, sir?

¶ MUSIC: *pause while music ends.*

Investigator. Where are we? I don't seem to remember.

Martin. You'll be all right in a moment. You've had a nasty shock.

Investigator. [*SUDDENLY*] The plane! Did we crash?

Martin. Yes, you crashed.

Investigator. Oh! I'm alive! I've got to send a wire.

Martin. There's no need for that now, sir.

Investigator. This is very important. Where's a phone I can use?

Martin. There's no phone, sir.

Investigator. There must be a phone around here somewhere. What is this dump anyway? I can't see anything. It's so foggy.

Martin. The fog will lift soon.

Investigator. Where are the other passengers? How many survivors were there?

Martin. There were no survivors, sir.

Investigator. You mean I'm the only one?

Martin. [*WITH EMPHASIS*] There were *no* survivors . . .

Investigator. What are you talking about? Are you crazy? I'm alive, aren't I? Come on, now, I want a straight answer. No double talk. You know who I am?

Martin. Yes, sir. I know all about you.

Investigator. [*SNAPPING*] Well, let's have it then.

Martin. [*PATIENTLY*] It would be a lot easier for you if you figure it out for yourself.

Investigator. What is your name?

Martin. Inspector Martin of the Immigration Service.

Investigator. All right, Martin. You say you know all about me. Then you must be aware of the importance of the work I'm engaged in. In view of this, your refusal to co-operate can only cast grave doubts on your motives. I can assure you this incident will be investigated thoroughly. Now you'll make things a lot easier on yourself if you answer my questions in a straightforward manner. Any attempt at evasion on your part can only lead me to infer that you have something to conceal. Now then. I've been in a plane crash. I ask you where I am . . . how I got here . . . where the other passengers are, and you tell me there were no survivors. And you . . . [*BREAKS OFF*]

¶ MUSIC: *a brief phrase: in sharply.*

Investigator. [*REALIZING NOW*] Oh . . . I see.
Martin. Yes. And the fog has lifted, hasn't it?
Investigator. But . . . [*SELF-PITYINGLY*] I had so much to do yet. Why me? Why? All my plans . . .
Martin. I know how you feel, sir. Everybody feels like that at first. But you'll snap out of it. [*CHEERFULLY*] After all, you're one of the lucky ones. You're *Up Here*. Of course, you've only got a temporary visa but I'm sure you won't have any trouble in getting a permanent visa at the *main gate*.
Investigator. The *main gate*???
Martin. Yes. [*FADING*] Just follow me, sir, to the Head Gatekeeper.

¶ MUSIC: *bridge: briefly.*

Gatekeeper. [*FADING IN: HE'S A QUERULOUS, TIRED OLD MAN*] Well, it's about time, Martin.
Martin. Sorry I'm late, sir. I was delayed at the border.
Gatekeeper. You're always delayed at the border, Martin. Why don't you tell these immigrants where they are right off instead of beating around the bush?
Martin. I've found it's better to break it gently. Regulations don't forbid it, and . . .
Gatekeeper. I know all about regulations. I've been Gatekeeper for a long time. It's gross inefficiency. You young fellows think just because you've got civil service jobs you can get away with anything. When I started in the Immigration Service we had to keep on our toes, believe me. I don't know why I stay on this job. No efficiency . . . no co-operation . . . I ought to hand in my resignation. [*STUBBORNLY*] But I won't. I won't give some people the satisfaction.
Martin. Sir, I have an applicant here.
Gatekeeper. Oh yes, yes yes.
Martin. Here's the file, sir.
Gatekeeper. [*READING*] Applicant for permanent entry #578293B021. Where is he? — Oh there you are! Welcome, welcome.
Investigator. My name is . . .
Gatekeeper. [*TESTILY*] Yes, yes. I know who you are . . . it's all down here in the record. Now if you'll just sign this . . .

¶ SOUND: *rustle.*

Investigator. What is this document?
Gatekeeper. Standard form. Application for permanent entry. Sign right there.

¶ SOUND: *writing.*

243

Investigator.   There you are.

Gatekeeper.   Fine. Martin will show you to your quarters.

Martin.   [*FADES SLIGHTLY*] This way, sir.

Investigator.   Just a minute. Why are we going this way? Isn't that the Main Gate over there?

Gatekeeper.   Oh you can't go through that yet.

Investigator.   Why not? I signed that document.

Gatekeeper.   That's just an application. Before you can go through the Main Gate we've got to investigate you.

Investigator.   [*INCREDULOUS*] Investigate *me*?

Gatekeeper.   You'll be investigated thoroughly by the Permanent Investigating Committee on Permanent Entry. I am the chairman.

Investigator.   And what happens if I do not get a clean bill of health from this committee of yours?

Gatekeeper.   In that case it means . . . deportation.

Investigator.   Deportation? To where?

Gatekeeper.   [*SURPRISED AT THE QUESTION*] Why . . . *Down There.*

Investigator.   [*PAUSE*] I want to state at this time most emphatically that I refuse to submit to any investigation by any committee whose members, for all I know, may be completely unqualified to pass judgement on me.

Gatekeeper.   [*SHOCKED*] My good sir, are you questioning the integrity of my committee?

Investigator.   I make no allegations. I am making a statement on policy . . .

Gatekeeper.   But you've *got* to be investigated.

Investigator.   I raise no objections to an investigation. In fact, I welcome an investigation. My record is clean. I am perfectly willing to subject that record to the scrutiny of any competent body. Before I do so, however, I must be satisfied as to the competence of that body. If you will submit to me a list of the names of persons eligible to sit on this tribunal together with a list of alternate nominees, I will inform you of my approval or disapproval in each individual case, and we can then determine the composition of the committee.

Gatekeeper.   [*AGHAST*] My dear sir, you can't select the committee that is going to investigate you. That's unheard of *Up Here*!

Investigator.   Well, it's not unheard of where I come from!

Gatekeeper.   You're a newcomer. You can't just barge in here and expect to change things overnight!

Investigator.   I am aware of that, sir. I assure you that I have no wish to disrupt the work of your committee. I am merely making this request in order to provide a safeguard which will guarantee fair play and justice. Nor am I attempting in any way to put any pressure of any kind on either you or the members of your committee. However, may I point out that your refusal to even consider it might be construed wrongly, and might lead to speculation that certain members of your committee fear that their impartiality might be challenged.

¶ MUSIC: *transition.*

Oates. [*SLY AND SLIMY*] May we enter?

Investigator. [*FADING IN*] Why certainly, certainly.

Oates. Forgive the intrusion. My companions and I come here on a matter of grave import.

Investigator. Come right in.

Oates. [*FADING IN*] My name, sir, is Oates. Titus Oates. Doctor of Philosophy.

Investigator. This is a rare privilege. I've read about your career with great interest, Doctor Oates.

Oates. In a certain sense we pursued the same line of endeavour . . . as did my companions. [*UP A LITTLE*] May I present Torquemada, Inquisitor-General of the Spanish Inquisition.

Torquemada. [*AUSTERE, COLD*] I am honoured, sir.

Investigator. I'm very happy to make your acquaintance Mr. Torquemada.

Oates. [*UP A LITTLE*] And this is another distinguished member of our — ah — profession — so to speak — Mr. Cotton Mather — formerly of Salem, Massachusetts.

Mather. [*PIOUS*] I bid you welcome sir.

Investigator. [*DELIGHTED*] Cotton Mather! Well! This *is* a privilege.

Oates. And this gentleman is the distinguished jurist, Baron George Jeffreys.

Investigator. [*HE'S NOT IMPRESSED*] How do you do, Judge?

Jeffreys. [*GRUFF, BRUTAL*] Your servant, sir.

Oates. I see his Lordship's name is not as familiar to you as that of Torquemada and Mather. His Lordship's fame would have been instantly known to you had I presented him as . . . The Hanging Judge . . . formerly of the Bloody Assizes.

Investigator. [*ENTHUSIASTICALLY*] Oh! The Hanging Judge! This *is* a pleasure. I should have remembered the name, Judge.

Oates. [*NASTILY*] No need for apology. So few people do.

Jeffreys. [*FURIOUSLY*] The devil take you Oates. I've had enough of your jibes. The fame of the Bloody Assizes will live long after your confounded Popish Plot will have been forgotten. Miserable little sneak! Informer!

Oates. [*LIVID*] You dare call me that! Butcher!

Torquemada. My friends . . . I beg of you. We shall be giving our new friend a false impression.

Mather. *Up Here* we live in peace and brotherly love.

Investigator. Don't apologize. You should hear what some of my pals used to call me! Well, I'm really flattered by this visit, gentlemen. Of course, I'm not really in, yet. I understand I've got to be investigated first. I'd like to ask your advice. I raised a point with the Gatekeeper in connection with . . .

Oates. The committee has already met in executive session and your proposal has been rejected.

Investigator. You seem to know a great deal about it.

Oates. That is hardly surprising, sir. We are on the committee.

Investigator. [SURPRISED] You are?

Torquemada. We have served on it for a considerable length of time.

Investigator. Oh, I assume there won't be any obstacles to my entry?

Jeffreys. None whatever, sir. Your permanent entry is assured.

Investigator. You constitute a majority of the committee?

Oates. Yes. However, we merely serve in an advisory capacity.

Torquemada. The Gatekeeper makes all final decisions.

Mather. We, of course, play no small part in influencing those decisions.

Jeffreys. The Gatekeeper has never, to my knowledge, used his veto.

Investigator. And you gentlemen see eye to eye on most matters?

Torquemada. On all matters.

Oates. Invariably.

Investigator. I don't want to embarrass you, but it does seem peculiar to find Titus Oates, an enemy of popery, in complete agreement with Torquemada, the founder of the Inquisition.

Oates. Your point is well taken, sir, but *Up Here* one's perspective changes. We rise above our differences.

Mather. Say rather that we have submerged our differences in the face of a treacherous and powerful enemy.

Investigator. And that enemy is . . . ?

Mather. *Down There*!

Investigator. Hmmm. I see. A foreign Power!

Oates. It is our high purpose to awaken the apathetic multitudes to the imminent danger of an attack from within by this foreign Power, which has never renounced its goal of complete domination.

Torquemada. We believe that purpose can best be accomplished by exposing the extent to which agents of this foreign Power have infiltrated into our midst, spreading their noxious doctrine, and enlisting the aid of unsuspecting dupes in a monstrous conspiracy.

Investigator. But how have these subversive elements managed to enter? Who is responsible?

Oates. The Gatekeeper.

Investigator. The Gatekeeper!

Jeffreys. In my considered opinion, speaking as one trained in jurisprudence, the evidence is overwhelming.

Investigator.   Then why has he been permitted to remain in his present high position of trust?

Oates.   For some time now we have been considering ways and means of exposing the Gatekeeper and forcing his resignation. We have hesitated to do so until a man could be found to take his place. Your arrival at this time is most opportune.

Investigator.   [*OVERWHELMED*] Gentlemen, surely you don't mean . . .

Torquemada.   There is no doubt you are the man.

Investigator.   I am honoured. But I am, after all, a newcomer. Surely one of you would be better qualified. You are familiar with the local political situation, you have studied the available evidence.

Oates.   One factor outweighs all other considerations. In you we have a man who can bring to the committee's work the latest inquisitorial techniques.

Torquemada.   Compared to you sir we are mere untutored novices, and we bow to your superior knowledge and experience.

Investigator.   Gentlemen, I cannot find the words to express my feelings of humble gratitude at the signal honour you are conferring upon me.

Jeffreys.   Then you accept? In that case we propose . . .

Investigator.   Just a minute, Judge. It seems to me this undertaking of ours is not without certain dangers.

Mather.   We can expect to rouse some disapproval and even active opposition, but nothing so serious that we cannot cope with it.

Investigator.   I wasn't thinking of the lower levels of the administration, Mr. Mather. I was referring to . . .
Pause.

Oates.   [*SOFTLY*] You are concerned about The Chief?

Investigator.   Frankly, yes.

Oates.   You need have no fear on that score. The Chief never interferes.

Torquemada.   Rest assured, sir, we will have a free hand, provided of course we do not overstep legal boundaries.

Investigator.   Then in all humility I dedicate myself to the task of bringing to light the facts of this monstrous conspiracy that threatens our way of life *Up Here*. I shall pursue this objective relentlessly disregarding all attempts at intimidation by persons in high places who may be implicated by these facts; and I shall not cease until I have fixed the blame for a thousand years of treason!

¶ MUSIC: *transition: suggestive of band at rally: plenty of brass.*

Crowd.   [*IN THE HEARING ROOM: EXCITED BUZZ OF CONVERSATION*]

¶ SOUND: *gavel: noise subsides.*

Gatekeeper.   The committee will come to order. Let the record show that a full quorum of the committee is present. We have before us an application for permanent entry . . . #578293B021. Is the applicant present?

Investigator. I am ready. [*THROUGH THE FOLLOWING*] Mr. Chairman . . . Mr. Chairman . . . Mr. Chairman . . .

Gatekeeper. There are a number of rules governing the conduct of these hearings. It is our purpose on this commitee . . .

Investigator. Mr. Chairman. On a point of order.

Gatekeeper. Sir, I was about to inform you of the rules.

Investigator. Sir, I believe my point of order takes precedence.

Gatekeeper. As I understand it, a point of order is usually raised in connection with procedure. Since I have not yet informed you of the rules, I fail to see how a point of order is . . .

Investigator. Mr. Chairman. My point of order is not raised in connection with rules of procedure. It goes much deeper than that: the competency of this committee to conduct an investigation.

Gatekeeper. Sir you have raised . . .

Investigator. Please do not interrupt.

Gatekeeper. But the committee has already considered your proposal . . .

Investigator. Mr. Chairman, I must insist that I be allowed to finish my point of order without interruption from the chair.

Gatekeeper. Oh, very well.

Investigator. Today I am prepared to bring specific charges concerning the fitness of a certain member of this committee to sit in judgement upon me or any applicant.

Crowd. [*EXCITED REACTION*]

¶ SOUND: *gavel.*

Gatekeeper. This is a very serious charge.

Investigator. Mr. Chairman, may I suggest you ask me against whom these charges are being preferred?

Gatekeeper. Er . . . yes, yes. I was about to do so. Against whom are you preferring these charges?

Investigator. I bring these charges which, if proven — and I have no doubt that they will be fully substantiated — in which event the member of the committee who has been found to be derelict in his duty should be removed from this committee. I think you will agree to that, Mr. Chairman.

Gatekeeper. Certainly. Any member who has been proven to be unfit to serve on this committee will not be allowed to continue to sit upon it. But will you please state against whom you are bringing these charges?

Investigator. Against the chairman of this Committee — the Gatekeeper!

Crowd. [GREAT EXCITEMENT]

¶ SOUND: *gavel.*

Gatekeeper. You charge *me* with unfitness? [STAMMERS INCOHER-ENTLY] Why, that is . . . that . . . that is preposterous.

Investigator. [THROUGH THE NEXT SPEECH] Mr. Chairman . . . Mr. Chairman . . .

Gatekeeper. It's ridiculous . . . it's completely out of order. The applicant will be seated and the hearing in his case will proceed.

Investigator. Mr. Chairman . . .

¶ SOUND: *gavel.*

Gatekeeper. You are out of order.

Investigator. Mr. Chairman . . .

Gatekeeper. You are out of order.

¶ SOUND: *gavel.*

Investigator. Mr. Chairman I cannot accept that ruling. You stated just now, did you not, that any member of the committee who is proven to be unfit will be removed?

Gatekeeper. Yes I did. However . . .

Investigator. Your statement carried the clear implication that charges of such a nature, in order to be proven or disproven, must first be fully heard.

Gatekeeper. Yes, in the sense that . . .

Investigator. And yet when you learn that these charges are directed against yourself, you refuse arbitrarily to even hear these charges. Now I ask you, sir . . . was your first statement a true statement of the position of this committee with respect to the airing of charges of unfitness in connection with any member and his consequent removal from this committee in the event such charges were found to be true; and if it is true, then is your second statement to the effect that I am out of order in preferring charges against you consistent with the first statement alluded to or did you mean in your earlier statement to exclude yourself from the category of members against whom charges can be preferred, and if that was the meaning of the statement upon what precedent do you base such a flagrantly improper ruling?

Gatekeeper. Well, I — I — I don't follow your question.

Investigator. Now come, you know that's a perfectly simple question. Is your statement true — the statement that proven charges of unfitness would result in removal of the member concerned.

Gatekeeper. [CONFUSED] The first statement?

Investigator. Or were you lying?

Gatekeeper. How dare you accuse me of lying!

Investigator. Then it *was* true.

Gatekeeper. It most certainly was.

Investigator. Then how do you reconcile it with your present position?

Gatekeeper. I merely stated . . .

Investigator. You must realize that it cannot be reconciled unless of course you were deliberately creating a false impression.

Gatekeeper. I deny that. I was stating the truth.

Investigator. I am glad to hear you so positive about it. If, as you say, you were telling the truth then you do not, in fact, you cannot refuse to consider charges against *any* member of this committee including yourself.

Gatekeeper. Well that would seem to be . . .

Investigator. I am not asking you what it seems to be. I am asking you to state the position of the chair. Are you refusing now to allow me to air these charges.

Gatekeeper. No, no . . . of course not . . . that would not be consistent . . . I concede that. But I am objecting on grounds of proper procedure. I am the chairman of this committee. You now propose to investigate me. Clearly as long as I am in the chair it would be most improper . . .

Investigator. I agree completely.

Oates. Mr. Chairman . . .

Gatekeeper. Yes, Doctor Oates.

Oates. May I suggest that the matter would be expedited and the interests of propriety best served if you were to relinquish the chair temporarily while these charges are placed before the committee? Would this be satisfactory to the applicant?

Investigator. I have no objection whatsoever.

Gatekeeper. Well . . . it's completely without precedent. However, if it will expedite matters . . . Doctor Oates, will you take the chair?

Oates. I shall consider it a privilege.

Gatekeeper. [*FADING*] It's most unusual . . . most unusual.

¶ SOUND: *gavel.*

Oates. You may proceed with your charges.

Investigator. I wish to call as my first witness . . . Inspector Martin of the Immigration Service.

Oates. Is Inspector Martin present?

Martin. [*FADING IN*] I am, sir.

Oates. You may proceed with your examination of the witness.

Investigator. Inspector Martin. I have just a few questions . . . I'm sure you can answer them quite easily. Were you the Officer who conducted me to the Gatekeeper's office yesterday.

Martin. I was.

Investigator. Were you present throughout the interview?

Martin. I was.

Investigator. Isn't it a fact that the Gatekeeper stated at that time that there was gross inefficiency in the Immigration Service?

Martin. Well, er . . . what he meant . . .

Investigator. I am not asking you what he meant. Confine yourself to facts. Is it a fact that he said there was gross inefficiency?

Martin. Well, yes he did, but . . .

Investigator. Those were his exact words . . . ? Gross inefficiency.

Martin. He did use those words but . . .

Investigator. In reference to the Immigration Service of which he is the head?

Martin. Yes but if I may say so . . .

Investigator. There is no need for statements. Confine yourself to answering my questions. Now then. Did he also make a statement at that time to the effect that the way things were going in the Immigration Service you can get away with anything nowadays?

Martin. I think he said something like that.

Investigator. You think? Isn't it a fact that those were his exact words . . . "you can get away with anything" . . .

Martin. Well he may have . . .

Investigator. Come now, you're hedging Martin. Did he say it or didn't he. Yes or no?

Martin. [RELUCTANTLY] Yes, he used those words.

Investigator. Did he also make a statement to the effect that he feels unable to cope with the disorganized state of the Immigration Service and that he felt he should hand in his resignation? Is that true?

Martin. Well, that's true to an extent.

Investigator. To what extent? He complained about the disorganization in the Service?

Martin. Yes.

Investigator. And he made a statement about handing in his resignation?

Martin. Yes he did.

Investigator. Then your answer to my previous question which was . . . "that's true to an extent" . . . was not a completely truthful answer . . .

Martin. Well, if you want to put it that way . . .

Investigator. I am putting it that way. Your answer to my question as to what extent the statement I attributed to the Gatekeeper is true — should have been that it is entirely true.

Martin. Well, I suppose it should have been.

Investigator. Then you were lying.

Martin. No sir. I was not lying.

Investigator. Not deliberately, Inspector. Let us say you were confused.

Martin. Yes, I suppose I was.

Investigator. On reconsidering the question then . . . and take all the time you want before you answer . . . you would say that it is entirely and completely true that the Gatekeeper made all the statements attributed to him . . . [*PAUSE*] Please answer the question.

Martin. [ANXIOUS TO GET IT OVER WITH] Yes . . . yes yes. It is entirely true.

Crowd. [EXCITED REACTION]

¶ MUSIC: *briefly.*

Investigator. Sir, you have heard the testimony of the previous witness?

Gatekeeper. Yes.

Investigator. Was his testimony true?

Gatekeeper. Well I want to be fair to Inspector Martin . . .

Investigator. I think up till now we have all been so.

Gatekeeper. I would say that his testimony is true insofar as the actual words I used. However, the intent . . .

Investigator. I think the committee can draw its own conclusions as to the intent.

Gatekeeper. That may be sir. But the point is . . .

Investigator. The point is that you actually used those words.

Gatekeeper. Well, yes, I must say I did. However . . .

Investigator. Very well then. If, as you admit, your department is grossly inefficient . . .

Gatekeeper. But I do not admit . . .

Investigator. [GOING RIGHT ON] . . . is it not possible that certain subversive individuals have managed to infiltrate *Up Here* by taking advantage of this laxness and gaining permanent entry.

Gatekeeper. That is absolutely impossible. I deny it.

Investigator. You deny they have gained entry by taking advantage of your laxness? How then did these subversives gain entry?

Gatekeeper. Well they got in — [CHECKS HIMSELF] I deny that any subversive elements gained entry at all. I never said they did.

Investigator. But if certain undesirable elements have infiltrated here you admit the responsibility would be yours and yours alone?

Gatekeeper. Yes it would. But I again deny that such a thing is possible. Every applicant must undergo the usual routine investigation.

Investigator. [POUNCING] Routine! Don't you think the applications of — let us say — of heretics, dissenters, rebels — many of them with prison records — should have been given more than *routine* consideration.

Gatekeeper. Sir, I . . .

Investigator. Don't you think you should have exercised the most careful vigilance in cases of this kind?

Gatekeeper.   Sir . . .

Investigator.   That you should have subjected such individuals to the most intensive scrutiny?

Gatekeeper.   All our investigations follow the standard pattern. That is what I meant by routine.

Investigator.   In other words, you admit that cases of individuals most likely to be subversive *Up Here* were investigated with no more thoroughness than you would use in the case, say, of an applicant whose record was without a blemish.

Gatekeeper.   I did not consider it necessary.

Investigator.   What was your motive in coddling known subversives?

Gatekeeper.   There was no evidence that any of them were subversive.

Investigator.   Do you deny the possibility that a more complete investigation would have brought forth facts which would have possibly exposed their affiliations with a foreign power? Do you deny that possibility?

Gatekeeper.   How can I answer . . .

Investigator.   Do you deny that possibility?

Gatekeeper.   I cannot answer such a question. No one can.

Investigator.   Then you do not deny such a possibility.

Gatekeeper.   Obviously I cannot deny it. I neither deny it nor admit it.

Investigator.   Can you deny it?

Gatekeeper.   No matter how many times you ask me that question my answer must be that . . .

Investigator.   Mr. Chairman the witness is not being responsive. I ask that the chair direct him to answer the question.

Gatekeeper.   I must protest Mr. Chairman. The nature of the question ...

¶ SOUND: *gavel.*

Oates.   In the opinion of the chair the question is a proper one. Witness is directed to answer.

Investigator.   Can you deny such a possibility?

Gatekeeper.   [*WEARILY*] I neither deny nor admit it.

Investigator.   But you do not deny it?

Gatekeeper.   [*DEFEATED*] No, I do not deny it.

Investigator.   Mr. Chairman, members of the committee. In view of the admission of gross inefficiency by the Gatekeeper — in view of the fact that he cannot deny there is a possibility that subversive persons likely to be agents of a foreign power — by taking advantage of the Gatekeeper's laxness — if indeed it is mere laxness and not a deliberate and treasonable coddling of such persons — have succeeded in infiltrating *Up Here* for the purpose of undermining our way of life — in view of these facts this committee has no alternative but to re-open for complete and thorough investigation a number of cases . . .

253

Gatekeeper. I protest! This is a deliberate attempt to discredit the Immigration Service. I insist that we proceed with the regular business of the committee immediately.

Investigator. May I remind the Gatekeeper that he has temporarily relinquished the chair?

Gatekeeper. Mr. Chairman I appeal to you. How much longer are the members of this committee going to tolerate these disruptive tactics?

Crowd. [*EXCITED BUZZ*]

¶ SOUND: *gavel.*

Oates. The chair agrees that this committee has no alternative but to re-open a number of cases in order to determine the truth of the allegations which have been made. It therefore rules . . .

Gatekeeper. [*SHOUTING*] I will not be a party to any such undertaking! I will resign first!

Oates. If the Gatekeeper feels that this is the only honourable course open to him . . .

Gatekeeper. That is exactly how I feel. I am resigning . . . do you hear? I resign . . . I resign!!

¶ MUSIC: *bridge.*

Investigator. The committee will come to order. Let the record show that a full quorum of the committee is present. This is the first open session of this committee under my chairmanship and I wish to announce that hearings on new applications will be suspended temporarily in order to enable the committee to re-open for investigation a number of cases in which permanent entry has been granted and where the committee has reason to believe there is evidence of disloyalty, actual or potential. Mr. Oates, who is our first witness?

Oates. Socrates.

Crowd. [*MURMURING*]

Investigator. Please state your full name for the record.

Socrates. I am called Socrates.

Investigator. Mr. Socrates, what is you occupation?

Socrates. Philosopher.

Investigator. Mr. Socrates, this committee has heard certain testimony in closed session concerning your activities. An accusation has been made against you to this effect: that Socrates is an evil-doer, and a curious person, who searches into things under the earth and in heaven and he makes the worse appear the better cause. Do you care to deny that statement?

Socrates. While I have the life and strength I shall never cease from the practice and teaching of philosophy exhorting anyone I meet after my manner and convincing him saying . . .

Torquemada. Witness is not being responsive to the question. Mr. Chairman I request that he be ordered to answer yes or no.

Investigator. Witness will answer the question. Is this accusation true and if so, are you still engaged in these subversive activities?

Socrates. I do nothing but go about persuading you all young and old alike not to take thought for your persons and your properties but first and chiefly to care about the greatest improvement of the soul. I tell you that virtue is not given by money but that from virtue come money and every other good of man, public as well as private. This is my teaching and if this is the doctrine which corrupts the youth my influence is ruinous indeed. But if anyone says that this is not my teaching he is speaking an untruth.

Investigator. Come on now, Socrates, don't hand me that. You know that's not an answer to my question. Unless you're responsive to the question, the committee can draw only one inference.

Socrates. Acquit me or not, but whatever you do, know that I shall never alter my ways, not even if I have to die many times.

Investigator. Mr. Socrates, your failure to clear yourself of the charge of subversion, although given a fair opportunity to do so, can leave no doubt in the minds of the members of this committee that granting you permanent entry was a serious mistake. Any questions. Mr. Oates?

Oates. No questions.

Investigator. Mr. Torquemada?

Torquemada. No questions.

Investigator. Judge Jeffreys?

Jeffreys. No questions.

Investigator. Mr. Mather?

Mather. No questions.

Investigator. Mr. Socrates, it is the ruling of this committee that pursuant to Section 28A Article 4B Paragraph Two of the Internal Security Regulations you be handed over to an officer of the Immigration Service for the purpose of deportation from *Up Here* to *Down There*.

¶ MUSIC: *descending in scale to illustrate where Socrates is going.*

Investigator. Is the next witness ready, Mr. Oates?

Oates. He is.

Investigator. Please state your full name.

Marx. [SLIGHT GERMAN ACCENT: HE IS MEEK AND MILD] My name is Karl Marx.

Investigator. Mr. Marx, I hand you a pamphlet written by one Karl Marx. Now you wrote this pamphlet didn't you Marx?

Marx. Oh no.

Investigator. You deny that you wrote this pamphlet.

Marx. I did not write it.

Investigator. Now come, Marx. You know that won't get you anywhere here. We know you wrote this. There's no use denying it.

Marx. No, no, I didn't write . . . I am not a writer.

Investigator. You say you're not a writer but you *are* Karl Marx.

Marx. Yes, but . . . I am Karl Marx, the watchmaker.

Crowd. [EXCITED BUZZ]

Investigator. Just a moment. Mr. Oates. [AN INDISTINGUISHABLE WHIS-PERED CONVERSATION] Mr. Marx . . . there seems to be some confusion as to whether or not the committee has subpoenaed the right Karl Marx. The witness is excused for the time being. . . . do not leave the hearing room. Mr. Oates, do you have another witness?

Oates. We do.

Investigator. All right. Please state your full name.

Jefferson. Thomas Jefferson.

Investigator. Your occupation?

Jefferson. President.

Investigator. Did you engage in any other occupation Mr. Jefferson?

Jefferson. I was a gentleman farmer.

Investigator. I am not referring to that. Is it not a fact that you were an active revolutionary?

Jefferson. Mr. Chairman . . .

Investigator. That in fact you were one of the leaders of a movement which had as its aim the overthrow of established government by force and violence?

Jefferson. Mr. Chairman. When in the course of human events it becomes necessary for one people to dissolve the political bands which have connected them with another . . .

Investigator. Come on now, Tom, you know you're stalling. Just answer the question. You don't have to make a speech.

Oates. Mr. Chairman, perhaps if you made the question more specific? We all want to be fair to Mr. Jefferson.

Investigator. Your point is well taken Mr. Oates. Mr. Jefferson, I hand you a statement purported to have been made by you in a letter to a Mr. William Stevens Smith. Will you read it please?

¶ SOUND: *rustle of paper.*

Jefferson. What country before ever existed a century and a half without rebellion. . . . The tree of liberty must be refreshed from time to time with the blood of patriots and tyrants. It is its natural manure.

Investigator. Did you or did you not make that statement? And if you did do you still subscribe to those views?

Jefferson. If there be any among us who wish to dissolve this Union . . . let them stand undisturbed as monuments of the safety with which error of opinion may be tolerated where reason is left free to combat it.

Investigator. Who are you trying to kid, Tom? I've asked you a simple question. Why don't you co-operate with this committee? Are you opposed to the work of this committee? Don't you think this committee has a right to expose subversives like this Socrates? Now where do *you* stand, Tom?

Jefferson. It behooves every man who values liberty of conscience for himself, to resist invasions of it in the case of others; or their case may, by change of circumstances, become his own. It behooves him, too, in his own case, to give no example of concession, betraying the common right of independent opinion, by answering questions of faith, which the laws have left between God and himself.

Investigator. I think it's a waste of time to question this witness any further . . . unless the committee has some questions.

Committee. No questions . . . no questions.

Investigator. Mr. Jefferson . . . it is the ruling of this committee that pursuant to . . .

¶ MUSIC: *descending theme as before sneaks in here.*

Investigator. . . . Section 28A Article 4B Paragraph Two of the Internal Security regulations that you be handed over to an officer of the Immigration Service for the purpose of deportation from *Up Here* to *Down There*!

¶ MUSIC: *up and out.*

Investigator. Who is the next witness Mr. Oates?

Oates. Karl Marx.

Investigator. Is this the right Karl Marx this time?

Oates. We believe it is.

Investigator. Your name is Karl Marx?

Marx 2. [*MEEK AND MILD: SLIGHT ACCENT*] Yes.

Investigator. I hand you this pamphlet and ask you if you are the author.

Marx 2. Oh no.

Investigator. You deny it?

Marx 2. I am not a writer.

Investigator. But you are Karl Marx.

Marx 2. Yes. But I am Karl Marx the piano tuner.

Crowd. [*EXCITED BUZZ.*]

Investigator. There's obviously a misunderstanding here. Witness is excused temporarily.

Marx 2. [*FADING*] Thank you.

Investigator. Mr. Oates, let's try to have this cleared up before our next session. Do you have another witness?

Oates. Yes we do.

Investigator. Then we'll proceed . . . [*PAUSE*] Please state your full name.

Milton. John Milton.

Investigator. Occupation?

Milton. Poet.

Investigator. Have you ever engaged in any other activity, Mr. Milton?

Milton. For a short time I was Latin secretary to the Lord General Cromwell.

Investigator. I don't think that's quite accurate, Mr. Milton. Would it not be more accurate to say that you were one of the chief propagandists for a man who led a bloody revolution and later became a ruthless dictator? Is that not a fact Mr. Milton? That was your chief activity. Not poetry. Poetry was a sideline wasn't it? You wrote political pamphlets, didn't you?

Milton. I did but prompt the age to quit their clogs
By the known rules of ancient liberty
When straight a barbarous noise environs me
Of owls and cuckoos asses apes and dogs.

Investigator. Strike that from the record! You won't get anywhere, Milton, by insulting the members of this committee. Now we're giving you an opportunity to clear yourself. [*COAXING*] Why don't you play ball with us, John? Why are you trying to protect this two-bit General? . . . a man who was a disgrace to his uniform. [*AGREEABLY*] Now if you wrote those pamphlets on Cromwell's order we can understand that. We understand you had some personal difficulties with Mrs. Milton. You probably needed the money. We don't wish to pry into your personal affairs, John. This isn't one of those Star Chambers like they used to have in your time. Just tell us where you stand in your own words.

Milton. Give me the liberty to know, to utter and to argue freely, according to conscience above all liberties. . . . And though all the winds of doctrine were let loose to play upon the earth, so Truth be in the field we do injuriously by licensing and prohibiting, to misdoubt her strength. Let her and falsehood grapple. Who ever knew Truth put to the worse in a free and open encounter? Her confuting is the best and surest suppressing. . . . For who knows not that Truth is strong next to the Almighty? She needs no policies, nor stratagems, nor licensing to make her victorious; those are the shifts and defences that error uses against her power; give her but room and do not bind her when she sleeps.

Investigator. Well there's no doubt where you stand, Jack.

Committee. [*MURMUR ASSENT*]

Jeffreys. He's saying the same thing this Jefferson fellow said. All these fellows say the same thing.

Investigator. Naturally they say the same things. They're part of the same conspiracy. John Milton . . .

¶ MUSIC: *sneaks in.*

Investigator. . . . it is the ruling of this committee that pursuant to Section 28A Article 4B Paragraph 2 of the Internal Security regulations that you be handed over to an Officer of the Immigration Service for the purpose of deportation from *Up Here* to *Down There*!

¶ MUSIC: *up and out.*

Investigator. Who is the next witness, Mr. Oates.

Oates. Karl Marx.

Investigator. Well let's hope we've got the right one this time. Now then. . . . Your name is Karl Marx?

Marx 3. [MEEK AND MILD] Yes.

Investigator. I hand you this pamphlet and ask you if that is your name on the title page.

Marx 3. Yes that is my name. Karl Marx.

Investigator. [TRIUMPHANTLY] Then you are *the* Karl Marx. You are the man who wrote this!

Marx 3. Oh no . . . no.

Investigator. You have just admitted that your name is on this pamphlet. Do you now deny that statement?

Marx 3. Oh no, that is my name there . . . Karl Marx. But I am not a writer. I am Karl Marx . . . the pastry chef.

Crowd. [BUZZ]

Investigator. Pastry chef? Now just a minute. This is going too far! One of you Karl Marxes is lying!

The 3 Marxes. Oh no . . . no . . . no.

Investigator. Just a moment.

Committee. [CONFERRING IN WHISPERS]

Investigator. [AFTER CONFERENCE] There is some doubt in the minds of the members of the committee as to whether we have the real Karl Marx here. The committee wishes to be fair. We don't want innocent people to suffer. However, security is the paramount issue. It is therefore the ruling of this committee that *all* persons by the name of Karl Marx be deported [MUSIC SNEAKS IN] from *Up Here* to *Down There* pursuant to Section 28A Article 4B Paragraph 2 of the Internal Security Regulations.

¶ MUSIC: *up and out.*

Investigator. William Lyon Mackenzie!

259

¶ MUSIC: *punctuate: hold under:*

Mackenzie.   Let the farmer leave his husbandry, the mechanic his tools, and pour forth your gallant population animated by the pure spirit of liberty; be firm and collected; be determined . . . be united . . . never trifle with your rights; . . . Strive to strike corruption at its roots; to encourage a system calculated to promote peace and happiness; to secure as our inheritance the tranquil advantages of civil and religious freedom, general content and easy independence.

¶ MUSIC: *descending theme.*

Investigator.   François Marie Arouet de Voltaire!

¶ MUSIC: *punctuate: hold under.*

Voltaire.   Liberty of thought is the Life of the Soul!

¶ MUSIC: *descending theme.*

Investigator.   John Stuart Mill!

¶ MUSIC: *punctuate: hold under:*

Mill.   If all mankind minus one were of one opinion and only one person were of the contrary opinion, mankind would be no more justified in silencing that one person, than he, if he had the power, would be justified in silencing mankind. We can never be sure that the opinion we are endeavouring to stifle is false opinion; and if we were sure, stifling it would still be evil.

¶ MUSIC: *descending theme.*

Investigator.   Martin Luther!

¶ MUSIC: *punctuate: hold under:*

Luther.   It is neither safe nor prudent to do aught against conscience. Here stand I . . . I cannot do otherwise!

¶ MUSIC: *descending them.*

Oates.   Baruch Spinoza!

¶ MUSIC: *punctuate: hold behind:*

Torquemada.   Thomas Pain!
Investigator.   [OFF] It is the ruling of this committee that pursuant to Section 28A Article 4B Paragraph 2 of the Internal Security regulations that you be handed over to an officer of the Immigration Service for the purpose of deportation from *Up Here* to *Down There*.
Jeffreys.   Oliver Cromwell!
Mather.   Guiseppe Garibaldi!

Torquemada.   Victor Hugo!
Oates.   Abraham Lincoln!

¶ MUSIC: *descending theme: a conclusion. Fade in violin and cello tuning up.*

Wagner.   [*SPEAKS WITH SLIGHT GERMAN ACCENT AS DO THE OTHERS*] [*COMING IN*] Good morning, Ludwig.
Beethoven.   Good morning, Wagner.
Wagner.   How are you this morning, Johann Sebastian?
Bach.   Quite well, thank you. [*LOWERING HIS VOICE*] Have you heard what happened yesterday at the invest . . .
Wagner.   Please, Johann, no politics. Our little club is devoted soley to music. . . . Shall we try the new quartette.
Beethoven.   Chopin is not here yet.
Wagner.   [*HESITANTLY*] Er . . . er . . . yes. I am afraid he will not be coming here any more.
Bach.   [*SURPRISED*] Why not?
Wagner.   I have taken the liberty to ask him to resign.
Bach.   [*SHOCKED*] How could you do such a thing, Richard? We have played with Frederic for ages.
Wagner.   I hated doing it. He is a fine musician, but we must be realistic. There have been certain rumours about Frederic. I don't believe them of course . . . but in his youth he *had* certain political tendencies. And even some of the titles of his compositions . . . like the Revolutionary Étude . . . well, I thought it would be safer not to be associated . . . you know . . . just until this blows over. Now, the quartette.
Beethoven.   How can we play the quartette? There are only three of us.
Wagner.   I have invited someone to take Chopin's place. A fine pianist . . . a great musician.
Bach.   Who? Lizst?
Wagner.   [*HORRIFIED*] No, no. *He* was a friend of Chopin.
Beethoven.   Schubert?
Wagner.   Oh no. *He* was a friend of *Lizst.*
Bach.   Then whom did you invite?
Wagner.   [*EAGERLY*] Otto Schmink!
Bach.   [*DUBIOUSLY*] Otto Schmink?
Beethoven.   I have never heard of him.
Wagner.   That is exactly why I have chosen him. *No one* has ever heard of him!

¶ MUSIC: *an accent: briefly and out.*

¶ SOUND: *rattling doorknob.*

Guard.   Pardon me sir . . . that door is locked.
Old man.   But this is my laboratory. It has never been locked before.

Guard.   Sorry sir, orders.

Old man.   But I am engaged in important research.

Guard.   My orders are that you are to be refused admittance.

Old man.   Why?

Guard.   You are a security risk. I'm sorry Mr. Galileo.

Old man.   But my research project . . .

Guard.   That has been taken over by someone else.

Old man.   Taken over? By whom?

Guard.   Professor Schmink!

¶ MUSIC: *an accent: briefly and out.*

Wordsworth.   [*RECITING*] O blithe newcomer! I have heard
　　I hear thee and rejoice
　　O Cuckoo! Shall I call thee bird,
　　Or but a wandering voice?

Cast.   [*SCATTERED APPLAUSE*]

Tennyson.   May I express our gratitude to you, Mr. Wordsworth, for gracing our Poet's Circle tonight. And now, we are privileged to hear some new poems by the author, Percy Bysshe Shelley, one of our most distinguished and . . .

Coleridge.   [*INTERRUPTING: IN A WHISPER*] Psst . . . psst . . . Tennyson. No . . . no . . .

Tennyson.   Your pardon . . . one moment. [*LOW*] Yes, what is it Coleridge?

Coleridge.   [*LOW*] Haven't they told you about Shelley? [*MUMBLES INDISTINCTLY*]

Tennyson.   [*AS COLERIDGE MUMBLES: SHOCKED*] No! Dear me! I didn't know . . . yes, yes, of course. I see the necessity. [*TO THE AUDIENCE: CLEARING HIS THROAT*] Ladies and gentlemen. I regret to announce that Mr. Shelley will not be with us tonight . . . er . . . in fact, Mr. Shelley has been dropped from membership in the Poet's Circle. May I also say at this time that any opinions expressed by Mr. Shelley in the course of his association with our Circle did not reflect the views of the other members. [*CLEARS THROAT*] Now then. To continue . . . in Mr. Shelley's place we shall hear a newcomer to our circle — the distinguished and inspired poet — Mr. Schmink.

¶ MUSIC: *an accent: briefly then segue to transition: setting stage for the committee.*

¶ SOUND: *(over music) gavel: several times: music out.*

Oates.   Galileo!

¶ MUSIC: *punctuate: hold behind.*

Torquemada. Percy Bysshe Shelley!

Investigator. [OFF: DRONING] . . . that pursuant to Section 28A Article 4B Paragraph 2 of the Internal Security regulations that you be handed over to an officer of the Immigration Service for deportation from *Up Here* to *Down There*.

Jeffreys. Frederic Chopin!

Oates. Ludwig Van Beethoven!

Mather. Johann Sebastian Bach!

Torquemada. Richard Wagner!

Jeffreys. Otto Schmink!

¶ MUSIC: *descending theme: conclusion.*

Investigator. Is that you Oates?

Oates. [OFF] Yes.

Investigator. Well, come in, come in.

Oates. [COMING IN: UPSET] I must talk to you.

Investigator. I've just been going over the list of tomorrow's witnesses. Small potatoes. Can't we jazz the hearing up with a few names? I don't want them to think we're scraping the bottom of the barrel. What's the matter with you Oates?

Oates. There is someone you must see.

Investigator. Who?

Oates. [NERVOUSLY] I . . . er . . . I'd rather not mention any names.

Investigator. [CHUCKLES] Mystery witness, eh? All right, bring him in.

Oates. No — you must go to him.

Investigator. What? Are you kidding?

Oates. I assure you, the matter is most urgent.

Investigator. All right, I'll take your word for it. This guy better be important.

Oates. Believe me he is. . . . Come, just outside the Main Gate.

¶ MUSIC: *mysterious: briefly.*

The Voice. [MENACING] You're late Oates. You know I don't like to be kept waiting. You stupid oaf.

Investigator. Now just a minute . . . just a minute here. Mr. Oates is a member of my staff and I will not have a member of my staff spoken to in that fashion. I don't care who you are . . .

The Voice. You don't? [A LOW FIENDISH CHUCKLE BUILDING TO A SUSTAINED LAUGH]

Investigator. [SLIGHT PAUSE] Oh . . . I see. [LOW: OUT OF CORNER OF MOUTH] Oates, we must watch what we say. How do we know this conversation isn't being recorded?

The Voice. You have my word of honour, as one gentleman to another.

Investigator. What do you want?

The Voice.   You must stop these investigations.

Investigator.   Are you giving me orders? Apparently you have some hold over Oates but you're not running my committee. If you think you can put pressure on me . . .

The Voice.   Stop this orgy of deporation. Stop sending those crackpot reformers *Down There.*

Investigator.   I will make no deals.

The Voice.   [*FRANTIC*] But you don't know what's been going on! Jefferson and Milton are calling for a Congress; Martin Luther and John Stuart Mill are making speeches about the Rights of the Damned; Cromwell and William Lyon Mackenzie have recruited a Lost Souls Militia; that madman Socrates keeps asking me if I know what virtue is. [*INCENSED*] ME?? And that lunatic Karl Marx . . .

Investigator.   Which Karl Marx?

The Voice.   How should I know? There are hundreds of them — all over the place. Remember those pamphlets you handed them at their hearings? They took them with them when they got deported. They printed thousands of copies, and you know what their slogan is? "Workers of the Underworld Unite. . . . You have nowhere to go but UP!" Now they've gone and organized a union and they have the gall to want me to negotiate with them. Before I do that I'll see them in . . . [*CHECKS HIMSELF: EXHALES NOISILY: ALMOST IN TEARS*] I can't cope with it! Stop the investigations! You're bungling it. There are ways of doing these things . . .

Investigator.   Are you criticizing my methods?

The Voice.   At first they didn't take you seriously . . . good! Then they began to be frightened . . . good! They kept their opinions to themselves . . . good! They stopped joining clubs . . . good! They informed on their friends . . . good! But you went on and on and on. Now they're beginning to ask themselves . . . maybe I'm next? Where will it lead to?

Investigator.   Nowhere. After my next hearings they won't dare open their mouths. When I started I said that I wouldn't rest until I had fixed the responsibility for thousands of years of treason. Certain personal investigations I've made have led me to an inescapable conclusion. Oates, you will issue the subpoena immediately.

Oates.   For whom?

Investigator.   Who do you think? The Chief!!

¶ MUSIC: *transition: melodramatic: fade for:*

¶ SOUND: *gavel: repeatedly.*

Committee.   [*OVER SOUND: AD LIB CONSTERNATION: PROTESTS*]

Investigator. [SHOUTING OVER THE OTHERS] I am the chairman of this committee . . . I will decide who is to be investigated . . .

Torquemada. But you should have consulted the members of the committee before . . .

Investigator. The subpoena has already been issued.

Jeffreys. You must quash it!

Investigator. There is no point in further discussion.

Oates. There is still time . . .

Investigator. The subpoaena will not be quashed!

Committee. [AD LIB: ALL TALKING AT ONCE: PROTESTING]

Investigator. No . . . no . . . no . . . no!

¶ SOUND: *pounding of gavel.*

¶ MUSIC: *in suddenly: religious, awesome: wrathful, but as if heard from a distance: complete silence.*

Oates. [LOW: FRIGHTENED] HE is coming!

Torquemada. Quickly . . . before it is too late.

Jeffreys. Cancel the hearing!

Mather. We dare not do this!

Investigator. The subpoena stands!

Committee. [PROTESTING]

Investigator. [SHOUTING] No, no, no.

¶ SOUND: *gavel.*

¶ MUSIC: *louder now: closer: even more wrathful.*

Oates. You must! You must!

Torquemada. This is madness!

Jeffreys. You cannot investigate the Chief.

Mather. You've gone too far!

Investigator. [SHOUTING] There is no one so high as to be immune from investigation, where there is the slightest . . .

¶ MUSIC: *a tremendous burst: drowns the investigator's voice.*

Oates. The Chief is the supreme Power!

Torquemada. There is no greater Power!

Investigator. This committee is a greater Power! *I* am a greater Power!

Jeffreys. But He is the Chief!

Investigator. [HYSTERICAL] No! I am the Chief! I am the Chief! I am the Chief! I am the . . .

¶ MUSIC: *the climax: overpowering: out completely: pause: then the celestial theme: soft, gentle.*

Martin. Good morning, sir.

265

Gatekeeper. [*FADING IN: CHEERFULLY*] Good morning, Martin. Lovely morning, isn't it?

Martin. Beautiful. . . . Glad to see you back on the job, sir.

Gatekeeper. Thank you, Martin. It's good to be back. [*BRUSQUELY*] Well, it's all over and done with. Now we've got to look ahead. We're going to have our work cut out for us. All these people to be re-located. Oh dear, when I think of the paper work alone. Martin, I have an interesting assignment for you. I think you're going to enjoy it.

Martin. A re-location?

Gatekeeper. No . . . a deportation.

Martin. I see.

Gatekeeper. Here is the file. . . . And let us hope this is the last deportation we'll ever have.

¶ MUSIC: *brief transition: fade under.*

Martin. [*FADING IN*] This way . . . come along now.

Investigator. [*FADING IN: BABBLING INCOHERENTLY: QUIETLY*] I am the Chief . . . the Chief . . . answer the question . . . point of order . . .

¶ MUSIC: *segue to descending theme: sustain under.*

Investigator. [*BABBLING*] I am the Chief . . . treason . . . that's a simple question . . . just answer yes or no . . . I am the Chief . . . *Up Here* . . . deported . . . *Down There* . . . Article 2B Section 48 . . . I am the Chief . . . point of order.

Martin. [*DURING THE ABOVE*] Just follow me . . . take it easy . . . that's right . . . this way now . . . come along . . . just a little farther . . .

¶ MUSIC: *descending theme up and out.*

The Voice. [*SMOOTHLY*] Ah, I was expecting you, Inspector Martin. *And your charge.*

Investigator. [*DURING THE ABOVE AND THROUGH FOLLOWING CAN BE HEARD BABBLING IN BACKGROUND EVERY NOW AND THEN*]

Martin. [*RATTLING IT OFF*] Pursuant to Section 28A Article 4B Paragraph 2 of the Internal Security regulations I now hand over to you rejected applicant #578293B021. That is all.

The Voice. Not quite, Inspector. I *now* inform *you* that I refuse entry to the applicant.

Martin. [*ASTOUNDED*] You refuse. . . . But you can't refuse!

The Voice. I can and I do refuse. I have certain rights too, you know. [*WITH A CHUCKLE*] You must give me my due, as the saying goes.

Martin. But you're never refused before.

The Voice. That is true. In the past I have invariably prepared a warm welcome for rejected applicants — a very warm welcome. [*A FLASH OF ANGER*] But I will not have *him* set foot on my territory. That is final.

Martin. But I can't go back with him. What am I going to do?

The Voice. [*SUAVELY*] May I suggest you look up Article 35C paragraph 4A.

Martin. Article 35C Paragraph 4A?

¶ SOUND: *pages in book being turned.*

The Voice. That's right.

Martin. Here it is. [*READS*] "In the event that rejected applicant is refused entry *Down There*, after deportation, the Inspector in charge is required to return said applicant to his place of origin at the point where applicant first crossed the border."

The Voice. Exactly.

¶ MUSIC: *transition: to earth.*

Garson. It's incredible, Doctor.

Doctor. Those are the facts, Mr. Garson.

Garson. He was the only survivor?

Doctor. No doubt about it. Are you a close friend, Mr. Garson?

Garson. Yes, I am.

Doctor. I think you ought to know, Mr. Garson. The crash seems to have affected his mind.

Garson. Well, after all, the shock . . .

Doctor. It's a little more complicated than that, I'm afraid. He keeps babbling about being the Chief . . . and something about no one being too high and phrases like *up here* and *down there* . . . completely irrational.

Garson. But he isn't violent?

Doctor. Oh no . . . quite docile . . .

Garson. This condition is temporary?

Doctor. It's hard to say.

Garson. Well at least his life was spared.

Doctor. Mr. Garson, the plane crashed on top of a mountain, thousands of feet high. Yet he was found wandering about at the *foot* of the mountain.

Garson. What of it?

Doctor. The authorities say it's absolutely impossible for any human being to get down that mountain in the dark by himself.

Garson. [*FERVENTLY*] It was an act of God, Doctor . . . an act of God!

¶ MUSIC: *curtain.*

Announcer. *Stage* 54 . . . Item 35 . . . "The Investigator," a new play by Reuben Ship . . . was produced and directed by Andrew Allan, with music composed and conducted by Lucio Agostini. The Investigator was played by John Drainie. The other people were: Linda Ballantyne, Larry McCance, Fred Diehl, Eric Christmas, James Doohan, Barry

Morse, Alan King, Tommy Tweed, Frank Peddie, Richard Gilbert, Budd Knapp, Howard Milsom, Gerard Sarracini, John Colicos, and Paul Kligman. Sound effects by David Tasker. Technical operation by Andrew Stewart.

The Jinker

JOSEPH SCHULL

Production

Producer: Andrew Allan
Music: Lucio Agostini
Sound: David Tasker and Bill Roach
Operator: John Sliz
Announcer: Lamont Tilden
Program: Stage 55
Broadcast: March 20, 1955, 9:00–10:00 pm EST
Studio: Toronto
Network: Trans-Canada

Cast

Budd Knapp *as* Charles Torrance
Douglas Rain *as* Bob Torrance
Ruth Springford *as* Maura
Alan King *as* Tim Mahan
J. Frank Willis *as* Ernest Johns
Frank Peddie *as* David Hardy
Murray Westgate *as* the Barrelman
William Shatner *as* Parker
Richard Gilbert *as* Johnson

•

THE JINKER

Preface

"Of our regular writers, Joseph Schull was the romantic one: he wrote fine parts for women," says Andrew Allan, cryptically, of a writer he greatly admired, one of the most talented of the serious writers in Allan's team. Of the 80 original plays Schull wrote for radio, Allan produced about 30. The universality of Schull's themes, along with his dramatic and narrative gifts, made his plays popular with all of the major Golden-Age radio-drama producers across Canada. His radio play "The Concert" was the only one of the dozen *CBC Stage* plays submitted by Allan to the BBC to be produced in England. Schull's dramatic writing for radio includes documentaries and biographies, allegories and satires, and serious and tragic plays. "The Jinker" is a magnificent example of Schull's tragic vision, and one of the very best serious dramas ever produced on *Stage*.

Schull was born in South Dakota in 1919, and the family moved to Moose Jaw, Saskatchewan when he was three. He began writing plays in university, and in 1935 he came to Montreal to begin a career as a dramatist, novelist, and historian. During the war this man of the prairies was a naval intelligence officer. He returned to Montreal after the war to continue his career. In addition to his original radio plays and adaptations, Schull wrote five stage plays, a number of dramas for television, and ten histories of Canadian figures and institutions, including the official history of the Canadian Navy.

"The Jinker" is a powerful and moving play, both a traditional and a modern tragedy. Based on a turn-of-the-century Newfoundland seal-hunt through the treacherous arctic seas, it portrays an epic conflict between two contending leaders of the sailors' tribe, with inevitable tragic consequences. It also exhibits a colossal struggle with opposing Nature, in the form of the irresistible and threatening ice-floe which finally grinds up the antagonist. This powerful arctic symbol of tragic Nature is in a particularly Canadian tradition, as the great frozen universe of "Mr. Arcularis" shows. "The Jinker" displays Schull's strong narrative and lyrical skills, especially in the central passage describing the giant ice-floe moving irresistibly through the northern sea. Such skills are part of the secret of the power and distinctiveness of the radio-drama medium. The excellence of "The Jinker" is enhanced by its translation into epic and dramatic terms of a major social concern of the time. Schull's prairie origins familiarized him with rural life and a regional culture, while his east-coast navy experience provided the authentic details of Newfoundland life and of the sealing expeditions which dominate the play. Dwelling in Montreal must have shown him the effects on our rural and regional cultures of post-war, sophisticated urban life, and the effects of the increasing tendency towards the centralization of the Canadian polity and economy. The loss of crucial cultural and social traditions was experienced in the 1950s by all the regions of the country — as also seen in "The Macdonalds of Oak Valley." Schull's work, then, is a prime example of that combination of art and social comment towards which Allan was always aiming.

JOSEPH SCHULL

The Jinker

Charles. [*MIDDLE-AGED*] Not until the night of my seventeenth birthday did I ever hear my grandfather mention the name of Tim Mahan. He had told me many stories of his father and brothers — the Torrances of Newfoundland — and of the sealing voyages and northern ice that in the end had claimed them all. But the memory of his own last voyage to the ice — fifty years before, when he was twenty-six — had been a thing long stored up between my grandfather and my grandmother to be told me when the right time came. And so this night it came.

¶ MUSIC: *title cue up and under.*

Announcer. *Stage* 55 . . . Item 26 . . . "The Jinker" . . . a tale of the Newfoundland sealers many years ago, written by Joseph Schull. Starring Budd Knapp, Douglas Rain, Ruth Springford, and Alan King. Produced and directed by Andrew Allan, with music composed and conducted by Lucio Agostini. . . . "The Jinker," by Joseph Schull.

¶ MUSIC: *up and out.*

Charles. We sat on the wide porch of the old house, Robert and Maura Torrance and myself, looking to the sunset and the calm sea. I remember the deep and joining look which passed between that old woman and that old man as Robert Torrance began the story — not as he had told me other stories, in casual fragments between long sessions with his pipe; but this time laying the pipe away, beginning and carrying on with slow, deliberate effort. And I remember how his words, as he went deeper into the tale and the spectral memories took on flesh and blood for him, grew richly tinged with his own way of speech, echoing across the centuries and the stormy seas the voices of the Bristol men and Devon men who sailed with Cabot and with Drake.

¶ MUSIC: *sneak background.*

Charles. It has been long with me, that story; and the voice — stilled now — is often in my ears. Perhaps it is a story now more mine than his, even as the voice is mine; and the burden laid down in the telling has become my burden, though a lighter thing, and changed. As Newfoundland is changed — St. John's — the harbour — and the hunt. I have seen Water Street often enough, loud with the bustle of men preparing for the journey to the ice; on many March days since I have been a part of it. But it is this one March day, more than seventy years ago, the day I never saw and know of only through his telling, that is most alive for me. They are all dead now — long since — those jubilant throngs of outport swoilers who crowded through the street.

¶ MUSIC: *out.*

¶ SOUND: *crowd background.*

Charles. But they live for me with a thought, and with a thought Robert Torrance walks among them. And then another figure — tall and lithe, a cap pushed far back on riotous hair, shouldering aside the jostlers on the walk, his wild black eyes defiant of the eyes that follow him and turn from him.

¶ SOUND: *slight, startled stir of crowd, then murmur of uneasy men dies out.*

Charles. Suddenly the face of Robert Torrance is a graven mask. The crowd gives back about him, heads turn, laughter falls to an uneasy silence. It is Tim Mahan standing before him — Tim, as I have seen him from that first and last day on which my grandfather spoke his name — and over the defiant eyes has crept a film of deadly watchfulness.

Mahan. [*TENSELY BLAND: A DEFIANT CASUALNESS*] Well, Robert, so tomorrow we're off for the front.

Torrance. [*TENSE: GRIM*] Aye.

Mahan. You go master of the *Jean Bright*?

Torrance. [*DEEP, RESTRAINED ANGER*] You know that well enough. [*DELIB-ERATE SIGNIFICANCE*] My father is not here this year to master her.

Mahan. [*DEFIANT HYPOCRISY*] A shame it is. He was a good man, John Torrance.

Torrance. And taught you all you know — to his cost.

Mahan. [*SHARPENING: SOFT MENACE*] And what d'ye mean by that?

Torrance. Take what meaning you wish.

Mahan. I hear you have been asking wunnerful strange questions of the lads from the outports. They have given *Kestrel* a bad name, Robert.

Torrance. There are questions still to be asked, Mahan. And the name your *Kestrel* wears she has earned. You're going master of her again?

Mahan. I am.

Torrance. And you've a crew to sail with you?

Mahan. I have. More men than I need. More than I can carry. Did ye not think I'd get a crew?

Torrance. It would be better for 'em to sail with another master. But I've no quarrel with them.

Mahan. But with me . . . ?

Torrance. [RESTRAINED: HARD] What's between us will be settled here, later. Keep off from me while we're in the ice, Mahan. That's all I have to say to you — now.

Mahan. [SOFT, SARDONIC LAUGH] We'll see, Robert.

Cast. [DISTURBED MURMUR OF MEN RISES A LITTLE UNDER MAHAN'S LAUGH: FADES OUT]

Charles. He passed along the street and came up the rocky cliffside path from the harbour towards the lights of the little house. The sound of that laugh, familiar from his boyhood, with its mingling of defiance and of deadliness and madness, lingered in his ears. His own stern words were softening within him; the old, impotent, grieving fury was giving place to the old fear.

¶ SOUND: *house door pushed open.*

Charles. And as he pushed open the door of home and Maura stood before him in its light and warmth, he knew that Maura knew.

¶ SOUND: *door closed.*

Maura. [SOFT: TENSE CONCERN] It is Tim Mahan again?

Torrance. [SULLEN CASUALNESS] I met him on Water Street — yes. What of it?

Maura. He is going on the hunt?

Torrance. [MORE SULLENLY] Yes. But so am I. Ye need not worry about that.

Maura. [TENSE RELIEF] Ah. [TURNS AWAY] Your supper is ready.

Torrance. [SULLEN ANGER: SARCASM] Did ye think I'd not? You know well enough that I *must* go now. A week ago it would have been an easy matter to find another master for the *Jean Bright*. Now it's too late.

Maura. [TENTATIVE: NOT MEANING IT] There is Ernest Johns. He knows as much of swoilin' as any man on the island and should have had his own ship long ago.

Torrance. And he is my mate. What would be said of me if I stepped down now? You did not speak seriously of him, anyhow. I'm going. It's settled. You'll have your way.

Maura. [SOFTLY] *My* way? Is it only mine?

Torrance. [ANGRY EVASION] You know well enough that this swoilin' is a fool's life — and grows more so every year — a game for children!

275

There's better money in fish — better money in trading — even behind the counter of a store I could sit easy and make my way, and there'd be money in the bank for us and for the children when they come along. But no — the Torrances have always gone to the ice, even though they do not always come back. This year a Torrance must go again, to show the island there is no fear in the tribe. Is that no how ye see it? Isn't it?

Maura.   [*QUIETLY*] You know it's not. If you don't wish to go, it is your affair.

Torrance.   But Mahan is going — and so I must. That is how you see it. I know you well enough. No one here — neighbour or stranger — must be able to say that Tim Mahan kept a Torrance from the ice!

Maura.   I have never said such words, nor thought them. Why do you spend your anger and your fear on me?

Torrance.   Fear!

Maura.   [*STEADILY*] Fear. It is not for yourself alone. It's not a shameful thing. I know that. I know what Tim Mahan has done — I am more certain of it than you. And I know what he may do. But . . . [*VOICE BREAKS A LITTLE*] what you must do lies in your own heart. I will say not one word to decide you.

¶ MUSIC: *an accent: to background.*

Charles.   She set his supper on the table, and they ate in silence. Afterward, she sat in the kitchen knitting as he went about seeing to the last bits of his gear. They went to bed, and he lay beside her in the darkness, his eyes open. The face of his father came to him. And the face of Tim Mahan. All came back — the year-long welter of fact and fancy and agonized suspicion he had lived with since the *Jean Bright* returned last April, masterless, flying no flags.

¶ MUSIC: *out.*

Charles.   Towards dawn he was unable to endure the bed longer. Maura made no sound as he drew his clothes on and left the bedroom, but he knew that in the dark her eyes were open too.

¶ SOUND: *fade in sound of sea booming at foot of cliffs.*

Charles.   On the cliff it was the chill moment when false dawn gives way for a while to deeper darkness. He heard the tide in the throat of the cove, a hundred feet beneath him. The gleam of the ice-blink in the north seemed filled with pale menace. He tried to shrug away the cold heaviness that possessed him, but it would not go.

¶ MUSIC: *dawn strain punctuates: to background.*

Charles.   The eerie ice-blink fading, as real dawn creeps along the horizon . . .

Torrance. [*DEEP, SOFT, APPRECIATIVE BREATH*]

Charles. A pet day coming, lifting the heart with the thought of it. From the north the smell of the great ice-floe coming on the light wind, and as the sun strides inward a white glitter twinkling below the cliffs from the stringing pans of slob ice — the outriders of the floe. Up the shore behind them, above Baccalieu and Bonavista and the Funks and the Horse Islands, along all the miles of the Newfoundland coast and around the shoulder of the Labrador, the floe itself — the ice — moving down from the darkness of the Pole. Cradled in the arms of the great current; a continent neither sea nor land, rocking, moaning southward. In the harbour below, the men of the city and the out-ports, the Tickles and the Guts and Reaches and the Coves of New-foundland — all astir now, boarding the coal-black ships to go north-ward for the seals. And he a Torrance; and no living man in Newfoundland able to remember a sealing season when there was not a Torrance in command or at the mainmast barrel of one of the ships. Yet it would take but one softening look, one touch of Maura's hand . . .

¶ MUSIC: *out.*

Maura. [*OFF: SOFT, RESTRAINED CALL*] Your breakfast, Robert.

Charles. Below the rocky path, longers for the flakes stood beside the crazy lean-to of the gutting shed, and the smell of salt and fish was brisk on the air. On the slope beyond the house the snow had not yet left the thin and starving soil that clung upon the rocks and yielded up so grudgingly its turnips and potatoes. All this he loved in that moment as he had never loved it before, and a cold rage rose in him and turned on Maura.

¶ SOUND: *house door opened: closed: soft stir of cooking..*

Charles. There was fish boiling in the iron pot and tea on the stove, and bread and molasses set out on the clean oilcloth of the table.

Maura. Sit to now. It is ready.

Charles. Her slim body stirred him, moving lithely and familiarly between table and stove. The love that joined them ached in him, and still the cold anger held them apart. He sipped his tea and looked straight ahead of him through the open doorway of the little parlour, shining like a ship's cabin. A walrus tusk surrounded by figures carved from whales' teeth by the Eskimos of Northern Labrador stood on the table inlaid with a thousand pieces of sandalwood which his great-grandfather had brought from India. It was good, it was all good — the warm, tight house and the shining cleanliness of it, and the old strong sureness of the lives that had been here before them. A man would keep it. A man would stay with it, possess it.

¶ SOUND: *slight stir of teacup.*

Charles.   He looked at her, pretending to sip her mug of tea, with eyes averted; and the thought died against her silence.

¶ SOUND: *chair pushed back.*

Torrance.   [*RISING: SULLEN SIGH*] I must see to my gear . . .

Charles.   She moved about the kitchen and to and from the bedroom and the shed outside, putting the heavy sweaters and the socks and oddments into his clothes bag. Only once she paused with something in her hands, and her head bent over it.

Maura.   [*QUIET: EFFORT*] If Mahan's *Kestrel* is near you in the ice, look to yourself. [*PAUSE*] I don't know what the *Kestrel*'s owners are thinking of, to send him master of her again.

Torrance.   [*SHORTLY*] They are thinking of the fat and the money, like all owners. [*GRIMLY*] He did well enough for them last year.

Maura.   I have seen the evil growing in him since we were children together.

Torrance.   [*AS BEFORE*] So have I.

Maura.   And always his life has been twined somehow with yours — since you played and fought when you were little — since the two of you sailed first with your father. [*PAUSE: EFFORT*] I had hoped that when he became master of his own ship, and you of yours, there would be no more of it. But — there is a fate about it all — a darkness that he brings wherever he comes, whether he wishes it so or not.

Torrance.   [*GRIMLY*] Tim knows well enough what he does.

Maura.   [*SOFT INTENSITY*] There is a devil in Tim Mahan, and a little of madness. He is the one man on earth I could wish dead, and not think it a sin. [*PAUSE: LITTLE CATCH*] I shall be watching from the cliffs the ships go.

Torrance.   [*MOVED GENTLENESS*] I know. [*TAKING HER IN HIS ARMS: FIERCE PLEADING*] Maura — Maura — even yet, if it were not what I see in your eyes!

Maura.   You see only what is in your own heart. Do you not know that?

Torrance.   [*BREAKS AWAY: SULLENLY*] No.

Charles.   They stood together in the doorway at last, and he kissed her and she clung to him with her whole body calling on him to live and stay. But still she would say no word. He put her from him at last, gently; turned, and without looking back went down the rocky path toward the harbour.

¶ SOUND: *fade in sporadic ships' whistles: harbour sounds.*

Cast.   [*HARBOUR BUSTLE: LAUGHTER AND BUSTLE OF EXCITED CROWD*]

Charles.   The flag-hung buildings — the brisk March air — the men, women and children streaming to the waterside. The old excitement of the hunt stirring in spite of all as he came up the *Jean Bright's* gangway.

¶ SOUND: *steps up the gangway.*

Cast. [MEN ON BOARD: EXCITED WELCOME] The skipper — the skipper! Marnin', Cap'n? Is it to be a log-load this year, Bob?

Torrance. [PUSHING AMONG THEM: GOOD NATURED] Give me room to come aboard, boys. [CLEARER] Where's Ernest Johns?

Johns. [ELDERLY: CALM: FADING UP] Here, Bob.

Torrance. Ah. What's to be done?

Johns. Nothin' for the moment. We're shipshape. Ten minutes to go.

Torrance. I'll stow my gear.

Charles. The hands of the church clock creeping towards ten. Fifty ships in the harbour — low in the water, bunkered with coal, ballasted with rocks. Decks piled high with timber and stores and gear — sides of bacon hung in the rigging along the lower yards, and higher above them over each ship the bright strings of flags which bloom above the sealing fleet each spring.

¶ SOUND: *ship and harbour background in again.*

Torrance. [FADING UP] Well — near time.

Johns. Aye [VOICE RAISED] Cast off them lines, there!

Cast. The lines, there! Let go lines . . .

Charles. All about them other ships — casting lines, weighing anchor, spurting up anxious puffs of smoke — and then — ten o'clock.

¶ SOUND: *sudden clamor of church bells, town bells, sirens.*

Cast. [CHEERS OF CROWD]

Charles. Smoke billows in sudden clouds above the stubby funnels of the ships. They swing, jockey for position, and nose away in a stringy pack — out through the narrows and clear of the harbour, then hard to port for the north.

¶ MUSIC: *out to sea.*

¶ SOUND: *steamship under way.*

Cast. [MEN MURMURING: EXCITED AND HAPPY: BACKGROUND.]

Johns. [ORDER] There's your course. Steady as she goes now. [MORE QUIETLY: TO TORRANCE AT HIS SIDE] Taking her straight up the cut. All right?

Torrance. That'll do. We'll run with the rest of the pack for a while.

¶ MUSIC: *theme coming into background over fading sound.*

Johns. [*PLEASED SIGH*] Well, boy — off again.
Torrance. Ayah.
Johns. Feels good.
Torrance. It does, at that.

¶ MUSIC: *up and fade to background.*

Charles. And so it did. It moved in his blood for a moment, this annual migration of men outward and northward to meet the southern moving ice and the seals. It caught him out of himself and lifted him to the cold fellowship of the winds and tides. It went on; it went on forever; and he lived and breathed, a part of it.

¶ MUSIC: *theme in: the cold, slow-moving ice: background under.*

Charles. Deep in the sea and writhing outward from the Pole, the mighty Labrador Current sets towards the south, the winds and storms scarring the surface above it, contending always vainly with its relentless might. And riding gripped in its arms comes the great, thousand-mile-square ice raft, fed from the polar seas and the northern glaciers. It moved, treacherous, deadly, unpredictable, making its own weather, driven aside by cross winds of its own breeding yet always returning to the south'ard route. The ageless bergs, snapped off from the seaward-crawling fingers of the Greenland Cap, tower amid its jagged dunes, contemptuously smashing out great lakes for themselves as they move with sinister docility to the wind and sea. Frozen rain and snow add glittering miles to its expanse as it moves down from Baffin Bay and beyond Cape Mercy towards the Labrador coast. Islands of fresh water ice from the mouths of emptying rivers join as the bleak sun grows warmer. Formations of pulpy sludge ice crawl out ahead in the early days of March to warn of its coming. And as it moves, a solid white desert groaning in majestic agony, or breaking and rejoining in a thousand jig-saw patterns, somewhere within its expanse the seals come with it — riding the great raft, whelping on the ice, at a season which has varied by hardly so much as a week in all the years that men have known of them.

¶ MUSIC: *out.*

Cast. [*ANGRY SHOUTS OF ALARMED MEN: FADING*]
Johns. [*ANGRY AND ALARMED*] *Kestrel*! That damned jinker, Mahan!
Torrance. [*CALMLY*] Aye — he's passed us. Let him go. He came by so close aboard of us he near took our yards . . .

¶ MUSIC: *tympani punctuation.*

Johns. [*ANGRILY*] Well ahead now, and pleased with himself.
Torrance. [*REPEATING CALMLY*] Let him go, I say.

Charles. Robert Torrance, standing on his quarterdeck in the bright sunshine, smelt the sea and the ice, and it was good. It brought, for the moment, a hard serenity which nothing could disturb. The ceaseless rhythm of it all, vast and inexorable, in which man's life and death were as the falling of a snowflake, gave him a pride and a lightness. It was no man he feared; he had always known that. He was a match for Tim Mahan or any other; and it seemed a small thing in that moment to go down, if he must go down, before the power that moved the seas and the great ice.

¶ MUSIC: *an accent: then background.*

Charles. Three days north, through the open channel of the "Inside Cut" with the jagged edges of the floe looming heavier and darker on their starboard hand. There were few ships in company now — the pack was dwindling, as captain after captain set his helm to starboard and bore away for the ice.

¶ MUSIC: *out.*

¶ SOUND: *ship's labouring progress: water: bumping ice: background.*

Charles. The fourth day. Heavier ice in the Cut now. Yesterday the pans and clumps of sludge had drifted by like rafts in the sea. Today the sea flowed in lakes and rivulets among a moving land of ice. Entering the floe.

Johns. You've taken more no'thing this year, Bob. The other lads have broke off a good bit to the south'ard of us.

Torrance. Aye.

Johns. I think ye've made a good guess. There've been no sign of seals yet that I'd trust. I think ye'll find the pack to the north.

Torrance. What d'ye make of that astern there?

Johns. The smoke? It's well to the east. It's the three ships that broke off ahead of us this morning.

Torrance. I don't mean them. The other — dead astern.

Johns. [PAUSE: SOFT, ANGRY EXCLAMATION] Ah-h. So he dropped back and let us go by him in the night.

Torrance. Aye. It's *Kestrel*, all right. Riding in our wake.

¶ MUSIC: *punctuation: into:*

¶ SOUND: *labouring ship: smashing ice: dead sound.*

Charles. Heavier ice with another morning, as they bite deeper into the floe. The bruising, crushing stuggle begins. The course is north by east, but hour by hour the ship zig-zags along the open cracks of the floe, riding down the drifting pans with her armoured bow.

¶ SOUND: *roaring of engines: crushing of ice.*

Charles. Engines at full speed, safety valves spurting, men labouring and cursing the demonic bucking of the ship. Ice, moving with the light breeze, locks close against the sides of the ship, churns away before its onward thrust, swirls astern into the turmoil of the wake. The sun sliding down with late afternoon; the steely day closing about them. And men of watch drifting aft now, to gather in little knots, their faces darkening at the sight of smoke and a low-lying hull astern.

Cast. [*LOW, ANGRY MURMUR OF MEN*]

Johns. [*SOFT ANGER: OUT OF IT*] Damn his eyes! Was there ever a sealer but Mahan would ride so cool in another man's wake?

Hardy. [*GRIMLY*] There'll be trouble over this.

Johns. [*HARD EMPHASIS*] There'll *not* be trouble, Hardy, and see you make sure there's not. It's trouble he's looking for.

¶ MUSIC: *punctuation into:*

¶ SOUND: *labouring ship: noise of spars and deck beam strain: background.*

Charles. Eight — nine — ten days, northward and eastward into the floe. Somewhere in its depths the harp seals barked and slithered beside the whitecoats, their newborn young. Thousands upon thousands of them together, the pack spread out from its centre to the limits of every horizon; yet for all its vastness it was a speck in the greater vastness of the floe. And the barrelmen, swaying at the masthead, changing their watches in weary rotation through the daylight hours, had seen no sign of it yet. Men gathered oftener and oftener in knots around the foot of the masts, looking up at the watching barrelmen scanning the horizon. And the hope in those upturned faces was beginning to give way to a troubled discontent.

Cast. [*MURMUR OF DISGRUNTLED MEN*]

Man. [*OUT OF MURMUR*] Come by d'wrong ship, dis time.

Man 2. Jinker on our tail — da's why — see that smoke astern?

Man. Torrances has always been good swoilers before.

Man 2. Aye, when their heart's in it. Bob's isn't.

Charles. There was something wrong with this voyage. Robert knew that the men felt it as surely as himself; though they had not the grim certainty which filled him every time he looked astern at that smudge on the horizon. The men no longer had their blithe, childish confidence in the captain's luck; they were wishing they had sailed in another ship. And yet — on the twelfth day . . .

Cast. [*TENSE, EXCITED MURMUR*]

Man. [*OUT OF MURMUR*] Lookit Danny aloft there — he's got his glass on something . . .

Man 2. Why's he take so long? [*CALLS*] Danny! Hoi! Have you gone to sleep? What d'y see from that barrel, yu scut?

Barrelman. [*FOR THOSE DIRECTLY BELOW*] Avast below, will ye? — I'm not sure — [*BREAKS: MORE LOUDLY FOR SHIP: THOUGH STILL TENTATIVE*] Four miles on the starboard bow — looks like it might be bobbin' holes — aye! — there's a harp and a whitecoat . . .

Cast. [*EXCITED CRIES*] Swoils! We're into the fat!

Charles. It was "seal ice" now — snow crusted, punctured here and there with bobbing holes — and yes — beyond them here a stray seal, there a tri-form blot against the white surface — a family of harp seals, lifting their heads, wrinkling their noses, gazing in the direction of the ship with their ineffectual liquid brown eyes.

¶ SOUND: *ship under easy way.*

Torrance. It's a patch, all right. And from the look of it, it might be the fringes of a big one.

Johns. Aye. I think so. There's too many families about for it to be a clump of strays.

Torrance. [*CALLING ALOFT*] What d'ye say, barrelman? Is it a big patch?

Barrelman. [*OFF: WATCHING INTENTLY*] Tell ye in a minute, skipper — there's a ridge of ice ahead for a bit — [*CATCH: JOYFUL SHOUT*] Aye! I see 'em now. It's de main patch — must be! T'ousands of 'em, sor — far as I can see! Swoils!

¶ MUSIC: *up with excitement: down into:*

Cast. [*ANGRY MUTTERING OF CREW*]

Johns. [*GRIMLY*] That's changed their mood in a hurry.

Torrance. What is it?

Johns. Look astarn. There's your friend, *Kestrel*, just liftin' over the rim again. The men have no liking for this business, Bob.

Torrance. Neither have I. [*PAUSE*] He's five miles astern of us. He can't have sighted the patch yet. I've a notion . . .

Johns. Well?

Torrance. [*CONSIDERING HALF-HEARTEDLY*] I could reverse engines — nose away to the west'ard till nightfall. If he followed I'd have him miles away from the patch by dark, and I could slip back . . .

Johns. And if he did not follow? He's no fool, Bob. And if he came here first after we found the patch, you'd have an ugly crew on your hands.

Torrance. [*HEAVILY*] Aye, you're right. Well, here's where we start our killing tomorrow sunrise. Burn her down.

Johns. [*TURNING AWAY: CALLING ORDER*] Burn her down.

¶ MUSIC: *punctuation.*

Charles. Nightfall. *Kestrel* dark against the ice a half mile away —

burned down too, fires banked and riding at rest. Anger had been loud in the *Jean Bright* as she came up, but now jubilant commotion takes over the ship. Decks and 'tween decks are loud with the bustle of preparations for the hunt — sealing knives to be sharpened, gaff points and boot cleats to be filed up, bread bags to be stuffed with the next day's rations. Hunters' voices and a clatter of similar preparations drift faintly from the other ship, but between them are the night dark, the voices of the seals, the restless moaning of the ice.

¶ SOUND: *wind: wash of water: seals: groan of ice.*

Charles.   Snow in the middle watch; but towards dawn the light breeze wears round to south of west. A clear day.

¶ SOUND: *ship getting into motion: siren.*

Cast.   [*VOICES OF EXCITED MEN*]

Charles.   The ship moves among the seals, following the cracks and lanes of open water that lead to the heart of the seal patch. The men of the hunting watches — fifty men to a watch — drop overside onto the ice, stream off in excited files, racing each other across the treacherous, yielding pans. In half an hour they are laying about them among the bawling whitecoats, and the mounds of pelts are piling up under the panflags that mark the ship's property like a miner's claim stakes.

¶ SOUND: *siren: ship under way.*

Johns.   Shall I wear round for loading, Bob?

Torrance.   [*GRIM: ABSTRACTED*] Aye . . .

Johns.   The First Watch will have a good lot of pelts for us by now . . .

Torrance.   [*SHARP: ANGRY EXCLAMATION*] D'ye see that? — off astern there?

Johns.   [*QUICKLY: CALMINGLY*] Aye, I see it. And there's nothing to be done about it, Bob.

Torrance.   Mahan's dropped every one of his watches alongside ours. Look there! — his men and ours are not a hundred yards apart.

Johns.   There's no law says they must be. And there's swoils enough for the lot of us.

Torrance.   Enough for five ships! He could work from the other side of the patch — ten miles away — if it was only fat he's after.

Johns.   Leave em be, Bob. We'll keep our heads, get our own load, and clear out.

Torrance.   [*GRIMLY*] If it's a simple as that, I'll be well content.

Johns.   I'll wear round for the panflags of Number One watch.

Torrance.   And ye'll find *Kestrel* panflags planted side by side with 'em. That's the way he's ardered it.

Johns. Maybe. But leave em bide, till we're out of the ice.

¶ MUSIC: *punctuation: to background.*

Charles. A full moon riding above the ice, silhouetting the two motion-less ships. Northern lights climb jaggedly along the horizon, whisper up the sky in fangy arcs of blue, green and yellow. Eerily complaining, the great floe rocks southward in the arms of the Labrador current. Light and darkness, shadow and gloom, chase each other in a weird dance along the *Jean Bright*'s quarterdeck. From the 'tween decks beneath the snores of two hundred sleeping men billow up in a soft wave.

¶ MUSIC: *out.*

Johns. You've need of sleep, Bob.

Torrance. In a spell.

Johns. [*AFTER A PAUSE: EFFORTFUL CASUALNESS*] It's been a great day's killing. There's three thousand pelts stowed down. Another two thousand still on the ice.

Torrance. You're dead sure of where your panflags are? — every one of 'em?

Johns. I am.

Torrance. [*SOFT START: SHARP BREATH*]

Johns. [*QUICKLY*] What is it?

Torrance. [*RELAXING*] Nothing. I — thought something moved out there. [*PAUSE*] It's not far from here that the thing happened a year ago.

Johns. [*SLIGHT PAUSE: QUIET: HARD*] If it's Mahan you're thinking of, leave him be.

Torrance. Why?

Johns. Because you're captain of this ship. With two hundred men depending on you.

Torrance. I mind it.

Johns. And there's another two hundred in *Kestrel*. Good men — friends and neighbours, half of 'em, to our crew. They've no part in what's between you and Mahan.

Torrance. [*QUIET: SARDONIC: BITTER*] And what would that be? You've never spoken of it before.

Johns. I've known what's been in your mind this past year.

Torrance. And what's been in yours? Did you ever before know John Torrance to leave his ship when he was in the ice.

Johns. No, I did not.

Torrance. Why should he have done it last year? Why should he have gone over the side in the middle of the night and onto the floe alone?

Johns. [*PAUSE: QUIETLY*] I don't know. Maybe I've the same thoughts as

285

you. [*URGENT, INTENSE PLEADING*] But I put 'em from me while we're in the ice, Bob! And so should you. They'll not bring back your father.

Torrance. No. They'll not. And there's but one thing will put 'em at rest. [*PAUSE*] I should not have come to the ice this year, Ernest. I'd the notion not to.

Johns. [*QUIETLY*] I know.

Torrance. [*SURPRISED*] Maura told you?

Johns. She did.

Torrance. [*GRIM QUIET*] It's a heavy weight you'll bear, then — both of you.

Johns. No man can shift the weight from his own back, Bob. Nor set it down and run from it.

Torrance. [*BITTERLY*] So it's myself I'm afraid for? You talk two ways at once. All this day you've been telling me — "Leave him be — have no trouble with him in the ice."

Johns. And you've listened. There's been no trouble this day.

Torrance. But it's breeding. It has been since morning. You know that as well as I.

Johns. And still there need be no trouble. I don't talk two ways at once, Bob. You must settle with him — I know that well enough. But here in the ice, with all depending on you, you are not your own man. [*GOING*] Remember that.

Torrance. [*HARSH SIGH*]

¶ MUSIC: *slight tympani punctuation: background roll.*

Torrance. [*A QUICK, TENSE GASP*]

Charles. A movement? A hardening of shadow upon the gloom and glitter of the ice?

¶ MUSIC: *out.*

Torrance. [*HARSH, RELAXING SIGH*]

Charles. No. Formless shadows crawled every where across the gleaming face of the floe as the pans shifted. Now and then from the distance came the loom of a great berg riding down a lesser barrier. The ice was a breeding ground for fancies as well as seals; a cold, miasmal fairyland where every man's thoughts walked out of his head and took on strange shapes before him. He went below at last, flung himself onto his bunk, and fell into exhausted sleep.

¶ MUSIC: *alerting dawn strain: into:*

¶ SOUND: *muffled stir of voices and feet on deck, heard from cabin.*

Johns. [*FADING IN GRIMLY*] Bob . . .

Torrance. [*LEAPING FROM SLEEP*] What is it?

Johns. Trouble. Half a dozen panflags been shifted in the night.

Torrance. [*STARING UP: GRIM SATISFACTION*] Ah! So he *was* on the ice!

Johns. [*HARD: STEADY: DETAINING HIM*] Hold on!

Torrance. [*TURNING BACK*] Well?

Johns. You were waiting for this last night. Hoping for it.

Torrance. Maybe I was.

Johns. Then wait a bit longer. Deal with Mahan when you get your men home.

Torrance. He's making the time. Not I.

Johns. [*INTENSELY*] And will you let him? [*PAUSE: EARNESTLY*] Changing panflags is a bad business, Bob. But a fight between ships in the ice could be worse.

Torrance. [*BREAKING AWAY GRIMLY*] There'll be no fight between *ships* . . .

¶ SOUND: *fade in stir of angry voices: men shuffling on deck.*

Cast. Cap'n! Here's the Skipper. Bob, that divvil of Mahan's been at it again!

Torrance. [*STERNLY: SURE OF HIMSELF: OVER IT*] Well now — what's it all about? Quiet, the rest of you!

Man. Look there, skipper — on the ice — our Number One Watch, and *Kestrel's* . . .

¶ MUSIC: *tympani punctuation.*

Charles. A mile away on the ice, the fifty men of *Jean Bright's* first hunting watch, milling beside their panflags. And hard by, the first watch from *Kestrel.* A hundred men, broken into six angry groups shuffling with cocked fists and an air of furious mystifaction, each about a mound of pelts. Even from a mile away the dangerous electricity in the air could be felt. It could be felt among the men of the three watches still on board. It was plain in the face of David Hardy, master of the first watch, as he came panting back across the ice to the ship's side.

Hardy. [*ANGRY: BREATHING HEAVILY*] Ye'd better come out here, skipper. There's *Kestrel* flags been set on six of our piles. Near a thousand pelts swiped.

Torrance. What do the *Kestrel* lads say?

Hardy. No one says he knows anything about it. And they'll not give up a pelt under their flags.

Cast. [*ANGRY MURMUR FROM DECK*]

Torrance. [*LOUD*] Quiet! [*TO HARDY*] No more would you. And there's no proving anything now.

Hardy. [*ANGRY FLARE*] You know who's done it! And so do we! It's happened before to ships lying near him.

Torrance. [*STERNLY*] I say there's no proving it. Leave all as it is, set up new flags, and get on with the killing.

Hardy. The men'll not go.

Torrance. You'll tell 'em it's my orders! And you'll see that they go.

Cast. [*RISING MURMUR OF PROTEST*]

Torrance. [*TURNING ON THEM: STERN: SURE*] And the rest of you make ready your gear now! We'll get on with the hunt.

Johns. [*PAUSE: LOW: WARM APPROVAL*] Good work, me son!

Torrance. [*BRUSQUELY*] Get the ship under way.

¶ MUSIC: *punctuation into:*

¶ SOUND: *ship under way: bumping ice: background.*

Cast. [*VOICES OF MEN SETTING OFF FOR HUNT: IN DISTANCE: FADING*]

Johns. Well — there's the last of the watches away.

Torrance. Aye. And well spread about the ice. See they're kept that way.

Johns. Wear back for loading now?

Torrance. Come alongside the edge there, first.

¶ SOUND: *metallic clink: a gaff taken from a rack of them.*

Johns. What do you want with that gaff? You're not going on the ice?

Torrance. I am. We're well clear of the men now. They'll not notice.

Johns. [*PROTEST*] Bob . . .

Torrance. [*STERNLY*] Come alongside the ice, I say, and drop me.

¶ SOUND: *ship's side grates gently against the ice.*

Johns. [*GRUFFLY*] You've acted like a captain, so far. Now you're a fool.

Torrance. [*GRIM: SARDONIC*] Is this not what Maura wanted? — and you too?

Johns. [*ANGRILY*] I'll not speak for her. For myself, I thought you'd a clear head — and the strength to hold on to yourself. D'ye not see you're playing his game?

Torrance. Is he to go on with this business of the panflags forever?

Johns. We're in a rich patch. A few pelts either way is no matter. And it's not the pelts you're thinking of.

Torrance. Maybe it's not. Maybe I'm thinking there'll be more flags changed tonight if he's not stopped, and more again the next night — till we've four hundred men at each others' throats. [*SLIGHT PAUSE*] Stand clear . . .

¶ SOUND: *clunk as he drops to ice.*

Torrance. Ah. [*SPEAKS UPWARD TO JOHNS ON DECK*] Get on with the loading. If the wind works round to the nor'west we'll be in for thick weather. Don't wait too long to call the men in.

Johns. [*CURTLY*] I won't. And I hope you're *sure* of what you go to do. For you've no choice now.

Charles. *Kestrel* a mile away — grating gently against the ice too — down now, like his own ship, to a skeleton crew of ship-handlers and loaders. His gaff felt out the flaky sish which looked like solid ice but lay, a yielding film above open water. The sun still cast a dazzling glare on the floe, but the mood of the day was changing. He could feel the uneasiness of the weather, and smell snow riding far off in the wind.

¶ MUSIC: *slight tympani punctuation.*

Torrance. [*SOFTLY*] Ah . . .

Charles. A tall figure had dropped to the ice and was separating now from the loom of *Ketsrel*'s side. But Mahan was not coming to meet him. Gaff in hand, moving with elaborate casualness, he was heading off into the floe, away from the hunting watches. It would be better this way.

¶ MUSIC: *tympani.*

Charles. A broad, jagged ridge, where wind and swell had lifted the pans to a height of nearly thirty feet. And down the other side, a small lake of black water — and Mahan, resting on his haunches at the edge of it — the place he had chosen. His eyes not on the man that followed him, but on an ice pan in the middle of the lake, joined to its edge by a narrow neck. He was looking at a pair of Hood seals — the watchdogs and warriors of the breed — aloof and dangerous. Torrance felt a cool, warning tremor run through him. Mahan had known the Hoods were here.

Mahan. [*OFF: BLAND: DANGEROUS*] Ah, Robert — welcome to my lake.

¶ MUSIC: *tympani background.*

Charles. He was at the water's edge now. The big form was moving toward him over the jagged footing of ice with its familiar, lithe grace. The cap on the head pushed far back as always, a lock of black hair curling beneath the peak. He was a little mad, and there was no doubt about it. The madness flickered in his black eyes; it showed in the restless lift and turn of his head. Even before last year the ugly, sullen name had trailed him about the city and the outports — Jinker — the man who brings the feel of evil, for himself and all those who sail with him.

Mahan. [*NEARING: SOFTLY AND DANGEROUSLY*] Well, Robert? I think you wanted a word with me.

Torrance. [*GRIMLY*] I did. I wanted to tell you that you've changed your last panflag.

289

Mahan.   So? And who says I've done such a thing?

Torrance.   You'll come back with me this instant, before the loaders get to 'em, and take down the flags you shifted last night. Or we settle our business here and now.

Mahan.   [*SLIGHT PAUSE: MORE SOFTLY AND DANGEROUSLY*] Our business, Robert? I've been thinkin' about that. Indeed, I'd say it's more the reason than the seals why I clung to ye on the way north. There's been something troubling you this year past. I'd a mind to hear it where we're alone.

Torrance.   [*SUDDEN, FLARING INTENSITY*] You've no need to hear it! You know. You went onto the ice to shift panflags last year. But my father saw you. He came over the side and was onto you before you got fairly started. You let him have it with a gaff or a knife, and you shoved his body into a crack in the floe and crawled back in the dark to your ship!

¶ SOUND: *in the pause water laps gently: off the throaty growl of the hood seals.*

Mahan.   [*DEADLY SOFTNESS*] So that's what's been on your mind. You're a hard thinker, Robert, and the truth will out, they say. Queer, isn't it? It's why I wanted ye north this year . . .

Torrance.   [*GRIM AND WATCHFUL*] I know that . . .

¶ SOUND: *seals bark.*

Mahan.   And why I was glad when I found the Hoods. [*CHUCKLE*] Look at 'em out there — already stirring — they'll be after us in a minute — if we don't move.

Torrance.   We'll not move till we've settled our business.

Mahan.   No, we'll not. [*SOFTLY: TENSING*] It was rash of ye, Robert, to tell me all this — out here — where if one of us comes back bleeding and one does not come back — [*SUDDEN EFFORT*] — it can all be blamed on the Hood!

Torrance.   [*STARTLED LEAP ASIDE*] Oh!

¶ SOUND: *simultaneously the sing of the flying gaff: metallic clank and quiver as it strikes in the ice.*

¶ MUSIC: *tympani punctuation.*

Charles.   The flash of the gaff head seemed to streak from beneath Mahan's arm before the rippling movement of his turn. The shaft whistled within an inch of Torrance's side, shuddering in the ice behind him. Mahan was scrambling towards him — off balance — pulled forward by the throw. He drew back his arm, his own gaff level across his shoulder, and suddenly was overwhelmed by the one thing he had never bargained for. He could not make himself drive that steel-headed spear into the shape lunging towards him. It quivered in his grasp for a second; and in that second Mahan was upon him . . .

Torrance.   [*JOLT AND GROANS OF STRUGGLE AS HE GOES DOWN*]

¶ SOUND: *rattle of gaff on ice.*

Charles.   He sank groggily under the rain of blows that beat at his head, his shoulders, his neck — started to his feet, slipped, and was on his knees again. Mahan loomed mistily above him, a block of ice in his arms now, raised to crash down on his skull and that would be the end. But Mahan's towering form and bloody face were suddenly darkened by the shadow looming behind him . . .

Mahan.   [*STARTLED CRY*]   The Hood — the Hood! [*A SCREAM OF PAIN*]

¶ SOUND: *growling bark of seal.*

Charles.   Moving on the ice with twice the speed of a man, the beast lashed out with one of its flippers to open a long, ugly gash in Mahan's cheek. He reeled back, his head bobbing drunkenly from the blow, and as he did so the other flipper swept in with full force, knocking him to the ice.

¶ SOUND: *thud of blow.*

Mahan.   [*GROAN*]

¶ MUSIC: *tympani punctuation: to background.*

Charles.   Torrance, half conscious, was slithering across the ice to his gaff — flinging it with all the strength he had, low at the belly of the seal.

¶ SOUND: *gaff strikes: coughing whinny of seal.*

Charles.   With the gaff-handle quivering in its front, the seal shuled to the ice in a red-streaming mass.

¶ SOUND: *another bark: off.*

Charles.   The other Hood, the mate, was shambling in from the ice-pan now. He wrenched the gaff from the steaming body and ran to the water's edge to deal with her. The gaff plunged, but she was quicker than the male. He felt the shoulder of his jacket go, then pain screamed through his body as her teeth tore the flesh of his arm. He plunged the gaff into her again and again. She quivered, settled on the ice . . .

¶ SOUND: *weird, throaty moan of dying seal.*

Charles.   . . . and it was over.

¶ MUSIC: *tympani out with punctuation.*

Torrance.   [*GASPING BREATHING: NAUSEA*]

¶ SOUND: *distant, muted siren of a ship.*

Charles.   He must not faint. Something was telling him he must not faint.
Torrance.   [*THE GASPING BREATHING: BEGINNING TO STEADY AGAIN*]
Charles.   He raised his head. The day had changed about him.

¶ SOUND: *siren.*

Charles.   From the nor'west, still beyond the ships and the ridge that hid him from them, a filmy wall walked inward, topped with light. The snow as closing in. He was hearing the warning signals of the two ships. It had been a sound instinctively registering in his mind through all the fight. Between the bodies of the seals Mahan lay, still unconscious. It would have been so easy in that moment — he cursed himself for what he could not do. The breathing carrion could be shoved to the edge of the ice, kicked into the water like a sculped seal, and that would be the end. Instead, he bent low, heaved the inert body to his shoulders. Staggering and vomiting, grateful for the lightning flashes of pain which cleared his head, he made his way to the ridge over which they had come, down the other side to a sound of voices nearing, and into blessed darkness.

¶ MUSIC: *up and in to eerie suggestion of fog: background.*

Charles.   He was in his bunk; his wounds throbbing beneath clean bandages. Ernest Johns stood in the cabin, his face shadowed and sombre in the light of the dim oil lamp.

¶ MUSIC: *out.*

¶ SOUND: *gurgling of John's pipe.*

Charles.   The old man's pipe sucked noisily as he drew on it; and the gurgling had a familiar realness which was somehow comforting. Even in the warm and reeking cabin there was the feel of weather on the make. Everything — ship and crew, the animal voices and the moaning ice — seemed trapped at the centre of a vast, malign silence which was swallowing the earth.
Johns.   Ye've a bad gash in the shoulder, but it's clean now.
Torrance.   [*SLIGHT GROAN: THEN BLEAKLY*] Well — say what's in your mind.
Johns.   [*QUIETLY EARNEST*] Either ye should not have gone, or ye should have finished him. [*SLIGHT PAUSE: MORE INTENSELY*] It's more than a matter of Mahan and yourself, Bob. Neither the men in this ship nor

his own are safe now.

Torrance. I know.

Johns. Tomorrow, if the weather lifts, we should clear out. Leave the pelts we haven't picked up. Holds are full, and the deck pounds near full. Couldn't take more'n another thousand anyway.

Torrance. [*PAUSE: IMPRESSED*] What about the men? How will they feel if we run away from out pelts?

Johns. The men know better. They've more'n a glim of the truth of it. But here's not the place to settle it, Bob! They want to get back with the fat we have.

Torrance. [*SOFT GROAN*] I could not tell her how it would be. But I knew.

Johns. Maura again? Are ye blaming *her* for your coming? What are you, man? You could not let Mahan drive you from the ice — but this fullishness is another matter. And if there was not the iron in you to end it, you should not have begun. What's that . . . ?

¶ SOUND: *alarmed stir overhead on deck.*

Torrance. [*LISTENING*] Snow lightened?

Johns. [*ANXIOUSLY*] Gave no sign of it ten minutes ago — [*GOING QUICKLY*] I'll have a look . . .

Cast. [*FADE IN: ANXIOUS MEN SHUFFLING ON DECK*]

Torrance. [*FADING IN*] What is it?

Johns. [*ANXIOUS*] Ye should not have left your bunk, Bob . . .

Torrance. [*MORE URGENTLY*] What's the trouble?

Man. [*OUT OF MURMUR*] I seen something between the ships — 'twas moving . . .

Man 2. 'Twas a light, sor — I seen a masthead light, hard by . . .

Man. Listen!

¶ SOUND: *off: muffled in fog: ship's engines: crash of ice.*

Johns. [*SOFT EXCLAMATION*] *Kestrel*! She's under way.

Man 2. [*ANGRY: ANXIOUS*] Aye — it's her! They're crazy — all on board of her this trip. Moving off in the starm. 'Twill be the end of her.

Man. And a good t'ing. Serve her right. Serve Tim Mahan right, and the fools that sailed wit' him. Jinker, he is!

Johns. [*SUDDENLY*] The horn! Git that horn going!

Cast. [*ALARMED SHOUTS: SUDDENLY RISING*]

¶ SOUND: *ship nearing suddenly: crashing in over ice: ship's siren on board.*

Charles. Immense, vague, magnified to giant size in the thickness, *Kestrel* was bearing down on them.

¶ SOUND: *peaks.*

Charles. Its hugeness lessened as it drew near — narrowed to a looming wedge, crawling forward with deadly menace.

¶ SOUND: *Kestrel's bow noses into* Jean Bright's *side: climbs up the bulwark: slides off gratingly.*

Cast. [*ANGRY, PANICKY SHOUTS OF FALLING MEN*]

Charles. Among a sprawling, yelling tangle of men knocked flat by the impact, Torrance struggled to his feet, made his way to the port bulwark. *Kestrel's* bow had grated down, sheered off from the side of the ship. But suddenly the great, iron-clad wedge was thrusting through the snow once more . . .

Men. [*PANIC*] She's comin' again!

Charles. Lower this time — level with the side . . .

¶ SOUND: *above roaring of steam.*

Charles. . . . she struck. He felt the port side lifting with the thrust . . .

¶ SOUND: *crash of the bow: heave of the ship before a steady, grating thrust.*

Cast. [*SCREAMS OF MEN FALLING: SLIDING: GURGLING OF WATER*]

¶ MUSIC: *punctuates: to background.*

Charles. *Jean Bright* heeled drunkenly to starboard before the unrelenting thrust — men grabbed desperately at each other as they slid along tilting planks. Water climbed the bulwarks — the ship took on a sagging deadness. Jagged sticks of timber, loose mounds of pelts, slithered down the canting deck, carrying the men with them, surged over the side in a helpless, tangled mass among the washing pans of ice. Fires flared and were smothered by engulfing water. Below decks the pounds gave, and the whole tonnage of fate drove against the sides.

¶ SOUND: *slow, gurling, creaking rush of overturning ship.*

Charles. The mastpeaks swept downward, cutting a great, slow arc through the gloom. They came level with the ice, resting for a moment quivering on its edge. Then they broke through, and amid a lashing hail of ice fragments and flying wood the *Jean Bright* turned over and sank.

¶ MUSIC: *up to end it.*

Johns. [*SOMBERLY FINISHING A ROLL CALL*] Parker . . .

Man. [*OFF: DULLY*] Here . . .

Johns. Davis . . . [*PAUSE*] Kelvin . . . [*PAUSE*] Johnson . . .

Man 2. [*WEARILY*] I'm here, Ernest.

Johns. [*TURNING TO TORRANCE*] Fifteen gone, far as I can tell.

Torrance. [*DULLY*] Aye.

¶ SOUND: *a bleak wind: near lap of water.*

Cast. [*OFF: SOFT WEEPING OF ONE OR TWO SHAKEN MEN*]
Torrance. [*DULLY: UNABLE TO TAKE IT IN*] No food, no gear. All we've come for gone, and all that would take us home with our lives.
Johns. [*SLIGHT PAUSE: SOFTLY: A THING TOO HORRIBLE TO BELIEVE*] It was Mahan alone — Tim Mahan that ordered up the steam and come in on us in the starm and rammed us. Tim Mahan giving the steering orders, and no man else in the ship knowing what he was about.

¶ SOUND: *the wind.*

Johns. [*SOFTLY: SNIFFING THE WIND*] Changing, the wind. Veering to the nor'west. [*PAUSE*] They might ha' known. The Lard does not let such a thing be done unpunished.

¶ SOUND: *wind more loudly.*

Charles. And so it was. For at the break of the bitter morning the wind was blowing sharp from the north, and the outward channels of the floe had closed in iron-hard.

¶ MUSIC: *tympani punctuation.*

Cast. [*SURPRISED*] Kestrel! She didn't get out!
Charles. Kestrel lay not a mile away, already locked in from open water. The face of the floe was alive with slithering pans, hurled in like huge projectiles by the force of wind and sea.

¶ SOUND: *wind: storm: crashing ice: background.*

Charles. Kestrel's men were on the floe fore and aft of her and to loo'ard, with axes and ice chisels and dynamite, but their work was useless there. The trap had closed on her to winnard, and on the winnard side no man could live among the ice blocks charging in with flying chips and powdering snow.

¶ SOUND: *storm up.*

Torrance. [*SLIGHTLY OFF: TO ANOTHER MAN*] What have ye got there? — that stick of timber. Let's have it.
Johns. [*COMING UP TO HIM*] What now, Bob?
Torrance. The thing I did not do before.
Johns. We must save their ship for 'em. There's no hope else for any of us.
Torrance. [*GRIMLY: STARTING AWAY*] This comes first. For all else depends on it.

¶ SOUND: *storm in.*

295

Cast. [*SLIGHT, GRIM MURMUR OF MEN AS THEY FOLLOW HIM*]

¶ MUSIC: *tympani rhythm background.*

Charles. The purpose was sure in him as he started on his way against the lashing wind and skidding fragments of the ice. He could not bring himself to speak to his men; but they streamed behind him, heads bent against the gale, carrying the few poor tools which were left them. They knew, he thought, as he worked his stiff fingers around the splintered club. They knew what must be done, and if *he* did not do it, *they* would. But he would not fail them twice.

He passed among the *Kestrel* men working on the ice, and without looking he felt them draw apart and leave a lane for him. Their faces, he knew, like those behind him, would wear a look of stony assent.

Mahan. [*OFF: SHOUTING: LUNATIC DEFIANCE*] Stay clear o' my ship, ye squid-squaws! [*CHUCKLE*]

Charles. There was a gaff in Mahan's hand, a knife at his belt; and he came down the listing deck towards Torrance with quick, careful steps. No man of either crew stirred a foot to come between them. Amid the gale, the sway of movement gathering along the deck and gathering in from the ice was a soundless, inexorable thing; a multiplying of eyes watching with steely intentness a work that must be done.

¶ MUSIC: *out.*

Mahan. [*THE SOFT, LUNATIC CHUCKLE*] This is the end of it, Robert. And time.

Torrance. High time, Tim.

¶ MUSIC: *low tympani punctuation.*

¶ SOUND: *wind: creak of ship: smash of driving ice cakes: background.*

Charles. The two in the cleared space circled each other as the ice battered the ship and the snowy wind swept the deck. The thing would be swift, for there was no flaw of mercy in the one, no hope of mercy in the other.

Cast. [*A SUDDEN GASP*]

Charles. Suddenly Mahan lunged, driving his gaff before him like a spear . . .

¶ SOUND: *wood cracking wood: then rattle of gaff on deck.*

Charles. . . . and Torrance swung his club to break it from his hand and break the wrist with it.

Mahan. [*A CHOKED SCREAM OF PAIN*]

Charles. Mahan's right hand dropped to his side, but he plunged on with his left hand clawing for the knife in his belt . . .

¶ SOUND: *clatter of knife on deck.*

Charles.   It slipped from his fumbling fingers, but he turned from a vain dive after it to tear off his cap, fling it at Torrance's face and follow it in . . .

Torrance.   [*SMOTHERED GASP: THEN CHOKING: STRANGLING*]

Charles.   Torrance swung the club again — blindly — and a searing shock ran up his arms as Mahan kicked it from his hand.

¶ SOUND: *club falls to deck.*

Charles.   Mahan's left hand was at his throat, bending him backward. He beat out with fists and feet, but could not break that terrible, single-handed grip. His eyes were starting from their sockets and his tongue forcing its way between his teeth when his fingers, groping for Mahan's shattered wrist, found it and twisted with all the strength he had left.

Mahan.   [*SCREAM OF AGONY*]

Charles.   He wrenched from the loosened grip, scrambled along the deck for the club, turned, swinging low . . .

¶ SOUND: *breaking wood: breaking bones.*

Charles.   . . . felt the crash of breaking wood and breaking bones. Then, as Mahan's trunk crumpled onto the shattered legs, he raised his stump of wood for the last time and brought it down with all the hate that was in him on the black head.

¶ SOUND: *the blow.*

Mahan.   [*GROAN: CHOKED OFF*]

Cast.   [*HORRIFIED MURMUR: THEN DEAD SILENCE*]

Charles.   [*AFTER A PAUSE*] As he bent over the smashed thing quivering on the deck before him, his eyes cleared. He saw the white line of the neck beneath the jacket collar. A shaggy curl of dark hair twisted down over the young flesh, untouched by the clotting ooze above. He had the strange feeling, in that passing second, that he was standing once again in the schoolyard where they had first played and first fought. Suddenly a terrible haste possessed him. He lifted the body in his arms, staggered up the deck through an opening lane of men, and with a great, sobbing heave flung it over the windward bulwark.

Cast.   [*STARTLED MURMURS ABOVE: GASP*]

¶ SOUND: *wind and ice.*

Charles.   He saw the groaning, tortured mass of the ice receive its offering; and then the thundering pans came driving inward to grind it among them and over it from sight.

¶ MUSIC: *up for the climax: background.*

Charles. She rode high and sorrowful into St. John's at last — the burdened *Kestrel* — clean — stripped of her last pelt, but heavy with the weight of four hundred men who had lost their spring.

¶ MUSIC: *out.*

Charles. He thrust himself among the crowd, thrusting aside the anxious questions, limped alone from the jetty and took the path towards home.

¶ SOUND: *house door pushed open: closed after pause.*

Torrance. [*VOICE A LITTLE RAISED: ANXIOUS: QUESTIONING*] Maura . . .
Maura. [*OFF: FADING IN: A GASP*] Robert! [*INCREDULOUS*] Robert!
Torrance. [*SUDDEN UNDERSTANDING: GOING TO HER: TAKING HER IN HIS ARMS*] Maura! How could you know?
Maura. [*TEARFUL: FAINT*] I was gathering my things — to leave the island forever. It seemed that all the deaths I have died these weeks had become the real death at last. [*SOB*] I saw the *Kestrel* from the hill — and I thought it was him coming home. And I knew that if he came back, you would not.
Torrance. Aye. I know.
Maura. [*TEARFUL INTENSITY*] And yet I knew that you must go. For there *was* fear in you, Robert. And if you had turned your back on it you would have found it all the days of your life, everywhere, waiting . . .
Torrance. [*GENTLY*] There. There is no fear any more.

¶ MUSIC: *punctuates: to background.*

Charles. I remember the deep and joining look which passed between that old woman and that old man. The sureness of it. Or was it the memory of a sureness which had ebbed and flowed with the years? — in her as in him, for there was no ripple of his soul whose impulse did not stir her. Perhaps that is why he told me the story, why she listened so intently. Weighing again its cost — that hard-won, hard-held sureness: the stout ship sucking down in the black water, the roll call in the windy night, the silences — the crumpled thing on deck, the dark curl, the white line of flesh beneath the jacket collar. Too great a cost? No sureness yet — no sureness ever. Only the knowledge of what cannot be changed. Only the hard, spent calm of the great ice moving with the great current on the breast of the greater sea.

¶ MUSIC: *up to conclusion.*

Announcer. Stage 55 . . . Item 26 . . . "The Jinker" . . . a tale of the

Newfoundland sealers many years ago . . . was written by Joseph Schull . . . and produced and directed by Andrew Allan, with the assistance of Jimmy James, and with music composed and conducted by Lucio Agostini. Charles Torrance, the storyteller, was Budd Knapp; Bob Torrance was Douglas Rain; Maura, his wife, was Ruth Springford; Tim Mahan was Alan King; Ernest Johns was J. Frank Willis; David Hardy was Frank Peddie; the Barrelman was Murray Westgate; Parker was William Shatner; and Johnson was Richard Gilbert. Sound effects by David Tasker and Bill Roach. Technical operation by John Sliz.

Full Speed Sideways

TOMMY TWEED

Production

Producer: Andrew Allan
Music: Morris Surdin
Sound: Fred Tudor
Operator: Terry Ruslin
Announcer: Ken Haslam
Program: Stage 61, Playbill 9
Broadcast: November 26, 1961, 8:00–9:00 pm EST
Studio: CBL Toronto
Network: Trans-Canada

Cast

John Drainie *as* Captain Jim Sheets
Ed McNamara *as* Melchisedek Seager
Arch McDonell *as* Amateur Historian
John Bethune *as* Footnote
Frank Perry *as* Harold Talbot
Alan King *as* Pierre
Tommy Tweed *as* Thomas Tweed
Geoffrey Alexander *as* G.A. Henty

Norman Ettlinger *as* General Middleton
Ruth Springford *as* Minnie Buffalo Chip
Joseph Shaw *as* Captain Haig de Haig
Hugh Rose *as* Lieutenant Hugh John Macdonald
Alan Pearce *as* Colonel Sam Bedson
Bernard Johnson *as* the Singer

•

FULL SPEED SIDEWAYS

Preface

Although Andrew Allan retired as Head of the Drama Department and as producer of the *Stage* series at the end of the 1954–55 season, he did return for one last *Stage* season in 1961–62. Tommy Tweed's "Full Speed Sideways" was one of its highlights. It illustrates not only Tweed's genius at pricking serious Canadian clichés in the most hilarious and disarming manner, but also Allan's genius at choosing plays which combine sharp social comment with dramatic effectiveness. The play concerns, of all things, a naval battle in the middle of the prairies during the Riel Rebellion.

It is hard to believe, but there really was a naval battle on the Canadian prairies. In April 1885, shortly after Riel and his Métis had seized the town of Batoche and formed a provisional government, General Middleton, who was beseiging Batoche, commandeered the freighter s.s. *Northcote* to transport troops and material down the South Saskatchewan River to his army. Unknown to Middleton, the river was difficult to navigate, and this strategy seemed far more promising than it turned out. As the *Northcote* moved slowly downstream, its voyage was aborted by a ferry cable placed across the river by the defenders of the Métis stronghold. It was only weeks later that Canadian troops managed to capture Batoche and end the fighting.

Tommy Tweed was born in Medicine Hat, Alberta, the very town from which the *Northcote* had departed 23 years before. He studied science at University of Manitoba, Winnipeg, and started his radio career there at station CKY. Between 1935 and 1941 he wrote and acted in many local and network shows, including *The Youngbloods of Beaver Bend*, with Esse W. Ljungh. He moved to Toronto in 1941 to continue his career. Tweed played a major role as an actor and script-writer during the Golden Age of radio drama. He also wrote an acted in a number of CBC television plays. In the two decades following 1941, not less than 130 of his plays were broadcast by the CBC, of which about 50 were originals. His satiric

303

documentaries on Canadian history were prominent among these. He was one of Allan's favorite actors on the *Stage* series, and Allan produced 12 of Tweed's original plays.

TOMMY TWEED

Full Speed Sideways

Announcer. [COLD] CBC *Stage* tonight submits the fourth in a quartet of plays especially commissioned and written to commemorate the 25th Anniversary of the CBC and the 19th consecutive season of our radio drama showcase.

¶ SOUND: *eight bells.*

¶ MUSIC: *a robust entry of sailing sailing over the bounding main . . . no repeat . . . out.*

¶ SOUND: *toot.*

Announcer. Tonight, on CBC *Stage* — our Radio Drama showcase — Playbill No. 9 "Full Speed Sideways," being the incredible log of the s.s. *Northcote,* the first and only gunboat to navigate the Canadian Prairie, wherein General Middleton attacked Batoche from the sea, thereby adding another chapter to the glorious record of the Senior Service. Herewith — extracted painstakingly from various sources, including the Saskatchewan Archives, the Militia Reports, Personal Reminiscences and obscure Footnotes, "Full Speed Sideways." Music composed, arranged, and conducted by Morris Surdin. Production and direction by Andrew Allan.

Singer. [HEARTS OF OAK ARE OUR SHIPS: ONE VERSE: OUT]

Announcer. Presenting John Drainie as Captain Jim Sheets and Ed MacNamara as Co-captain Melchisedek Seager in "Full Speed Sideways" by Tommy Tweed.

¶ MUSIC: *a short jolly hornpipe tie-off.*

Amat[*eur*]. As an Amateur Historian, I do for fun what the Professional Historian does for the record. And in some stubborn case, for money. Gramatically speaking, he deals in the past tense; while I deal in the Past Imperfect. I am such stuff as footnotes are made of . . . and this is the way of it.

305

¶ SOUND: *rifle shot with a wicked ricochet.*

Amat. The Opening shot of the Northwest Rebellion was fired at Duck Lake in the Territory of Saskatchewan on March 26th, 1885. While too modest to be "heard round the world," it was loud enough to startle procrastinating, official Ottawa.

¶ MUSIC: *an explosion on the side drums: to a background of boodle doodle doop dop boodle doodle doop.*

Amat. [*ON CUE*] On March 27th, the news of the defeat of the Mounted Police and the Prince Albert Volunteers, produced frantic telegrams from the Minister of Defence, Adolphe Caron, to Militia Commanders throughout the Dominion. Their quotas were fixed for twenty-four hour mobilization. The West was aflame.

¶ MUSIC: *another explosion on the side drums: top it with the bugle call "charge".*

Amat. The sixty year old warhorse, bogey moustachioed General Frederick D. Middleton, Commander-in-Chief of Canadian Militia, heard the call and detrained the first detachment of Winnipeg's 90th at Quappelle and then sat back nearly two hundred miles southeast of Batoche to await reinforcements.

¶ SOUND: *train whistle: the crossing signal one: to a train background running.*

Amat. In a short twelve days they came, thanks to Van Horne of the CPR. Five hundred raw troops there were, not to mention a mountain of supplies including 6,000 rifles, a million cartridges and a quarter of a million pounds of canned rations. Even so, if it hadn't been for Van Horne, his superintendents and station masters, including one who baked fresh bread daily for the boys, they would have starved to death. As it was they nearly perished in the bitter, spring cold. In fact when the Surgeon-General submitted his final report, he noted:

¶ SOUND: *out at end of narration.*

Surg[*eon-general*]. That rheumatism, bronchitis, pleurisy, tonsillitis, and pneumonia have put more men out of action than the enemy did.

¶ MUSIC: *bloop: should be close on: with at least two instruments (wind): small and pert.*

Foot[*note*]: although General Middleton, like Queen Victoria, would not have been amused, one Toronto contingent found it hilarious that one of their outfit had forgotten to leave the combination of his safe with his employees. Another had left the gas burning in his home, while a third was paying a fine of three cents a day on an overdue library book. Proceed.

Amat.   Thank you. Like Wolesley's "Jolly Boys" of 1870, this latest batch of raw untrained, but enthusiastic volunteers could still sing. Given a fire, a rock-hard, enweeviled Army biscuit, they would swing into their favorite.

All.   [WITH MUSIC]   The volunteers are all fine boys
and full of lots of fun,
It's mighty little pay they get for carrying a gun:
The Government has grown so lean, the CPR so fat
Our extra pay we did not get —
You can bet your boots on that!

To annexate us some folks would, or independent be,
And our Sir John would federate the colonies, you see;
But let them blow till they are blue and I'll throw up my hat
And give my life for England's flag —
You can bet your boots on that!
The flag that's waved a thousand years,
You can bet your boots on that.

Amat.   By April the 6th, most of the Expeditionary Force was in the Northwest, and beginning its 200 mile march on the Métis head-quarters at Batoche. All citizens felt happier and breathed easier. Except those few, those happy few, who had settled at Medicine Hat where the CPR crosses over the South Saskatchewan River. No troops had been alloted for their protection. Even the Hudson's Bay Company's river streamer, the *Northcote*, had been ruled out as a possible means of evacuating the women and children, for on the previous days her personnel had received this telegram:

Sheets.   Lessee, it says here, "s.s. *Northcote* will load supplies as per attached memo and proceed down river to Saskatchewan Landing. Rendezvous with Col. Otter and transport his men and supplies across the river and see him safely on the way to relieve Battleford. Signed, Frederick Middleton, Officer Commanding Northwest Field Force."

Amat.   That is Captain Jim Sheets, and his reaction was typical of a for-mer Mississippi riverman:

Sheets.   Judas H. Mahogany Priest.

Amat.   He folded the message and looked at his second in command. His reaction was also typical of a former Mississippi riverman, although it had the pious overtones of the deep, Southern Baptist.

Mel.   Almighty Moses, Jim, who wants to go to war. Like the good book says, leave us take off for the land of Egypt where we won't see no war, nor neither hear the sound of the trumpet. I think.

Amat.   The Co-captain's name, by the way, was Melchisedek Seager. The third member of the crew of the 160 foot *Northcote* was a rather insignificant and worried bookkeeper cum purser whose reaction was typical of his breed:

Harold.   [*AS ADVERTISED*] Oh dear. More work.

Amat.   His name was Harold Talbot, and he hailed from Kansas City, Kansas.

Harold.   Excuse me, sir. Kans City, Missoura.

Amat.   Oh. I'm sorry.

Harold.   Nobody ever gits it right.

Amat.   I beg your pardon. The fourth member of the crew was down in the engine-room minding his business . . . his all important business, so we will get to know him later. His name, for the record, was Pierre; and I can discover no other. I assume he was a French half-breed. He was the *de jure* First Engineer. He was also, *de facto,* Second Engineer, Third Engineer, Oiler, Wiper Water-Tender and Fireman of the fast and commodius s.s. *Northcote.* And thus it was, at 6:30 on the bitterly cold morning of April the 6th, that the *Northcote* waited, with steam up, at Medicine Hat landing. The crew had loaded supplies all night according to the telegraphed instructions. The First Engineer, etc. was about to blow the whistle (which incidentally could be blown both from the engine room and the bridge) when his practiced eye noticed with horror that an all important length of copper tubing was allowing precious liquid to escape. And under high pressure, too. He hailed the bridge on the engine room howler.

¶ SOUND: *shreep.*

Sheets.   [*THROUGH A PIPE*] Jim Sheets listenin'. What's eatin' at you, Pierre, me and Mel was all set to have breakfast.

Pierre.   Oh, M'sieu Capitaine Sheets, the business, she has sprang a leak!

Sheets.   [*GALVANIZED AT ONCE*] Bad!

Pierre.   Bad! *Mon Dieu,* she's terrible, I'm tole you the business is leak so fas' we never make hit roun' dat first bend!

Sheets.   Watch yer steam gauge, I'm gonna blow a general alarm.

¶ SOUND: *whistle begins to toot frantically: establish: to background.*

Amat.   To us landlubbers, it is a source of ever increasing wonder and admiration to watch how men, who, so to speak, go down to the sea in ships, face an emergency. When the danger was explained to them they sprang ashore as one man, some with unmanly tears of anxiety in their eyes.

308

¶ SOUND: *whistle out.*

Amat. They roused the sleeping citizens of Medicine Hat and thus began the frantic search for copper pipe. And because Captain Sheets ran, as they say, a tight ship, they found it. Or rather young Thomas Tweed, the General Merchant, found it for them. He came aboard with it at 7:30 and he went straight to the Pilot House . . .

¶ SOUND: *knock.*

Sheets. Come in!

¶ SOUND: *door opens.*

Tom. Ah, Captain Sheets and Co-captain Seager.
Sheets. Howdy, Tom.
Mel. Glad to have you aboard, Tom.
Sheets. I hope an' trust you got good news, Tom.
Tom. Blessed if I know. But its a length of copper tubing.
Sheets. [*FERVENTLY*] Saved, saved!!
Mel. Praise be, Tom, you'll never know what you have did.
Tom. It's just a length of copper tube.
Sheets. Jest a length o' copper toob, he says.
Mel. Tom, as the good book says, who kin find a length o' copper toobin'. Its price is far above rubies. I think.
Tom. Oh, I wasn't going to charge for the tube. It's on the house. You gave me a nice order, I consider it a favour.
Mel. Oh now, Tom.
Sheets. [*HASTILY*] Take it easy, Mel. Never look a gift horse in the . . . if Tom wants to make us a present, we'll take her as specified.
Tom. Look, I don't want you fellahs to be embarrassed. There's a war on, and if a piece of copper tubing will help us win it, who am I to stand in the way?
Sheets. Oh, we didn't aim to fight with that toob.
Mel. Nosirree bob.
Tom. Oh I know that. But if you've had trouble in the engine room and a copper tube will repair a broken boiler, then I say it's the duty of every citizen who can, to help.
Sheets. Er . . . how's that again?
Tom. After all, we're going to stay and make ready to defend our women and children. You and your crew are going to war. Now, I wouldn't want to see a warship like the *Northcote* in jeopardy because of a defective boiler.
Mel. [*MYSTIFIED*] They ain't nothin' wrong with our boiler.
Sheets. [*SAME HERE*] Yeah. She's as sound as a dollar.
Tom. But your man said the business in the engine room was leaking

like a sieve.

Sheets. Oh. *That* business.

Mel. Tom, don't tell me you ain't wise?

Tom. But your man said . . .

Sheets. It ain't the boiler Donald McIver was talkin' about.

Mel. No! He was talkin' about our private still.

Tom. A private still!

Sheets. Sure.

Mel. That way we don't pay no never mind to your prairie drought.

Sheets. An' we allus try to keep about twelve bottles ahead o' the still. Jest in case.

Tom. But you're never that many miles away from a steamer landing.

Sheets. Oho, takin' too much of a chance that away.

Mel. Yep. Learned to be careful when Jim an' me was working the Mississippi and Missouri.

Sheets. Specially when we was runnin' contraband past Grant when he was layin' seige to Vicksburg. They wasn't no chanct o' gittin' the goods jest ony ole wheres.

Mel. That was when we learned to rely on ourselves. No more store goods.

Sheets. Bein' a land lubber, Tom, you ain't got no idea jest how demoralizin' it is to run short on a long voyage.

Mel. I pray to the good Lord you never will.

Sheets. Why . . . I mind the time in '62 when the Sioux Injuns was on the radan in Minnesota. Me an' Mel here got our steamer stuck on a sandbar spang in the middle o' them hostiles. An' do you know what?

Tom. No, what.

Sheets. [*WITH HORROR AND REVULSION*] Me and Mel here, and Harold Talbot and the rest o' the crew run outta store goods and we lived fer two whole weeks on literally nothin' but food and water.

Mel. I tell you, bein' scalped is a sight bettern that.

Sheets. So that's why we run a still.

Mel. Sides, store goods is gettin' all fired costly.

Sheets. Wicked. Ever since that John A. MacDonald went in fer that there National Policy five years ago, the cost of livin's gone up about 15 cents a quart.

Mel. Sides, when you make it yerself, you know what you're gettin'. Lot healthier that way. Never know what them foxy perfessional likker makers is up to.

Tom. Ahem, fellahs, this copper tube. Er, it's not what you'd call pristine. We've been using it at the store to siphon coal oil. And stuff.

Mel. Fine! Couldn't be better. We allus flavour our goods with coal oil. Gives it zing and keeps it exclusive.

Sheets. Sure. And if we ever run short on fuel, it makes her burn better in the lamps.

Tom. Well, if it's all right with you, it's all right with me.

Mel. Almighty Moses, look what time it's gettin' to be.

Sheets. Blasted war's liable to be over, we don't git a wiggle on.

Mel. Tom, why don't you stay and have breakfast. We ain't leaving till after.

Tom. Look, you fellahs don't feel you have have to . . .

Sheets. Nonsense.

¶ SOUND: *bottle and glass.*

Sheets. Say when, Tom.

¶ SOUND: *there is a large pouring into a large tumbler.*

Tom. Hey wait. . . . Oh no, I . . . oh dear. I din't think you fellahs . . . I mean before breakfast!

Sheets. Natcherly. I never like to eat on an empty stomack. Mel, say when.

¶ SOUND: *pouring.*

Mel. Just a tumblerful, Jim, I don't wanta spoil my appetite.

Sheets. There you go, Melchisedek.

Mel. Thanks. Hey Jim, ain't you forgot Pierre.

Sheets. Judas Priest, so I did. Scuse me, Tom, you're right in front o' the engine room howler.

Tom. Sorry.

¶ SOUND: *shreep.*

Pierre. [AT THE OTHER END OF A PIPE] Allo, allo, Pierre down 'ere. I am listen. Who is dere?

Sheets. Jim Sheets talkin. Like a shot o' breakfast?

Pierre. Ho, for sure. About five fingers, me.

Sheets. Assoom the position, then, she's acomin' down. Mel, hand me the funnel.

Mel. Yep.

¶ SOUND: *funnel into pipe: pours the drink into it.*

Tom. Holy smoke Jim go easy. You'll choke him to death.

Sheets. Not a chance. Listen.

Pierre. [ALMOST CHOKES TO DEATH] *Merci Beaucoup, m'sieu.*

Sheets. See, what'd I tell you.

Pierre. Now de chaser, *s'il vous plait.*

Sheets. Hand me that other tumblerful, Tom.

Tom. Great Scott. Not more liquor!

¶ SOUND: *shreep.*

Sheets.   Assoom the position, Pierre. Chaser comin' down.

¶ SOUND: *funnel in pipe: hootch poured it.*

Tom.   Jim you'll kill him for sure this time.
Sheets.   Not Pierre.
Mel.   He's half French and half Injun. Indestructible.
Tom.   Incredible.
Sheets.   Listen, Tom.
Pierre.   [*THROUGH PIPE: WITH GREAT RELISH*] Ahhhhhhhhhhh!
Mel.   That's the French half.

¶ SOUND: *whistle gives a glorious blast: then two short toots.*

Sheets.   That's the Injun half. Pierre, don't waste all your steam, you'll
   still got coffee to make and then we take off. Listenin' out.
Tom.   And I've got to take off too. Helen and the kids'll wonder what's
   happened.
Sheets.   Let's go then, Mel and we'll see youse offa the boat.

¶ SOUND: *door opens.*

Mel.   I'll say so long now, Tom. I wanta take another gander at me
   charts. Water's awful low. Them sand bars is real wicked this time o'
   year. Prolly have to walk this tub mosta the ways.
Tom.   Sure. I'll see you next time, Mel.

¶ SOUND: *Sheets and Tom start to clump down the inside companionway.*

Sheets.   Tell me, Tom, how are the youngsters.
Tom.   Fine as frog's hair.
Sheets.   How old are they now.
Tom.   Harry's rising five and too young to know what all this trouble's
   about. Jean's old enough but she's mad because we won't let her carry
   a rifle.
Sheets.   I hope and trust none of youse hasta.
Tom.   We'll put our trust in the CPR Freight Shed. I'm barracking all the
   men there until this blows over. That and keep our powder dry.
Sheets.   Which last ain't gonna be no problem in a prairie summer.
Tom.   Here comes your Purser.
Sheets.   [*PROJECT*] Nearly left without you, Harold.
Harold.   [*WORRIED AS USUAL: FADING IN*] Oh now, you wouldn't do that.
   I'm terribly sorry, Captain Sheets but I jest couldn't fine no copper
   toobin. [*ON NOW*] I ben all over this here town too. Oh, hello, Mr.
   Tweed.
Tom.   Mr. Talbot.

312

Sheets.   Oh. You all, know each other.

Tom.   Not officially. We passed each other looking for copper pipe.

Sheets.   Mr. Tweed, this here's my purser, Mr. Harold Talbot.

Tom.   How do you do.

Harold.   That's all right.

Sheets.   Harold here comes from Kans City, Kans.

Harold.   [*HIS ETERNAL CROSS*] No, Kans City, Missoura.

Sheets.   Oh yeah. Always gettin' them two mixed up. Well, see you next time, Tom, an' good luck.

Tom.   [*FADING*] So long, Jim. We may need it yet.

Sheets.   [*INTO HIGH AND PROFESSIONAL GEAR*] Ahoy there at the back end o' the boat. Haul in them back lines, we're leavin' pronto. Harold, haul in that there gangplank, will yuh?

Harold.   Oh yeah, sure.

Sheets.   PIERRE! Get the lead out! Throw her into ree-verse and back outta here.

Pierre.   [*OFF: SHOUTING*] Sure ting M'sieu Capitaine Sheets.

¶ SOUND: *some fumbling with the gangplank.*

Sheets.   Harold, fer gosh sakes, when you're haulin' in the gangplank, watch what you're doin'. You'll scratch the paint offen the gun-whale.

¶ SOUND: *the whistle toots twice: the engines start.*

Sheets.   [*ROARING PLEASANTLY*] Mel, you still in the wheel house?

Mel.   [*OFF*] Yeah. What's eatin' at you. You comin' up?

Sheets.   Yeah. Watch when you swing her tail around. She's as heavy as a brood sow with them two barges lashed to her sides.

¶ SOUND: *steps running up stairs.*

Mel.   [*HALF OF THE FADE IN: OFF*] Shucks, Jim, I reckon I kin back outta any o' these river towns with my eyes closed.

Sheets.   [*FINAL FADE IN*] By the living, I must be slipping, Mel. So intrusted in gettin' the show on the road, I plumb fergot my eye opener.

Mel.   Bottle's right there, holdin' my chart down. Where you left her.

Sheets.   Ain't you had yours yet?

Mel.   Jest the first course. Never like to drink my main course alone.

Sheets.   Good rule. Me neither. So let her rip.

¶ SOUND: *glass and bottle: pouring.*

Mel.   Say when.

Sheets.   Oh jest a tumblerful. Don't wanta spoil my appetite. Thanks.

¶ SOUND: *another glassful.*

Mel. Jim, if this war don't turn out to be too warlike, we stand to make a potful of spondulucks runnin' supplies.

Sheets. Jest what I was thinkin'. Cheers. [*PAUSE: HE CHOKES TO DEATH*] Sm . . . sm . . . smooth.

Mel. Health. [*PAUSE: SO DOES HE*] Yeah . . . but not so smooth as the last batch. You suppose Pierre's been fiddlin' with the recipe?

Sheets. Could be. Pierre never was one to leave well enough be.

¶ SOUND: *shreep.*

Pierre. [*THROUGH TUBE*] Allo, allo, Pierre down here. I am listen, me. Who is dat?

Sheets. Jim Sheets. Throw her into go ahead. And don't be all day lessen we back into the CPR bridge and a lawsuit.

Pierre. Hat once, M'sieu Capitaine Sheets.

¶ SOUND: *the distant engines stop: pause: then pick up speed: through following:*

Sheets. Start spinnin' the wheel, Mel.

Mel. Yep. Figger to take her close to the south shore when we hit Police Point.

Sheets. Not too close. Don't fergit that deadhead.

Mel. I don't know but what we shoulda put off sailin' till tomorra. These here ice-floes is thickern flees onto a houn' dawg.

Sheets. We ain't got time. It'll take us week easy to make Saskatchewan Landin', what with the water so low and the sand bars so high.

Mel. Too late now anyways. Turnin' in these ice-floes'd take our paddle wheel off fer sure. She's jest as dangerous to quit as she is to go ahead.

Sheets. Do the best you kin. When we tie up fer the night a lot of 'em'll pass. They won't be so many in the A.M.

Mel. Figger to have another?

Sheets. Why not.

¶ SOUND: *pouring two glasses.*

Mel. Say when.

Sheets. Jest a tumblerful. When I'm on dooty, I always figger to set a good example to my crew. Health. [*PAUSE: HE CHOKES TO DEATH*] You're right, Mel. She ain't so smooth as the last batch.

Mel. Cheers. [*PAUSE: SO DOES HE*] Nope, she definitely ain't. Do you espose we got a bad order of potatoes?

Sheets. Well, they was old. They was last fall's.

Mel. No, I mean do you figger mebbe they had Paris Green onto 'em?

Sheets. Can't blame the Paris Green. That'd only give her bokay.

Mel. Could be the wire worm.

Sheets. Nope, ner not that neither. You know what I think.

Mel.   Nope.

Sheets.   Give her a coupla left hand spokes. There's the dead head, dead ahead. I think we're not gettin' to drink her soon enough.

Mel.   Mebbe.

Sheets.   Mind the time we tried a tumblerful right outta the business?

Mel.   [*WHO CAN SEE IT AND TASTE IT*] Yeah.

Sheets.   The mash writhin' gently to herself inside.

Mel.   Smoothern honey on a Sunday afternoon.

Sheets.   [*WAXING LYRICAL*] Drip, drip drip, she come outta the copper toob. The engine room fire ree-flected in every drap. Half a tumblerful . . . hold her up to the light. Clear as gristle. Drink her down. Warm alla ways. Then you're eyes'd water and durned if wouldn't run right out yer toes.

Mel.   Should try that this afternoon when we whomp up the next batch.

Sheets.   We'll do that. Cause this batch is definitely tainted. And there ain't nothin' like tainted hospitality to give a riverman a bad name. Sides, it's hard on the bronical toobs.

Mel.   Well, as the good books says, waste not lest ye be wasted by drought. I think. Bottoms up.

Sheets.   All the way.

¶ SOUND: *both choke to death.*

Sheets.   No doubt, she must have went bad in the bottle.

Mel.   Like the good book says, thou knowest not the way of the spirit. I think.

Sheets.   Mel, you take the first trick. I think I kin face one of Hank's breakfasts now. I jest hope and trust it ain't bannock and sowbelly agin.

¶ MUSIC: *bugle call: "Come to the Cook House Door" into "Steamboat Bill Steaming Down the Missisippi": to background for:*

Amat.   On April the 13th, precisely seven days and several batches later, the s.s. *Northcote* made Saskatchewan landing, which is about 30 miles north of Swift Current. Modern trains make the same distance in about three hours. But there was a good reason for this snail's pace. Lack of water. The *Northcote* drew thirty-four inches of water and at that time of year before the spring run-off, the South Saskatchewan river only provided a bare thirty inches. Therefore, the *Northcote* 'crutched her way along, grounding on sand bars every ten miles and hauling herself off by "sparring."

¶ MUSIC: *pauses: bloop.*

Footnote: this operation was used in all river steamboating. It consisted of setting the vessel's spars — tall, heavy timber like telegraph poles —

in the channel, on either side of the boat, with their tops inclined to the bow. High on each spar was a tackle block, through which a stout manilla rope was threaded. One end of each cable was attached to the gunwhales, and the other ends were wound around a steam winch. As the winch turned and the paddle wheel revolved, the boat was lifted and thrust forward a few feet. The spars were then reset farther ahead and the operation was repeated until the steamer cleared the bar. The grotesque appearance of the boat during the sparring gave this operation the nickname of "grasshoppering." Proceed.

¶ MUSIC: *resumes in background.*

Amat. [ON CUE] Thank you. For once the *Northcote* was ahead of herself. Col. Otter's column, on the way north to relieve Battleford, had not yet arrived. Captain Sheets nosed his vessel into the landing and prepared to wait.

¶ MUSIC: *out at the end of narration.*

Mel. But fer how long, do you reckon, Jim?
Sheets. Search me. I don't see no Army hereabout.
Mel. Mebbe they're figgerin' to have their war somewhere's else.
Sheets. That don't cause me no ondue heartburn.
Mel. Ner me neither likewise.
Sheets. And we're gettin' paid, so we kin wait till hell freezes over.
Mel. Pervidin' we don't run short o' supplies.
Sheets. What's the last check-over say.
Mel. Six quarts and a heel.
Sheets. Better we should go on half rations. The next batch ain't gonna be ready fer 12 hours.
Mel. Oh now, Jim, leave us not panic. Remember what the good book says, the night cometh when no man can drink. I think.
Sheets. All the same that's runnin' things too close to the wind. I best whistle up Pierre and check into it.

¶ SOUND: *shreep.*

Sheets. It ain't that hard to get the stuff perdooced. It's all a question of organization. Where is that bloodstained half-breed engineer anyways!

¶ SOUND: *shreep: shreeep.*

Harold. [OFF OUTSIDE: FADING IN] Help . . . help . . . help.
Mel. Now what.
Sheets. It's Harold.

¶ SOUND: *door burst open.*

Sheets. What's eatin' at you, Harold?

Harold. You and Mel better get to the Engine room quick. The business is acting mighty queer.

Mel. What!

Harold. Yeah, the pot's kinda jumpin' up and down. I don't like the looks of her.

Sheets. What's the matter with Pierre!

Harold. I don't know for sure. He's just lyin' on the floor. Out cold or mebbe dead.

Mel. Why didn't you tell us about Pierre before.

Harold. First things first.

Sheets. Did you kick him to bring him around.

Harold. Yeah, he didn't move a muscle.

Mel. I'll bet he's been dippin' into the stuff before she's ready fer publication.

Sheets. Stop talkin' and come on! I don't like the sound o' this!

¶ MUSIC: *fast and short downstairs type: out clean.*

¶ SOUND: *a queer blumping from the business.*

Sheets. She don't sound too healthy to me, Mel.

Mel. Me neither. I had one of 'em go on me when I was working outta Memphis. Got a potato stuck in her throat and built up a powerful head o' steam fore she went to glory.

Harold. I'm gettin' outta here.

Sheets. Oh no you ain't, you're gonna help turn her off!!

¶ SOUND: *a couple of really bad blumps: some escaping steam maybe.*

Mel. It's too late. I know them signs.

Sheets. Hit the deck, boys. Dive Harold or you ain't never again gonna lay eyes on Kans City, Kans.

¶ SOUND: *they scrabble for the deck just in time: vrooooom: as loud as we should artistically: a shower of hardware: then the inevitable last late piece.*

Harold. [*WHEN THERE IS COMPLETE SILENCE*] Kans City, Missoura.

Sheets. [*HORRIFIED*] Oh, Mel!

Mel. Yeah?

Sheets. Don't look! The business has went to glory!

Mel. Oh no! [*HE SEES IT: ALMOST BREAKS DOWN*] Oh no, no, no, no.

Sheets. I got nothin' bust. You all in one piece, Mel?

Mel. Yeah, but who wants to live now. Like the good book says, anguish is come upon me, because my life is yet whole in me. I think.

Sheets. Harold, what are you tryin' to do to Pierre!

Harold. Bring him round with this dipper o' water.

317

Sheets. Water!!

Mel. You wanta kill him, Harold!

Sheets. Here, try my flask, least ways it won't poison him.

¶ SOUND: *the crew begins to gather in the background: what happened? etc.*

Harold. Easy now, Pierre.

Sheets. Don't waste it.

Harold. He's comin' round, Jim.

Sheets. Natcherly. Our stuff would most bring a corpse round.

Pierre. [*WEAKLY*] Allo, M'sieur Capitaine Sheets.

Sheets. So you figger to stick with the ship a spell longer, hey?

Pierre. Oh, mon capitaine, I have for you the bad, bad news, me.

Sheets. So have I, but les' have yours first.

Pierre. When we landed here, you hit the deck so hard, you spill all my
pile of cord wood dere. When the cord wood spill over, the bag of
sugar on top jump hout de window. She bust hup when she jump
hout. *Voilà*, no more sugar.

Sheets. But what happened to you, sticka cord wood hit you?

Pierre. I am a woman, me. When de suger jump hout I was 'orrified
me. I must have fainted. But whatever, I got one beeg bump on my
head, me.

Mel. Jim, we're finished. This is the end. No sugar.

Sheets. Pierre, when the business went to glory, she took our last
charge o' potatoes.

Mel. And they prolly won't have none in this hell hole. Like the good
books says, there is no joy in Israel, when their ain't no corn in Egypt.
I think.

Sheets. Men. It's your captain talkin'.

All. [*MUMBLE A BIT IN BACKGROUND TO ESTABLISH THEM*]

Sheets. What I'm gonna ast you to do now is above and beyond the call
o' dooty. We're short o' stuff. Despirit short. With only six bottles and
a heel left and on half rations, that ain't gonna last no moren twelve
hours. Under them conditions, I'm askin' you to stay.

Crew. [*MUMBLE: MUMBLE*]

Sheets. Any man who don't wanna stay is free to go. I won't report him
to the Company, ner neither will I hold it agin him personal.

All. We'll stay.

Sheets. Good men. [*MOVED*] I don't deserve a crew like you.

Harold. [*SOTTO*] Why shouldn't they stay with me holdin' back their
pay until this trip's over.

Sheets. Ach, you got no romance in your soul Harold. You're all the
same, you rats from Kans City, Kans.

Harold. Kans City, Missoura.

Sheets. Now men, it's gonna be a long dry spell until we git things organized agin. So I want everybody to go ashore and tear the place apart till you find sugar.

Crew.   [*AGREE: FADE OFF*]

Sheets.   Harold, I want you to take Duncan McIvor and Charlie Mac-donald with you and beg borry or steal some kinda kettle we kin make a new business outta.

Harold.   Sure. But if its all the same to you, we'll just steal it. Faster.

Sheets.   Good man. No, wait. Just take Duncan, bein' a blacksmith he'll reconize the right thing when he sees it. I want Charlie to stay here and carpenter up another business stand.

Harold.   I'm on my way. Meanwhile, what're you and Mel gonna do.

Sheets.   Shovel up this mash into a wash tub, picker over fer nuts and bolts, then wring her out and save what juice we kin. Beggars can't be choosers.

Harold.   [*FADING*] Okay, see you later.

Sheets.   Hand me that scoop shovel, Mel.

Mel.   [*DISTRAUGHT*] Huh?

Sheets.   I said hand me that scoop shovel.

Mel.   Oh. Sure.

Sheets.   What in the nation's eatin' at you now.

Mel.   [*COMING OUT OF HIS REVERIE*] Jim, bein' a Southerner, I never figgered to admit William Tecumseh Sherman was anything' but a low down skonk.

Sheets.   That's what we all figger.

Mel.   But he sure said a mouthful, all right.

Sheets.   Huh?

Mel.   Jim, he was dead right. War sure *is* hell!

¶ MUSIC: *"Marching Through Georgia": to a background for:*

Amat.   It is a heart rending thing to see brave men facing stark famine. But they did it without a murmur. And their fortitude was rewarded. The scroungers came back, not with sugar, but with molasses. Col. Otter's army arrived the next day carrying not potatoes but hard tack. No matter that it was vilified by all the Army except Middleton, it was starch and it was pressed into service, by Captain Sheets and his haggard men. In no time a new business was opened up and in short order was producing a rum flavoured staff of life. After testing, the pious Melchisedek Seager remarked to his Captain:

¶ MUSIC: *out at the end of narration.*

Mel.   Jim, leave us face it, she ain't so good as the potato stuff and she tastes like rum but you'll get used to her in a couple hours. A change is as good as a rest, and like it says in the good book, man ain't expected to live by bread alone. I think.

Sheets. Mel, I'm worried. I sure hope and trust them weevils in them biscuits don't cut the strength down none. I ain't never heard tell o' fermented weevils.

Mel. Me neither. Anyways we ain't dry, praise be.

Sheets. Amen to that.

Mel. Now, lessee, we got Otter and his men ferried over the river and on their way; all 745 officers and men not to mention 450 horses. What now.

Sheets. We load more supply for Middleton and start down river as soon as we kin.

Mel. What's the cargo this time?

Sheets. Accordin' to orders a hundred men from the Midland Battalion, all the supplies we kin carry, along with two barge loads of stuff as well.

Mel. Jim, that's too heavy, we'll never make her.

Sheets. You tell that to the Army.

Mel. We'll be scraping bottom all the way.

Sheets. You tell that to the army too. Oh, I almost forgot. One Gatling gun and its trainer.

Mel. What's a Gatling gun.

Sheets. Search me.

¶ MUSIC: *bloop.*

Foot.: this machine gun, the first successful one of its kind to become operational, was invented in 1862 by Dr. R.J. Gatling. It had ten barrels in a circle which were loaded, fired, and emptied automatically. The rate of fire depended upon the speed with which the operator turned the crank handle. Proceed.

Mel. [*A SLIGHT PAUSE*] Jim, did you hear somebody talkin'?

Sheets. Yeah, thought fer a bit I heard music too. But I ain't sure.

Mel. Me, too. Suppose it's the new batch hittin' at us.

Sheets. How could it. We only had two tumblers apiece.

Mel. Anyways, who did you say this gun's trainer was.

Sheets. I didn't, but the Army says his name's Captain Howard of the Connecticut Home Guard.

Mel. Almighty Moses, how did an American soldier get to fightin this war.

Sheets. Must be on account of him bein'a dam yankee. They'll sneak in anywheres. Well standin' chewin' the fat won't load no cargo. Let's round up the crew.

Mel. First let's keep our strength up with a fresh bottle o' lunch.

¶ MUSIC: *"How Dry I Am": then to a neutral background.*

Amat. The steamer *Northcote* was by now so heavily laden that she

fairly wallowed down the river. The two barge loads of troops gave
her a sluggish helm and what with one thing and another, she was
from the 23rd of April until the 5th of May getting to Saskatoon, a distance of 200 miles. During this time, Middleton, who needed a victory
but was too politically cautious to go all out, engaged Riel's forces at
Fish Creek with no credit to himself.

¶ MUSIC: *pauses: bloop.*

Foot.: if the morale of the eager-to-fight volunteers was bad, that of the
officers was worse. The General, many of them felt, was a pompous
ass and a chucklehead. There had been no excuse for the setback at
Fish Creek. There was no excuse they could see, despite difficulties
with the wounded, for the long delay before the advance on the rebel
stronghold at Batoche. Proceed.

¶ MUSIC: *sneaks in background.*

Amat. Thank you. It was about this time that the following conversation between General Middleton and a certain War Correspondent
must surely have taken place.

¶ MUSIC: *out at the end of narration.*

Henty. [AS IN G.A. BELIEVE IT OR NOT] May I present myself and my
credentials, General.
Mid. [MATCHING HENTY'S STUFFINESS] Pray do, sir.
Henty. I am the correspondent from the *London Standard*. My card.
Mid. Ah yes. G.A. Henty.
Henty. Quite. Boys books, you know.
Mid. I say, what brought you here, Mr. Henty?
Henty. On an assignment to cover the California Goldfields. Heard
about your little war. Dropped in, so to speak. Two birds with one . . .
eh, what, hm?
Mid. Quite. Surprised the *Times* didn't send a man over.
Henty. Believe me, sir, the *Standard* will give you every bit as good a war
as the *Times*!
Mid. Oh, I have no doubt, sir.
Henty. [A BIT UMBRAGEOUSLY] Don't forget, General, I have been, as it
were, with Clive in India. Good show, that. I have been with Wolfe at
Quebec. Good show there, too. Very difficult on the whole.
Mid. Oh quite.
Henty. [SURELY HENTY'S FINEST HOUR] I have also been with Nelson at
the Nile. Splendid Victory. I was also with Nelson at Trafalgar. Bad
show that. Lost him. Pity.
Mid. But those last two were at sea. This is prairie land and very dry
land at that.

Henty. I merely mentioned the sea, because you, sir, have served time at Gibraltar.

Mid. Quite.

Henty. I don't mean to impugn the ability of the Army, sir, but you must admit that on more than one occasion, the Army has been helped no end by the Navy.

Mid. Quite. But I repeat, we are not at sea, nor even near it.

Henty. Pity.

Mid. Quite. No, we have only a few miserable river steamers and an even more miserable South Saskatchewan River.

Henty. Pity.

Mid. Quite.

Henty. Oh, that's vastly different. Of what possible use is a river steamer. Even if you had sea room and she were armour plated. Tcha, no possible use at all.

Mid. Pity.

Henty. Quite.

Mid. No, Henty, the Prairie is no place to . . . I say, would you mind repeating your last remark!

Henty. Not at all. I merely said; even if she were armour plated, of what possible use is a river steamer.

¶ MUSIC: *"Rule Britannia": maestroso to a hornpipe background.*

Amat. I repeat; this conversation cannot be documented, but whatever was said, the result proved to be little short of amazing to one and all. But I'm ahead of myself. On the afternoon of the 6th of May, the *Northcote* left Fish Creek. Along with the Army, there were a handful of settlers returning home. One of these last, a Scots half-breed, proved especially interesting to the Crew.

¶ MUSIC: *out at end of narration.*

¶ SOUND: *vessel running in background.*

Sheets. Well, fry me fer a prairie oyster, if it ain't Minnie Buffalo Chip.

Chip. Jim Sheets, as I live and breathe.

Sheets. Minnie, you're a sight fer sore eyes. All three hunnert pounds of you.

Chip. You're downstream terrible early this season.

Sheets. Couldn't help it. Been freightin' war supplies and soldier boys.

Chip. Would you be headed down where the war is?

Sheets. Not on yer tintype. When we get to Gabriel's Crossin', I'm staying right there.

Chip. Gosh, I hope Middleton gets a wiggle on, business is roont.

Sheets. Too bad.

Chip. Aye, everything' goin' oot and naethin' coming in.

Sheets. Are you still a widda, Minnie?

Chip. I am that! And now I've achieved a state of unwedded bliss again I'll be a long while changin. Hey, whose yon fancy sojerboy coming along the deck.

Sheets. He's comin' to have a council of war with me and my boys.

Haig. [*YOUNG: A PUKKA: SHORT FADE IN*] Ah there, Sheets, I perceive you are engaged.

Sheets. Good Lord, no!! Minnie and me's jest good friends. Lemme me make you acquainted. Captain, this is Mrs. Minnie Buffalo Chip. Minnie, this here's Captain Haig de Haig.

Chip. Is that so. Well, many happy returns of the day to both of you, Captain.

Haig. Herrumph. How do you do, madam. Sheets, I think we'd better have our conference now.

Sheets. Sure thing. Minnie, you beat it over to the engine room. Pierre's whompin' up a new batch.

Chip. Grand. I've been a long, dry two hours without a drink. [*FADING*] See you at testing time.

Haig. See here, Sheets, you're not in the Army so I can't discipline you. But do you have to fraternize with the enemy. The woman's obviously a native judging by her barbarous speech.

Sheets. Lissen, Captain, Minnie's all right.

Haig. [*STIFFENING*] She's a Métis and they are the enemy.

Sheets. She's a Métis, all right. But she's a Blackfoot. You boys is fightin' Poundmaker's Crees.

Haig. I don't like it. Probably a spy.

Sheets. Ach! That's army stuff. Come on, son, let's get the meetin' over with.

¶ MUSIC: *music up: the first bars of a hornpipe.*

Haig. Ah, the Messrs, Sheets, Seager and Talbot . . . Oh, I say, where's Pierre?

Sheets. Oh er . . . he's in the engine room, getting things . . . er, oiled up.

Haig. Splendid fellow. As Middleton's A.D.C., I bring you his latest strategy.

Sheets. Shoot, Captain.

Haig. Oh, I shall be in two days. And so shall you or my name isn't Haig de Haig.

Mel. Jim what's this here double-barrelled soldier boy talkin' about.

Harold. Yeah. We're civilians and we ain't shooting nothin'.

Mel. I'll drink to that. Break out the stuff.

Haig. No thank you. We plan to armour plate the *Northcote* and attack

Batoche from the sea, so to speak.

Sheets.   Not with my ship, you ain't.

Haig.   This is insubordination.

Mel.   Haig, you ain't givin' orders here.

Harold.   Yeah, I'm only a bookeeper.

Sheets.   Poor Harold if he'da knowed he was going to be shanghai-ed like this, he wouldn't of never left Kans City, Kans.

Harold.   Kans City, Missoura.

Mel.   Come on, Harold, you and me's gettin' outta here.

Sheets.   Wait, fellahs, what am I supposed to do.

Mel.   Jim, like the good books says, tarry thou here with the ass, whilst I and the lad go yonder and pray. I think.

Haig.   [BOILING UP] I don't like your tone, Seager.

Mel.   That's tough!

Harold.   I second the motion. In spades.

Haig.   But you can't leave General Middleton's Army high and dry.

Sheets.   Ain't that what an Army's supposed to be!

Haig.   But this is war! We simply must have a Navy!!!

Mel.   Come on, Harold, let's skedaddle.

Harold.   Second the motion.

¶ SOUND: *door opens.*

Haig.   I repeat, sir, we intend to have a Navy and we intend to use it in the best traditions of Nelson at Trafalgar!

Mel.   An' I repeat, no soap. Or in the words of John Paul Jones, "I don't even intend to fight."

¶ SOUND: *door slams.*

Haig.   I mean to say.

¶ SOUND: *door opens fast.*

Mel.   I think.

¶ SOUND: *door slams.*

¶ MUSIC: *tops this with the next few bars of the hornpipe: out clean.*

¶ SOUND: *engine room background.*

Chip.   As I live and breathe, Melchisedek Seager.

Mel.   Afternoon, there, Minnie.

Chip.   Come on in. Just minding the boiler while Pierre's minding the business.

Mel.   Jim told me you was aboard. Goin' home?

Chip.   Certainly am. And what are you lookin' so sad about?

Mel.   Young Captain double-barrelled Haig wants to armour plate this tub and open up on them rebels when we go by Batoche.

Chip. By the bones of Malcolm Canmore, that sounds like bloody good fun.

Mel. Not to me it don't.

Chip. Bye the bye, Mel, I hate to bring this up the noo, but you and the boys must be makin' a pile of money with all your haulin'.

Mel. Why?

Chip. Would it no be a good time for you and rest of the boys to settle the board bill you owe me for last season?

Mel. [SADLY] Like the good book says, Minnie, Oh, how sharper than a servant's tooth it is to have a thankless creditor! I think.

¶ MUSIC: *final bars of hornpipe: comes out clean and has taken out sound.*

Haig. Captain Sheets, I'm sorry to invade the privacy of the bridge, but how long until we sight Gabriel's Crossing.

Sheets. Not long. And when we git thar, you'll be minus one crew.

Haig. We shall see about that, sir!

¶ SOUND: *shreep.*

Chip. Hello up there. That you, Jim.

Sheets. Minnie, what are you don' in the engine room.

Chip. Firin' the boiler, whilst Pierre has lunch.

Sheets. I mighta knowed it was you the way this old tub is shaking. How'd you like a snack while you wait.

Chip. Send her down.

Sheets. Assoom the position. Haig, hand me that funnel.

Haig. Certainly.

¶ SOUND: *business with voice pipe: pouring.*

Haig. [HORRIFIED] Are you trying to drown that woman in coal oil.

Sheets. Simmer down, soldier boy, it ain't coal oil. How's that, Minnie?

Chip. [CHOKES TO DEATH] Smooth. Guid loash, I could fight Culloden all over again. And win.

¶ SOUND: *whistle gives two joyous toots.*

Sheets. Swell. Now get back to work.

Chip. Avast you swab, I'm doin' this for free, gracious and fer naethin'. So how about that board bill you owe me.

Sheets. Oh sure. Remind me about it soon's we hit Gabriel's Crossing. [HASTILY] Listenin' off! Now where was we, Captain.

Haig. I was on the point of discussing the armour plating of this vessel.

Sheets. Nope. Absolutely. No hard feelin's though. Have a jolt.

Haig. Of that!

Sheets. It just smells like coal oil. It's ashully a kinda rum we make here on the premises. Help yourself.

¶ SOUND: *bottle: pours modest dollop.*

Haig.   I suppose it's all right. Sun's well over the yardarm. And we are, as it were, at sea. Nelson's blood and all that.
Sheets.   I'll join you.

¶ SOUND: *pours out the tumblerful.*

Haig.   I say, all that! But you're navigating!
Sheets.   Sure, that's why I dassent take moren a tumblerful.
Haig.   Well, down the hatch.
Sheets.   Up your kilt.
Haig.   [*CHOKES TO DEATH: ENDS WITH A LONG DRAWN OUT WHEEZE*]
Sheets.   Smooth, ain't she.
Haig.   [*GULP*] I say, it's none of my business but you aren't even watching where you're going.
Sheets.   Don't halfta. Know every sand bar in this river.

¶ SOUND: *a large crunch: short and swift however (which is cheating).*

Sheets.   [*PLEASED*] What'd I tell you. There's one of 'em now!

¶ MUSIC: *"Many Brave Hearts Are Asleep in the Deep So Beware, Beware"; then to a narration background built on "Life on the Ocean Wave."*

Amat.   After this and many more sand bars, the *Northcote* finally made Gabriel's Crossing. There, certain economic pressures were brought to bear on Captain Sheets and his crew. The Army won and the *Northcote* was armour plated with two inch planks which had been "liberated" from the barn of Gabriel Dumont, the Rebel Adjutant. There was no "armour" left for the Pilot House, so they made do with sacks of flour, tins of Bully Beef and hard tack. Adequate, I suppose, but it put the guesswork back into navigating. Thirty-five officers and men of 'C' Company Infantry School Corps were doubling as Royal Marines. Dr. Moore was in charge of the sick officers, one of whom was Lieut. Hugh John Macdonald, son of Old Tomorrow, the Prime Minister. There was one small cannon, which nobody trusted, and one Gatling gun left behind by Captain Howard, which nobody understood.

¶ MUSIC: *pause: bleep.*

Foot.:   Middleton put the *Northcote* in charge of Col. Sam Bedson, who, in civilian life, was the Warden of Stony Mountain Penitentiary in Manitoba. This probably made Col. Sam the first and only penologist in all history to command a warship. Certainly of all the fantastic expedients resorted to by either side in the Northwest Rebellion of

326

1885, converting a sternwheeler into a battleship was the most ludicrous. To make matters worse Riel's spies knew all about the operation and were ready with a warm welcome. Proceed.

¶ MUSIC: *"A Capital Ship for an Ocean Trip Was the Walloping Window Blind": out clean.*

Amat. [COLD] At 6:00 a.m. on the morning of the fateful 9th of May, armed to the teeth, safety valve popping, Captain Sheets swearing, and Melchisedek Seager muttering what he was sure were prayers, I think, H.M.S. *Northcote*, so to speak, stood out to sea, as it were, for her unwilling appointment with destiny.

¶ MUSIC: *a rollicking "Life on the Ocean Wave": to background for:*

Amat. And from then on, as in every one of Her Majesty's ships-of-the-line when preparing for action, things began to happen with frightening speed.

¶ MUSIC: *out at end of narration.*

Amat. At 6:15 in the sick bay: Minnie to Hugh John.
Chip. Well, young sojer boy, what's your name.
Hugh. Lieut. Hugh John Macdonald
Chip. Och losh, you're young day *after* Tomorrow. I'm Minnie Buffalo Chip.
Hugh. I know.
Chip. What's wrong wi' your face laddie?
Hugh. Erysypalis.
Chip. Looks like glanders to me.
Hugh. And Dr. Moore is treating it.
Chip. Dr. Moore, eh? Horse or people?
Hugh. Oh, people.
Chip. Great swith no wonder you're ill. I've suffered with glanders for years and it's horse doctors give me relief every time.
Hugh. Thank you.
Chip. That and the rum I'm even now putting up in bottles in the engine room. I'll bring you a tumblerful and if you're anything like your auld mon, it'll cure you at once.

¶ MUSIC: *foreboding type: pa da doomp dum dum: out.*

Amat. At 6:30 on the bridge: Bedson to Sheets. No pun intended.
Bed. Jim, just before we get opposite Batoche we'll signal with our whistle that we're ready to open fire on the Rebels.
Sheets. [SOUR] Uhuh.
Bed. Our boys will answer with their bugle and open fire. We'll have Riel's outfit caught between us.

Sheets. Uhuh.

Bed. In case of an accident here, I'll give Pierre a copy of the signals for the engine room.

Sheets. Col. Sam, it'll have to be me or Mel, else it won't work.

Bed. Why not. A signal's a signal.

Sheets. In the first place all Middleton's buglers is rabid Ontario Orangemen.

Bed. So?

Sheets. So, *our* side's liable to open fire on *us* on account of Pierre blows the whistle with a mighty powerful French Canadian accent!!!

¶ MUSIC: *foreboding type: up a third: pa da doomp dum dum: out.*

Amat. At 6:50 on the bridge:

Sheets. Mel, I make it one hour and ten minutes and we'll be where the war's gonna be.

Mel. I ain't cheerin' none. Ask me, we ben sold down the river.

Sheets. If we could only find a sand bar for we git to Batoche.

Mel. I been lookin'. We ain't like General Forrest, we're gonna git thar fust with the leastest.

Sheets. Seems as though.

Mel. Jim, I'm as good a Confederate as Robert E. Lee, but right now I wisht I was over to Edmonton, runnin' on the — I hate to say it — the Nawth Saskatchewan River.

Sheets. Mel, that's blasphemeous. I didn't know you felt that-away.

Mel. Like the good book says, what the hell doth Melchisedek doeth in the land of the Hitite. I think.

¶ SOUND: *a muffled shot: rifle.*

Sheets. Judas H. Mahogany Priest, they started the war afore they said they would!

Mel. Get down, they started firin'.

Bed. [*OFF: LOUD*] Action station. Drummer, beat to quarters!!

¶ SOUND: *three more rifle shots: some running: a scuffling on deck: shouts: off.*

Sheets. Is that them, or us.

Mel. Sounds like them. Better whistle Pierre, tell him to open her wide and we'll run fer it.

¶ SOUND: *a perfect fusilade of shots: off.*

¶ SOUND: *shreep.*

Sheets. Holy smoke, he's callin' us! Take the wheel, I'll git it. Jim Sheets . . . all right down there?

Chip. Certainly we're all right.

Sheets.   Minnie! You ain't hurt?
Chip.   Guid losh, no. I just soakin' wet.
Sheets.   Great snakes, Mel, we ben holded below the water line. Every
   man for himself. Abandon ship.
Chip.   Jim, hold on, that was no rifle fire.
Sheets.   What!
Chip.   Pierre bottled the last batch too soon and everyone o' they corks
   blew out.

¶ MUSIC: *stern and foreboding: up a third: pa da doomp dum dum.*

Amat.   Seven oh Five. Ahead of schedule for the war. Start slowing up.
   Behind schedule in the engine room; start mopping up.

¶ MUSIC: *same: up a third.*

Amat.   7:15: still too fast. Anchor two miles above Batoche.

¶ MUSIC: *same: up a third.*

Amat.   7:40: weigh anchor for the last lap. Minutes pass. There is a tense
   whispering on deck as the boys finger their rifles and wait. And on the
   bridge there is a curious silence between two comrades, as the
   moment of truth approaches. Two men who go down to the sea in
   ships. What words can take the place of the flickered eyelid, the
   restrained gesture, the curt nod. Perfect communion.

¶ SOUND: *two large glasses filled with the stuff: the hand that pours is shaking badly.*

Both.   [*THEY DRINK DEEPLY: NO CHOKE THIS TIME*] Ahhhhhhhhh.

¶ SOUND: *a single rifleshot: with a wicked ricochet.*

Sheets.   Judas Priest, Pierre's bottled her too soon again.

¶ SOUND: *fusilade of shots.*

Mel.   Seems as though . . .

¶ SOUND: *bridge window smashes close on.*

Mel.   Hey, Jim, that ain't the stuff. That's the bloody Rebs. Look at 'em.
   South side the river, there.
Sheets.   South side. North side, you mean!
Mel.   No, by heck, both sides!!!
Sheets.   My gorsh, we're surrounded. Take the wheel, Mel.

¶ SOUND: *the ship begins to return the fire: shreep.*

Sheets.   Pierre, how's she don' down there!
Pierre.   [*PLEASED*] Tres magnifique, M'sieu Sheets. She's hall mopped hup.

Sheets. Not the stuff, the boiler!!

Pierre. Oho, she is beginning to bulge, *M'sieu*. I got two lance corporal sitting hon de safety valve.

Sheets. Then full speed ahead, we're goin' right through!

¶ SOUND: *door opens.*

Mel. Harold, what are you doin' here. [*FRANTIC*] An' quit pointin' that squirrel rifle at me, wanna kill somebody.

Harold. Col. Bedson, he says whatever you do, mind the sunken ferry cable ahead.

Mel. We know. Tell the Colonel to mind his own business.

Sheets. And Harold, keep your stoopid bookeepin' head down, if you wants to see Kans City, Kans.

Harold. Kans City, Missoura.

¶ SOUND: *door shuts.*

Sheets. Mel, start blowin' the whistle. Let Middleton know his war's early.

¶ SOUND: *whistle begins to toot frantically: ad lib to window smash.*

Sheets. Lissen fer the bugle to answer.

¶ SOUND: *another window smashed: on.*

Sheets. Oh, what a glass bill we got.

Mel. Glory be, them Rebs is good shots.

Sheets. Look, with that ferry cable sunk, I figger to run right over her. But how kin I steer sittin' on the floor.

Mel. Jump up every so often and take a squint.

¶ MUSIC: *bugle well off: sound the charge.*

Sheets. They heard us. There's the bugle.

¶ SOUND: *shreep.*

Sheets. Yeah, what is it!

Pierre. *Sacre Bleu, M'sieu Capitaine* Sheets. My steam gauge she's drop fifteen pound. Do you got to blow that whistle too much, hein!!

Sheets. Stoke her faster. I gotta have the pressure.

Pierre. But I cannot keep hup wid dat whistle.

Sheets. Then tell them two lance corporals on the safety valve to move over and make room for Minnie. That'll do her.

Pierre. She is right here. You tell her. She is biger dan me.

Chip. I heard the proposition, Jim. You pay that board bill, I'll see that you get more steam.

Sheets. You're a hard woman Minnie, but I gotta have steam. It's a bargain. Pierre!

Pierre. You are de Boss. Now we go full speed straight hup hin de hair.

Mel. Jim, look! What's them Rebs doin' just over yonder.

Sheets. Mel, we're done for, they're pullin' up that ferry cable.

Mel. If we kin just run over it for she gits too high outta the water.

Sheets. Nope, too late. We ain't runnin' fast enough.

¶ SOUND: *shreep.*

Pierre. Allo, allo.

Sheets. Full speed backwards, we got trouble.

Pierre. You got trouble! Hokay, sure t'ing, full speed backwards.

Mel. That ain't gonna work neither. Safer to hit the cable head on.

¶ SOUND: *shreep.*

Pierre. Allo, allo. Don' you see I ham busy like hell, me.

Sheets. Shut up. Full speed ahead.

Pierre. [*FURIOUS*] But I ham full speed ahead.

Sheets. Well, then, full speed ahead faster.

Mel. Watch her Jim. Here comes the cable.

¶ SOUND: *there is wrench as the cable hits the ship: distant recorded cheer from the rebels.*

Sheets. Now we're up the crik good. She's comin' up and over.

Mel. An' we got such lovely smoke stacks.

Sheets. Jest pray she don't take this wheelhouse too.

Mel. Duck behind them flour sacks an' hang to the grass girls.

¶ SOUND: *the cable hits the twin stacks: they are wrenched off at their base: crash to the deck with a hell of a row: like two imperial oil drums on the loose: they bounce about a bit: reaction from the boys downstairs, etc.*

Sheets. Oh Mel, now we're in for it. They's a fire in Pierre's boiler what'll make hell feel chilly.

Mel. Too late, sparks fallin' on the deck already.

Crew. [*AND THE SOLDIERS SHOUT "FIRE, FIRE" . . . AD LIB*]

Sheets. Oh mother, war is hell, but a fire at sea is a terrible thing.

Mel. Hey, spin your wheel, she's turnin; right. We're headed fer shore. Full speed.

Sheets. Call Pierre. Tell him full speed backwards.

Mel. You cain't they still got that cable up. She'll tangle in the paddlewheel and we're roont!! Like the good book says . . .

Sheets. They ain't time fer the good book now. Take the wheel and gimme that speakin' toob. They's only one way an' she better work.

¶ SOUND: *shreep.*

Sheets.   Pierre!!!!

Pierre.   *Allo, allo.*

Sheets.   [*BESIDE HIMSELF*] You wanna job next season!!!

Pierre.   For sure, I gat 'ongry, me.

Sheets.   Then don't argue! FULL SPEED SIDEWAYS!!!

¶ MUSIC: *a strong entry of "No More I'll Go A-roving With You Fair Maid" to a background for:*

Amat.   Let us draw a quick and sympathetic veil across the red faces of all who suffered in this ghastly marine disaster. As a bucket brigade controlled the deck fire, the *Northcote* floundered ignominiously past Batoche and the War. And instinctively ran aground on a sand bar. There she spent the night. In time, with her funnels repaired, she steamed back to Batoche — late as usual.

¶ MUSIC: *out at this point.*

Amat.   [*NO PAUSE*] The war was over. Riel gave himself up. The show had cost Ottawa five milllion dollars. For the victory, the fed-up troops should have had the credit; Middleton desperately wanted it, but "Gatling" Howard spoiled the General's chances because of an odd bit of campaign doggerel which caught Canadian imaginations in 1885.

¶ MUSIC: *intro.*

Song.   Full many a line of expressions fine
And of sentiments sweet and grand
Have been penned of our boys, who from homes' dear joys
Set out for the Northwest land.
We've been told how they fought for the glory sought,
We've heard of the deeds they've done;
But it's quite high time for some praise in rhyme
For the man with the Gatling gun.

All honour's due — and they have it too —
To the Grens and the Q.O.R.
They knew no fear but with British cheer,
They charged and dispersed afar
The Rebel crew; but twixt me and you
When all has been said and done,
A different scene well there might have been
But for Howard and his Gatling gun.

Amat.   And even the *Northcote* had her brief moment in the sun, for she carried the defeated Riel upstream to the Elbow, where he was taken by wagon to Regina and his appointment with Fate.

¶ MUSIC: *sneaks "Oh Shenandoah": background.*

Amat. The *Northcote* was conceived by the Hudson's Bay Company who pioneered river steamers on the Prairies. She was born in 1873 at Grand Rapids, Manitoba, where the South Saskatchewan discharges into Lake Winnipeg. She was christened *Northcote* after Sir Stafford Northcote, Governor from '69 to '74. She lived a busy life until the CPR undermined her usefulness. There is a picture of her in the *Beaver Magazine.* It was done with house paint upon linoleum — which seems fitting. Old Timers, mispronouncing her name, called her the "North Goat," imagining she was named after some Arctic Nanny. She died on the shores of Cumberland Lake in 1900. Fire, relic hunters, and the elements did their deadly work, and all that remains are parts of her shattered deck timbers, the framework of her sternwheel, the massive cylinders, and her boiler. But long may she cruise in the happy Hunting Ground of Prairie schooners and river steamers.

¶ MUSIC: *full up for a finale based on the last line of "No More I'll Go A-roving."*

Announcer. Playbill Nine of *CBC Stage* . . . "Full Speed Sideways" . . . was written for this occasion by Tommy Tweed. Music composed, arranged, and conducted by Morris Surdin. Production and direction by Andrew Allan. In the cast were John Drainie as Captain Jim Sheets; Ed McNamara as Melchisedek Seager; Arch McDonell as Amateur Historian; John Bethune as Footnote; Frank Perry as Harold Talbot; and Alan King as Pierre. The part of Thomas Tweed was played by his bona fide grandson, our author, Tommy Tweed. G.A. Henty was Geoffrey Alexander; General Middleton was Norman Ettlinger; Minnie Buffalo Chip was Ruth Springford; Captain Haig de Haig was Joseph Shaw; Lieutenant Hugh John Macdonald was Hugh Rose; Colonel Sam Bedson was Alan Pearce; and the Singer was Bernard Johnson. Sound effects by Fred Tudor. Technical operation by Terry Rusling.

ALL THE BRIGHT COMPANY

Selected Bibliography

Andrew Allan's signed original production scripts for the complete *Stage* series and most of his other productions are housed in the CBC Radio Drama Archives, Centre for Broadcasting Studies, Concordia University, Montreal. The Centre is the official repository for all English-language CBC radio-drama scripts, departmental correspondence, and other ancillary materials. The instrument of access for the scripts, from the beginnings, is the bibliography *Canadian National Theatre on the Air*, cited below. The Archives also house twelve substantial personal collections of those who were involved in the production of Canadian radio drama, from the beginnings in 1925 to the present, as well as research papers and recent Ph.D and M.A. theses concerning a number of the playwrights in this anthology.

Allan, Andrew. *A Self-Portrait*. Ed. and Intro. Harry J. Boyle. Toronto: Macmillan, 1974.

Fink, Howard. "Canadian Radio Drama and the Radio Drama Project." *Canadian Theatre Review*, 36 (Oct. 1982).

———. "Critical Introduction." *Words on Waves: Selected Radio Plays of Earle Birney*. Kingston: Quarry Press and Toronto: CBC Enterprises, 1985.

———. "Radio Drama, English-Language." *The Canadian Encyclopedia*. Edmonton: Hurtig, 1985.

———. "The Sponsor's v. the Nation's Choice: North American Radio Drama" [an analytical history]. Ed. Peter Lewis. *Radio Drama*. London: Longmans, 1981.

———. "Tyrone Guthrie's Radio Theatre and the Stage Production of Shakespeare." *Theatre History in Canada*, 2, No. 1, (Spring, 1981).

Howard Fink, with Brian Morrison. *Canadian National Theatre on The Air 1925–61 / CBC-CRBC-CNR Radio Drama in English / A Descriptive*

335

Bibliography and Union List. Toronto: University of Toronto Press, 1983.

———. *Canadian National Theatre on the Air, II: 1962–85 / CBC Radio Drama in English* (TBP, 1988).

———, and John D. Jackson. "Radio Drama and Society, Homologies: An Analysis of Joseph Schull's *The Jinker*." *Canadian Drama*, 9, No. 1 (1983).

———, John D. Jackson, Gregory M. Nielson, and Rosalind Zinman. "Literary and Sociological Analysis of English-Language Radio Drama." *Culture*, 1, No. 2 (1981).

Frick, N. Alice. "Andrew Allan Remembered." *Performing Arts in Canada*, 23, No. 3 (November, 1986).

Jackson, John D. "On the Implications of Content and Structural Analysis." In Liora Salter, ed., *Communication Studies in Canada*. Toronto: Butterworth's, 1981.

———, and Gregory M. Nielsen. "Toward a Research Strategy for the Analysis of CBC English-Language Radio Drama and Canadian Social Structure." *The Canadian Journal of Sociology*, 9, No. 1 (1984).

Oxford Companion to Canadian Drama and Theatre. Eds. Eugene Benson and L.W. Conolly. Don Mills: Oxford, TBP 1988.

Page, Malcolm. "From *Stage* to *Sunday Matinee*: Canadian Radio Drama in English, 1981–82." *Canadian Drama*, 9, No. 1 (1983).

Wallace, Robert, ed. "Radio: Canada's Voice." *Canadian Theatre Review*, 36 (Oct. 1982).

Weir, Austin E. *The Struggle for National Broadcasting in Canada*. Toronto: McClelland and Stewart, 1965.